The Future of Large, Internationally Active Banks

World Scientific Studies in International Economics

(ISSN: 1793-3641)

Vol. 45 Trade Law, Domestic Regulation and Development
by Joel P. Trachtman (Tufts University, USA)

Vol. 46 The Political Economy of International Trade
by Edward D. Mansfield (University of Pennsylvania, USA)

Vol. 47 Trade-Related Agricultural Policy Analysis
by *David Orden (Virginia Polytechnic Institute and State University, USA)*

Vol. 48 The New International Financial System: Analyzing the Cumulative Impact of Regulatory Reform
edited by Douglas Evanoff (Federal Reserve Bank of Chicago, USA), Andrew G. Haldane (Bank of England, UK) & George Kaufman (Loyola University Chicago, USA)

Vol. 49 The Economics of International Migration
by Giovanni Peri (UC Davis)

Vol. 50 The Legal and Economic Analysis of the WTO/FTA System
by Dukgeun Ahn (Seoul National University, Korea)

Vol. 51 The Political Economy of Trade Policy: Theory, Evidence and Applications
by Devashish Mitra (Syracuse University, USA)

Vol. 52 Microeconometrics of International Trade
by Joachim Wagner (Leuphana University Lueneburg, Germany)

Vol. 53 Multinational Enterprises and Host Country Development
by Holger Görg (Kiel Institute for the World Economy, Germany)

Vol. 54 Globalization: The Macroeconomic Implications of Microeconomic Heterogeneity
by Andrei A. Levchenko (University of Michigan, USA)

Vol. 55 The Future of Large, Internationally Active Banks
edited by Asli Demirgüç-Kunt (World Bank, USA), Douglas D. Evanoff (Federal Reserve Bank of Chicago, USA) & George G. Kaufman (Loyola University Chicago, USA)

The complete list of the published volumes in the series can be found at
http://www.worldscientific.com/series/wssie

55
World Scientific
Studies in
International
Economics

The Future of Large, Internationally Active Banks

Editors

Asli Demirgüç-Kunt
World Bank, USA

Douglas D Evanoff
Federal Reserve Bank of Chicago, USA

George G Kaufman
Loyola University Chicago, USA

World Scientific

NEW JERSEY • LONDON • SINGAPORE • BEIJING • SHANGHAI • HONG KONG • TAIPEI • CHENNAI • TOKYO

Published by

World Scientific Publishing Co. Pte. Ltd.
5 Toh Tuck Link, Singapore 596224
USA office: 27 Warren Street, Suite 401-402, Hackensack, NJ 07601
UK office: 57 Shelton Street, Covent Garden, London WC2H 9HE

British Library Cataloguing-in-Publication Data
A catalogue record for this book is available from the British Library.

Cover illustration by Ping Homeric.

World Scientific Studies in International Economics — Vol. 55
THE FUTURE OF LARGE, INTERNATIONALLY ACTIVE BANKS

ISBN 978-981-3141-38-4

Desk Editor: Philly Lim

Typeset by Stallion Press
Email: enquiries@stallionpress.com

Printed in Singapore

Preface

The Great Financial Crisis of 2007–2010 had a major impact on large cross-border banks, which were widely blamed for the start and severity of the crisis. As a result, much public policy, both in the United States and abroad, has been directed at making these banks safer and less influential, by means of increased micro- and macro-prudential regulation. What is the current regulatory landscape for these institutions? How have modifications to that landscape affected the level of intermediation and changes in risk management? How has it affected service levels? What adjustments have been made to the bank safety net and failure resolution process? How effective are those adjustments thought to be — particularly those requiring international regulatory cooperation? What are the prospects for the new *single supervisory mechanism* introduced by the European Central Bank? What lessons can we draw from the changes in bank operations to date? What additional changes can we expect?

On November 5–6, 2015, the 18th annual International Banking Conference was held at the Federal Reserve Bank of Chicago, cosponsored by the World Bank, to analyze and develop answers to these and similar questions. Nearly 180 financial policymakers, regulators, and practitioners, as well as financial researchers, scholars, and academics from some 30 countries attended the two-day conference and engaged in a lively discussion. The conference concluded with a discussion of what should be done next. This volume contains the papers and keynote addresses delivered at the conference. It is intended to bring the analyses and conclusions presented at the conference to a wider audience in order to clarify and improve understanding of the issues, and to stimulate further discussion aimed at guiding future financial public policy.

Acknowledgments

Both the conference held at the Federal Reserve Bank of Chicago, November 5–6, 2015, and this volume represent a joint effort of the Federal Reserve Bank of Chicago and the World Bank. Various people at each institution contributed significantly to the effort. The editors served as the principal organizers of the conference and would like to thank representatives from both organizations who contributed their time and energy. We would particularly like to thank Julia Baker, Ella Dukes, and Othia Riley for their support. Special mention should also be accorded Sandy Schneider, who expertly managed the conference administration; Kathryn Moran, who managed the Chicago Fed's web effort; John Dixon and Ping Homeric who developed the artwork for both the conference program and the book cover; as well as Han Choi, Helen O'D. Koshy, and Sheila Mangler, who had responsibility for preparing the conference materials and the manuscripts for the volume. Finally, we also thank Philly Lim from World Scientific, who aptly guided us through the full editorial process.

About the Editors

Asli Demirgüç-Kunt is the Director of Research in the World Bank. After joining the Bank in 1989 as a Young Economist, she has held different positions, including Director of Development Policy, Chief Economist of Financial and Private Sector Development Network, and Senior Research Manager, doing research and advising on financial sector and private sector development issues. She is the lead author of World Bank Policy Research Report: *Finance for All? Policies and Pitfalls in Expanding Access.* She has also created the World Bank's *Global Financial Development Report* and directed the issues on *Rethinking the Role of the State in Finance*, and *Financial Inclusion.* The author of over 100 publications, Ms. Demirgüç-Kunt has published widely in academic journals. Her research has focused on the links between financial development and firm performance and economic development. Banking crises, financial regulation, access to financial services including SME finance are among her areas of research. Prior to coming to the Bank, she was an Economist at the Federal Reserve Bank of Cleveland. She holds a Ph.D. and M.A. in economics from the Ohio State University.

Douglas D Evanoff is a vice president and senior research advisor for banking and financial institutions at the Federal Reserve Bank of Chicago. He serves as an advisor to senior management of the Federal Reserve System on regulatory issues and chairs the Federal Reserve Bank of Chicago's 'International Banking Conference.' His current research interests include financial regulation, consumer credit issues, mortgage markets, bank cost and merger analysis, payments system mechanisms and credit accessibility. Prior to joining the Chicago Fed, Evanoff was a lecturer in finance at Southern Illinois University and assistant professor at St. Cloud State University. He currently is an adjunct faculty member in the School of Business at DePaul University and is associate editor of *the Journal of Economics and Business,* the *Journal of Applied Banking and Finance* and *the Global Finance Journal.* He is also an institutional director on the board of the Midwest Finance Association. His research has been published both in academic and practitioner journals including the *American Economic Review, Journal of Financial Economics, Journal of Money, Credit and Banking, Journal of Financial Services Research*, and the *Journal of Banking and Finance*, among others. He has also published in numerous books and has edited a number of books addressing issues associated with financial institutions; most recently: *New Perspectives on Asset Price Bubbles* (Oxford University Press), and *Dodd-Frank Wall Street Reform and Consumer Protection Act* (World Scientific Publishing). He holds a PhD in economics from Southern Illinois University.

George G Kaufman is the John F Smith Professor of Economics and Finance at Loyola University Chicago and a consultant to the Federal Reserve Bank of Chicago. From 1959 to 1970, he was at the Federal Reserve Bank of Chicago, and after teaching for ten years at the University of Oregon, he returned as a consultant to the Bank in 1981. He has also been a visiting professor at Stanford University, the University of California, Berkeley, and the University of Southern California, as well as a visiting scholar at the Reserve Bank of New Zealand, the Federal Reserve Bank of San Francisco, and the Office of the Comptroller of the Currency. He has also served as the deputy to the assistant secretary for economic policy at the US Department of the Treasury. He is co-editor of the Journal of Financial Stability; a founding co-editor of the Journal of Financial Services Research; past president of the Western Finance Association, Midwest Finance Association, and the North American Economics and Finance Association; president-elect of the Western Economic Association; past director of the American Finance Association; and co-chair of the Shadow Financial Regulatory Committee. Kaufman holds a PhD in economics from the University of Iowa.

Contents

Part I
Special Addresses

Shared Responsibility for the Regulation of International Banks

— Chapter 1

■ Daniel K. Tarullo
Board of Governers, Federal Reserve System

1. Introduction

The regulation of financial institutions is necessarily a dynamic exercise. Growth or innovations in banking may create new risks that prompt regulatory change. The new requirements, in turn, incentivize or disincentivize certain actions by financial institutions, including shifts in activity that may start anew the process of regulatory response. The regulation of international banking reflects this general pattern, but because internationally active banks can quickly transmit financial problems across national boundaries, it also features the question of who should be doing the regulating in a dynamic financial environment.

Following the financial crisis, during which some internationally active banks posed special problems for both home and host countries, this issue has commanded attention reminiscent of the aftermaths of the Herstatt failure of the 1970s and the Bank of Commerce and Credit International (BCCI) failure of the early 1990s. Unlike those earlier instances, though,

Daniel K. Tarullo is a Member of the Board of Governors of the Federal Reserve System. The views expressed here are authors and are not necessarily shared by other members of the Federal Reserve Board or the Federal Open Market Committee.

this renewed prominence of the "who does the regulating" question has accompanied a major reconsideration of what regulation is appropriate. Today I would like to address both the "who" and the "what" issues in the regulation of international banking. My theme is hardly an original one — namely, that in the absence of either a global regulator or completely insular national banking systems, we must continue to work toward a system of shared responsibilities to assure both home and host regulators that internationally active banks are subject to adequate oversight and controls.

I will begin by reviewing briefly the benefits and risks associated with international banking and then identifying the different models for allocating responsibility for the oversight of international banks. After noting the shortcomings of the system for regulating internationally active banks that prevailed before the financial crisis and developments in the intervening years, I will turn to a consideration of the challenges that remain, with a few suggestions on how we might make more progress.

2. Benefits and Risks of International Banking

It is worth at least briefly reminding ourselves of some of the more salient advantages and risks associated with cross-border banking as they help inform development of regulatory options.[1]

Among the potential advantages are facilitating productive capital flows, diversifying risks associated with growth in host countries, diversifying the earnings and thus the stability of the global bank, offering counter-cyclical lending through support from the parent when host country economic conditions constrain domestic banking operations, enhancing efficiency in financial intermediation in host countries, providing specialized financial services,[2] and providing price or product competition

[1] By "cross-border banking", I mean to refer broadly to activities carried on outside of a bank's home country through subsidiaries and branches. I do not include direct lending or other financial transactions across national borders, whether or not facilitated by an agency in the country of the bank's customer or counterparty. While such activities can raise concerns pertaining to investor protection, the volatility of financial flows, or foreign exchange policies, relevant prudential considerations will generally be limited to the country(ies) from which the bank is initiating the transaction and raising any funds needed to fund it. For references to many individual studies examining one or more the advantages or risks, see van Horen (2014).

[2] For an example, see Claessens, Hassib, & van Horen (2015).

for banking services in host countries. The magnitude of these benefits obviously differs from country to country, depending on a variety of factors. Some of these benefits can be greater if foreign banks have the freedom to deploy capital and liquidity to whatever markets offer the most attractive opportunities, whereas others are achievable simply through the bank's expertise, existing business relationships, and range of services.

On the other side of the ledger are the risks associated with foreign banking that are distinct from risks associated with banking more generally. These risks tend to be related to the parent bank's capacity to support the larger organization. Reversals in the home market or other significant foreign operations may reduce the ability of the parent to support its foreign affiliates with needed capital and liquidity. Even if the foreign affiliate is not itself under great stress, the weakened overall condition of the parent because of problems in other parts of the world may prompt it to retrench — often rather abruptly — by reducing activity in foreign markets in which it is active. This response may be driven either by bank management itself or at the instance of home country officials who want the bank to continue to lend in its home market. Especially in countries where foreign banks account for a significant part of financial intermediation and where the underlying problems are not idiosyncratic to a specific bank, the result may be a significant diminution in intermediation beyond what would have taken place because of macroeconomic developments.

Even more serious is the risk that the foreign bank will fail, and that the home country will lack the resources or the will to ensure either that it is recapitalized and continues to function or that it fails in an orderly fashion. If the foreign operation has been thinly capitalized and is lacking in liquidity, host country officials may face an unpleasant choice between supporting a foreign bank (including operations for which they have not had consolidated supervisory responsibility) or allowing it to fail in a disorderly fashion, with potentially serious knock-on effects in the host country's financial system.

Thus, what might have been economic advantages for host countries from foreign banks in reasonably good times can turn into substantial disadvantages in periods of idiosyncratic or generalized stress? As with the benefits of foreign banking, the risks vary considerably among host countries. Obviously, countries without well-developed domestic banking systems will both benefit more and be at greater risk. Yet even the most sophisticated domestic financial systems can be affected significantly. For example, the risks can be exacerbated by funding patterns and currency mismatches, as happened in the United States during the financial crisis. Foreign banks that had been using their U.S. branches to raise dollars in short-term markets for lending around the world were suddenly left without access to this funding and, as a result, made substantial and relative to their assets — disproportionate use of the Federal Reserve's discount window.

3. Approaches to the Regulation of Internationally Active Banks

As I mentioned at the outset, international banking raises the question of who should do the regulating, as well as the question of what regulation is appropriate. The two questions are related, of course. As I will explain shortly, the nature of regulations in part depends upon the perspective and aims of the regulator. There are essentially four models, each of which has benefits and shortcomings.

First, the home jurisdiction can have dominant or exclusive regulatory responsibility for all of its banks' global operations through application of consolidated regulation and supervision. Second, host jurisdictions can have dominant regulatory responsibility for all foreign banking operations within their borders. This approach requires foreign banks to charter locally and to meet the same regulatory and supervisory standards applicable to domestic banks. Third, there can be shared authority between home and host jurisdictions, whereby host countries do some regulating and supervising of foreign banks within their borders but do not require all foreign banking activities to be locally chartered and subject to regulation identical to that of home banks. Finally, there could be one global regulator to oversee all the operations of internationally active banks around the world.

There are almost unlimited number of variations on the shared approach and, in fact, one or another variants on that approach have been adopted by most jurisdictions during the modern banking era (though there have been instances of countries severely limiting or prohibiting foreign banking altogether). Before turning to a discussion of how the shared approach has evolved and may be further modified, I think it useful to identify both the appeal and the problems with the other three, conceptually purer, approaches.

Both the attraction and limitations of the host country model are fairly apparent. On the one hand, the host country is most likely to be attentive to the risks posed to its financial system by foreign banks. More generally, the host jurisdiction is at least presumptively best positioned to craft a regulatory and supervisory framework to protect its financial system from the particular risks engendered by economic and financial conditions. Having all foreign banking operations meet local capital and other standards helps achieve that end. The risks of abrupt shifts of capital and liquidity out of the country can be minimized, and depositors can be better protected.

On the other hand, a fully local regulatory system would make the costs of entry very high. For example, if no foreign branches were allowed, or were required to operate as if they were separately chartered and capitalized, the commitment of resources needed to enter a foreign market would be considerably higher than those typically associated with opening a branch. In addition, even complete local subsidiarization might not protect a foreign banking operation from suffering some contagion if its parent is under stress. Thus, the quality of home country regulation may have some bearing even under the host country model.

Not surprisingly, the home country model presents essentially the obverse set of advantages and limitations. Having a consolidated set of capital requirements and a single supervisor allows for the quickest deployment of capital and liquidity where it is most in demand, or most needed to relieve stress, and minimizes compliance costs. However, as has often been pointed out, the home country regulator will be most responsive to the impact of both regulation and distress of its banks on its own market. In its regulatory and resolution activities, it is likely to undervalue the potential risks and costs for host countries. In periods of stress, the home country regulator, accountable primarily to home country legislators or government officials, may concentrate on stabilizing its own financial markets and be more inclined to allow, or even demand, a sharp reduction in activity abroad. The result would, at a minimum, be an abrupt decrease in intermediation at particularly sensitive times. At worst, foreign operations could default on obligations and exacerbate financial stress.[3]

At first glance, it might seem that the home country and global regulatory approaches would yield similar substantive results, since in each case, there would be consolidated regulation and supervision. A global regulator, however, would at least in theory take the interests of all jurisdictions into account in regulating, supervising, and resolving a global bank. Of course, how to balance those interests, particularly in the face of unanticipated circumstances — would be a difficult, and almost invariably political, judgment. This reality raises the thorny issue of the accountability of a global regulator.

The political factor is one of many reasons why jurisdictions are likely to remain unwilling to cede much authority to global, as opposed to international, financial institutions. Indeed, quite apart from political considerations, there may be good reasons not to do so. For one, a single global regulator of internationally active banks would presumably be something close to a regulatory monopolist, whose policies and practices could be inappropriately uniform across quite different national markets and slow to adapt to changing conditions. Also, as with dominant or exclusive reliance on home country consolidated supervision, it seems unlikely that a global regulator — no matter how well-staffed — would be fully informed on the varieties of financial risks posed to regulated institutions across national markets.

A limited exception to the general disinclination to cede financial sovereignty, as in various other areas, lies within the European Union or, more precisely, the euro zone. With the creation of a Single Supervisory Mechanism (SSM) in the European Central Bank and a freestanding Single Resolution Mechanism (SRM), there have been important transfers of authority, though national regulators continue to play a supporting

---

[3] Mindful of the considerations lying behind the limitations of both models, Dirk Schoenmaker has offered his theory of the "financial trilemma". which states that a jurisdiction can only have two of the three objectives of a stable financial system, international banking, and national regulatory policies. Professor Schoenmaker introduced his theory at a conference in 2008 and subsequently formalized it in Schoenmaker (2011). See also Richard (2007).

role. Interesting and important as this regional initiative is, however, the unique European arrangement of shared sovereignty makes it less a model for the world as a whole than an extension of the single currency project, responding to some of the difficulties encountered during the financial crisis.

4. The Shared Model and Lessons of the Crisis

The shortcomings of each conceptually "pure" model explains why some version of a shared home/host model has prevailed over time. Given the range of variations in this model, however, it is useful to bear in mind the relative advantages and disadvantages of the cleaner models in choosing the elements of a specific shared approach. In considering recent developments, as well as what remains to be done, it is also useful to begin by recalling the situation that prevailed at the onset of the financial crisis.

In its early years, the Basel Committee on Banking Supervision's work focused on elaborating the responsibilities of home and host regulators of internationally active banks. The principle of consolidated supervision was developed in the early 1980s, and reinforced following the failure of the BCCI in the early 1990s, in an effort to ensure that some regulatory authority had an overview of a global bank's consolidated assets and liabilities. At the same time, though, the Basel Committee set out expectations for host country prudential oversight of foreign banks that would be similar to that for domestic banks.[4]

The financial crisis painfully demonstrated the inadequacy of both home and host country regulation. Home country regulators of some large, internationally active banks clearly did not appreciate the risks those firms were assuming overseas. Host country regulators, including those in the United States, had not exercised prudential oversight of some foreign bank activities and had not sufficiently appreciated the

[4]The current version of this obligation is set forth in Basel Committee on Banking Supervision (2012). I have addressed the issue of host state responsibility at somewhat greater length elsewhere. Daniel K. Tarullo (2014). "Regulating Large Foreign Banking Organizations", speech delivered at the Harvard law school symposium on building the financial system of the twenty-first century, Armonk, New York, March 27.

risks associated with the funding models and other activities of some foreign banks that were subject to consolidated prudential regulation. And there were indeed instances of international bank failures in which the home country authorities seemed to focus on domestic interests to the possible detriment of the interests of host countries.[5]

Of course, regulatory failures were far more pervasive than inattention to the specifically cross-border activities of banks. The substantive rules governing capital and other requirements for all banks were woefully inadequate, although the fact that most very-large banks around the world have significant cross-border operations exacerbated the shortcomings. While banks were growing in size, integrating traditional lending and capital markets in ever more complicated ways and relying increasingly on vulnerable short-term wholesale funding models, many regulators around the world were at best failing to keep up with these changes. At worst, they removed older prudential limitations without substituting new measures designed to address the new realities of banking. The Basel Committee spent most of the decade before the crisis dominantly focused on the Basel II framework, which was intended to *reduce* somewhat effective regulatory capital levels for large banks in return for their transition to an internal-models-based approach to capital requirements. This was a choice made by national regulators, led by those in the United States, and not a byproduct of the structure of the Basel Committee itself.

Adding the lessons of the 2007–2009 financial crisis to those of earlier episodes of financial stress, I think we can infer some guidelines on host and home responsibilities to help shape expectations for practice. For host countries, the overarching guideline is that each jurisdiction should take responsibility for protecting the financial stability of its own markets as its contribution to achieving global financial stability. The extent of this responsibility obviously increases with the size and significance of the jurisdiction's financial markets. Thus the United States and the United Kingdom, which currently have the greatest concentrations of capital markets activities — have a particular obligation to oversee the local activities of both domestic and foreign banks that

[5] For a review of these instances, see Schoenmaker (2013).

could pose particular risks to financial stability and are likely to be especially difficult to observe for a home country supervisor less familiar with those markets.

A corollary of this general guideline is that the scope of host country regulation might sensibly vary with the size and systemic importance of foreign banks. This notion is consistent with the principle embodied in the Dodd–Frank Wall Street Reform and Consumer Protection Act that prudential regulation should be progressively more stringent as banks pose greater risks to financial stability. As I will discuss in a moment, this principle also lies behind some of the post-crisis frameworks developed by the Basel Committee and the Financial Stability Board (FSB).

For home countries, the relatively longstanding principle that regulators should exercise effective consolidated supervision remains critical, though I would emphasize that the regulation imposed by home jurisdictions is of equal — if not greater — importance. It is important to emphasize that this obligation is not a substitute for host country regulation and supervision of foreign banking organizations (FBOs). The home jurisdiction regulatory structure must ensure that the banks are fundamentally safe and sound, and that the parent will generally be able to support its operations around the world. Here, of course, a major shortcoming of the pre-crisis regime becomes apparent, in that capital and other regulatory requirements for internationally active banks were simply not strong enough.

Consolidated supervision must contain the risks to the financial system created by banking activity that is not fully captured by regulations. It must also ensure that banks do not hide problems by shifting assets or liabilities around their global operations and, more generally, that the banks are fundamentally safe and sound so as to forestall possible contagion risk to foreign operations.

Within these admittedly broad guidelines, there is obviously room for host countries to balance the benefits and risks presented by FBOs in a number of different ways. Their choices will be affected by policy preferences, the characteristics of their domestic financial systems, and the relative importance of foreign banks in those systems. The host country choices will also inevitably be affected by how home countries are carrying out their regulatory and supervisory roles. This consideration includes, of course, not just regulations that are nominally applicable, but the manner in which those regulations are enforced.

Branching presents a particularly instructive example of the tension between assuring financial stability and permitting foreign banking operations that may carry economic benefits. Because branches are not separately chartered and capitalized, a bank can relatively easily enter a foreign market by opening a branch, through which it can make loans — often initially to companies from its home country — using funds from the home bank. Particularly where (as in the United States) foreign branches are forbidden by local law from accepting retail deposits, it might seem that there are minimal risks to the host country if the parent bank (and thus the local branch) fails. However, U.S. experience with foreign branches in the decade prior to the crisis shows the very real risks that can arise when a branch is used to raise funds in the host country (in the United States, in dollars) through short-term wholesale borrowing, and then directs those funds out of the host country for loans or asset purchases by other parts of the bank. As noted earlier, when short-term funding dried up, many foreign branches were left seriously short of liquidity and had to turn to the discount window.

A shared feature of the U.S. and European Union regulatory systems for foreign banks is that branching is permitted without requiring separate capitalization. Many other jurisdictions have similar policies. Thus opportunities for foreign bank entry and market access are provided. In the United States, larger branches do have to meet some liquidity requirements, though they are less restrictive than the standards applicable to domestic banks and intermediate holding companies. This requirement is an important example of a prudential measure that balances financial stability and the benefits of international banking. The degree to which we or, I presume, other jurisdictions will remain comfortable with this balance will depend on two factors. The first factor is the degree to which local branches are used by foreign banks as significant sources of unstable funding or for other risky purposes. While this has been a significant issue in the United States, it is less clear that other jurisdictions face similar risks. The second is the confidence host jurisdiction regulators have that the parent banks are subject to effective regulatory and supervisory oversight.

5. Developments Since the Crisis

The profound shift in political and policy environments as a result of the financial crisis has led to considerable strengthening of minimum international standards for internationally active banks, at both national and international levels. Basel III enhanced the quantity and quality of capital requirements and introduced, for the first time, quantitative liquidity standards. Following completion of Basel III, the Basel Committee developed a structure of slightly misleadingly named capital "surcharges", which requires global systemically important banks (GSIBs) to maintain higher capital levels.[6]

The Federal Reserve supported all these measures but was a particularly strong advocate of the capital surcharges, which established the new principle that some international prudential standards should be progressively more stringent as the systemic importance of a bank increases. In meeting its responsibility to promote domestic financial stability, the Federal Reserve last year followed the lead set by the European Union some years previously and adopted a regulation requiring subsidiaries of GSIBs engaged in traditional banking as well as those engaged in capital markets activities be covered by local capital requirements consistent with Basel III. But neither in the United States nor the European Union do the GSIB capital surcharges imposed at the consolidated level apply to foreign banking operations in their jurisdictions.[7] So even if the global bank has local capital requirements for most or all of its foreign operations, the parent still has some flexibility as to where the additional capital buffer can be maintained. More generally, our requirements for other prudential regulations applicable to FBOs are calibrated to the relative importance of the FBOs in the U.S. financial system. Thus the structure of surcharges also help to create a good mechanism for balancing host country interests in assuring financial stability and in realizing the benefits that can come from global banking.

---

[6] I say "misleadingly" called capital surcharges because that term implies the banks are faced with a "charge" that has to be paid to someone. In fact, of course, the requirement is that the bank retain higher capital buffers in order to increase its resiliency.

[7] 79 FR 17240 (March 27, 2014); and Tarullo, Regulating Large Foreign Banking Organizations.

Even with good standards, regulators in host jurisdictions will want assurance that these standards are being rigorously implemented and enforced. The relative opaqueness of bank balance sheets makes capital, liquidity, and other common banking regulations difficult to monitor effectively. This argues for complementing fairly complex regulation that seeks to track the often-complex activities of large banks with simpler regulations, such as the leverage ratio and a standardized risk-weighted capital floor. But it also argues for existing international fora such as the Basel Committee and the FSB to provide effective monitoring mechanisms. Even with higher standards in place, supervisors in home and host jurisdictions will still face challenges in assessing cross-jurisdiction vulnerabilities. More regular sharing of information and assessments among home and key host jurisdictions both formally and informally should be high on our shared agenda.

At present, both those groups have useful processes for overseeing the implementation of agreed upon international standards. But they tend to be a bit formalistic, concentrating on comparing the language of domestic implementation to that of the international standards, rather than examining whether domestic practice in fact ensures substantive compliance or gaining a shared understanding of the unique risks in each market.

It would, I believe, be counterproductive to establish in either the Basel Committee or the FSB the kind of adversarial dispute settlement process associated, for example, with the World Trade Organization. It is in the interest of all members of those bodies to cooperate in the shared task of overseeing internationally active banks. Thus, the better approach to compliance would be one that simultaneously provides regulators with a way to work with one another and to gain deeper insight into how their counterparts in other jurisdictions are applying prudential standards.

For example, there has been considerable documentation of the interjurisdictional divergence in risk weights for similar exposures under the internal models-based capital approaches of Basel II.[8] While the Basel Committee has been working on this issue,[9] I suspect that one of the most effective ways of promoting broadly comparable risk weighting

---

[8] See generally Le Leslé & Avramova (2012).

[9] See Ingves (2014).

would be to have technically competent supervisory staff from other jurisdictions participate with home regulators in the actual bank model validations, oversight, and related supervisory functions. Similarly, as stress testing becomes a more important global financial stability tool, it will be useful to have staff experienced in stress testing at home participating in the stress testing exercises of other jurisdictions. These kinds of interactions, along with the more traditional device of supervisory colleges, can help foster confidence among host jurisdictions in both the regulatory and supervisory activities of home country authorities.

Another useful practice for furthering mutual confidence would be a program for regular contact among the very top officials of key regulators. The original Basel Committee brought together these officials for what were usually relatively informal meetings. As one of the early participants in those meetings once told me, the relationships he built with his counterparts through these regular contacts served everyone well when issues concerning international banks arose. But with the concentration of the Basel Committee on sometimes highly technical standards, participation has generally drifted down to the senior staff level. The FSB was created in part to compensate for this change in the Basel Committee. And the FSB usually does garner higher levels of participation. However, other features of the FSB — such as, including market regulators and finance ministries in order to provide a broader range of views on financial stability issues — mean that the FSB cannot serve the original Basel Committee purpose either. Moreover, even when the right member agencies are represented, the actual individuals participating may not be the most senior officials in the supervisory function of those agencies. Finally, the near doubling in size of both the Basel Committee and the FSB, while again critical for ensuring a representative group to consider financial stability issues, further complicates the matter.

Thus, while a regular, high-level interaction among all key regulators would be optimal, for the foreseeable future, we will probably have to live with something less than optimal. Ad hoc meetings around the fringes of various Basel convocations and bilateral interactions may have to suffice. In this regard, I note the importance of the creation of the SSM within the European Central Bank as the supervisor for all larger banks in the euro zone. The Federal Reserve has already established instructive and productive relationships with the experienced and committed group of supervisors that have been brought in to lead the SSM.

6. The Limits of Shared Responsibility

It is important to recognize, though, that even with the best of intentions and actions in home country regulatory and supervisory regimes, there will be limits to how much responsibility can appropriately be shared for international banking activities. These limits are most apparent in the context of the possible insolvency of a major foreign banking organization.[10] The work of the FSB in promoting effective resolution regimes around the world and in seeking an international framework for building the total loss absorbing capacity (TLAC) of GSIBs are very good examples of cooperative efforts that promote the aim of ensuring that even the largest banks can fail without either causing financial disorder or requiring injection of public capital. My expectation is that the FSB's framework for TLAC will incorporate the principle of an extra buffer of loss absorbing capacity at the consolidated level beyond what may be required in the aggregate at local levels.[11] But the margin may be a little thinner here, precisely because of the circumstances in which the loss absorption capacity may be needed.

With respect to going concern prudential requirements such as capital levels, host countries have a continuing opportunity to observe how home country officials are regulating and supervising their banks. Particularly if effective monitoring mechanisms are developed, host countries may become comfortable with limited oversight of some or all domestic operations of foreign banks. If they see the rigor of home consolidated oversight waning, they will have a chance to intensify their own supervision. But with the prospect of a failed bank, there will be no time for such adjustments or, as a practical matter, the capacity to impose new requirements may become limited by the time the prospect of failure is looming. The imposition of requirements in the midst of a

[10] Indeed, Dirk Schoenmaker developed his notion of the financial trilemma around the conflicts of interest that arise in the context of the insolvency of a global bank.
[11] The TLAC proposal of the FSB contemplates that host authorities will set internal TLAC requirements at 75–90% of applicable external TLAC requirements.

crisis would in any event likely exacerbate stress. Even with the best of intentions, today's home country regulators cannot effectively bind their successors' response to the insolvency of one of their globally important banks when political and economic pressures are likely to be high.

The gone-concern loss absorbency requirement for FBO intermediate holding companies proposed by the Federal Reserve Board on October 30 should enhance the prospects for an orderly firmwide global resolution of an FBO by its home country resolution authority through increasing confidence that the U.S. operations of the FBO will obtain their appropriate share of the loss absorbency capacity of the consolidated foreign bank. Past experience suggests that host supervisors are most likely to ringfence assets when there is doubt that the local customers and counterparties of foreign banks will be adequately taken into account. Yet if, for any reason, the home jurisdiction resolution is unsuccessful, the internal long-term debt will be available to U.S. authorities for orderly resolution and recapitalization of the intermediate holding companies.

We have calibrated our proposed internal TLAC requirements slightly below our proposed external TLAC requirements for U.S. GSIBs. This slightly lower calibration for internal TLAC recalls the difference between local going-concern capital requirements and the GSIB surcharge, but the gap is somewhat smaller, reflecting the concerns I mentioned a moment ago. The proposal thus balances support for the preferred resolution strategy of the home resolution authority of the foreign GSIB with assurance of U.S. financial stability if that strategy cannot be executed successfully.[12]

7. Conclusion

My view of shared responsibility for overseeing international banks emphasizes the importance of financial stability even as it allows for benefits specific to international banking. For the reasons I have explained, in the end host countries need to make the judgments on the tradeoffs

[12] Our internal TLAC proposal effects this balance principally by not including parent GSIB surcharges in the calibration for FBO intermediate holding companies but also by lowering the baseline TLAC requirement for U.S. intermediate holding company subsidiaries of single-point-of-entry strategy FBOs from 18% of risk-weighted assets to 16% of risk-weighted assets.

between these goals. But I have also explained how a strong set of international prudential standards and good institutional relationships among regulators could help tilt this balance toward greater flexibility for internationally active banks.

In response to positions akin to what I have presented today, one often hears complaints that the emphasis on financial stability will result in the balkanization of international banking. I would note first that it is not at all clear that developments since the crisis have on net balkanized banking, so much as shifted some international banking assets from the Organisation for Economic Co-operation and Development (OECD) countries whose banks were disproportionately affected by the financial crisis to banks from some emerging market and developing countries.[13] This development probably reflects both needed changes in some of the OECD nation banks and a logical reflection of the increasing economic importance of the non-OECD countries.

Second, I wonder how these critics can think that the pre-crisis situation of supposedly consolidated oversight and substantial bank flexibility was a desirable one. At least some of the flexibility enjoyed by banks in shifting capital and liquidity around the globe was deployed in pursuit of unsustainable activity that eventually ran badly aground.

Third, as I suggested earlier, even where concerns about "trapped" capital or liquidity are more sensibly based, reasonable ex ante constraints by host country authorities in pursuit of a sound and stable domestic financial system are likely to be far preferable to ex post constraints — for example, ringfencing — that are imposed when the foreign bank is under the greatest pressure.

References

Basel Committee on Banking Supervision (2012). *Core principles for effective banking supervision.* (Basel, Switzerland: Bank for International Settlements, September).

Claessens, S. & van Horen, N. (2014). The impact of the global financial crisis on banking globalization. *IMF Working Papers 14/197*, (Washington: International Monetary Fund, October).

[13] For a discussion of these points, see Claessens & van Horen (2014).

Claessens, S., Hassib, O., & van Horen, N. (2015). The role of foreign banks in trade. *mimeo*, (Washington: Board of Governors of the Federal Reserve System and De Nederlandsche Bank, March).

Ingves S. (2014). Finishing the job: Next steps for the Basel Committee, keynote address to the ninth BCBS-FSI high-level meeting on "Strengthening financial sector supervision and current regulatory priorities", Cape Town, South Africa, January 30.

Leslé, V. L. & Avramova, S. (2012). Revisiting riskweighted assets. *IMF Working Paper No. 12/90*, (Washington: International Monetary Fund, March).

Richard J. H. (2007). Conflicts between home and host country prudential supervisors. In D. D. Evanoff, George G. K., & John R. L., (Eds.), *International financial stability: Global banking and national regulation* (pp. 201–220). (Hackensack, N.J: World Scientific).

Schoenmaker, D. (2011). The financial trilemma. *Economics Letters*, *111*, 57–59.

Schoenmaker, D. (2013). *Governance of International Banking: The Financial Trilemma*. Oxford: Oxford University Press.

Schoenmaker D. (2013). *Governance of International Banking: The financial Trilemma* (pp. 72–87). Oxford: Oxford University Press.

Post-Crisis Risks and Bank Equity Capital

— CHAPTER 2

■ Thomas M. Hoenig
Federal Deposit Insurance Corporation

1. Introduction

It has been a rugged decade for the global economy, its financial firms, and their regulators. The economy has experienced crisis, followed by bail-outs, followed by thousands of pages of laws and regulations designed to address the deficiencies. However, for all this activity, people remain highly uncertain about what to expect from our economic institutions in the decade ahead. The dimensions of this uncertainty ultimately will depend on the choices and standards of performance demanded of those institutions today. It is with this in mind that I want to discuss one such standard — the role of capital — in the context of the conference theme: the future of large, internationally active banks.

I acknowledge that progress has been made in strengthening our financial institutions. Capital and liquidity positions of large banking organizations have improved since the crisis. I also acknowledge that stronger rules and more demanding regulators have played a role in achieving this improvement. Nevertheless, progress has been modest at

---

Thomas M. Hoenig is the Vice Chairman of the FDIC and the former President of the Federal Reserve Bank of Kansas City. The views expressed are those of the author and not necessarily those of the FDIC. His research and other material can be found at http://www.fdic.gov/about/learn/board/hoenig/.

best, and with the rich incentives that come from the safety net, there is constant pressure to compromise boundaries intended to strengthen the system. An example of the important decisions pending in the international arena is the Basel Committee's announced intention to review the calibration of its leverage ratio framework, after only recently recognizing its importance. My message, therefore, is that while there has been progress improving capital, much remains undone and there is no place for complacency regarding the stability of our financial system.

2. Two Regulatory Options: Risk Prediction or Equity Capital

To begin, global banks are not as well capitalized as some within the industry would have you believe. The fact is they remain highly leveraged and highly complicated, and should one fail, it would have systemic, destabilizing consequences. There are two different ways to address these concerns. One would require detailed rules to control firms' behaviors, structure their balance sheets, and direct their activities. The latest example is the Federal Reserve's minimum debt proposal, recently put out for discussion, that would require firms to issue additional long-term debt that would turn to equity when needed in order to increase their "total loss-absorbing capacity". But it is costly to service this debt, putting earnings pressure on firms and their units that — all else being equal — could accelerate failure should an institution run into financial trouble. This goes to the core of our discussion about the fundamental need for equity, versus debt, to make a financial system strong. A question we must ask, then, is whether the effect of such a requirement that is designed to make a firm more resolvable once that firm has failed, could — prior to failure — increase the firm's leverage and thereby its likelihood to default. Our goal to prevent failure should be every bit as important as resolving failed firms.

The other way to promote stability would be to simply demand more equity capital to enable banking firms to better withstand a crisis, while allowing them to run their businesses with less government direction.

The first option would require regulators to predict what activities and investments might cause future crises. It also would require them to calibrate rules in a manner that would not give rise to subsequent crises. In other words, regulators would have to successfully anticipate the source of future crises, which as you know could arise from a number of activities, but mostly likely will come from something we fail to predict.

The second approach is based on equity capital and thus would not require such extraordinary insight from regulators. By design, it acknowledges that regulators cannot predict events and it ensures a safer system because well capitalized institutions are better able to withstand shocks and survive crises. Using simple leverage measures instead of risk-based capital measures eliminates relying on the best guesses of financial regulators to guide decisions.

3. Ever-Changing Sources of Risk

Bank balance sheets today hold a range of assets that are unavoidably more sensitive to changes in interest rates than even just prior to the crisis. The near-zero short term interest rates of the post-crisis period have boosted the value of stocks and bonds, and they have encouraged increased leverage through low-cost borrowing at extended maturities. For example, the average maturity of newly issued corporate bonds is approaching 15 years, according to SIFMA data.

What zero interest rates give, rising interest rates can take away. Bond arithmetic tells us that the value of many long maturity, low coupon fixed income bonds issued in recent years can be expected to decline sharply in response to increases in interest rates or credit spreads, or just the expectations of such changes. Experience also tells us that additional risk can come from unpredictable flash events of heightened volatility for those financial assets that are electronically traded and at high speed.

While financial institutions are used to dealing with changes in interest rates, keeping them artificially at the zero bound for so long changes the calculus of this risk. The volume of fixed income obligations in the system, whose value is highly sensitive to interest rates, is large and growing. For the largest banks, unrealized losses on available for-sale securities will be passed through to regulatory capital, appropriately so. But this is an added risk factor with which they have previously not had to deal. Also, during the next rising rate cycle, pent-up customer demand for yield may force banks to re-price their deposits faster than has historically been the case. Lastly, how retail investors in bond funds would respond to a rising rate cycle is uncertain, as are the knock-on effects of large selling pressure by these funds.

Then there is the derivatives market, which the largest global banks continue to dominate and where they hold significant exposures. Notional values of derivatives held by FDIC-insured institutions exceeded $200 trillion at mid-year 2015. It is often pointed out that most U.S. interest rate swaps and CDS index swaps are now cleared and information on these derivatives is reported to trade repositories. Notional volumes have come down as a result of trade compression, and an enhanced margin rule recently finalized should further encourage clearing. Still, by some measures, derivatives exposure is a larger exposure category for banks today than just prior to the crisis. Net current credit exposure for derivatives at insured U.S. commercial banks and savings associations is about twice the pre-crisis average, according to the OCC's most recent Quarterly Derivatives Report.

Further, while the increased use of clearing has changed the locus of these exposures, it has not lessened risks to the system. The migration of standardized derivatives to clearing was a policy decision intended to make the system safer, but without question it elevates the systemic importance of safe and sound operations by central counterparties (CCPs). The potential for unanticipated events and risks, including resolution challenges, associated with the growing use of CCPs is a subject of concern to many observers and is being studied by international groups.

One potential source of trouble, for example, involves CCPs lowering their margin requirements, which is analogous to banks competing for loans by weakening their underwriting standards. If underwriting or margins are lessened too much, exposures mount quickly and often unexpectedly. In this context the capital that a CCP holds typically is relatively small in relation to the volume of its derivatives business. The market tends to downplay this because clearing members' guarantees place the risk of client non-performance on their member banks rather than the CCP. However, this simply punts the risk down the field. The risk still ultimately is against the capital of the CCP's member banks. Thus, the use of CCPs may not provide as much comfort as we might have intended. The Basel leverage ratio, which has been adopted for the largest firms in the U.S., requires banks to hold a small amount of capital against the potentially unlimited guarantee they provide to the CCP. Nevertheless, efforts continue to try to reduce or eliminate the capital they hold against this guarantee. If this were to be allowed, large amounts of economic exposure to derivatives — significant financial leverage and risk — would vanish from the regulatory capital radar screen, encouraging even larger volumes of interlinked and opaque derivatives activity. Such an outcome strikes me as a counterintuitive abandonment of post-crisis regulatory initiatives.

Another troubling source of market volatility and uncertainty is "the great bear market in commodity prices" that has persisted throughout much of the post-crisis period. The Bloomberg commodity index, for example, which tracks the prices of major industrial raw materials, had — as of last week — declined 63% from its July 2008 peak to its lowest level since 2002.[1]

Important industry sectors such as energy and shipping have come under pressure, along with individual firms with leveraged exposure to commodities. Complicating matters further are the linkages in both directions between commodity prices and financial markets. For example, some analysts have suggested that a tremendous expansion and subsequent contraction of structured finance and swaps activity related to commodities was an important driver of the pre-crisis commodity price boom and its subsequent collapse.[2] In the other direction, lost revenues from the sale of commodities by emerging market countries can drain their reserves and affect currency prices and the performance of a variety of financial contracts.

Finally, we cannot ignore the reality that international financial linkages across countries are more important now than they were even just five years ago. For example, the deep concern expressed by policymakers that Greece, a country with a GDP smaller than that of Louisiana, might default or exit from the Eurozone suggests in part wariness about potentially unknowable financial linkages and knock-on

---

[1] Headline commodity index, http://www.bloombergindexes.com/resources/, accessed October 26, 2015.

[2] See, e.g., http://ftalphaville.ft.com/2012/05/08/990211/the-subpriming-of-commodities/ and http://www.cnbc.com/2015/01/06/not-just-oil-are-lower-commodity-prices-here-to-stay.html, accessed October 26, 2015.

effects in this interconnected world. The extent to which changes in Chinese economic activity can reverberate on Wall Street further emphasizes the fragility of such linkages. And of course, U.S. developments with respect to our own federal debt limit are closely tracked overseas, because of their potential ripple effects.

At another level, international linkages are growing not only across legal boundaries but also within our largest banking organizations. For example, the proportion of derivatives activity in the lead IDIs of the eight U.S. G-SIBs that is conducted from their foreign offices increased from 43% at yearend 2009 to 51%at yearend 2014. Exposures recorded as "net due from" amounts that these IDIs have to their Edge corporation subsidiaries and other foreign subsidiaries increased from less than $2 billion at yearend 2009 to almost $200 billion at yearend 2014. I am not suggesting any specific safety and soundness concerns by mentioning these numbers, but I am suggesting that the potential for transmission of unanticipated risks across international boundaries does not appear to be diminishing with time — quite the opposite. These are not risks that I suggest banks should run from, but they are risks that banks must acknowledge and be prepared to absorb. Saying your risk models take care of it is not credible.

Some of these sources of risk undoubtedly have been fed by current regulations designed to direct banks' activities in accordance with regulators' views. For example, banks levered up on sovereign debt of nations such as Greece due to the zero risk-weighting given by "risk-based" rules. Trying to avoid crisis by directing activity and favoring certain investments to avoid crisis has not proven successful so far, and I am doubtful it ever will. Rather, the banks that historically have best weathered crises are the ones with strong equity capital.

4. Trust Built on Equity Capital

We hear often that trust and confidence in a system is necessary for it to successfully grow and create wealth. In the last crisis, analysts didn't trust banks' risk models — they trusted equity capital. This capital is a necessary ingredient to building that trust. It will help to ensure that banks can survive liquidity runs because someone will continue to lend to institutions that are still demonstrably solvent, and it will make failure — or need for bailout — less likely. Perhaps most importantly, strong capital will not require regulators to pick favored investments and put strict, complicated restrictions on an ever-growing set of activities.

The next question, then, is how have we done at promoting this cushion of equity? I estimate that for the eight U.S. G-SIBs, a simple measure of tangible equity to tangible assets on the balance sheet comes to about 7.7% for the group as of mid-year 2015. When the firms' balance sheets and this ratio are adjusted, using estimates of International Financial Reporting Standards (IFRS), to measure derivatives exposure, the equity cushion for the group shrinks to about 5.7% of exposure.[3] That is barely two percentage points higher than what these largest banks held as an industry when they entered the crisis, and it is unlikely to be adequate to maintain market confidence should we encounter any major recession or significant deterioration in asset values.

I have been told that a G-SIB needs less capital because it is more diversified than smaller regional banks. But G-SIBs today are more exposed, not less, to the types of common market-based, interconnected, and opaque financial risks that move together and too often undermine stability. And of course, their operations now are more, not less, integral to financial markets that so decisively control the performance of the broader economy.

5. Costs of Capital

What about concerns for the costs of capital? The effect of higher capital on a bank's foregone tax deductions, cost of funds, return on equity, industry ranking, and management bonuses are important for banks, of course, but these factors cannot be judged in isolation. A more complete question from a system-wide perspective includes asking whether higher levels of bank capital affect sustainable levels of economy-wide consumption and output over time.

In this respect and for the ranges we are talking about, the system-wide benefits of strong equity capital would appear to far exceed the aggregate economic costs over the business cycle and thus should not be

[3] For further information and data, see the Global Capital index: https://www.fdic.gov/about/learn/board/hoenig/capitalizationratio2015-2.pdf.

ignored. In the last crisis, for example, data show that better capitalized banks failed less frequently and were able to maintain lending more effectively than their less well capitalized counterparts.[4] I would add further that, on a relative basis, current media coverage suggest that better capitalized U.S. banks are currently outperforming their less well capitalized European counterparts.

6. Conclusion

Let me end by emphasizing that in the absence of government bailouts, a successful financial industry requires strong equity capital — and then good assets and earnings supported by this capital. ROEs might be boosted in the short term using excessive leverage, but that is almost never sustainable in the longer run. Thus, bankers and their regulators cannot afford to fall into the old habit of thinking when times are good that equity capital is merely a cost to the system.

Policymakers involved in capital regulation, including the Basel Committee as it proceeds with its review of the calibration of the leverage ratio, should take seriously the benefits of a strong foundation of equity capital, best measured using a leverage ratio. Contrary to some claims, equity capital in fact supports sustainable risk taking over the course of the cycle by removing the necessity of regulators to pick winners and losers, thus allowing the owners of the capital to take their own risks, run their own firms, and absorb their own losses without public support.

[4] Capital and lending ratios: https://www.fdic.gov/about/learn/board/hoenig/Lending%20through%20the%20cycle.pdf; failed bank capital ratios: https://www.fdic.gov/about/learn/board/hoenig/Failed%20Bank%20Capital%20Ratios%20at%20YE%202007_03%2026%202015.pdf.

Reputational Risks and Large International Banks

— CHAPTER 3

▪ Ingo Walter
New York University

1. Introduction

Reputational or "franchise" risk has been a key attribute of banking from its inception. Perhaps more than some other businesses, the foundations of banking are built on duties of care and loyalty in the management of money and capital — at the limit, if trust dies, the bank dies.

This chapter considers the "special" nature of banking and financial services and challenges to their franchises that banks and other financial firms seem to encounter with growing frequency and intensity. What exactly is "reputational risk", and how is it driven by transactions costs and imperfect information in the financial industry? What empirical research is there on the impact of reputational losses imposed on financial intermediaries, and how are they different from accounting losses?[1] The paper concludes with some key implications for risk governance.

2. Lessons from the Past

Reputational risk in banking and finance is nothing new. It can be found in historical accounts dating at least to biblical times, cementing the

[1] Earlier studies focusing on reputation include Chemmanur & Fulghieri (1994), Smith (1992), Walter & De Long (1995) and Smith & Walter (1997).

"specialness" of banking in the public discourse and engaging thinkers as diverse as Machiavelli, Adam Smith, Walter Bagehot, Frederick the Great, and Alexander Hamilton.

Damage associated with banking issues tends to spread beyond those immediately involved to the broader economy, and reflected in episodic booms, busts and panics throughout financial history. In due course, regulation targeting individual firms and the financial system as a whole usually gained traction, ranging from honest dealing and "fitness and properness" reviews of banks and bankers to wholesale constraint-based approaches intended to match the ultimate financial backstop of the general public with the public's right to set the rules. Privatizing gains and socializing losses in the financial system has never been politically tenable for very long.

Fast-forwarding to recent times, banking and finance have continued to be dogged by reputational issues. Issues centered on with conflicted equity research, insider trading, late-trading in mutual funds, fee kickbacks to insurance brokers, mis-selling complex securities and worthless payment protection insurance, stock clearing for pump-and-dump brokerage scams erupted with alarming regularity — in each case eroding the vital trust attribute of the industry. Sometimes prosecutorial zeal perhaps went gone too far, extracting settlements from firms in no position to argue their case in open court. Too often, one eruption began to fade just as another was just over the horizon.

The global financial crisis of 2007–2009 inflicted enormous financial damage and arguably brought the financial industry and its professionals to a reputational nadir around the world. What has happened since that time to restore financial firms to their former glory near the top of the reputational food-chain? Boards and managers in the banking industry have little good to say about the massive taxpayer bailouts that rescued the system and inevitable regulatory tightening that followed in their struggle to get back to business as usual. Almost a decade after the financial turbulence began to unfold, the industry's reputation has not yet recovered.

Why? Maybe people have longer memories than they used to, or the "made in finance" crisis hit them harder and lasted longer than they had imagined. Maybe it's the old and new reputational carnage that seems to pop-up like clockwork, penetrating even corners of finance that had nothing to do with the crisis. Or maybe it's the finance industry itself, apparently not capable of learning past lessons, a no-holds-barred profile in politics, and an exaggerated sense of self-worth.

The blowback inevitably continues to damage the industry itself and its people, as layers of regulation are piled on, weighing on financial efficiency and passing the cost on to clients, employees and shareholders. Nobody knows how large these efficiency losses are or how they affect economic welfare and growth in the name of greater stability and robustness. But the legacy imbedded in people's memories that now passes to the next generation militates against taking chances on reversing excessive regulation, and the drumbeat of reputation-sensitive revelations keeps the flame alive.

3. Specialness

Financial services comprise an array of what are arguably "special" businesses. They are "special" because they deal mainly with other people's money and because problems that arise in financial intermediation can trigger serious external costs. In recent years, the roles of various types of financial intermediaries have evolved dramatically, as summarized in Figure 1.

Capital markets and institutional asset managers have taken a greater portion of the intermediation function from banks, who themselves have followed the money by grating "universal" banking firms. Insurance activities conducted in the capital markets such as credit default swaps (CDS) compete with classic insurance and reinsurance functions. Fiduciary activities for institutional and retail clients are conducted by banks, broker–dealers, life insurers, and independent fund management companies. Financial intermediaries in each cohort compete as vigorously with their traditional rivals as with players in other cohorts, catalyzed by deregulation and innovation in financial products and processes.

At the same time, the information infrastructure of financial intermediation has continues to evolve, driving down information costs and making available to market participants all kinds of interpretation of material developments. Equally, the system's "plumbing" (trading and payments, clearance and settlement, custody, etc.) has exploited economies of scale

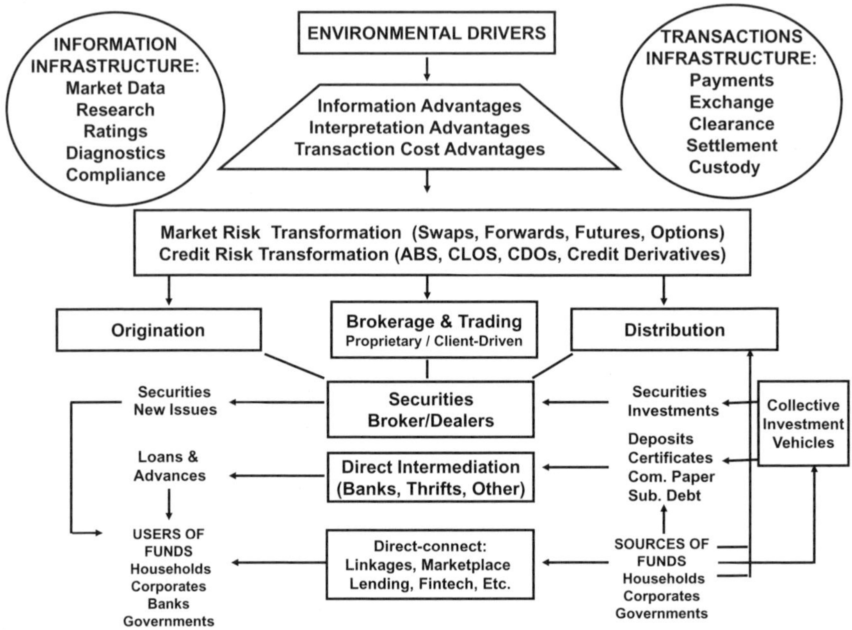

Figure 1. Schematic of financial functions.

as well as technology to lower transactions costs. The impact of improved information- and transaction-economies on financial efficiency have doubtless been dramatic, forcing firms in the industry into new strategies exploiting remaining anomalies and in particular their competitive advantages in *interpreting* market developments. This allows them to trade profitably against counterparties and add value for clients. The intensity of competition in this environment have made life as a financial intermediary a lot tougher, and sometimes the search for an "edge" leads over the edge.

In this dynamic, market developments have sometimes overtaken regulatory capabilities intended to promote financial stability and fairness alongside efficiency and innovation. The regulatory arbitrage that can result had a lot to do with the financial crisis and the ensuing Great Recession, and has been addressed in many of the regulatory measures that have been implemented or proposed. But it inevitably resurfaces in a perennial game of cat and mouse between the financial industry and its regulators. The next chapter in the evolution of the tableau in Figure 1 may be even more interesting as marketplace lenders, robo-advisers, and the rechanneling of intermediation through hedge funds and private equity funds, insurance companies, asset managers and others in shadow banking press competitive advantages provided attributable to differential regulatory costs.

Large international banks have traditionally dominated cross-border dimensions of the functions identified in Figure 1, especially in global wholesale financial activities. Many of them have been active as well in multi-local and regional businesses such as retail and private banking, middle-market lending and asset management. A relatively level domestic playing field that allows vigorous competition by foreign-based banks can be highly productive as it typically lifts the performance of all banks and improves local financial efficiency and innovation. At the same time it exposes international banks to country risk in a general sense as well as through the regulatory environment. Local political economics differ widely, and experienced international bankers soon become adept in striking a viable balance between the domestic regulatory setting and profitability.

These challenges can be summarized in Figure 2, a simple matrix that can be applied by partitioning specific client segments (C), geographic

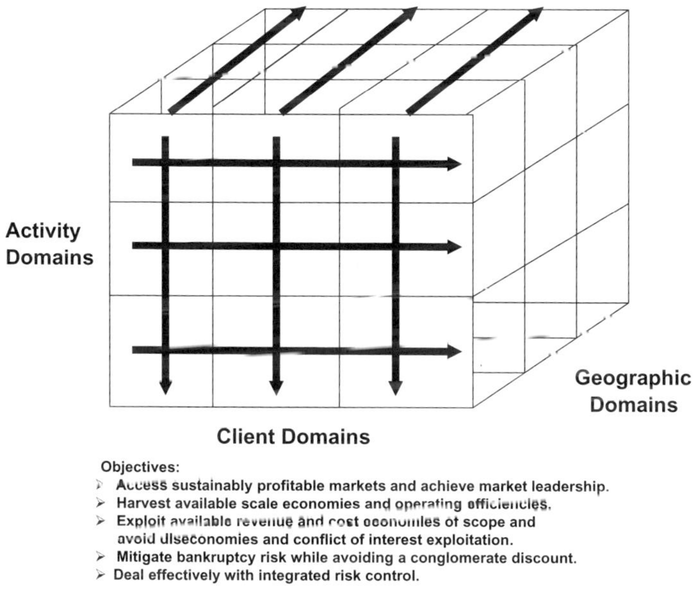

Figure 2. Creating value in a large internationally active bank.

arenas of operation (A) and financial products (P). Applying the (C–A–P matrix in the real world is anything but simple. The cells (individual markets) have to be calibrated in terms of size and growth potential (depending on classifications used, in many cases assigning a value of zero), competitive structure and conduct, ease of entry and exit, and other factors familiar in industrial organization. The cells are also linked within a given arena by product (scale economies) and clients (cost and revenue scope economies), as well as across arenas — which may run the gamut from seamless global platforms to highly specialized niche activities.

The extreme complexity of managing large international banks becomes clear by notionally superimposing the C–A–P matrix in Figure 2 onto the functional tableau of financial services in Figure 1 and imagining what separates more successful from less successful players in maximizing global risk-adjusted returns to capital that ultimately drives the value of the firm for its shareholders.

It is unsurprising that the global functional and activity models suggested above would give rise to significant reputational risk exposure for all financial firms, and perhaps especially large international banks. For their part, investors in banks and other financial intermediaries are sensitive to the going-concern value of the firms they own, and hence to the governance processes that are supposed to work in their interests. Regulators, in turn, are sensitive to the safety, soundness, and integrity of the financial system and, from time to time, will recalibrate the rules of the game. Market discipline, operating through the governance process, interacts with the regulatory process in ways that involve both costs and benefits to market participants and is reflected in the value of their business franchises. In turn, excellence in corporate governance is supposed to align the interests of shareholders — through the stock price — with the interests of other constituencies like managers, employees and clients in a sustainable way. But in the case of systemically important financial institutions like large international banks, the prevailing incentives have demonstrably left taxpayers exposed, allegedly "privatizing returns and socializing risks". So along with the inevitable regulatory reforms and tougher enforcement, the prospect of still further erosion of a bank's franchise through reputational losses can with proper governance improve financial stability going forward.

All the more curious, therefore, that large international banks have encountered a drumbeat of reputational losses, including new revelations having nothing to do with the financial turbulence. Some examples are listed in Box 1. Banks and bankers, some would argue, have somehow drifted in their key role as efficient allocators of capital

Box 1: Examples of Reputation-Sensitive Banking Practices: 2000–2015

- Mis-selling worthless payment protection insurance to retail mortgage and credit card customers.
- Promoting in-house products against superior (better-performing or cheaper) third-party products.
- Allowing hedge funds to trade in-house mutual fund shares after the NAV (net asset value) fixing at the close of market.
- Invading segregated customer accounts.
- Facilitating offshore clients' evasion of tax obligations in their countries of residence.
- Facilitating criminal money laundering.
- Evading bilateral and multilateral trade and financial sanctions — "wire-stripping.".
- Selling toxic securities to institutional investors.
- Taking proprietary trading positions against clients.
- Using client advisory relationship to earn kickbacks from product vendors?
- Designing off-balance-sheet structures for clients solely for purposes of financial misrepresentation.
- Submitting false libor quotes to support trading positions. Conspiring with competitors and brokers.
- Submitting false forex fixing quotes to support trading positions. Conspiring with competitors and brokers.
- Undermining primary-dealer or Dutch-auction government bond financings.
- Manipulating commodities markets to gain pricing advantage.
- Aiding and abetting government exchange-control evasion.

generators of social welfare towards wealth-redistributors from their clients to bank employees and shareholders. Among the reasons could be:

- Changing competitive market structure.
- Fiduciary obligations — from "client" to "transaction counterparty".
- Product complexity and erosion of transparency.
- Institutional size — too big to manage.
- Institutional complexity — too broad to control.
- Acquisitions-driven growth and poor merger integration.
- Underinvestment in compliance and risk management.
- Asymmetries in revenue-generation versus risk control.
- Regulatory capture, competence, resources, approach to settlement.
- Too systemic to prosecute — regulatory waivers.
- Adverse selection among bankers.
- Failure of market discipline.

If bank size, institutional complexity, potential conflicts of interest and the ability to manage and govern large international banks have been issues in the past, they may be even more compelling going forward as even bigger and broader financial conglomerates have emerged from governments' efforts to stabilize the system. In the process of consolidation some important things can get lost. An incumbent culture can get washed away in the integration. Underinvestment in risk management and compliance (the "defense") may come under the pressure of cost discipline. Revenue and earnings generation (the "offense") may be emphasized to justify new strategies, reinforced by compensation designs that tilt toward bonus as against malus.[2]

[2] In a large-sample empirical study of honesty in the professional conduct of bank and non-bank employees, Cohn, Fehr, & Maréchal (2014) find significant differences between the two samples. In the case of non-bank employees no relationship is found between honesty and their professional identification. In the case of banking their identification with the profession of banking is associated with increased levels of dishonesty. So instead of the "adverse-selection" notion that people tending to dishonesty are disproportionately represented among people selecting banking as a profession, this finding suggests that banking itself and its cultural norms are associated with increased dishonesty among otherwise honest individuals.

Boards, for their part, are supposed to set the tone that dominates everything a bank does and how that is projected into the marketplace. In some cases factors like gaps in industry knowledge of directors, imperial chairmen and a boardroom sociology that puts an excessive premium on "teamwork" can be a problem. Also at fault may be institutional investors who fail to use the power of the proxy to challenge errant boardroom behavior — possibly because they themselves face conflicts of interest doing other business with the banks in which they hold voting shares. This exposes the ultimate owners of the banks to a "double agency problem" — first via the fiduciary performance of their asset managers and second via those asset managers forcing bank boards to properly carry out their governance mandates. And not least, banking regulators have plenty of problems with conventional risk indicators in large, complex international banks so that adding often subtle qualitative factors that turn out to be highly reputation-sensitive is a real challenge.

4. What is Reputational Risk?

There are substantial difficulties in defining the value of a financial firm's reputation, the origins and extent of damage to that reputation, and by inference the sources of reputational risk.

Reputation may be defined as the opinion (more technically, a social evaluation) of the public toward a person, a group of people or an organization.[3] It is an important factor in many fields, such as education, business, online communities, and social status. In a business context, reputation helps drive the excess value of a business firm and such metrics as the market-to-book ratio. However, both precise definition and data are found to be lacking. Arguably many deficiencies in both definition and data can be attributed to the fact that theory development related to corporate reputation has itself been deficient. Such problems notwithstanding, common sense suggests some sources of gain/loss in reputational capital — the cumulative value of the franchise of the banking firm, including its self-defined principles of business conduct.

[3] For more detail, see the discussion of reputational risk issues in Walter (2010).

- Economic performance — market share, profitability, and growth.
- Stakeholder interface — shareholders, employees, clients, and suppliers.
- Legal interface — Civil and criminal litigation and enforcement actions.

Proximate losses in reputational capital are often reflected in:

- Client flight and loss of market share.
- Investor flight and increases cost of capital.
- Talent flight.
- Increases in contracting costs.

For practical purposes, reputational risk in the financial services sector is associated with the probability of loss in the going-concern value of the firm — i.e., the risk-adjusted value of expected future earnings. Reputational losses thus may be reflected in reduced operating revenues as clients and trading counterparties shift to competitors, increased compliance and other costs required to deal with reputational issues — including opportunity costs — and an increased firm-specific risk perceived by the market.

Reputational risk is often linked to operational risk, although there are important distinctions between the two. According to long-standing definitions under the Basle principles, operational risks are associated with people (internal fraud, clients, products, business practices, employment practices, and workplace safety), internal processes and systems, and external events (external fraud, damage or loss of assets, and force majeure). Operational risk is specifically *not* considered to encompass strategic and business risk, credit risk, market risk or systemic risk, or reputational risk.[4]

If reputational risk is bracketed-out of operational risk from an international regulatory perspective, then what is it? A possible working definition is as follows:

Reputational risk comprises the risk of loss in the value of a firm's business franchise that extends beyond event-related accounting losses and is reflected in a decline in its share performance metrics. Reputation-related

[4] Basel II at http://www.bis.org/publ/bcbs107.htm

losses reflect reduced expected revenues and/or higher financing and contracting costs. Reputational risk, in turn, is related to the strategic positioning and execution of the firm, conflicts of interest exploitation, individual professional conduct, compliance and incentive systems, leadership, and the prevailing corporate culture. Reputational risk is usually the consequence of management processes rather than discrete events, and, therefore, requires risk control approaches that may differ materially from operational risk.

According to this definition, a reputation-sensitive event might trigger an identifiable monetary decline in the market capitalization of the bank. After subtracting from this market-cap loss the present value of direct and allocated costs, such as fines and penalties and settlements under civil litigation, the balance can be ascribed to the impact on the firm's reputation. Firms that promote themselves as reputational standard-setters will, accordingly, tend to suffer larger reputational losses than firms that have taken a lower profile — that is, reputational losses associated with identical events according to this definition may be highly idiosyncratic to the individual firm.

In terms of the overall hierarchy of risks faced by financial intermediaries depicted in Figure 3, reputational risk is perhaps the most intractable among them. Market risk is usually considered the most tractable, with adequate time-series and cross-sectional data availability, appropriate metrics to assess volatility and correlations, and the ability to apply techniques such as value at risk (VaR) and risk-adjusted return on capital (RAROC). Credit risk is arguably less tractable, given that many credits are on the books of financial intermediaries at historical values. The analysis of credit events in a portfolio context is less tractable than market risk in terms of the available metrics, although many types of credits have over the years become "marketized" through securitization structures such as asset-backed securities (ABS) and collateralized loan obligations (CLOs), as well as derivatives such as CDS. These financial instruments are priced in both primary and secondary markets, and transfer some of the granularity and tractability found in market risk to the credit domain. Liquidity risk, on the other hand, has both pluses and minuses in terms of tractability. In continuous-time markets, liquidity risk can be calibrated in terms of bid-offer spreads, although in times of

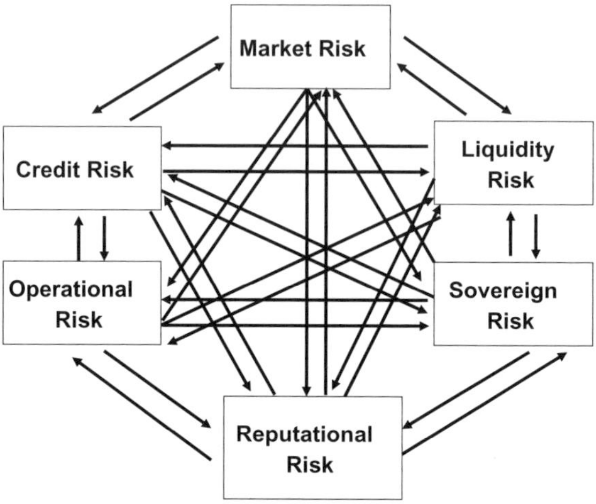

Figure 3. Key risk domains and their interrelationships.

severe market stress liquidity can evaporate and with it the ability to mark-to-market.

Operational risk is a composite of highly manageable risks with a robust basis for suitable risk metrics together with risks that represent catastrophes and extreme values — tail events that are difficult to model and, in some cases, have never actually been observed. Here management is forced to rely on either simulations or external data to try to assess probabilities and potential losses. Meanwhile, sovereign risk assessment centres on applied political economy and relies on imprecise techniques, such as "stylized facts analysis". so that the track record of even the most sophisticated analytical approaches is not particularly strong — especially under conditions of macro-stress and contagion. As in the case of credit risk, sovereign risk can be calibrated when foreign-currency government bonds and default swaps (stripped of non-sovereign attributes like external guarantees and collateral) are traded in the market. This leaves reputational risk as perhaps the least tractable of all — with poor data, limited usable metrics, and strong "fat tail" characteristics.

5. Sources of Reputational Risk

Where does reputational risk large international banks originate? To a large extent it appears to arise from the intersection between the bank

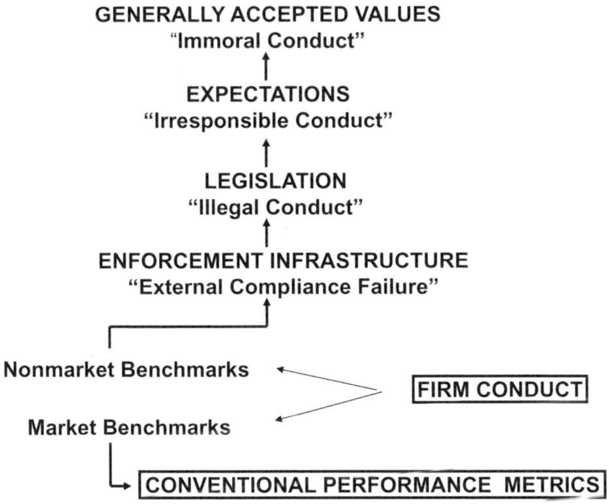

Figure 4. Reputational risk in context.

and the competitive environment, on the one hand, and from the direct and indirect network of controls and behavioral expectations within which the bank operates, on the other hand, as depicted generically in Figure 4.[5] The franchise value of a financial institution as a going concern is calibrated against these two sets of benchmarks. One of them, market performance, tends to be relatively transparent and easy to reward or punish. The other, performance against corporate conduct benchmarks, is far more opaque but potentially comparable in importance as a source of risk to shareholders.

Management must work to optimize with respect to both sets of benchmarks. If it strays too far in the direction of meeting the demands of social and regulatory controls, it runs the risks of poor performance in the market, punishment by shareholders, and possibly a change in corporate control. If it strays toward unrestrained market performance and sails too close to the wind in terms of questionable market conduct, its behavior may have disastrous results for the firm, its managers, and its shareholders.

Such are the rules of the game, and large international banks, along with all other firms, have to live with them. But they are not immutable. There is constant tension between firms and regulators about appropriate

[5]For an early discussion of external conduct benchmarks, see Galbraith (1973).

constraints on corporate conduct. Sometimes financial intermediaries win battles (and even wars) leading to periods of deregulation. Sometimes it is possible to convince the public that self-regulation and market discipline are powerful enough to obviate the need for costly external controls. Sometimes the regulators can be convinced, one way or another, to go easy in the interests of financial efficiency. Then along comes another major transgression, the constraint system reacts, and a spate of new regulations arises. A wide array of interests get into this constant battle to define the rules under which financial business gets done — managers, politicians, the media, activists, investors, lawyers, and accountants — and eventually a new equilibrium gets established which define the rules of engagement for the period ahead.

There is an array of more fundamental factors at work as well. Laws and regulations governing the market conduct of business firms are not created in a vacuum. They are rooted in social expectations as to what is appropriate and inappropriate, which in turn are driven by values imbedded in society. These values are rather basic. They deal with lying, cheating, and stealing, with trust and honor, with what is right and wrong. These are the *ultimate* benchmarks against which conduct is measured and which may be at the root of key reputational losses of large banks.

But fundamental values in society may or may not be fully reflected in people's *expectations* as to how a banking firm's conduct is viewed assessed. That is, there may be slippage between social values and how these are reflected in public expectations of business conduct. Build-up of adverse opinion in the media, the formation of special-interest lobbies and pressure-groups, and the general tide of public opinion with respect to one or another aspect of market conduct, can be reputationally debilitating even in the same underlying value system.

Neither values nor expectations are static in time. Both change. But values seem to change much more gradually than expectations. Indeed, fundamental social values are probably as close as one comes to "constants" in assessing business conduct. But here things do change. As society becomes more diverse and mobile, for example, values tend to evolve. They also differ across cultures, and are sometimes difficult to interpret. Is lying to clients or to trading counterparties wrong? What is the difference between lying and bluffing? Between lying and staking-out a negotiating position? The same conduct may be interpreted differently under different circumstances, so that interpretations of conduct may change over time and differ across cultures, giving rise to some unique contours of reputational risk.

There is additional slippage between society's expectations and the formation of public policy on the one hand, and the activities of public interest groups on the other. Things may go on as usual for a while despite occasional media commentary about inappropriate behavior of a firm or an industry in the marketplace. Then some sort of social tolerance limit or tipping point is reached. A firm goes too far. A consensus emerges among various groups concerned with the issue at hand. The system reacts through the political process, and a new set of constraints on firm behavior develops, possibly anchored in legislation, regulation, and bureaucracy. Or the firm is subject to class action litigation.[6] Or its reputation is so seriously compromised that its share price drops sharply.

As managers review the reputational experiences of their competitors, they cannot escape an important message. Most large international banks can endure a credit loss or the cost of an unsuccessful trade or a broken deal, however large, and still survive. These are business risks that banks have learned to detect and limit exposures before the damage becomes serious.

Reputational losses may in addition be the consequence of public reactions that may appear to professionals as unfocused, ambiguous or unfair. They may come from a new reading of the rules of the game, a new finding of culpability, something different from the way things were done before. Although regulators and litigants, analysts and the investigative media are accepted by financial professionals as facts of life, they in turn can be influenced by public uproar and political pressure, making a credible defense even more difficult.[7]

In the United States, for example, tighter regulation and closer surveillance, aggressive prosecution and plaintiff litigation, unsympathetic media, stricter guidelines for penalties and sentencing make it easier to get into trouble and harder to avoid serious civil penalties and even

[6] For a discussion, see Capiello (2006).

[7] For a full examination of these issues, see Smith & Walter (1997).

criminal guilty pleas. Global banking involves hundreds of different, complex, and constantly changing products that are difficult to monitor carefully under the best of circumstances. Doing this in a highly competitive market, where profit margins are under constant challenge and there is considerable temptation to break the rules, is even more challenging. Performance-driven managers, through compensation and other incentives, it is argued, have sometimes encouraged behavior that has inflicted major reputational damage on their firms and destroyed some of them.

The reality is that the value of large international banks to their investors suffers from such uncertain reputation-sensitive conditions. Since maximizing the value of the firm is supposed to be the ultimate role of management, its job to learn how to run the firm so that it optimizes the long-term trade-offs between profits and external control. It does no good to plead unfair treatment — the task is for management to learn to live within the constraint system, make its case when the system fails to serve the public interest, and make the most of the variables it can control.

The overall process can be depicted in Figure 5, which shows the firm and its internal governance processes in the center and various layers of external controls affecting both its conduct and the reputational

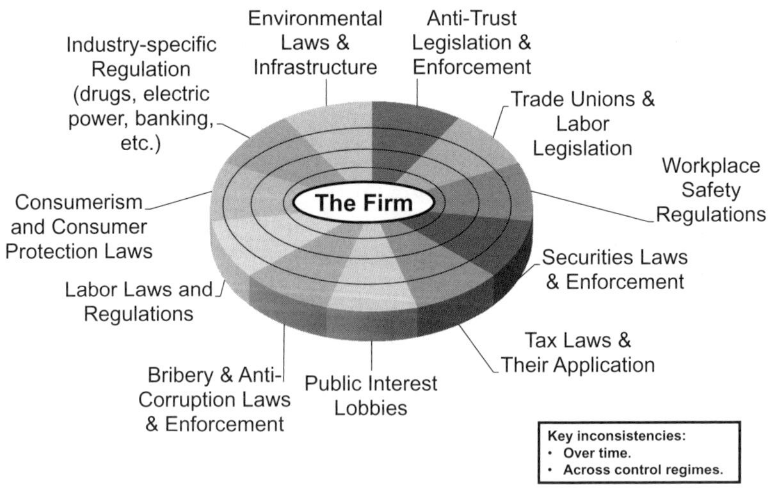

Figure 5. Reputational (franchise) risk through the lens of an external control web.

consequences of misconduct, ranging from "hard" compliance components near the center to "soft" but potentially vital issues of "appropriate" conduct on the periphery. Clearly, serious reputational losses can impact a large international bank even if it is fully in compliance with the multiple regulatory constraints it confronts around the world and its actions are entirely legal. The risk of reputational damage incurred in these outer fringes of the respective webs of social control in the various markets it serves are among the most difficult to assess and manage. Nor is the constraint system necessarily consistent, so conduct which is considered acceptable in a given environment may trigger significant reputational risk in others.

6. Valuing Reputational Risk

There have been a number of efforts to quantify the impact of reputational risk on share prices of financial firms beginning with widespread professional misconduct issues in the 1980s and 1990s.[8] Given the nature of the problem, most of the discussion has been anecdotal, although a number of "event studies" have been undertaken in cases where the reputation-sensitive event was "clean" in terms of the release of the relevant information to the market. In order to estimate the pure reputational loss associated with an adverse event, it is necessary to estimate the firm's cumulative abnormal market capitalization loss (CAR) and then deduct the present value of expected non-reputation-related costs including accounting write-offs, higher compliance costs, regulatory fines and legal settlements. The residual CAR can be considered associated with a loss of reputational capital.

Event studies in recent years have yielded a growing body of evidence on the share price sensitivity to reputational risk. For example, Cummins, Lewis, and Wei (2006) undertook a large sample study of operational and reputational events contained in the Fitch OpVar™ database. De Fontnouvelle, DeJesus-Rueff , Jordan, and Rosengren (2006) use loss data from the Fitch OpVar™ and SAS OpRisk™ databases to model operational risk for banks that are internationally active. In a

[8] For one of the early studies, see Smith (1992).

series of robust statistical estimates, they find a high degree of regularity in operational losses that can be quantified, underlining the importance of maintaining significant capital against operational risk. The paper goes on to segment the losses by event type and by activity line, as well as whether or not the operational losses occurred in the United States. The largest losses involve retail and commercial banking activities. As with other studies, the authors do not distinguish the associated accounting losses due to legal settlements, fines, penalties, and other explicit operational risk-related costs from reputational losses, so the estimates may understate the actual losses to shareholders.

Focusing on the differential impact of reputational shocks on accounting and market values, Gillet, Hübner, & Plunus (2010) attempt to isolate the pure reputational effect of the operational loss event on market returns by estimating for the difference between the market-value loss of capital and the announced accounting loss. The results show negative abnormal returns at the loss-announcement date, and in cases of internal fraud the loss in market value is larger than the announced accounting loss, interpreted by the authors as a sign of reputational damage.

Using a different approach, Fiordelisi, Soana, & Schwizer (2013) estimate the determinants of reputational risk for a sample of European and American banks during the period 2003–2008. The dependent variable is assigned a value of 1 if the bank experienced a cumulative abnormal return in the top third of the CAR distribution, a value 2 if the CAR fell in the middle third of the distribution, and a value 3 if the CAR fell in the lowest third of the distribution. The study concludes that reputational damage increases as bank profits and size increase, and that a higher level of bank capital and intangible assets both reduce the probability of reputational damage. In another study, Sturm (2013) concludes that firm characteristics are more important in explaining reputational damage than the specific characteristics of the loss event.

One study that tries to focus specifically on "pure" reputational losses is Karpoff, Lee, & Martin (2006). The authors attempt to distinguish book losses from reputational losses in the context of U.S. Securities and Exchange Commission enforcement actions related to earnings restatements or "cooking the books". The authors assemble a dataset of 2,532 regulatory events in connection with all relevant SEC enforcement actions from 1978 to 2002 and their respective monetary costs in the ensuing period through 2005. These monetary costs are then compared with the cumulative abnormal returns estimated from event studies to separate them from the reputational costs. The reputational losses attributed in the study (66%) are far larger than the cost of fines (3%), class action settlements (6%) and accounting write-offs (25%) resulting from the SEC enforcement actions.

In a pilot study of 49 reputation-sensitive events excluding operational events (Walter & DeLong, 1995) finds negative mean CARs of up to 7% of market capitalization, depending on the event windows used.[9] The results do not, however, distinguish between the overall CARs and the pure reputational loss components.[10]

Whereas such studies try to isolate the equity-price effects of reputation-sensitive events, one would expect the fixed income market to react as well through the affected firm's ability to maintain debt service — e.g., if the reputational shock triggers a revenue collapse. Plunus, Gillet, & Hübner (2012) examine bond market reactions to the announcement of operational losses by financial firms. They interpret the abnormal bond market returns for firms suffering reputational losses as part of operational loss announcements. Although less severe than in the case of stock prices, the time-series discussion in the study suggests that the bond price impact of reputational risk is indeed significant. In cross-sectional analysis, the study finds that high leverage has a negative impact on the performance of the bonds on the first press release of the reputational shock as well as on the settlement date. The absolute level of debt likewise affects the abnormal return on the event announcement.[11]

---

[9] Based on an empirical study of reputational risk conducted at the Stern School of Business, New York University.

[10] Ongoing empirical work on reputation-sensitive financial services events with Gayle De Long and Anthony Saunders.

[11] A paper by Bushman, Davidson, Dey, & Smith (2015) posits that bank CEOs who display extremely high consumption levels are associated with significantly higher bank risk-taking cultures. Materialistic bank CEOs became more numerous in the cohort after financial deregulation during the 1994–2004. At the same time, they pared-back attention to risk management and boosted downside tail risk in their banks, which surfaced particularly during the financial crisis of 2007–2009.

It is likely that the broader the range of a financial intermediary's activities, (1) the greater the likelihood that the firm will encounter exploitable conflicts of interest and reputational risk exposure, (2) the higher will be the potential agency costs facing its clients, and (3) the more difficult and costly will be the safeguards necessary to protect the value of the franchise. If this proposition is correct, costs associated with reputational risk mitigation can easily offset the realization of economies of scope in large global banking firms, scope economies that are supposed to generate benefits on the demand side through cross-selling (revenue synergies) and on the supply side through more efficient use of the firm's business infrastructure (cost synergies). As a result of conflict exploitation, the stand to gain initially but subsequent adverse reputational and regulatory consequences (along with efficiency factors such as the managerial and operational cost of complexity) can offset or reverse these gains.

It seems plausible that the broader the range of services that a financial firm provides to a given client in the market, and the greater the cross-selling pressure, the greater the potential likelihood that conflicts of interest and reputational risk exposure will be compounded in any given case, and, when these conflicts of interest are exploited, the more likely they are to damage the market value of the financial firm's business franchise once they come to light.

7. Conclusions

This chapter attempts to define reputational risk and to outline the sources of such risk facing large international banks. It then considers the key drivers of reputational risk in the presence of transactions costs and imperfect information, and surveys available empirical research on the impact of reputational losses imposed on banks.

Market discipline, through the reputation effects on the franchise value of large internationally active banks, can be a potentially powerful complement to regulation and civil litigation. Nevertheless, market

---

Replacing highly materialistic bank CEOs with more modest leadership reversed many of these effects.

discipline-based controls remain controversial. Financial firms continue to encounter serious instances of reputation loss due to misconduct despite the threat to the value of their franchises. This suggests material lapses in the risk management and corporate governance.[12]

Dealing with reputational risk can be an expensive business, with compliance systems that are costly to maintain, and various types of walls between business units and functions that impose significant opportunity costs due to inefficient use of information and resources within the organization. Moreover, management of certain kinds of reputational exposure in banking and financial conglomerates may be sufficiently difficult to require structural remediation by divesting or separating certain businesses. On the other hand, reputation losses can cause serious damage, as demonstrated by reputation-sensitive events that seem to occur repeatedly in the global banking industry. Indeed, it can be argued that such issues contribute to market valuations among financial conglomerates that fall below valuations of more specialized financial services businesses.[13]

One would like to believe that market discipline, through the reputation effects on the franchise value of financial firms, can be a powerful complement to regulation and civil litigation in avoiding or remedying damage created by unacceptable financial practices. Yet civil litigation seems ineffective in changing bank behavior despite "deferred prosecution" agreements not to repeat offenses, and market discipline-based controls remain controversial. Financial firms continue to encounter serious instances of reputation loss due to misconduct despite their effects on the value of their franchises.[14] This suggests continued material lapses in the governance and management process increasingly recognized in the "qualitative" components of stress tests applied annually to systemic banking organizations in the U.S., Europe and elsewhere.

---

[12] These issues are explored in Hoechele, Schmid, Walter, & Yermack (2002).

[13] Laeven & Levine (2005) and Schmid & Walter (2006). See also Kanatas & Qi (2003) and Saunders & Walter (1997).

[14] For an in-depth discussion of corporate culture, see Graham, Harvey, Popadak, & Rajgopal (2015).

In the end, it is probably leadership more than anything else that separates winners from losers over the long term — the notion that appropriate professional behavior reinforced by a sense of belonging to a quality franchise constitutes a decisive comparative advantage. The alternatives will rely even more on intrusive and sometimes possibly regulation to protect the general public from systemic risk, ultimately at substantial cost to financial efficiency and economic growth.

Managements and boards of large internationally active banks must be convinced that a good defense that incorporates reputational capital is as important as a good offense in determining sustainable competitive performance. This is something that is extraordinarily difficult to put into practice in a highly competitive environment for the banks and for its highly skilled professionals. A good defense requires an unusual degree of senior management leadership and commitment (Smith & Walter, 1997). Internally, there have to be mechanisms that reinforce the loyalty and professional conduct of employees. Externally, there has to be careful and sustained attention to reputational capital as a disciplinary mechanism.

References

Attorney General of the State of New York. (2003) *Global settlement: Findings of fact.* Albany: Office of the State Attorney General.

Brown, Stephen J., & Jerold B. Warner (1985). Using daily stock returns: The case of event studies. *Journal of Financial Economics*, 14, 3–31.

Bushman, R. M., Davidson, R. H., Dey, A., & Smith, A (2015). Bank CEO Materialism, corporate culture and risk. *Working Paper.* (University of North Carolina).

Capiello, S. (2006). Public enforcement and class actions against conflicts of interest in universal banking — The US experience vis-à-vis recent Italian initiatives. *Bank of Italy, Law and Economics Research Department, Working Paper.*

Chemmanur, T. J. & Fulghieri P. (1994). Investment bank reputation, information production, and financial intermediation. *Journal of Finance*, 49, 57–86.

Cohn, A., Fehr E., & Maréchal, M. A. (2014). Business culture and dishonesty in the banking industry. *Nature*, 516(7529), 86–89.

De Fontnouvelle, P., DeJesus-Rueff , V., Jordan, J. S., & Rosengren E. S. (2006). Capital and risk: New evidence on implications of large operational losses. *Working Paper*. (Federal Reserve Bank of Boston).

Fiordelisi F., Soana, M.-G., & Schwizer, P. (2013). The determinants of reputational risk in the banking sector, *Journal of Banking and Finance*, 37, 1359–1371.

Galbraith, J. K. (1973). *Economics and the public purpose*. New York: Macmillan.

Gillet R., Hübner, G., & Plunus S. (2010). Operational risk and reputation in the financial industry. *Journal of Banking and Finance*, 34, 224–235.

Graham, J. R., Harvey C. R., Popadak J., & Rajgopal S. (2015). Corporate culture: Evidence from the field. *Working Paper*. (Duke University).

Herman. E. S. (1975). *Conflicts of interest: Commercial banks and trust companies*. New York: Twentieth Century Fund.

Hoechle, D., Schmid M., Walter, I., & Yermack D. (2012). How much of the diversification discount can be explained by poor corporate governance? *Journal of Financial Economics*, 103(1), 41–60.

International Monetary Fund, Global Financial Stability Report (2009). Washington, DC: IMF, April.

Kanatas, G. & Qi, J. (2003). Integration of lending and underwriting: Implications of scope economies, *Journal of Finance*, 58(3), 1167–1191.

Laeven, L. & Levine, R. (2007). Is there a diversification discount in financial Conglomerates? *Journal of Financial Economics*, 85, 331–367.

Plunus S., Gillet R., & Hübner G. (2012). Reputational damage of operational loss on the bond market: Evidence from the financial industry. *International Review of Financial Analysis*, 24, 66–73.

Saunders, A. (1985). Conflicts of interest: An economic view. In I. Walter (Ed.), *Deregulating Wall Street*. New York: John Wiley.

Saunders, A. & Walter, I. (1997). *Universal banking in the United States: What could we gain? What could we lose?* New York: Oxford University Press.

Schmid, M. M. & Walter I. (2006). Do financial conglomerates create or destroy economic value? *Journal of Financial Intermediation*, 14(2), 78–91.

Smith, C. W. (1992). Economics and ethics: The case of Salomon brothers. *Journal of Applied Corporate Finance*, 5(2), 23–28

Smith, R. C. & Walter I. (1997) *Street smarts: Linking professional conduct and shareholder value in the securities industry*. Boston: Harvard Business School Press.

Sturm P. (2013). Operational and Reputational Risk in the European Banking Industry: The Market Reaction to Operational Risk Events, *Journal of Economic Behavior & Organization*, 85, 191–206.

Walter, I. (2004). Conflicts of interest and market discipline in financial services firms. In C. Borio, William C. Hunter, George G. Kaufman, & K. Tsatsaronis (Eds.), *Market discipline across countries and industries*. Cambridge: MIT Press.

Walter, I. (2010). Reputational risk and the financial crisis. In John R. Boatright (Eds.), *Business ethics*. London: John Wiley & Sons.

Walter, I. & DeLong, G. (1995). The reputation effect of international merchant banking accidents: Evidence from stock market data. *Working Paper*. (New York University Salomon Center).

Part II
The Cross-Border Banking Landscape

Cross-Border Banking Flows and Organizational Complexity in Financial Conglomerates

— CHAPTER 4

▪ Linda S. Goldberg
Federal Reserve Bank of New York and NBER

1. Introduction

Lending by global banks has been extremely volatile in the last decade. The cross-border banking landscape has been evolving rapidly, with changing volumes and composition of flows through internationally active banks, more volatility of these flows, and a recent increase in the importance of non-bank debt. These observations provide a backdrop to our focus on the increase in organizational complexity of financial organizations and potential consequences of this structure for international capital flows.

Several Figures illustrate these patterns in international capital flows through globally-active banks. Figure 1 presents the aggregate of international bank claims across internationally-active banks of countries that report to the BIS, with data shown for the mid-1990s through 2015. The dark hatch area shows credit extended internationally from these banks to

Linda Goldberg is Senior Vice President, Integrated Policy Analysis, Federal Reserve Bank of New York. Excellent research assistance was provided by Rose Wang. The views expressed in this chapter are solely those of the author and should not be interpreted as reflecting the view of the Federal Reserve Bank of New York or the Federal Reserve System.

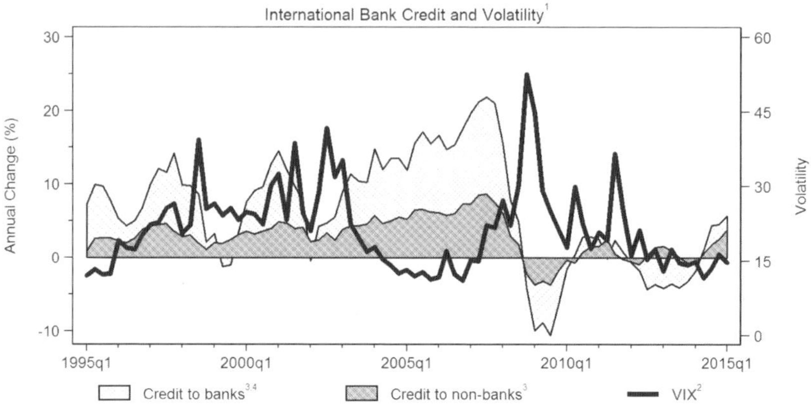

Figure 1. Bank and non-bank international claims of BIS-reporting banks.

Notes: [1]LBS-reporting banks' cross-border claims plus local claims in foreign currencies. [2] VIX refers to the Chicago Board Options Exchange Market Volatility Index. It measures the implied volatility of S&P 500 index options. [3]Contribution to the annual percentage change in credit to all sectors. [4]Including intragroup transactions.

Sources: Bloomberg; Dealogic; Euroclear; Thomson Reuters; Xtrakter Ltd; BIS locational banking statistics; BIS calculations; BIS Quarterly Review September 2015 "Highlights of Global Financing Flows".

non-banks, and the light hatch area shows changes in credit to banks over time. The black line is a measure of volatility, the VIX index. This figure shows that international bank credit grew sharply up until the crisis period in 2008, then collapsed, and is slowly recovering in aggregate. A comparison of the volumes to banks versus non-banks demonstrates that, during periods of stress, the bank-to-bank flows are considerably more volatile.

An additional window into relevant volatilities of flows is provided by decomposing banks' cross-border claims into its components, which are loans, debt securities, and other instruments. As evident from Figure 2, cross-border loans extended by banks are more volatile than the other components of claims. In terms of international assets, banks tend to have less stable funding flows to other banks, and, especially in periods of stress, the loan component is most volatile.

The composition and behavior of international debt securities contrasts the broad issuance trends of banks and non-banks. These corporate debt securities are depicted in Figure 3, with the darker area

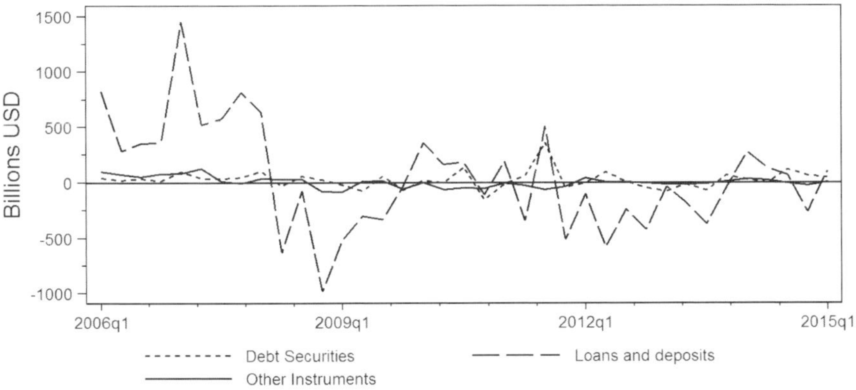

Figure 2. Composition of cross-border claims of BIS-reporting banks.

Source: BIS Quarterly Review Sept. 2015, BIS locational banking statistics by residence.

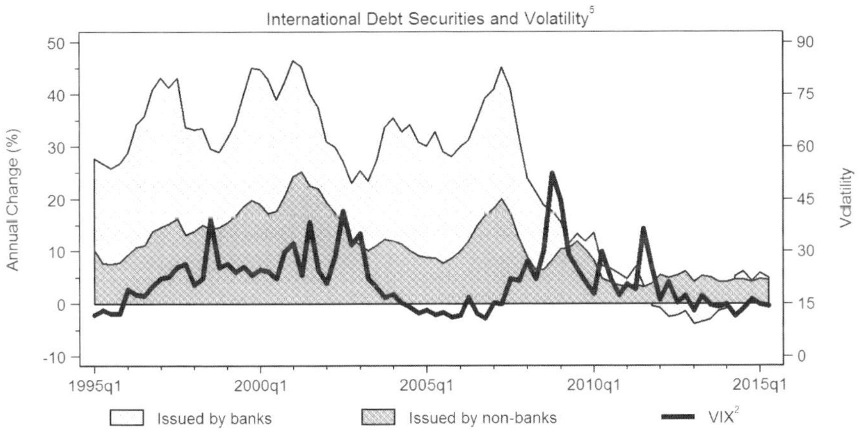

Figure 3. International debt securities issued by non-banks and banks.

Notes: [2]VIX refers to the Chicago Board Options Exchange Market Volatility Index. It measures the implied volatility of S&P 500 index options.

[5]Net issuance. All instruments, all maturities, all issuers.

Sources: Bloomberg; Dealogic; Euroclear; Thomson Reuters; Xtrakter Ltd; BIS locational banking statistics; BIS calculations; BIS Quarterly Review September 2015 "Highlights of Global Financing Flows."

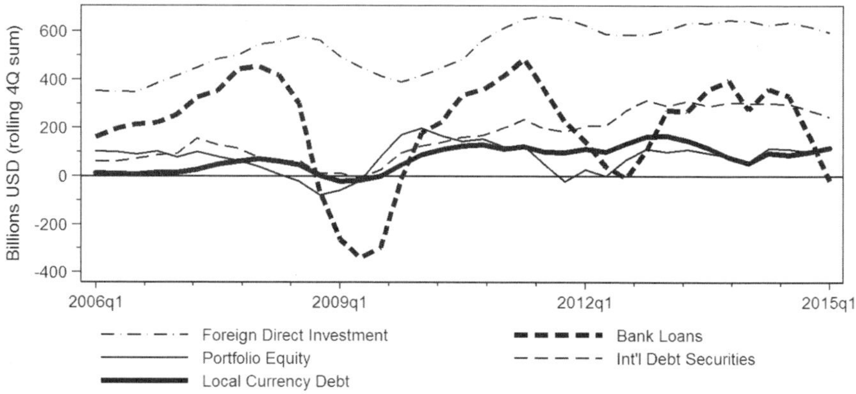

Figure 4. Volatility of private financing flows to EMEs.
Source: BIS, national authorities, Federal Reserve staff calculations.

in the figure showing issuance by non-banks, the lighter area showing issuance by banks, and a measure of volatility, the VIX, presented for context. Because international debt securities issuance by banks has fallen dramatically, non-bank issuance now dominates these instruments. By comparison, the securities issuance by non-banks appears more stable.

A final important contextual point concerns the structure and volatility of types of gross capital flows into emerging markets. A general observation historically has been that bank loans have been far more volatile than flows of other financing types. Figure 4 presents a relevant breakdown for the decade between 2006 and 2015. Foreign direct investment flows (dotted dash line) remain dominant in terms of volumes and recovered quickly post-crisis. International debt securities (thin dashed line), portfolio equity (thin solid line) and local currency debt (thick solid line) all collapsed during the crisis period and subsequently recovered. Swings in international bank loans (thick dashed line) dominate the overall volatility of credit to emerging markets. Together, these basic observations on cross-border financial flows underscore the importance of understanding the drivers of behaviors of internationally-active banks.

2. New Research on International Banking Organization Structure

A recent body of research has been developing to shed light on how global banks use internal capital markets to move liquidity across their international affiliates. This type of internal movement within the organization takes place alongside the more standard description of external capital market movements through global banks as described in Section 1. Indeed, at times, international gross flows through internal capital markets have been a similar order of magnitude as international bank-to-bank flows.

Among the key questions around internal capital market flows are its drivers and differences between these flows to related parties and flows to external parties through loans or other financing methods. What has been established is that internal capital market flows respond to shocks to parent organizations, as well as to funding conditions in domestic and foreign markets. In response to a shock, parent banks seem to prioritize some foreign affiliates relative to others, setting up a hierarchy of core and periphery business investment locations.[1]

Another question considers the observation that, while affiliate locations can be prioritized by individual global banks, differences in behaviors across global banks are observed even after conditioning on comparably sized shocks. In recent research we have been investigating a feature of global banks that has not previously been broadly explored, and which relates the structure of the organizations to which global banks belong. Each global bank is actually just a component of a much more complex organization comprised of many separate legal entities all under the umbrella of a bank holding company.

Below, we define organizational complexity in globally-active banks and discuss the findings of recent research that investigates how complexity influences bank balance sheet management. Previously, much of the discussion had focused on the role of size and business models of banks

[1]For example, see Cetorelli & Goldberg (2012a, 2012b, 2012c), De Haas & Lelyveld (2010), Düwel & Frey (2012), Kerl & Koch (2015) and Wong, Tsang, & Kong (2015).

for balance sheet management. For example, studies of the bank lending channel for international transmission of shocks show that larger banks are less responsive to shocks compared with smaller banks as in Kashyap and Stein (2000). Balance sheet composition matters as well: liquidity risk effects on lending are greater for banks with fewer liquid assets, more unused credit commitments, and less stable funding sources, as in Cornett, McNutt, Strahan, & Tehranian (2011). Compared with domestic banks, global banks have domestic lending activity that is less responsive to monetary policy and liquidity risk conditions, as in Cetorelli & Goldberg (2012a) and Correa, Goldberg, & Rice (2015). Our research on the implications of organizational complexity argues that a new dimension — the complexity and structure of financial conglomerates — should be considered as a factor in bank behaviors. In addition, in this work, we even conjecture that some of the empirical importance of size might instead be picking up the role of organizational structure.

2.1. *What is Organizational Complexity?*

Some of the thinking about what constitutes a bank and how banks behave is based on viewing the banks as simpleton organizations. While this type of perspective may be relevant for some banks, the larger banks — accounting for the majority of activity in the United States and other advanced economies — tend to be a part of much broader financial conglomerates. Accordingly, some perspectives might evolve from thinking about only the banking part of the business to considering the broader financial conglomerate to which this bank belongs and how the features of that broader financial conglomerate might influence bank behavior. The business of banking has evolved to become more complex, with many of the banks having moved from being stand-alone entities to becoming part of increasingly complex financial conglomerates (Herring & Santomero, 1990; Herring & Carmassi, 2010; Avraham, Selvaggi, & Vickery, 2012; Cetorelli, McAndrews, & Traina, 2014).

As the concept of complexity is not generally well defined, several alternative concepts from the perspective of organizational structure can be considered, as discussed in Cetorelli & Goldberg (2014). Organizational complexity indicates the degree to which the organization is structured through separate affiliated entities. "Business" complexity refers to the type and variety of activities that may be conducted within a given institution. While organizational measures have a more direct fit with the main concerns typically associated with complexity, such as resolution, fragmentation, cross-border systemic risk, internal liquidity dynamics, managerial agency frictions, and "too big to fail", business complexity relates more to the diversification and fragmentation of the type of production undertaken by organizations. In the context of global entities, organizational complexity can include geographic complexity, as captured by the span of the organization's affiliates across different regions or countries. These geographical attributes are dynamic; for example, the geographical spread of U.S. bank holding companies increased from 2000 to 2009, especially in tax havens and financial secrecy jurisdictions, while domestically located affiliates declined in the aftermath of the global financial crisis, as shown in Goldberg & Wang (2015).

We use the number of entities within a conglomerate as a measure of complexity. While this certainly is not a perfect measure that captures all dimensions of complexity, it provides an accessible and verifiable

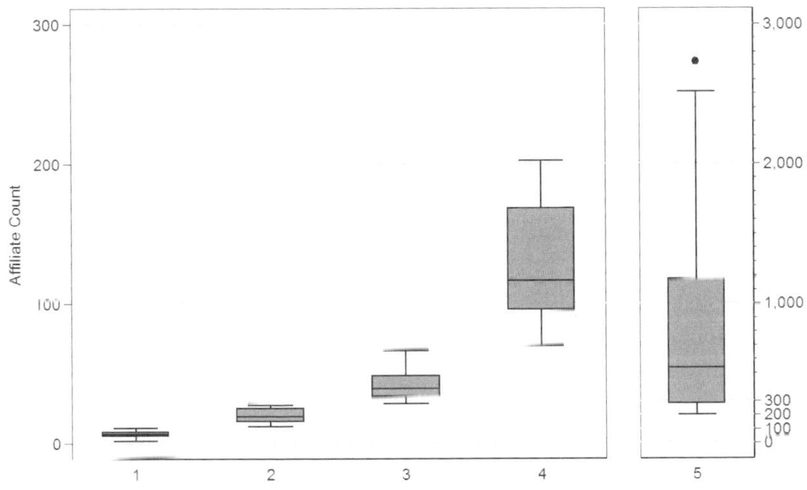

Figure 5. Counts of affiliated entities within foreign financial conglomerates in U.S.

Note: Quintiles are indicated along the x-axis.
Source: Cetorelli & Goldberg 2015, Bankscope.

metric given the type of information that can be accessed about holding company structure. The sample of entities considered is 132 foreign financial conglomerates with branches in the United States in 2012. For each of these financial conglomerates, the organizational structure is mapped using ownership tree information from Bankscope, with the constructed measure of counts based on the parts of the tree comprised of legal entities where the head of the tree controlled at least 50%.

As shown in Figure 5, in which the financial conglomerates are sorted by quintile based on the number of entities in each company, the first two quintiles both contain less than 50 entities. The third quintile has about 50–75 legal entities, and by the fourth quintile, the number becomes much more complex with 100–200 legal entities. The fifth quintile is on an entirely different scale that ranges from 200 to 2,500 or more entities. The size of these financial conglomerates, as measured by total assets, is correlated with complexity. However, for any given size, the conglomerates have a wide range of number of legal entities. Likewise, for a given quintile of number of legal entities, asset sizes vary dramatically.

2.2. *How Organizational Complexity Influences Balance Sheet Management*

Complexity may exist as a way to facilitate synergies across the different entities that are within a conglomerate.[2] The existence of organizational complexity may be associated with functional and horizontal specialization in these entities (Stein, 2002; Rajan & Zingales, 2000, 2001a, 2001b). Thus, the individual firms behave differently in a more complex conglomerate than they would if they were part of a simpler organization, as documented for firms in the manufacturing sector (Ozbas & Scharfstein, 2009).

In Cetorelli & Goldberg (2015), the specific conjecture is that, conditional on size, a commercial bank in a more complex financial

[2] Of course, this is not meant to argue that such synergies are the only drivers of organizational complexity. Other drivers include legal and regulatory considerations, tax incentives, tax avoidance, and residual effects of mergers and acquisitions.

conglomerate may maintain a more liquid balance sheet structure. Furthermore, the bank's activities may be more oriented towards the needs of its organizations, or alternatively, the bank's choices would be less oriented towards the local banking markets in which it is located than would otherwise be the case. The related conjecture is that the foreign bank hosted within a country may exhibit reduced sensitivities to shocks and opportunities in its host country. In this case, in response to monetary policy, regulatory instruments, or some other funding shock in the host country, the domestic bank lending channel is smaller, in line with the extent of organizational complexity, even beyond the pure effects of being global.

Cetorelli & Goldberg (2015) test the conjecture by exploring the *ex-ante* balance sheet composition of a sample of foreign financial organizations with branches in the United States, and examining the cross-sectional pattern of balance sheet adjustments in response to an exogenous shock. The particular shock is a deposit insurance assessment fee reform that occurred in November 2010 when the FDIC proposed and then passed a ruling that changed the way that deposit insurance was assessed in the U.S. This fee change made wholesale funding more expensive to U.S. FDIC-insured banks and reduced demand for and lowered the cost of wholesale funding. Since the U.S. branches of foreign banks are not subject to the FDIC assessment fee, these branches experienced a positive funding shock that lowered their cost of funding, as documented by Kreicher, McCauley, & McGuire (2014).

The analysis of the *ex-ante* balance sheets of these branches show that their balance sheet structures differ in accordance to the complexity of the organization to which they belong. Controlling for asset size of the financial conglomerate, branches that belong to more complex organizations are larger, engage in relatively less lending within the U.S., rely more on wholesale funding, and lend more to their own conglomerate. Around the time of the funding cost shock, cross-sectional differences are evident in the responses of these branches to the shock: also controlling for size, differences are strongly correlated with organizational complexity. The branches associated with more complex conglomerates exhibit weaker overall balance sheet sensitivity to the shock in terms of assets, funding and lending, and a weaker bank lending channel.

The complexity of the conglomerate imposes statistically significant and economically relevant constraints on the related banks' own balance sheets and the external bank lending channel. Both the external bank lending channel and internal lending channel to the organization reflect the bank having some relative specialization towards its parent organization.

3. Concluding Remarks

We began by observing that international lending flows through global banks can be quite volatile. As these banks actively finance banks and non-banks, both in their domestic markets and internationally, important questions arise about the drivers of this activity. A related set of questions arise around how financial firms use their internal capital markets domestically and internationally. The recent research on this topic contributes a new dimension by exploring the facts and implications around the complexity of the financial conglomerate. Foreign banks hosted by the United States partially relegate their balance sheet to the potential needs of the family in relation to the complexity of the family. The bank is set up for more internal capital flows, and it maintains operations in the U.S. operations that are structurally larger and more able to generate liquidity, even after controlling for the size of the overall conglomerate. In response to a positive funding shock, banks that are part of a more complex, larger organization have less growth in their balance sheet, less funding response, and less lending response. Once we add our measure of complexity into these specifications, size becomes less important in explaining the behavior of banks.

More analysis clearly is needed on the topic of complexity in financial organizations. First, complexity is a concept that must be clearly defined in relation to whichever economic or policy question is being considered. Depending on the question, the appropriate measure might be business complexity, organizational complexity, or geographic complexity. Second, improved complexity metrics are desirable, as the entity count-based metrics that are used thus far have obvious shortcomings. Third, more research is needed so that policy and research communities better understand the costs and benefits associated with each form of complexity. An improved understanding of complexity can yield important policy-relevant insights that inform the goals of global financial stability and sustainable maximum growth.

References

Avraham, D., Selvaggi, P., & Vickery, J. (2012). A structural view of U.S. bank holding companies. *Economic Policy Review*, *18*(2), 65–81.

Cetorelli, N. & Goldberg, L. S. (2012a). Banking globalization and monetary transmission. *Journal of Finance*, *67*(5), 1811–1843.

Cetorelli, N. & Goldberg, L. S. (2012b). Follow the money: Quantifying domestic effects of foreign bank shocks in the great recession. *American Economic Review*, *102*(3), 213–218.

Cetorelli, N. & Goldberg, L. S. (2012c). Liquidity management of U.S. global banks: Internal capital markets in the great recession. *Journal of International Economics*, 88(2), 299–311.

Cetorelli, N. & Goldberg, L. S. (2014). Measures of global bank complexity. *Economic Policy Review*, *20*(2), 107–126.

Cetorelli, N. & Goldberg, L. S. (2015). Organizational complexity and balance sheet management in global banks manuscript, Federal Reserve Bank of New York, October.

Cetorelli, N., McAndrews, J., & Traina, J. (2014). Evolution in bank complexity. *Economic Policy Review*, *20*(2), 85–106.

Cornett, M., McNutt, J., Strahan, P., & Tehranian H. (2011). Liquidity risk management and credit supply in the financial crisis. *Journal of Financial Economics*, *101*(2), 297–312.

Correa, R., Goldberg, L. S., & Rice T. (2015). International banking and liquidity risk transmission: Evidence from the United States. *IMF Economic Review*, 63, 626–643. Doi:10.1057/imfer.2015.28.

De Haas, R. & van Lelyveld I. (2010). Internal capital markets and lending by multinational bank subsidiaries. *Journal of Financial Intermediation*, *19*(1), 1–25.

Düwel, C., & Frey R. (2012). Competition for internal funds within multinational banks: Foreign affiliate lending in the crisis. *Bundesbank Discussion Paper*, No 19/2012. Economic Research Centre, Deutsche Bundesbank.

Goldberg, L. S., & Wang R. (2015). The moving geography of U.S. BHCs. Federal Reserve Bank of New York, *Liberty Street Economics* (December).

Herring, R. & Carmassi J. (2010). The corporate structure of international financial conglomerates: Complexity and its implications for safety and soundness." In A. Berger, P. Molyneux, & J. Wilson (Eds.), *The Oxford Bandbook of Banking*. Oxford: Oxford University Press.

Herring, R. & Santomero A. (1990). The corporate structure of financial conglomerates. *Journal of Financial Services Research*, 4(4), 471–497.

Kashyap, A. & Stein J. (2000). What do a million observations on banks say about the transmission of monetary policy? *American Economic Review*, *90*(3), 407–428.

Kerl, C. & Koch, C. (2015). International banking and liquidity risk transmission: Evidence from Germany. *IMF Economic Review*, *63*(3), 496–514.

Kreicher, L., McCauley, R., & McGuire P. (2014). The 2011 FDIC assessment on banks' managed liabilities: Interest rate and balance sheet responses. *Taxation and regulation of the financial sector*. Cambridge: MIT Press.

Ozbas, O. & Scharfstein D. (2010). Evidence on the dark side of internal capital markets. *Review of Financial Studies*, *23*(2), 581–599.

Rajan, R. & Zingales, L. 2000. The governance of the new enterprise. In X. Vives (Ed.), *Corporate Governance, Theoretical & Empirical Perspectives*. Cambridge: Cambridge University Press.

Rajan, R., & Zingales, L. (2001a.). The firm as a dedicated hierarchy: A theory of the origins and growth of firms. *The Quarterly Journal of Economics*, *116*(3), 805–851.

Rajan, R., & Zingales, L. (2001b). The influence of the financial revolution on the nature of firms. *American Economic Review*, *91*(2), 206–211.

Stein, J. (2002). Information production and capital allocation: Decentralized versus hierarchical firms. *Journal of Finance*, *57*(5), 1891–1921.

Wong, E., Tsang, A., & Kong, S. (2015). International banking and liquidity risk transmission: Evidence from Hong Kong S.A.R. *IMF Economic Review*, *63*(3), 515–541.

Global Banks: Good or Good-Bye?

— CHAPTER 5

- Thomas F. Huertas
  Ernst & Young

1. Introduction

Prior to the financial crisis and the Great Recession, global banks were big, broad, and borderless. They operated as integrated entities. Legal entities were an afterthought: the results that mattered were those for lines of business and for the group as a whole, not those for specific legal entities within the group.[1] And, global banks were reckoned to be good for growth, for they facilitated the allocation of capital to its most efficient uses.

Thomas F. Huertas is Partner in EY's Financial Services Risk Practice and chairs the firm's Global Regulatory Network. The chapter expands on his presentation to the 18th International Banking Conference at the Federal Reserve Bank of Chicago on November 5, 2015. These are his personal views.

[1] Regulation and supervision fostered this approach. Consolidated official supervision was the mantra: the home country had responsibility for the group as a whole. Host countries expected that the home country would act as a "source of strength". If needed, the subsidiary in the host country could turn to its parent and affiliates for capital and/or liquidity. If the parent itself needed capital and/or liquidity, it could turn to the home country for support, for home countries would regard their major banks as "too big to fail".

The financial crisis changed that judgment. Governments bailed out global banks,[2] and global banks came to be seen as a source of instability. Consequently, in 2009 G20 leaders mandated officials to devise a new regime, one that would assure financial stability without burdening the taxpayer. That regime is now largely in place and does three things. It makes banks less likely to fail.[3] It makes banks safe to fail.[4] And, it reduces reliance on banks, in particular with respect to derivatives.[5]

---

[2] In the financial crisis authorities found that they were damned if they didn't support their major banks, and they were damned if they did. Arguably, the U.S. authorities aggravated the crisis by not supporting Lehmans when market participants and host-country authorities expected the U.S. authorities to do so. Indisputably, jurisdictions that did provide support, found that it was very expensive and very unpopular to do so. In other words, too big to fail was too costly to call off in the midst of the crisis, but also too costly to continue after the crisis.

[3] Regulation is stricter: capital and liquidity requirements have increased very substantially. Supervision is tougher, more pro-active and more forward looking. Stress-testing is central to the new approach. It forces banks to hold excess capital today so that they could write off — without breaching minimum requirements — the losses that stress would cause, if it were to materialize. As a result of these initiatives, banks are safer and sounder, and the threat they pose to financial stability is much diminished.

[4] The objective is to end too big to fail, to make banks resolvable, so that a bank that reaches the point of non-viability can be recapitalized and restructured, without cost to the taxpayer and without significant disruption to financial markets or the economy at large. Although much remains to be done, very significant progress toward this goal has been made. Jurisdictions have introduced special resolution regimes, established resolution authorities, and initiated planning for resolution by both the banks themselves and the authorities individually and collectively within crisis management groups. Key to these plans is the concept of bail-in and the requirement that banks maintain an amount of TLAC (total loss-absorbing capacity) sufficient to allow its 'bail-in' (write-down or conversion to equity) to recapitalize the bank.

[5] Major jurisdictions have introduced mandatory clearing requirements for standard derivatives, so that a central counterparty becomes the seller to every buyer and the buyer to every seller. This reduces risk except at the tail of the distribution: at the tail the CCP becomes a single point of failure, a fact that makes it all the more important that CCPs become robust (able to withstand the simultaneous failure of their two largest participants) and resolvable

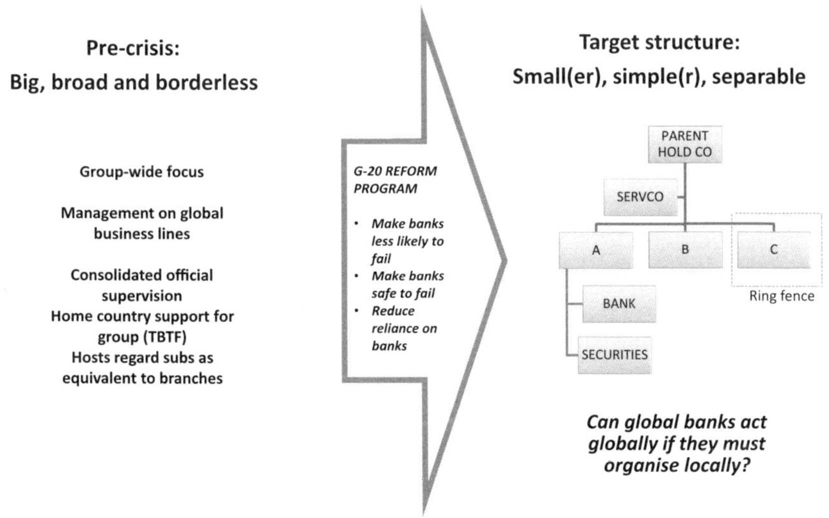

Figure 1. A new regulatory regime requires a new structure: will it force a new business model as well?

Implicitly, these reforms point toward a new business model for banks, one where they are small(er), simple(r) and separable (see Figure 1).

In this new regime resolvability and separability go hand in hand. The introduction of TLAC, together with the bail-in and the ordering of the creditor hierarchy under the resolution regime, goes a long way toward assuring resolvability. These changes also transform the liability side of the bank balance sheet into something akin to that found in a securitization structure (see Figure 2). Losses are absorbed in reverse order of seniority, starting with CET1 capital and then progressing to the "gone concern" elements of TLAC (AT1 and T2 capital plus qualifying senior debt [debt that is explicitly subordinated to operating liabilities]). These "gone concern" elements are subject to write-down or conversion into CET1 capital at the point of non-viability. This effectively recapitalizes the bank and facilitates its stabilization and restructuring. Only if losses exceed the amount of TLAC is it necessary to extend bail-in (write down) to operating liabilities such as derivatives and deposits.

In this new environment separability complements resolvability. Banking organizations increasingly have to put specific activities into

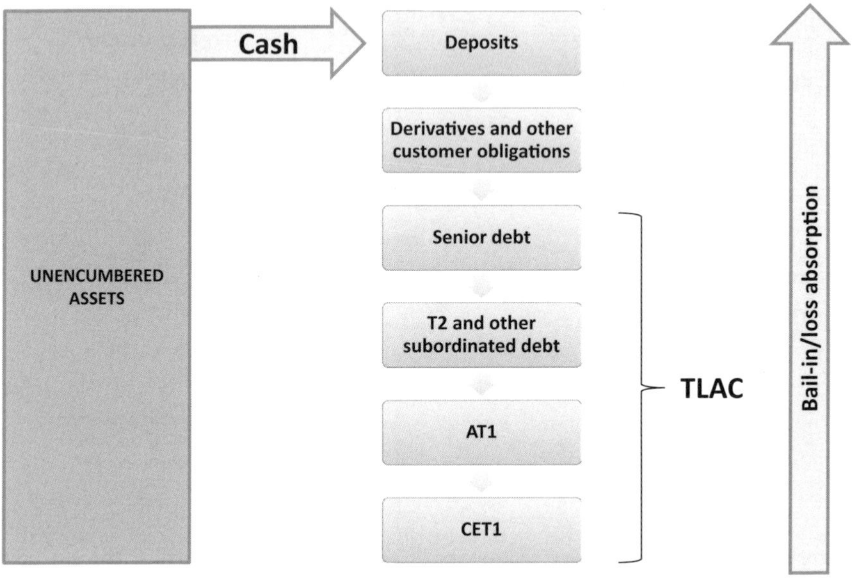

Figure 2. Introduction of TLAC aims to assure resolvability.

Table 1. Ring fence attempts to create 'independent' entity.

Capital	• Each entity to meet solo requirements • TLAC to be pre-positioned
Liquidity	• Each entity to meet LCR and NSFR requirements
Governance	• Subsidiary board must be independent from group
Dividends and distributions	• Payable only with permission of supervisor
Inter-affiliate transactions	• Affiliates treated as if they were third parties • Subject to capital requirements, large exposure limits and in some cases collateral
Service provision	• Service provider must be robust • Limit on obtaining services from banks within group

separate legal vehicles subject to regulation and supervision by local authorities. To various degrees such subsidiaries are required to be 'independent' from the group (see Table 1 for details). To this end, such subsidiaries must increasingly have a separate board with a number of directors who are independent, in the sense that their primary obligation is to the subsidiary itself rather than the group. In addition, such subsidiaries face restrictions on transactions with other affiliates within the group, including in some cases the ability to use other affiliates to make payments or settle securities transactions.[6]

There is a desire to be sure that each material legal entity can stand on its own, even if some or all of the affiliates in the rest of the group fail. Host country supervisors are likely to want material legal entities within their jurisdiction to have TLAC "pre-positioned". so that an appreciable amount of "gone-concern" capital is already in place, available for write-down or conversion, should the host-country authority be required to put that entity into resolution. Consequently, in this new regime banking groups will have to manage on a legal vehicle basis as well as on a line of business and group-wide basis.

If global banks have to be managed as a collection of 'independent' subsidiaries, will this mean good-bye to global banks? Certainly, the drive toward "separability" threatens to diminish the scale and scope economies that global banks have enjoyed. And, in a digital age, it will certainly be easier for new entrants to compete in specific lines of business, particularly if they can take advantage of the infrastructure that banks collectively provide and/or if the authorities fail to impose on the new entrants the same requirements that they impose on banks.[7]

Can new entrants also employ new forms of organization as well as new technology to challenge global banks? We offer three possibilities for consideration. The first is a unit bank model. In a digital age, it should be as possible for clients to go to the bank as for the bank to go

---

[6] Examples are the requirement for the largest UK and Swiss organizations to place their domestic retail and commercial banking activities into a separate legal vehicle as well as the U.S. requirement for foreign banking organizations to place all of their U.S. subsidiaries into an intermediate holding company.

[7] For example, many providers of payment services simplify the front end for the payment initiator; they continue to rely on the banking system to actually execute the payment. This threatens to push banks into simply providing the financial equivalent of band width. The customer relationship and revenues would increasingly flow to the new entrant or provider of the app. Lending platforms pose a similar threat.

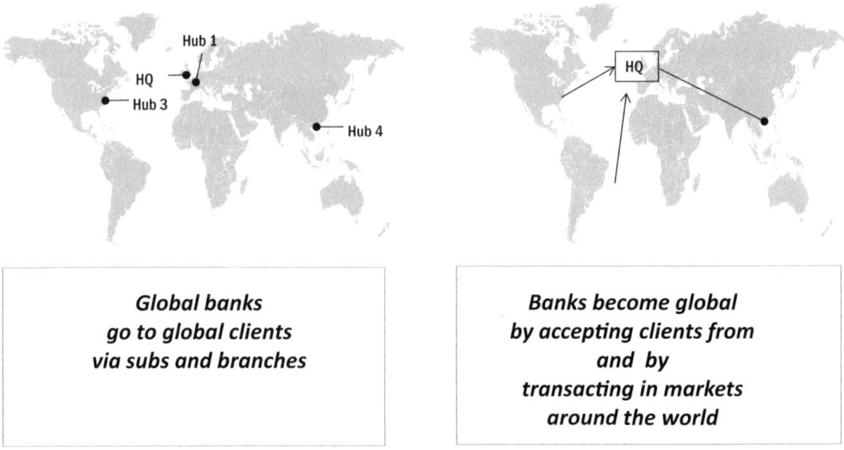

Figure 3. Unit Bank model: In digital age it may be easier for clients to come to the bank than for the bank to go to clients.

to clients (see Figure 3) From a legal vehicle standpoint, the unit bank would be the simplest structure of all: one vehicle, one jurisdiction, no branches, and no subsidiaries. It would comply with relevant capital and liquidity requirements. In particular, bail-in and TLAC would apply, so that the bank itself would effectively function like a securitization vehicle. Assets would generally remain unencumbered but available to pledge to lenders (private or official) should a need for immediate liquidity arise. Such a model is already the basis for a new entrant to consumer banking in the UK. And, such a model may be particularly appropriate for wholesale business. Indeed, such a model may give the jurisdiction that allows it some advantage in acting as a financial center.

The second model is essentially a private equity model (Figure 4). If banking regulation forces groups to treat their own subsidiaries as independent entities, much if not all of the rationale for a group goes away. It may therefore make sense to consider what might be called a private equity model, in which a private equity firm manages a fund on behalf of investors that takes stakes in various banks, each of which is independent from one another. As the manager of the fund that makes the investment in the bank, the private equity firm may exert a certain

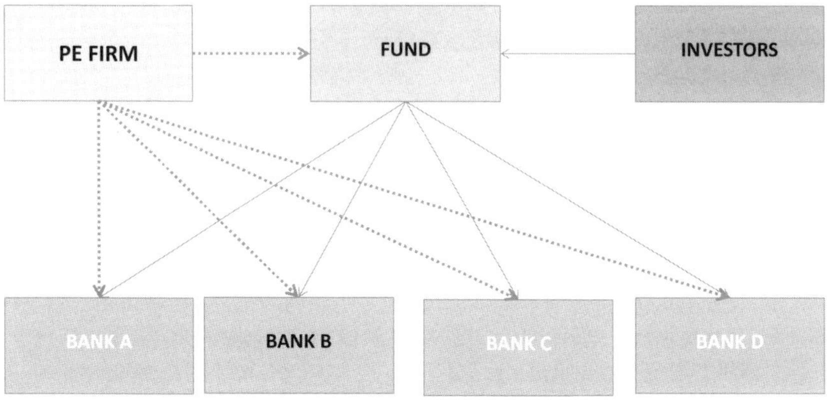

Figure 4. PE model: Fund manager directs separate independent banks owned by fund(s) managed by PE firm.

degree of control (such as appointing directors to the board) commensurate with the size of its stake in the bank.

Of particular interest is the possibility that firms could implement such a PE model on a contingent basis, i.e., as investors in "gone-concern" capital instruments such as T2 capital or qualifying subordinated debt that banking groups will issue to meet TLAC requirements. Such a fund might be particularly effective in monitoring and disciplining the bank, for it would in fact be prepared to step in and take control of the bank, if the bank were to enter resolution and its debt were converted into equity in the bank.

A third possible model is a limited liability partnership (LLP) (Figure 5). This entity would own the bank and be integrated for tax purposes with the tax returns of the limited partners. Note that the LLP need not manage the bank itself. That task can fall to a general partner which concludes a contract with the LLP to manage the bank. The LLP structure effectively eliminates the double taxation of corporate profits and very significantly reduces the incentive for the entity owning the bank (the LLP) to use debt to finance its investment in the bank. This would strengthen the banking group's CET1 capital and reduce the risk that the bank would fail. Consideration might therefore be given to allowing such structures to own banks, particularly if leverage at the LLP level were limited.

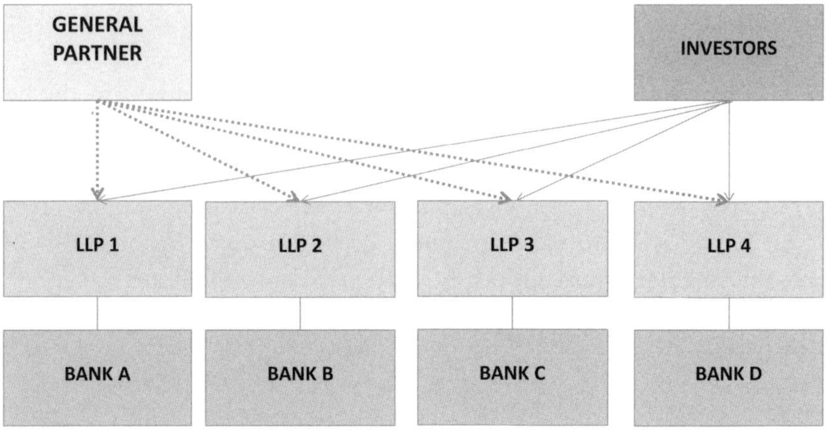

Figure 5. LLP model: General partner manages separate independent banks owned by limited liability partnerships.

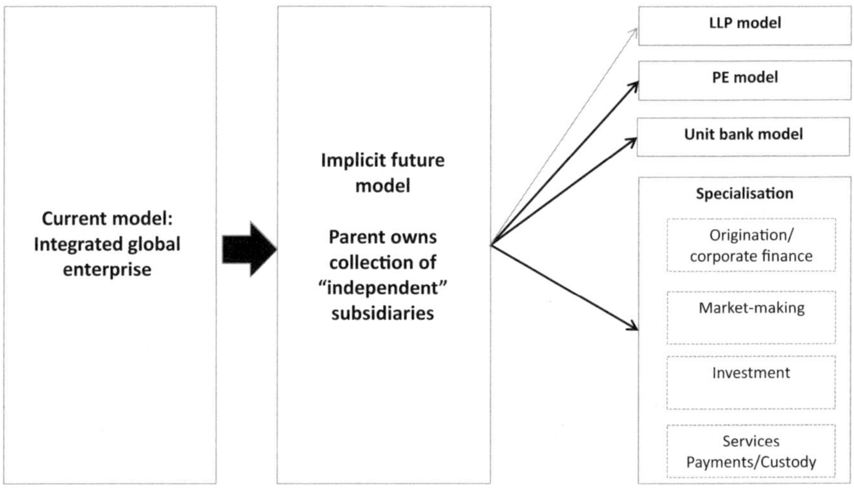

Figure 6. Change in regulation may open door to new business models suited for digital age.

In the face of new entrants using new technology and new business models, how might global banks respond? They are already seeking to make the existing model more efficient, to exit jurisdictions and/or lines of business in which they do not have a competitive advantage or in which the risk outweighs the reward. But this is not likely to be enough to protect them against new entrants employing new technology and new forms of organization.

Global banks already recognize that they need to adapt to the new technology (see Figure 6). Should they be looking at new forms of organization as well, ones more in accord with the new regulatory mantra of "small(er), simple(r), separable" mantra? That could enable global banks to continue to promote greater growth through the efficient intermediation of capital. In other words, to facilitate the good.

The Future of Large, Internationally Active Banks: Does Scale Define the Winners?

— CHAPTER 6

- Joseph P. Hughes
  Rutgers University
- Loretta J. Mester
  Federal Reserve Bank of Cleveland and The Wharton School, University of Pennsylvania

1. Introduction

In the wake of the 2008 financial crisis, the U.S. has taken a number of steps to limit the degree of systemic risk in the financial system. Some have called for limiting the size of large financial institutions deemed systemically important. Proposals to limit size have raised the

---

This chapter was prepared for the Conference on the Future of Large, Internationally Active Banks organized by the Federal Reserve Bank of Chicago and the World Bank. The views expressed in this paper do not necessarily reflect those of the Federal Reserve Bank of Cleveland or the Federal Reserve System. Hughes thanks the Whitcomb Center for Research in Financial Services at the Rutgers Business School for its support of data services used in this research.

question of whether size confers benefits in terms of the types of financial services and products uniquely offered by large financial institutions and whether large financial institutions can offer financial services at lower average cost due to technological scale economies, or whether lower costs of production, if they exist, are the result of safety-net subsidies rather than technological advantages. In other words, is there an actual trade-off between lower systemic risk and scale efficiency?

To the extent that technology accounts for scale cost economies, large financial institutions competing in global financial markets and operating in countries that impose such limits are likely to experience a competitive disadvantage compared to institutions operating in countries without limits. Moreover, such limits may not be effective if they work against market forces and create incentives for firms to avoid these restrictions, and could thereby push risk-taking outside of the regulated financial sector, without necessarily reducing systemic risk.

Earlier studies of banking costs often failed to find evidence of scale economies at large financial institutions. According to Greenspan (2010), "For years the Federal Reserve was concerned about the ever-growing size of our largest financial institutions. Federal Reserve research had been unable to find economies of scale in banking beyond a modest size." However, many more recent studies have found evidence of scale economies, even at the largest financial institutions, and often these economies increase with the size of the institution.[1]

Textbooks assert that scale economies characterize banking and justify the claim by pointing to such scale-related phenomena as the diversification of liquidity and credit risk, the spreading of overhead costs, and network economies in payments. Moreover, large institutions have historically continued to grow larger. Larger financial institutions

[1] A selection of papers that have found scale economies at large banks includes: Hughes, Lang, Mester, & Moon (1996, 2000), Berger & Mester (1997), Hughes & Mester (1998, 2013b), Hughes, Mester, & Moon (2001), Bossone & Lee (2004), Wheelock & Wilson (2012), Feng & Serletis (2010), Dijkstra (2013), Kovner, Vickery, & Zhou (2014), Becalli, Anolli, & Borello (2015), and Wheelock & Wilson (2015).

offer financial products not available at smaller institutions. And institutions have merged domestically and internationally, resulting in larger institutions.

Of course, it is possible that financial institutions expand in spite of scale diseconomies to obtain too-big-to-fail subsidies whose benefits outweigh any scale diseconomies, as pointed out by critics of the largest financial institutions.[2] The claim by these critics that breaking up the largest financial institutions would create shareholder value appears to either reject the finding of scale economies at these institutions or to conclude that the social benefit of breaking up the banks in terms of reduced systemic risk would outweigh the cost of forgone scale economies. For example, a recent analysis by Goldman Sachs indicates that JPMorgan Chase experiences $6–7 billion in "net income synergies," but that the new capital surcharge imposed on global systemically important banks (G-SIBs) could outweigh this cost benefit and make break-up a value-enhancing strategy.[3] The CFO of JPMorgan Chase rejected Goldman's analysis.[4]

---

[2] For example, see Richard Fisher, former President of the Federal Reserve Bank of Dallas, and Harvey Rosenblum, former Director of Research at the Federal Reserve Bank of Dallas (Fisher & Rosenblum, 2012): "Hordes of Dodd-Frank regulators are not the solution; smaller, less complex banks are. We can select the road to enhanced financial efficiency by breaking up TBTF banks — now." See Sheila Bair, former chairman of the Federal Deposit Insurance Corporation (Bair, 2012): "The public-policy benefits of smaller, simpler banks are clear. It may be in the enlightened self-interest of shareholders as well." See Purcell (2012), former chairman and CEO of Morgan Stanley, 2012: "Breaking these companies into separate businesses would double to triple the shareholder value of each institution."

[3] According to the Goldman Sachs analysis (Ramsden, Fitzgerald, Parls, & Senet, 2015, p. 1), "The Fed's recent G-SIB proposal raises JPM's capital requirement to 11.5%, 100–200 bp higher than money center peers, reigniting the debate about whether a breakup could unlock shareholder value given that size is now a regulatory negative. A breakup could create value ... as each standalone business would face a lower G-SIB surcharge."

[4] See Popper (2015): "... Ms. [Marianne] Lake, the chief financial officer, said JPMorgan should keep its current mix of businesses because it had around $18 billion in cost synergies from having all its business lines under the same roof. 'Scale has always defined the winner in banking,' Ms. Lake said."

2. What are Scale Economies?

Scale economies describe how cost varies with outputs — the measure of scale economies is the inverse of the measure of cost elasticity. If a proportional increase in all outputs results in a less than proportional increase in cost, the elasticity of cost is less than one, and there are scale economies or, equivalently, increasing returns to scale. If cost increases in the same proportion, the elasticity equals one, and there are constant returns to scale. If cost increases more than proportionately, the elasticity exceeds one, and there are scale diseconomies or decreasing returns to scale.

The calculation of the cost elasticity follows from the specification and estimation of cost. The specification is critical. The specification includes output quantities, $\boldsymbol{q}$, variable input quantities, $\boldsymbol{x}$, variable input prices, $\boldsymbol{w}$, and fixed input quantities, $\boldsymbol{k}$. The expenditures on the variable inputs define (variable) cost: $\boldsymbol{w}\cdot\boldsymbol{x}$. In many analyses, outputs usually include loans, liquid assets, securities, trading assets, and off-balance-sheet activities. Inputs include deposits and other types of borrowed funds, labor, equity capital, and physical capital. Equity capital is usually treated as a fixed input, k, so its price and the cost of equity are not required. However, a shadow price and cost of capital can be computed from this formulation. The standard formulation of the equation to be estimated includes some version of these outputs and input prices as well as the level of equity capital. A control for asset quality, often the amount of non-performing assets, n, may also be part of the specification. The econometric estimation of the cost function,

$$C_i = C(q_i, w_i, n_i, k_i) + \varepsilon_i, \tag{1}$$

where i designates the ith firm, allows the calculation of how a proportional variation in the output quantities affects cost. The cost elasticity of the ith firm is the sum of the individual elasticities of cost with respect to each output j:

$$\text{cost elasticity}_i = \sum_j \frac{\partial C}{\partial q_{ij}} \frac{q_{ij}}{C}. \tag{2}$$

The measure of scale economies is the inverse cost elasticity: scale economies = 1/cost elasticity.[5] Hence, a value of cost elasticity less than one implies a value of scale economies that exceeds one — scale economies.

It is important to note that the estimated cost elasticity of each bank is conditioned on the input prices the bank faces. Conditioning banks' cost on input prices takes into account phenomena such as regional differences in wages and rents. To the extent that financial markets are integrated, regional differences in interest rates on borrowed funds should be eliminated, but differences may arise due to differences among banks in the composition of their borrowed funds in terms of maturities, types of collateral, and the market's perception of banks' default risk. In the case of financial institutions thought to be too big to fail, the interest rates they pay on borrowed funds may be lower than those of other institutions. Conditioning the cost function on these rates, in effect, levels the "playing field". The estimation of cost elasticities accounts for such differences in input prices.

3. Why are Scale Economies so Hard to Detect in Banking?

Greenspan's quote above accurately summarizes the common finding of earlier studies that used the standard specification of the cost function: slight scale economies at smaller banks and scale diseconomies at the largest banks. However, the standard cost function that accounts for outputs and input prices and some conditioning arguments such as a measure of loan quality and the quantity of equity capital fails to account for endogenous risk taking. Cost expressed as a function of any given quantities of outputs varies with the amount of risk taken in producing those outputs. For example, raising the contractual interest rate

[5] In the case of a variable cost function conditioned on the quantity of equity capital, a shadow price of equity can be computed so that the cost elasticity can be derived from total economic cost defined as the sum of variable cost and the cost of equity capital. For the details of this calculation, see Hughes, Mester, & Moon (2001).

charged on loans generally increases expected return but also return risk because loan applicants with better credit quality seek out other lenders, while those with poorer credit quality remain. The lower quality of loan applicants requires devoting additional resources to credit evaluation and loan monitoring. Thus, for the same quantities of outputs produced with higher credit risk, a higher return is expected, but at a higher cost.

Consider two sets of output quantities, one proportionately larger than the other. Figure 1 illustrates a hypothetical risk-expected return frontier for the smaller output quantity bundle. Expanding the outputs, in this case, in equal proportions, improves the banks' diversification and spreads overhead over a larger scale, which results in the higher frontier — an improved risk-expected return trade-off. Suppose the bank produces the smaller output quantities with the risk-expected-return exposure at point *A*, which reflects a particular mix of loans, contractual interest rates, and resources allocated to managing risk. The investment strategy at *A* gives rise to a particular probability distribution of loan default. At point *B* the bank maintains the mix of loans and contractual interest rates as it increases the outputs in equal proportions. Thus, at point *B* the bank

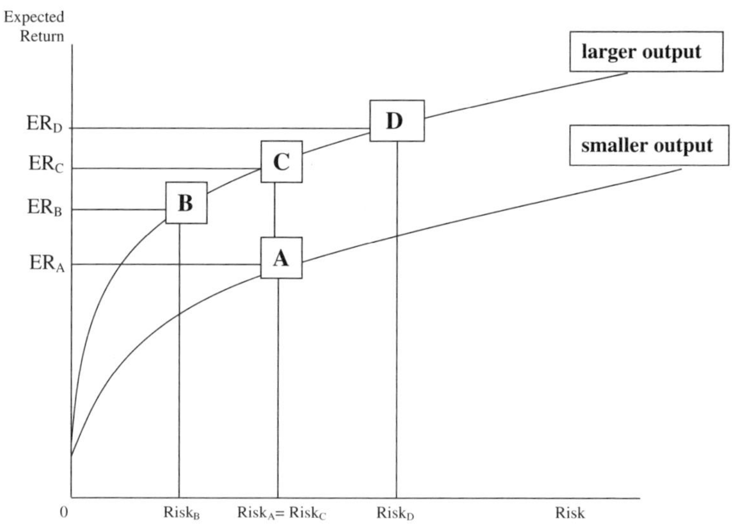

Figure 1. Scale economies as a function of risk-expected return trade-off from Hughes & Mester (2013b).

continues the investment strategy of point *A*, but better diversification due to the expanded scale and spreading overhead costs results in a higher expected return accompanied by a lower return risk. The proportionate expansion of outputs from point *A* to *B* while maintaining the same investment strategy results in a less-than-proportionate increase in cost, which implies the cost elasticity is less than one or, equivalently, there are scale economies. The less-than-proportionate increase in cost results from spreading the overhead costs over the larger scale and from reduced risk-management costs due to improved diversification. Other factors may be at play, too, such as enhanced network economies in payments.

But in response to the improved risk-expected return trade-off at the larger output scale, the bank might adopt a riskier investment strategy. For example, it might raise the contractual interest rate on loans, which produces a higher expected return but also higher return risk since loan quality will drop. To the extent that the additional risk-taking in moving from point *B* to, say, point *C* involves extra costs of risk management, the increase in cost from point *A* to point *C* may be in proportion to the increase in output — giving the appearance of *constant returns to scale*. However, moving from point *A* to point *D*, the additional risk compared to point *B* may occasion an increase in cost that is more than proportional to the increase in output — giving the appearance of *scale diseconomies*.

But it is important to note that despite the appearance of constant returns to scale at *C* and scale diseconomies at *D*, the underlying *production technology* exhibits scale economies, which are apparent in the improved risk-expected return frontier. It is the bank's choice of risk-management investment strategy interacted with the underlying production technology that gives the appearance of constant returns to scale or scale diseconomies. The improved frontier associated with the production technology can be detected when, holding constant the investment strategy at *A* and proportionately expanding outputs, the expected return increases and return risk decreases — point *B* on the improved frontier. The estimation of the standard cost function does not control for the investment strategy. Consequently, it is likely to identify constant returns or scale diseconomies for banks producing a larger output with more costly risk. How can these scale economies be identified when risk-taking obscures them?

Identifying scale economies requires controlling for the investment strategy at point *A* so that the proportional increase in outputs being investigated moves the bank to point *B* where the investment strategy remains the same but better diversification reduces risk, while spreading overhead costs, reducing risk-management costs, and exploiting increased network economies increase expected return. Calculating scale economies based on the standard cost function fails to control for the investment strategy because the standard cost function does not include arguments characterizing expected return and return risk, or managerial preferences for risk and return. If, instead, an expected-return or profit function is estimated rather than a cost function, the investment strategy can be taken into account.

4. How Can the Cost Elasticity be Estimated While Accounting for the Investment Strategy?

The expected-return or profit function must account for managers' choice of expected return and risk. In effect, it is a demand function for return and risk. Such a demand function can be derived from a managerial utility function that ranks, not return and risk, but production plans. Production plans (q, n, x, k) consist of a vector, q, of outputs made up of financial products and services; a measure of asset quality, n; a vector, x, of variable inputs, consisting of funding sources, labor, and physical capital; and the amount of equity capital, k.[6] Production plans are more basic than these first two moments of the subjective

[6] Typical types of outputs include balance-sheet loans and sold loans, either in aggregate or disaggregated into types of loans, liquid assets, securities, trading assets, and off-balance-sheet activities measured either by the amount of non-interest income or by the credit-equivalent amount. Typical inputs consist of sources of borrowed funds: insured deposits, uninsured deposits, and other borrowed money, labor, and physical capital. The expenditures on these inputs comprise interest and non-interest expense.

distribution of returns. In ranking production plans, managers must translate plans into realizations of profit for any given state of the economy, s.

Let (p, w, r) represent, respectively, the prices of outputs, the prices of inputs, and the risk-free rate of interest. Managers' beliefs about the realizations of after-tax profit conditional on the state of the economy, $\pi = g(q, n, x, k, p, w, r, s)$, plus their beliefs about the probability distribution of states of the economy combine to imply a subjective distribution of after-tax profit that depends on the production plan: $f(\pi; q, n, x, k, p, w, r)$. Under well-known restrictions, this distribution can be represented by its first two moments, $E(\pi; q, n, x, k, p, w, r)$ and $S(\pi; q, n, x, k, p, w, r)$.

While managerial utility could be defined over these two moments, a more general specification defines utility over profit and the production plan, $U(\pi; q, n, x, k, p, w, r)$, which is equivalent to defining it over the conditional probability distributions $f(\cdot)$. If only the first moment influences utility, utility maximization is equivalent to profit maximization. However, the generality of this specification allows higher moments to influence managers' ranking of production plans. Thus, bank managers with high-valued investment opportunities might trade expected profit for reduced risk to protect their valuable charters. On the other hand, managers whose banks face low-valued investment opportunities might adopt higher-risk investment strategies to exploit a mispriced bank safety net.[7]

Let π designate after-tax profit, t, the tax rate on profit, and $p_\pi = 1/(1 - t)$, the price of a dollar of after-tax profit in terms of before-tax dollars. Then the before-tax accounting or cash-flow profit is defined as $p_\pi \pi = p \cdot q + m - w \cdot x$, where m equals other sources of revenue so that $p \cdot q + m$ gives total revenue. Maximizing the utility function subject to the technology and this definition of profit — conditional on the vector of outputs — gives the demand for profit $\pi^*(q, n, v, k)$, where $v = (w, p, r, m, p\pi)$. The cost function follows:

$$C^*(q, n, v, k) = p \cdot q + m - p_\pi \pi^*(q, n, v, k). \tag{3}$$

[7] See Marcus (1984) and Hughes and Mester (2013a).

Note that conditioning the profit function on outputs permits the derivation of the cost function from the conditional profit function. When only the first moment of the profit distribution influences the ranking of production plans that produce the conditioning outputs, then utility maximization implies profit maximization so that the standard cost function can be obtained from the conditional profit function. However, when higher moments of the profit distribution influence the ranking of production plans that produce the conditioning outputs, the cost function that is derived from the conditional profit function contains arguments that characterize the investment strategy. In this sense, it is a *risk-return-driven cost function*.[8] The production plan that solves the utility maximization problem defines cost and the investment strategy related to the outputs. Thus, in asking how cost varies with a proportional change in outputs, the investment strategy is held constant so that the proportional variation captures the cost elasticity between points *A* and *B*, not *A* and *C* or *A* and *D*, and so the cost elasticity measure (and, therefore, the scale economy measure, its inverse) calculated from this risk-return-driven cost function appropriately uncovers the degree of scale economies associated with the underlying production technology.

5. Do Big Banks Have Lower Average Operating Costs?

Operating costs or, equivalently, non-interest expenses, include corporate overhead — accounting, advertising, auditing, insurance, utilities, legal, advisory, and consulting. Additional categories include the expenses

[8] For details on the specification and estimation of the risk-return-driven cost function, see, for example, Hughes & Mester (2013b) and Hughes, Lang, Mester, & Moon (1996, 2000). Tests of profit maximization conducted by these authors in all their studies have always rejected profit maximization — implying that higher moments of the profit distribution influence the ranking of production plans. The utility framework from which the risk-return-driven cost function is derived is adapted from the Almost Ideal Demand System (Deaton & Muellbauer, 1980) used to estimate consumer demands. In the complete banking framework, a first-order condition defining the optimal amount of equity capital is also estimated.

involved with information technology and data processing, compensation and benefits, and expenses for the physical building and other fixed assets. In studying operating cost economies — spreading the overhead — Kovner, Vickery, & Zhou (2014) show that identifying the full extent of such economies requires controlling for the bank's investment strategy. They ask how the efficiency ratio, the ratio of non-interest expense to the sum of net interest income and non-interest income, varies with the natural log of assets. With no controls in the regression, they find that a 1% increase in assets implies a decrease of 1.32% in the efficiency ratio. When they control for the asset allocation component of the investment strategy, they obtain a decrease of 1.892%. From their most complete characterization of the investment strategy — controlling for the asset allocation, revenue sources, funding structure, business concentration, and organizational complexity — they obtain a decrease of 4.52% in the efficiency ratio, over three times larger than the decrease estimated without controls for the investment strategy.

They also regress the natural log of operating costs on the natural log of assets to obtain an operating cost elasticity — the regression coefficient on the log of assets. Without controls, a 10% increase in assets is associated with a 9.93% increase in operating costs — essentially constant returns to scale; with controls for asset allocation, a 9.79% increase in operating costs; and with controls for asset allocation, revenue sources, funding structure, business concentration, and organizational complexity, an 8.99% increase.

While they do not report how the operating cost elasticity varies with the size of the bank, they find that the efficiency ratio decreases with size. A 1% increase in assets implies the ratio decreases about 4% for banks between the 50th and 95th percentiles and 8% for the largest 1% of banks.

6. Does Endogenous Risk-Taking Obscure Scale-Related, Improved Diversification?

The importance of controlling for endogenous risk-taking is illustrated in a related study of the relationship between bank size and diversification — a study by Demsetz & Strahan (1997) that considers the question of the choice of investment strategy as a bank increases its output and obtains better diversification. A naïve hypothesis might contend that better scale-related diversification implies that larger banks operate with less risk. In terms of Figure 1, the bank at point *A* operates at the less risky point *B* as it increases its scale. However, an empirical examination is likely to find that larger banks are riskier. As the bank at point *A* increases its scale and achieves the higher frontier, it may choose an investment strategy with more risk than the strategies at points *A*, *B*, and *C*.

Demsetz & Strahan (1997) contend that better diversification gives banks the incentive to take more risk, and this endogenous increase in risk-taking is likely to obscure the exogenous reduction in risk — the improved risk-expected return trade-off generated by the improved scale-related diversification. They estimate several asset pricing models to obtain measures of bank-specific risk which they then regress on asset size and controls for the investment strategy. With no controls, risk and asset size are weakly negatively related; however, when the controls for the investment strategy are included in the regression, the negative relationship between risk and size becomes strong and large. As in the case of estimating cost economies, finding clear evidence of size-related diversification requires controlling for the investment strategy.

7. Do Big Banks Experience Overall Scale Economies?

The estimation of the risk-return-driven cost function in Equation (3) reveals the scale economies that elude the standard cost function. Dijkstra (2013) estimates both the standard cost function and the risk-return-driven cost function for European banks in 2003, 2007, and 2010. Table 1 reports the cost elasticities he obtains. For the standard cost function, the cost elasticity is either 1 or very close to 1 for the three years — essentially constant returns to scale. By controlling for the investment strategy, the risk-return-driven cost function yields estimates of the cost elasticity that imply a 10% increase in outputs is associated with an 8.56% increase in cost in 2003, an 8.30% increase in 2007, and

Table 1. Comparing scale economies estimates.

		Cost Elasticity		
		2003	2007	2010
	European Banks			
Dijkstra (2013)	Standard Cost Function	**0.983**	**0.997**	1.000
Dijkstra (2013)	Risk-Return-Driven Cost Function	**0.856**	**0.830**	**0.820**
	U.S. Banks			
Hughes and Mester (2013b)	Standard Cost Function	**1.070**	1.026	1.016
Hughes and Mester (2013b)	Risk-Return-Driven Cost Function	**0.845**	**0.878**	**0.798**

Note: Estimates of scale economies derived from the standard cost function and from the risk-return-driven cost function are shown for European and U.S. banks in three years. Values in bold are significantly different from 1 at better than 10%.

an 8.20% increase in 2010 — evidence of large scale economies that elude the standard cost function.

Hughes & Mester (2013b) find similar results for the same three years for top-tier U.S. bank holding companies. The standard cost function yields cost elasticities that imply either scale diseconomies or constant returns to scale: in 2003, a 10% increase in outputs results in a 10.7% increase in cost; in 2007 and 2010, the cost elasticities are not statistically different from one. In contrast, after controlling for the investment strategy, the risk-return-driven cost function provides evidence of substantial cost economies: a 10% increase in outputs implies an 8.45% increase in cost in 2003, an 8.78% increase in 2007, and a 7.98% increase in 2010.

Not only do Hughes & Mester (2013b) find evidence of substantial scale economies for all three years, they also find that the largest banks experience the largest scale economies. In Table 2, the estimates of cost elasticities are broken down by size groups. Consider a comparison of the mean cost elasticities of banks in the range of $2–10 billion in assets to those of banks whose assets exceed $100 billion. For a 10%

Table 2. Cost elasticities estimated from the risk-return-driven cost function from Hughes and Mester (2013b).

Consolidated Assets	Cost Elasticity		
	2003	2007	2010
< $0.8 billion	**0.855**	**0.891**	**0.815**
$0.8–2 billion	**0.833**	**0.882**	**0.814**
$2–10 billion	**0.834**	**0.870**	**0.754**
$10–50 billion	**0.731**	**0.846**	**0.763**
$50–100 billion	**0.711**	**0.812**	**0.701**
> $100 billion	**0.737**	**0.749**	**0.700**

Note: Estimates of scale economies derived from the risk-return-driven cost function are shown for U.S. banks in three years. Values in bold are significantly different from 1 at better than 10 percent.

increase in outputs, in 2003 cost increases by 8.34% for the smaller banks and 7.37% for the very large banks; in 2007, 8.70% for smaller banks and 7.49% for the largest; and in 2010, 7.54% for the smaller banks and 7.00% for the largest.[9]

8. Are the Scale Economies Found for the Largest Financial Institutions Generated by a More Efficient Production Technology or by Cost-of-Funds Subsidies Because of Being Perceived as Too Big to Fail?

Hughes & Mester (2013b) conduct tests to determine whether technology or cost-of-funds subsidies due to too-big-to-fail account for the

[9] The estimate of a mean cost elasticity of 0.700 in 2010 for banks whose assets exceed $100 billion is consistent with approximately $14–19 billion in cost synergies at $2.4 trillion in consolidated assets, the size of JPMorgan Chase at the time of the Goldman report on breaking up JP Morgan Chase and the response by CFO Marianne Lake that JPMorgan Chase has approximately $18 billion in cost synergies.

estimated scale economies of the largest financial institutions. Using the 2007 data on U.S. banks, they re-estimate the cost function after dropping banks larger than $100 billion in assets, the so-called too-big-to-fail banks.[10] They then calculate the cost elasticity for the largest banks whose assets exceed $100 billion out-of-sample based on the fitted cost function. Compared to the baseline cost elasticity of 0.749 for these banks reported in Table 2, they obtain a cost elasticity of 0.742. If the largest institutions benefit from a lower cost of funds because of being perceived as too big to fail, their elimination from the estimation and the out-of-sample calculation of nearly the same value of cost elasticity provides compelling evidence that the study's estimated scale economies at the largest institutions are not being driven by the perception of being too big to fail.

The authors also performed an additional test to see whether the estimate of scale economies at banks whose assets exceed $100 billion is being driven by a cost-of-funding advantage from being perceived as too big to fail. They recalculated estimated cost elasticities for these banks, replacing their actual cost-of-funds with the median cost-of-funds for banks in the sample with $100 billion or less in assets. The mean cost elasticity for the too-big-to-fail banks with these pseudo-prices is 0.743 compared to the baseline 0.749. This is suggestive that it is production technology, not perceptions about being too-big-to-fail, that generates the scale economies of the largest financial institutions.[11]

---

[10] See Brewer & Jagtiani (2009) for a discussion of the definition of the too-big-to-fail classification.

[11] Davies & Tracey (2014) estimate a standard cost function for European banks and obtain significant scale economies. They test the robustness of this result by replacing the interest rate paid on borrowed funds with the interest rate implied by Moody's rating, assuming no government or outside assistance in the case of financial distress. While using the actual observed price of borrowed funds yields evidence of scale economies, these economies disappear when the pseudo-price is used in the estimation. They assume that this difference in measured scale economies is due to a too-big-to-fail subsidy. Hughes & Mester (2013b) point out some weaknesses of the Davies & Tracey (2014) approach. While Hughes & Mester use a pseudo-price strategy, they substitute the pseudo-prices into the equation for the

Thus, while there may be a funding cost advantage among the largest banks (perhaps because they are perceived as being too-big-to-fail), the risk-return-driven cost function controls for this funding advantage when computing scale economies, and there is no evidence that a funding cost advantage influences the estimates of scale economies.

9. How Would Restrictions on the Size of the Largest Financial Institutions Affect their Global Competitiveness?

Tarullo (2011) describes the trade-off between systemic risk and efficiency: "An additional concern would arise if some countries made the trade-off by limiting the size or configuration of their financial firms for systemic risk reasons at the cost of realizing genuine economies of scope or scale, while other countries did not. In this case, firms from the first group of countries might well be at a competitive disadvantage in the provision of certain cross-border activities."

Wheelock and Wilson (2012) compare the cost of the four largest institutions in 2009 ($1.244–2.225 trillion) with a number of $1 trillion institutions equaling the total assets of the four largest institutions. The combined cost of the scaled-down institutions is 9% higher.

Hughes and Mester (2013b) compare the cost of the 17 largest institutions whose assets exceeded $100 billion in 2007 with these institutions scaled back to half their size with the same product mix. They increase the number of smaller institutions so that the combined assets equal the assets of the 17 largest institutions. The cost of the scaled-down institutions is 23% higher.

---

cost elasticity derived from the cost function estimated with the observed prices. In contrast, Davies and Tracey re-estimate the cost function using the pseudo-prices and the total cost and input expenditures that correspond to the original observed prices. Their model assumes that cost is minimized with respect to the pseudo-prices, but the total costs and cost shares belong to the observed prices, not the pseudo-prices. Since the pseudo-prices do not give rise to the total costs used in the re-estimation, the evidence obtained from the re-estimation is hard to interpret and cannot be considered evidence that the too-big-to-fail policy generates the scale economies.

Proposals to limit the size of banks or to break up existing large institutions to reduce systemic risk face the problem that economic incentives reward scale and scope. Smaller institutions will produce at higher average cost and will likely not be able to provide the variety of financial products and services that characterize larger institutions. Because such size restrictions would work against market forces, they would create incentives for companies to avoid them. An obvious strategy entails operating outside the more regulated sector where there is no assurance that new sources of systemic risk will not develop. Thus, the incentive to escape regulatory restrictions on the size and configuration of financial institutions would require intensive research and monitoring, roles currently assigned in the U.S. to the Office of Financial Research and the Financial Stability Oversight Council.

10. Conclusions

Scale economies are hard to detect empirically because costly endogenous risk-taking interacts with the production technology, which tends to obscure them. Empirical results based on models that account for endogenous risk-taking indicate that the largest financial institutions experience the largest scale economies and that technological advantages, such as diversification and the spreading of information costs and other costs that do not increase proportionately with size, rather than safety-net subsidies appear to generate the scale economies.

It is very important to note that the literature does not indicate whether these benefits of larger size outweigh the potential costs in terms of the systemic risk that large scale may impose on the financial system. More research is needed to calibrate efficiency benefits against potential system risks posted by large, complex institutions. However, the finding of significant scale economies does suggest that if public policy considerations imply that society would be better off with smaller financial institutions, restrictions that limit the size of financial institutions, if effective, may put large banks at a competitive disadvantage in global markets where competitors are not similarly constrained. Moreover, size restrictions may not be effective since they work against market forces and create incentives for firms to avoid them. Avoiding the restrictions could thereby push risk-taking outside of the more regulated financial sector without necessarily reducing systemic risk. These factors need to be considered when evaluating policies concerning financial institution scale.

References

Bair, S. (2012). Why it's time to break up the 'too big to fail' banks. *Fortune*. Available at: http://fortune.com/2012/01/18/why-its-time-to-break-up-the-too-big-to-fail-banks/

Becalli, E., Anolli, M., & Borello, G. (2015). Are European banks too big? Evidence on economies of scale. *Journal of Banking and Finance*, *58*, 232–246.

Berger, A. N., & Mester, L. J. (1997). Inside the black box: What explains differences in the efficiencies of financial institutions? *Journal of Banking and Finance*, *21*, 895–947.

Bossone, B. & Lee, J.-K. (2004). In finance, size matters: The 'systemic scale economies' hypothesis, *IMF Staff Papers*, 51(1), 19–46.

Brewer, E. & Jagtiani, J. (2009). How much did banks pay to become too-big-to-fail and to become systemically important? *Federal Reserve Bank of Philadelphia Working Paper* No. 09-34.

Davies, R. & Tracey, B. (2014). Too big to be efficient? The impact of too-big-to-fail factors on scale economies for banks. *Journal of Money, Credit, and Banking*, *46*, 219–253.

Deaton, A. & Muellbauer, J. (1980). An almost ideal demand system. *American Economic Review*, *70*, 312–326.

Demsetz, R. S. & Strahan, P. E. (1997). Diversification, size, and risk at bank holding companies. *Journal of Money, Credit, and Banking*, *29*, 300–313.

Dijkstra, M. (2013). Economies of scale and scope in the European banking sector 2002–2011, *Amsterdam Center for Law & Economics Working Paper* No. 2013-11.

Feng, G. & Serletis, A. (2010). Efficiency, technical change, and returns to scale in large US banks: Panel data evidence from an output distance function satisfying theoretical regularity. *Journal of Banking and Finance*, *34*, 127–138.

Fisher, R. & Rosenblum, H. (2012). How huge banks threaten the economy. *The Wall Street Journal*. Available at: http://www.wsj.com/articles/SB10001424052702303816504577312110821340648.

Greenspan, A. (2010). The crisis. *Brookings Papers on Economic Activity*. Spring 2010201–246.

Hughes, J. P., Lang, W., Mester, L. J., & Moon C.-G. (1996). Efficient banking under interstate branching. *Journal of Money, Credit, and Banking*, *28*, 1045–1071.

Hughes, J. P., Lang, W., Mester, L. J., & Moon C.-G. (2000). Recovering risky technologies using the almost ideal demand system: An application to U.S. banking. *Journal of Financial Services Research*, *18*, 5–27.

Hughes, J. P. & Mester, L. J. (1998). Bank capitalization and cost: Evidence of scale economies in risk management and signaling. *Review of Economics and Statistics*, *80*, 314–325.

Hughes, J. P. & Mester, L. J. (2013a). A primer on market discipline and governance of financial institutions for those in a state of shocked disbelief. In F. Pasiouras (Ed.), *Efficiency and Productivity Growth: Modelling in the Financial Services Industry* (19–47). West Sussex, U.K.: John Wiley and Sons.

Hughes, J. P. & Mester, L. J. (2013b). Who said large banks don't experience scale economies? Evidence from a risk-return-driven cost function. *Journal of Financial Intermediation*, *22*, 559–585.

Hughes, J. P., Mester, L. J., & Moon, C.-G. (2001). Are scale economies in banking elusive or illusive? Evidence obtained by incorporating capital structure and risk-taking into models of bank production. *Journal of Banking and Finance*, *25*, 2169–2208.

Kovner, A., Vickery, J., & Zhou, L. (2014). Do big banks have lower operating costs? *Economic Policy Review*, 20(2), 1–27.

Marcus, A. J. (1984). Deregulation and bank financial policy. *Journal of Banking and Finance*, *8*, 557–565.

Popper, N., (February 24, 2015). JPMorgan Chase insists it's worth more as one than in pieces. *The New York Times*.

Purcell, P. (June 25, 2012) Shareholders can cure too big to fail. *Wall Street Journal*. Available at: http://www.wsj.com/articles/SB10001424052702304765304577480743265772620.

Ramsden, R., Fitzgerald, C., Parls, D., & Senet, K. (2015). New capital rules reignite the JPM breakup debate. *Goldman sachs equity research*. United States: Banks.

Tarullo, Daniel K. (2011). Industrial organization and systemic risk: An agenda for further research. *Conference on the Regulation of Systemic Risk, Federal Reserve Board*. Washington, D.C.

Wheelock, D. & Wilson, P. (2012). "Do large banks have lower costs? New estimates of returns to scale for US banks. *Journal of Money, Credit, and Banking*, *44*, 171–199.

Wheelock, D. C. & Wilson, P. W. (2015). The evolution of scale economies in U.S. banking. Federal Reserve Bank of St. Louis, *Working Paper* No. 2015-021A.

The International Banking Landscape: Developments, Drivers, and Potential Implications

— CHAPTER 7

▪ Juan A. Marchetti
World Trade Organization

1. Introduction

A cursory look at the press over the last couple of years gives the impression that internationally active banks have been shaken by a tsunami and that, as a consequence, the industry's landscape has been fundamentally transformed. These seemingly tectonic shifts in the banking industry have affected not only investment banking, or investment banking operations of universal banks, but also international banks' retail operations worldwide.[1]

Marchetti is Counsellor, Trade in Services Division, WTO. The views expressed in this chapter are personal and should not be attributed to WTO Members or the WTO Secretariat. This chapter is based on a presentation made by the author at the Conference on 'The Future of Large, Internationally Active Banks', cosponsored by the Federal Reserve Bank of Chicago and the World Bank (Chicago, November 5–6, 2015).

[1]See, for example, The Economist (2012, 2015a, 2015b), Financial Times (2014, 2015a, 2015b), Moneyweb (2015).

The purpose of this short chapter is to document recent trends in international banking, particularly since the global financial crisis, to look into the drivers of those developments, and to discuss the potential implications. The paper does not attempt to present new evidence but, rather, draws from existing evidence.

The chapter is organized as follows. Section 2 will provide an overview of the main developments in international banking since the global financial crisis. Section 3 will review the main drivers identified by the literature. By way of conclusion, Section 4 will discuss the potential implications of these developments.

2. Developments in International Banking Since the Global Financial Crisis

For the purposes of the current discussion, an internationally active bank[2] is defined as a bank that conducts operations or transactions in foreign markets. The term includes banks that conduct foreign business through establishments abroad, e.g., by establishing a subsidiary or a branch, and/or that provide services on a cross-border basis (e.g., cross-border lending).

The global financial crisis of 2008–2009 shook the banking industry worldwide, and prompted noteworthy changes. Four facts stand out among the developments in international banking since the crisis. First, direct cross-border lending as a share of total banking assets has declined. Second, the share of local lending by foreign bank affiliates has remained steady. Third, international banks have refocused their activities — withdrawing from some markets — and have been replaced by other banks with a more regional focus. Fourth, banks are being disintermediated by other forms of corporate financing, in particular bond markets.

[2] Some would refer to these banks as "global", but whether an 'internationally active bank' is really 'global', or whether some are more 'global' than others (in terms of their reach to, or penetration in, foreign markets), remains a matter of degree.

a. The decline of cross-border lending

Global gross capital flows remain well below their peak before the global financial crisis, which was reached after an unusual period of expansion. Those developments have been well documented (Allen & Gale, 2015). Changes in cross-border banking flows explain a substantial part of this rise and fall.

Figure 1, which has been drawn from Forbes (2014), shows the total global gross capital inflows broken into three categories of assets: banking flows, portfolio flows, and foreign direct investment (FDI).[3] As can be seen, all types of capital flows declined during the crisis, but cross-border banking flows did not only fell to zero, but actually reversed, indicating that banks not only stopped lending money abroad, but also liquidated foreign exposures to bring money home. Since the crisis, both portfolio flows and FDI have stabilized at positive but lower levels, while banking flows have continued to contract.

The contraction of international bank lending concerns mainly flows between unrelated banks resident in different jurisdictions. This has been

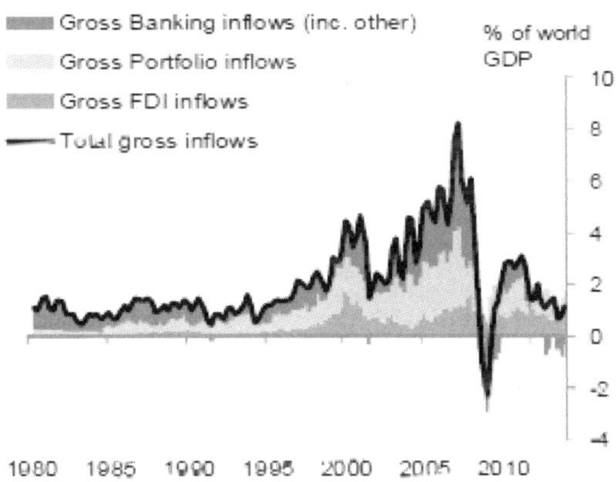

Figure 1. Global gross capital inflows, by asset.

Source: Forbes (2014).

[3] "Banking flows" is, in fact, the "other" category of the IMF International Financial Statistics. As explained by Forbes (2014, footnote 37), this category is primarily banking, but the data also include transactions in currency and deposits, and trade finance.

argued by Reinhardt and Riddiough (2014), who separate cross-border banking flows into interbank and "intragroup" transactions,[4] and show that while interbank flows fell drastically in the immediate aftermath of the Lehman Brother's collapse, intragroup funding actually increased after that event and was stable for the remainder of the crisis period. Furthermore, they find that this contrasting behavior in interbank and intragroup flows is a response to fluctuations in global risk — hence, more of a permanent feature than a one-shot event.

A further look into banking data shows cross-border lending has evolved heterogeneously across regions. Breaking down BIS data by country groups confirms the rise and fall of cross-border lending before and after the global financial crisis, but also reveals that while cross-border lending to developing and emerging economies has increased again, foreign bank claims to developed economies have rather continued to decrease or stabilized at a lower level (see Figure 2, from Bremus & Fratzscher, 2014).

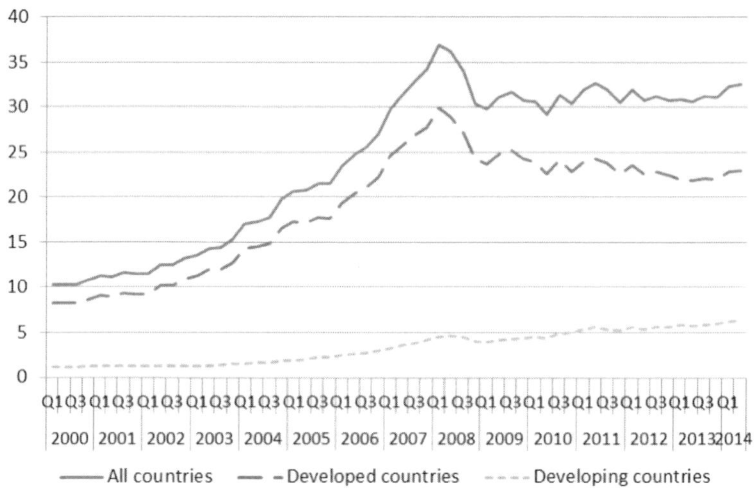

Figure 2. Total foreign claims of BIS reporting countries, in trillion USD.

Source: Bremus and Fratzscher (2014), on the basis of BIS Consolidated Banking Statistics, on an immediate borrower basis.

[4] Interbank refers to arms-length transactions between unrelated banks resident in different jurisdictions; while "intragroup" refers to transactions between affiliates belonging to the same banking group, and occurring through so-called "internal capital markets".

b. The resilience of lending through branches and subsidiaries in foreign markets

While cross-border lending has fallen since the global financial crisis, international banks have reshaped their international business models, relatively privileging operations through branches and subsidiaries in host countries. As can be seen in Figure 3, cross-border claims as a share of total banking assets of host countries have not recovered to their pre-crisis level, while loans extended in host countries by affiliates of foreign banks did fall slightly from the peak in 2007, and have been rather stable since about 2009. According to the IMF (2015), the share of local lending in total foreign claims (the sum of cross-border claims plus loans extended through affiliates abroad) has thus grown from less than 43% to about 49%, and most of those loans are in local currency.

c. The inrush of emerging-market banks, and the regionalization of international banking

International banks are withdrawing, but they are being replaced by other banks, usually from emerging economies and with a more

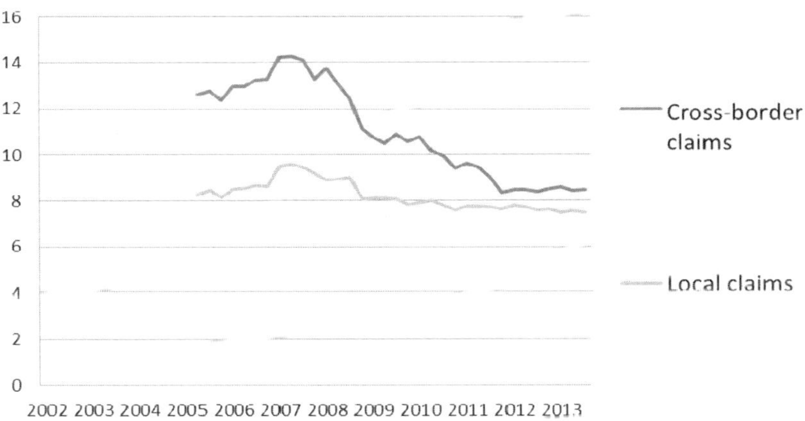

Figure 3. Cross-border and local claims relative to total banking assets of recipient countries

Source: Based on BIS data for Chart 2.1 in IMF (2015), available at http://www.imf.org/external/pubs/ft/gfsr/2015/01/.

regional focus. As explained by Claessens & van Horen (2014), the total number of foreign banks in host countries has fallen since 2009, but given that the number of domestic banks also declined, the market share of foreign banks has stabilized at about 35%. And although the total number of foreign banks declined, many of the operations of departing banks have been acquired by other foreign-bank parents, often from emerging and developing economies. Indeed, after rising continuously before 2008, the number of foreign banks from high-income countries declined from 948 in 2008 to 814 in 2013, while banks from emerging and developing economies has continuously increased their presence, owning now 441 foreign banks, which represents 8% of all foreign assets, double what they accounted for in 2007 (Figure 4).

As these banks tend to invest mainly in their own geographical regions, we may be witnessing further regionalization of international banking. Asia-Pacific is a case in point. Remolona & Shim (2015) show

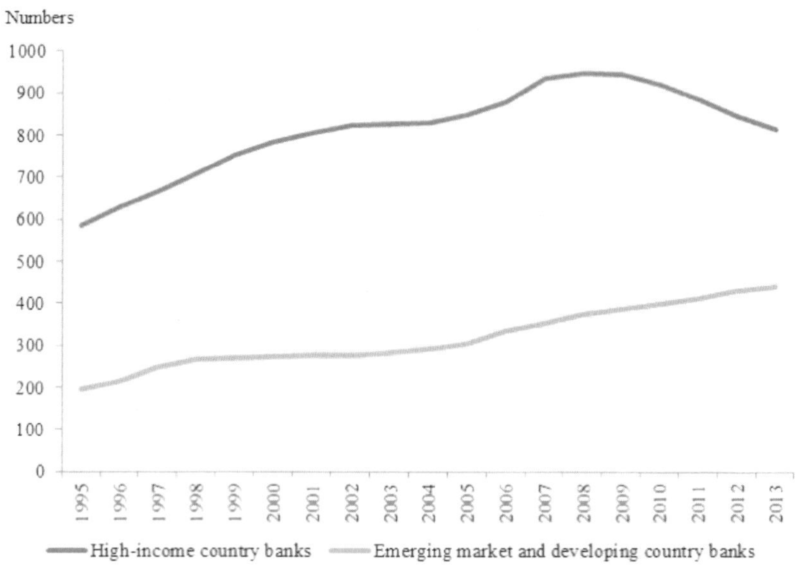

Figure 4. Number of foreign banks from high-income and developing economies.
Source: Claessens and Horen (2014).

that, while in the years leading up to the crisis, much of the cross-border activity in the region had been driven by dollar credit intermediated largely by European banks, since the crisis European banks have held back and banks from Asia-Pacific have stepped in, so that the bulk of banking intermediation (and thus cross — border flows) is now conducted within the region. The IMF (2015) makes a similar point, and argues that regionalization is also taking place in other regions, in particular Latin America and Africa (through the expansion of pan-African bank groups), albeit not to a degree comparable for the time being to that of the Asia-Pacific region.

d. Banking disintermediation

The decline in cross-border bank lending has been accompanied by bank disintermediation, i.e., funding of the global corporate sector shifting away from banks and towards international bond issuances (IIF, 2015b; IMF, 2015). This 'disintermediation' can take many forms, from traditional bond issuance (Figure 5) to direct lending to companies by non-bank financial institutions, such as insurers and pension funds. This surge has been driven to a large extent by the rapid increase in bond issuances from emerging markets.

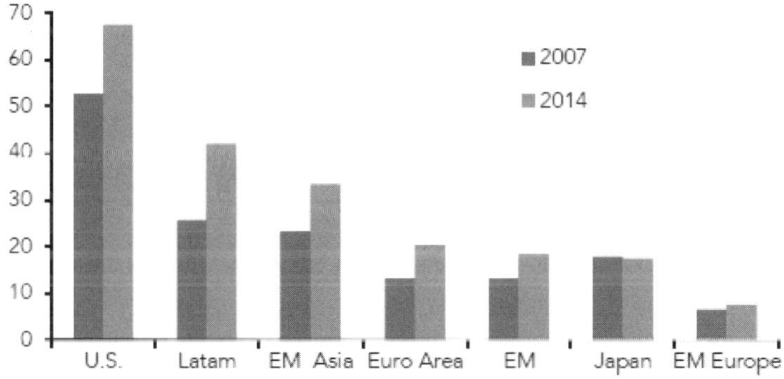

Figure 5. Non-financial corporate sector: share of bond market funding, percent.
Source: IIF (2015b).

3. Explanations for the Changes in International Banking

Regulatory reform following the global financial crisis explains, in my view, most of the developments highlighted in the previous section. The general regulatory reaction following the global financial crisis has been a mix of national and internationally coordinated policies aimed at three closely related objectives: reducing the likelihood of failure by a large international institution, reducing the risk of cross-border transmission of such a failure, and dampening the effects of those shocks. Reforms have therefore aimed at both ensuring the prudential safety of individual banks (through, e.g., stricter capital and liquidity requirements), and introduction structural changes (such as limits on proprietary trading or the separation of proprietary trading from retail deposit taking) so as to avoid contagion within banking groups and across the system (Claessens & Marchetti, 2013). Many of these reforms have emphasized local operations: ring-fenced local capital and liquidity, local governance and systems, limits on cross-border intra-group funding, and national and cross-border recovery and resolution regimes.

Recent research has shed further light on the actual impact of recent regulatory reforms on international banking in the aftermath of the global financial crisis. Bremus & Fratzscher (2014) found that regulatory policy has been an important driver of adjustments in cross-border banking since the crisis, but the effects depend on the measure considered. More independent and powerful supervisory authorities tend to promote international lending, while increasing capital requirements in the home country reduces cross-border claims.

Recent research by the IMF (2015) is also worth highlighting. A survey conducted among bank supervisors in 40 countries shows that many countries tightened regulations on banks' international operations or strengthened their supervision between 2006 and 2014 (through for example limits on banks' activities, and requirements on foreign bank branches), while a more limited number loosened regulations regarding foreign banking presence and activities. Moreover, the proportion of countries that tightened regulation on banks' international operations is higher in advanced economies than in emerging market economies.

According to the IMF, changes in regulations targeting banks' international operations, as well as more general regulatory changes (e.g., stricter bank capital requirements), can affect foreign banking lending in at least three ways: (1) tighter regulations may reduce foreign bank lending just because bank activities in general are curtailed; (2) regulatory arbitrage may induce a countervailing effect, in so far as banks in countries that tighten banking regulations may increase their claims on countries that are less regulated; and (3) regulatory changes may bring about a substitution effect between various types of lending because their effects may differ across types of exposures.

The IMF analysis shows that regulatory changes can explain a sizable fraction — roughly half — of the decline in cross-border claims on recipient countries (as a percentage of GDP) since the pre-crisis years (2005–2007). Tighter regulations on banks' international operations or capital regulations in home countries are associated with a reduction in lending from those countries.

These results should not come as a surprise. Regulation affects cross-border lending of international banks in many ways. For one, if banks have difficulty in raising more capital to comply with higher capital requirements imposed by Basel III, they may resort to "deleveraging", and, in so doing, the assets of more distant or less profitable markets become prime candidates for shrinkage. Secondly, as pointed out by *The Economist* (2012), some regulators have been reported as treating foreign exposures more harshly in stress tests, that is, to assume that foreign assets will not be as easily available as domestic ones for meeting liabilities, thus affecting international banking.

Apart from regulation, political factors may have also contributed to the reassessment and downsizing of international networks by some banks. In fact, in some cases banks — particularly banks having benefited from capital infusion or bailouts by governments — have been under pressure to give priority to domestic credit needs, and therefore refocus their operations towards the home market (*The Economist*, 2012).

Another factor that may be playing a role in the developments outlined in the previous section is the defensive reaction to be expected from international banks in the even to global shocks, particularly those affecting home headquarters. In that regard, Claessens & Van Horen (2014) found that banks headquartered in a country that experienced a crisis are more likely to exit from any host country. Looking at bilateral home-host relationships, they find that banks from a particular home country are more likely to completely pull out of a particular host country when the latter is less developed, when the home country is more developed, when the home country banks only represent a small share of the host country banking system, and when the distance between the home and the host country is large. In their view, their results suggest that, under pressure to consolidate, foreign banks from richer countries pulled out of countries where they only had a small presence, and out of poorer and more distant countries.

One other factor affecting international banking is the pressure from shareholders to improve returns that took a beating following the financial crisis. This is certainly a significant factor driving the retreat of various 'global' banks from overseas markets, particularly from those that may represent a drag on the bank's profits (*Financial Times*, 2015b). It has been reported that the return to profitability has been perhaps substantially being achieved by shrinking balance sheets and geographical footprints (*The Banker*, 2015). The high costs of compliance with new regulatory requirements both at home and abroad may also be a contributing factor.

Regulation has focused on avoiding negative outcomes, not on defining desired international banking business models. However, intentionally or not, all these reforms are forcing international banks to revisit business models and organization structures.[5] It is worth noting in that regard that the decentralized multinational model of banking (whereby banks match assets and liabilities in each country, with liabilities consisting largely of local deposits) proved more robust in overcoming the credit crunch in wholesale funding markets during the recent global financial crisis than the "international banking model", whereby banks employ funds raised in one country to lend in another,

[5] Banks that could have portrayed as "global" right before the crisis are now jettisoning international operations.

often relying on wholesale funds or foreign exchange swap markets (McCauley, 2014).

4. Conclusions and Potential Policy Implications

The previous sections have reviewed recent developments in international banking and suggested some explanations, but the factors at play, as well as the data, are complex and hard to interpret. From that perspective, I concur with Allen & Gale (2015) that "[d]rawing firm conclusions is premature at best and foolhardy at worst". Nevertheless, by way of conclusion, I would like to briefly discuss some potential implications of recent developments, not only for policymakers but for markets and financial institutions as well.

What are the effects of these developments on financial stability? Again, no definitive conclusions can be drawn at this stage. The IMF (2015) analysis referred to above finds that the greater the international claims on an economy as a result of cross-border banking flows, the more exposed the economy is to international shocks. Moreover, and somewhat surprisingly, the IMF also found that exposure to cross-border lending does not necessarily insulate an economy from domestic shocks. In fact, countries with high cross-border lending appear as suffering a greater contraction in credit in the face of domestic shocks. However, where foreign bank lending is through local branches or subsidiaries, domestic shocks are not amplified. The IMF suggest that this could be because intra-group funding makes up for disruptions in local funding. So, as concluded by the IMF, "[w]ith regard to financial stability, the findings of the empirical analysis in this chapter lends support to a "multinational" banking model rather than a cross-border one...All else equal, the shift to more local as opposed to cross-border operations results in a decline in the sensitivity of capital flows to global shocks and yields a reduction in contagion. Foreign banks operating locally rather than through cross-border transactions tend to contract credit much less following domestic shocks in host countries."

Broadly, therefore, the changes in the international banking landscape that have occurred since the crisis — basically a reduction in cross-border banking flows and more emphasis on lending through branches and subsidiaries in host countries — might contribute positively to financial stability. However, also as recognized by the IMF (2015), limiting cross-border lending may jeopardize other benefits and create new risks. For one, cross-border flows play a positive role in the allocation of global savings across countries, thus facilitating investment and contributing to economic growth. Hence, a reduction in those flows may lead to a reduction of those benefits. In addition, changes in the sources of supply of cross-border credit might raise new financial stability risks. Increasing global bank disintermediation — i.e., a decline in direct cross-border lending to corporates by banks and a concomitant increase in international issuances of corporate bonds among other forms of financing — implies that the locus of risks is shifting away from banks to non-banks. Such a shift, as recognized by the IMF, may complicate surveillance of the global financial system.

Does the retrenchment of banks in developed countries make the global system more stable? The rising importance of banks from emerging markets and developing countries, through foreign presence abroad and — very likely as well, although data is more limited — through cross-border lending, is a natural development, reflecting their growing roles in the world economy and global financial markets. The retrenchment of banks from developed countries and their replacement by banks from emerging economies represents a replacement of one set of banks by another, but it may also represent a shift from set of borrowers to another. Current data does not allow for a full assessment of the kind of reallocation that has occurred. Therefore, it is premature to assert whether these changes have made the global financial system more stable (Allen & Gale, 2015). In any case, these specific developments raise may challenges, including (i) the need for policy makers in emerging and developing economies to participate actively in international deliberations concerning financial regulation about financial reforms, to upgrade their regulatory frameworks and, in particular, to adequately perform their role as home regulator and supervisor of foreign branches and local subsidiaries, including inter alia by ensuring the solvency of their banks; and (ii) the need to improve data coverage so as to encompass additional emerging markets and developing countries as creditor countries (Claessens & van Horen, 2015).

Does greater regional banking integration lead to greater financial stability? Caution is necessary here as well. First, regionalization may make the global banking system more prone to shocks, as diversification will be more limited and some newly emerging players may be less capitalised (Claessens & van Horen, 2014). Second, it may increase vulnerability to regional crises (IMF, 2015). Third, it may not lead to the use of the best banking technology and know-how in every market (Claessens & van Horen, 2015). In any case, we lack all the data necessary to make a more definitive conclusion (Allen & Gale, 2015), and further analysis of banking regionalization, as well as its pros and cons, is badly needed.

Finally, the (potentially negative) effects of these developments on the financing of emerging markets and developing economies should not be overlooked. While recent international regulatory reform (e.g., higher capital and liquidity requirements, leverage ratios, ring-fencing initiative) has been pursued and will hopefully strengthen the resilience of global banks, it could also have a significant impact on the financing of these economies. As explained by Carstens (2015), global banks are subject to consolidated supervision, and manage their risks and maximise their expected risk-adjusted returns by consolidating all their subsidiaries' assets and liabilities with those of the parent bank. Risk-weighted assets, liquidity coefficients and leverage ratios are calculated on a consolidated basis under the rules and supervision of the home jurisdiction's regulator. Assets held by subsidiaries result in capital charges and liquidity requirements for the global group as a whole. Therefore, the treatment given by home-country regulations to risk exposures registered at foreign subsidiaries, if they lead to disproportionate increases in capital charges for the bank, could significantly increase the costs of operating foreign subsidiaries and the financing costs of emerging and developing economies. The challenge ahead is to ensure an adequate balance between financial stability and the lending capacity of the financial sector, particularly in emerging and developing economies.

References

Allen, F. & Gale, D. (2015). Cross-border banking since the crisis — what does it mean for stability? *Banking Perspective, the Quarterly Journal of the Clearing House*, 3(1). Available at: https://www.theclearinghouse.org/publications/2015/2015-q1-banking-perspective/allen-gale-crossborder.

Bremus, F. & Marcel F. (2014). Drivers of structural change in cross-border banking since the global financial crisis. *CEPR Discussion Papers* No. 10296.

Carstens, A. (2015). Global banks and the adoption of the new regulatory framework: effects on the financing of emerging markets and developing economies. In Banque de France, *Financial stability review*, No. 19, April 2015.

Claessens, S. & Marchetti J. A. (2013). Global banking regroups. *Finance & Development*, 50(4). Available at: http://www.imf.org/external/pubs/ft/fandd/2013/12/claessens.htm.

Claessens, S. & Van Horen, N. (2014). The impact of the global financial crisis on banking globalization. *IMF Working Paper* No. 14/197.

Financial Times (December 9, 2014). Big banks are giving up on their global ambitions, by M. Arnold and C. Hall.

Financial Times (April 17, 2015a). HSBC Speeds up exit from emerging markets, by P. Jenkins and M. Arnold.

Financial Times (August 25, 2015b). Investment banking: Titans retreat, by L. Noonan.

Forbes, K. (November 18, 2014). Financial deglobalization?: Capital flows, banks and the Beatles, speech at Queen Mary University, London.

Institute of International Finance (January, 2015a). Capital flows to emerging markets.

Institute of International Finance (June, 2015b). Capital markets monitor — key issues.

International Monetary Fund (2015). International banking after the crisis: Increasingly local and safer? *Global Financial Stability Report*. pp. 55–91.

McCauley, R. (2014). De-internationalizing global banking? *Comparative Economic Studies*, 56(2), 257–270.

Moneyweb (March 7, 2015). Global banks look local these days. Available at: http://www.kpmg.com/za/en/issuesandinsights/articlespublications/financial-services/pages/global-banks-look-local-these-days.aspx.

Remolona, E. & Shim, I. (September, 2015). The rise of regional banking in Asia and the pacific. *BIS Quarterly Review*.

Reinhardt, D. & Riddiough, S. (2014). The two faces of cross-border banking flows: An investigation into the links between global risk, arms-length funding and internal capital markets. *Bank of England Working Paper* No. 498.

The Banker (2015). Top 1000 World Banks 2015: A new global picture, by Philippe Alexander, June 29, 2015.

The Economist (April 21, 2012). The retreat from everywhere.

The Economist (March 7, 2015a). Cocking up all over the world.

The Economist (March 7, 2015b). A world of pain.

Part III
Banking Activity Trends Following the Financial Crisis: Expansion? Retrenchment?

How Did Foreign Bank Lending Change During the Recent Financial Crisis: An Overview

— CHAPTER 8

- Allen N. Berger
  University of South Carolina, Wharton Financial Institutions Center and European Banking Center
- Tanakorn Makaew
  Securities and Exchange Commission
- Rima Turk-Ariss
  International Monetary Fund

1. Introduction

Foreign bank lending during financial crises is an important policy issue. Foreign banks are often accused of either spreading or exacerbating

This document summarizes the findings of a comprehensive research paper by the authors; see Berger, Makaew, & Turk Ariss (2016). The views expressed are those of the authors and do not necessarily reflect the views of the Securities and Exchange Commission, the IMF, or of the authors' colleagues at those institutions. The Securities and Exchange Commission, as a matter of policy, disclaims responsibility for any private publication or statement by any of its employees. The authors thank Stijn Claessens, Ricardo Correa, Asli Demirguc-Kunt, Gabriele Gelate, the economic consequences of crises by significantly cutting back credit supply in host countries. Specifically, foreign banks are alleged to cut bank lending in host nations in response to adverse balance sheet conditions at home, spreading crises from country to country (De Haas & Van Horen, 2012a). They are also purported to decrease credit to businesses in the host country more than do domestic banks during financial crises, perhaps because they suffer from more serious informational opacity problems, or because they are less willing to take significant risks in host nations. We argue in this paper that the issue of foreign banks reducing credit during financial crises is more nuanced and requires use of a more comprehensive dataset than has been employed in most of the existing literature.

Many research papers address these issues, but have frequently been handicapped by the use of incomplete datasets. These studies typically analyze loan quantity effects only, rather than including loan pricing, which would help to develop a fuller picture of changes in credit supply. They often use aggregate- or portfolio-level information, rather than studying individual loans, which sacrifices a significant amount of relevant information. In some cases, they analyze the effects on publicly-listed borrowers only, rather than including private firms for which bank credit is more important. They usually do not control for borrower characteristics, and so have difficulty distinguishing between the effects on safer versus riskier borrowers and differentiating between loan supply and demand effects. The research often does not distinguish between relationship and non-relationship borrowers, making it difficult to explore the informational opacity question. Finally, many of the

---

Linda Goldberg, Todd Gormley, Neeltje van Horen, Juan Marchetti, Sole Martinez Peria, Mark Mink, Denise Streeter, Fedrica Teppa, Anjan Thakor, Gregory Udell, Larry Wall as well as conference and seminar participants at the European Central Bank, the Dutch National Bank, the Bank of Finland, Financial Intermediation Research Society, Chicago Federal Reserve International Banking Conference, Financial Management Association, and the IMF Research Department for helpful suggestions. Samarth Kumar, Ashleigh Poindexter, Raluca Roman, Marshall Thomas, and Emily Zhao provided excellent research assistance. We thank the Darla Moore School of Business and CIBER for research support.

studies include data from only one or a small set of countries, making it challenging to draw general conclusions.

We address these data deficiencies in this study by using a very comprehensive dataset that combines information from a number of sources using a substantial amount of human resources. Data on bank ownership and other characteristics and condition are taken from Bureau van Dijk's, BankScope. Additional information on foreign versus domestic ownership is from Claessens & van Horen (2014), which is considered to be the more accurate source. These data are hand-matched with Thomson's Loan Pricing Corporation DealScan dataset, which provides loan characteristics and bank-borrower relationship information. We use computerized fuzzy matching in combination with manual verification to map borrowers in DealScan with the Bureau van Dijk's Orbis database, allowing us to obtain borrower characteristics and listing status. The computerized matching is required because of the size of the Orbis database, which contains data on over 10 million private and public firms. Since Orbis only contains the most recent listing status, additional information on historical listing status is obtained from Bureau van Dijk's Osiris. The final dataset contains over 18,000 loans with bank, loan, borrower, and relationship information from 2004 to 2011 for 50 countries (25 developed and 25 developing) around the world. The data collection, matching, and processing consumed three economists and five research assistants who jointly speak over 10 languages several years to complete.

This chapter contributes to several strands of the literature on the costs and benefits of foreign banks. Although there are some micro studies using data from a specific country,[1] most papers on foreign banks rely on cross-country aggregate data. For example, Detragiache, Gupta, & Tressel (2008) use country-level data to show that credit to the private sector is lower in countries with more foreign banks. Bruno

[1] Mian (2006) uses loan data from Pakistan to show that greater distance between foreign bank headquarters and their local branches lead foreign banks to avoid lending to small borrowers. Gormley (2010) uses foreign bank entry data at the district level from India to show that the presence of foreign banks may adversely affect the performance of small local firms.

& Hauswald (2008) use country-level data on foreign bank entry to show that external-finance-dependent industries grow faster in countries with more foreign banks. Feyen *et al.* (2014) use country-level data to show that credit growth is highly sensitive to cross-border funding shocks and this sensitivity is higher in Eastern Europe and Central Asia. Instead of country-level data, our paper uses loan-level data from 50 developed and developing countries to examine differences between foreign and domestic banks. Studying a large panel of loans from countries with varying degrees of economic development allows us to draw more general conclusions about foreign bank behavior.[2]

Some recent research also uses information on individual loans, but does not have borrower characteristics, and instead uses borrower fixed effects as controls (e.g., De Haas & van Horen, 2012a, 2012b). Because we have detailed information on borrowers, we are able to examine the effects of individual borrower characteristics, including whether the borrower is publicly listed, which turns out to be crucial to our results. We are able to allow borrower conditions and the sensitivities of loan spreads to these to change during the financial crisis, which indeed occurs in our dataset. In addition, we are not restricted to look only at borrowers with multiple loans as is required by the use of borrower fixed effects. Borrower with multiple loans may not be representative of borrowers as a whole. A few papers use borrower information, but they analyze either a single country or a limited set of developing countries (e.g., Ongena, Peydro, & van Horen, 2013). Our dataset contains over 18,000 loans with information on banks, loans, borrowers, and relationships.

Our paper is closely related to the recent work of Giannetti & Laeven (2011). They show that foreign banks rebalance their loan portfolios in favor of domestic borrowers during the crisis period (flight home). Consistent with their finding, we find that foreign lending is

---

[2] Other papers that discuss the benefits and costs of foreign banks include Levine (1996); Berger, DeYoung, Genay, & Udell (2000); Claessens, Demirgüç-Kunt, & Huizinga (2001); Beck, Demirgüç-Kunt, & Maksimovic (2004); and Giannetti & Ongena (2008).

affected by the crisis more than domestic lending. Our paper adds to their work by documenting the interplay between flight home and flight to quality. For example, we show that the contraction in foreign lending is concentrated among private borrowers.

One of the most popular topics in the financial crisis literature is the balance-sheet effect. In foreign bank context, the balance-sheet effect refers to the notion that foreign banks may behave differently from domestic banks because of their balance-sheet conditions at home. Foreign banks may cut their lending in host countries to accommodate adverse balance-sheet conditions at home (e.g., Peek & Rosengren (2000); Schnabl (2010); Popov & Udell (2010)).[3] The balance sheet channel is also recently extended to include bank losses in some foreign markets affecting lending in other foreign markets. Popov & van Horen (2015) show that lending by foreign banks with sizeable holdings of sovereign bonds of Greece, Ireland, Italy, Portugal, and Spain was significantly reduced relative to non-exposed banks. However, the balance sheet channel may be offset in some circumstances. Claessens & van Horen (2013) find that foreign lending is not much reduced in countries where the foreign banks have dominant roles or are funded locally. Our paper documents that foreign and domestic banks differ not only during financial crises, but during normal times as well. In addition to balance-sheet conditions, we find that foreign and domestic banks react differently to crises due to the difference in information problems between the banks and their borrowers (e.g., whether borrowers are public or private).

This chapter is also related to the literature on credit rationing. Starting with Stiglitz & Weiss (1981), numerous papers, including those in the relationship lending literature, document the importance of asymmetric information on bank lending.[4] More recent papers introduce the recent financial crisis as a quasi-natural experiment to test

[3] An interesting counterexample is Detragiache & Gupta (2004), who document that foreign banks in Malaysia did not abandon the local market during the Malaysian financial crisis despite receiving less government support than domestic banks.

[4] See, for example, Berger & Udell (1992, 1995) and Petersen & Rajan (1994).

credit rationing theories and find that the effects of the recent financial crisis are not uniform across borrowers. De Haas & van Horen (2012b) find that foreign banks reduce lending by more in geographically distant countries and in markets where they are less experienced or connected. Claessens and van Horen (2015) similarly find that foreign banks are shifting lending to a more regional focus. The crisis tends to have more severe impacts on borrowers with no access to bond markets (Santos, 2011), riskier borrowers with fewer tangible assets (Popov & Udell, 2010), and borrowers applying for new loans (Ivashina & Scharfstein, 2010).[5] In this chapter, we take advantage of the informational heterogeneity between foreign and domestic banks, between U.S. and non-U.S. banks and borrowers, between safer and riskier borrowers, and between relationship and non-relationship borrowers as additional layers of identification. Our results support the notion that credit rationing differs across all of these dimensions.

Finally, there is a recent interest in the corporate finance literature on differences between public and private firms (e.g., Gao, Li & Harford, 2013; Maksimovic, Phillips, & Yang, 2013; Michaely & Roberts, 2012). Our paper contributes to this literature by studying credit availability to these two types of firms using a dataset that includes borrower and bank characteristics.

Our main results are consistent with the main findings in the literature — that foreign banks contract their supplies of credit more than domestic banks during financial crises. However, our details on loan quantities, spreads, and other contract terms; borrower characteristics; and bank-borrower relationships in many countries allow us to draw additional conclusions about the nature of this contraction in credit and provide a more complete picture than this literature. We find important differences between quantity and price effects, between listed and private firms, between safer and riskier borrowers, and between relationship and non-relationship borrowers. Finally, because the recent

[5] Other papers that study the effect of financial crises on bank lending include Bae, Kang, & Lim (2002); Ongena, Smith, & Michalsen (2003); Gan (2007); Puri, Rocholl, & Steffen (2009); Carbó-Valverde, Rodríguez-Fernández, & Udell (2012); and Presbitero, Udell, & Zazzaro (2012).

financial crisis originated in the U.S. and because this country has the most developed capital markets, we also distinguish between the effects involving U.S. banks and borrowers versus the rest of the world and find some additional interesting differences.

To sample some of the new results in the paper, the net reduction in lending by both foreign and domestic banks during the recent financial crisis was primarily concentrated among private borrowers, which tend to be riskier than public borrowers. Surprisingly, credit increased slightly for public borrowers. The decline in lending during the recent financial crisis was substantially greater for non-relationship borrowers than for relationship borrowers. The declines were also greater for poorly-rated firms than investment-grade firms, although both experienced declines in credit. Declines were larger for U.S. banks and U.S. borrowers reflecting that the impact of the crisis was more severe in the U.S.

In term of pricing, all-in spreads (total fees and interest paid over LIBOR) increased the least during the crisis for foreign banks and private borrowers, consistent with significant quantity rationing by foreign banks and of private borrowers, which tend to be relatively risky. The difference in spread between public and private borrowers increased during the crisis, and was larger among non-U.S. borrowers, consistent with expectations that that information problems may be more severe outside the U.S. Lending by U.S. banks domestically to public borrowers appears to be associated with interest-rate insurance (spreads that did not increase as much as in other cases). The sensitivities of spreads to borrower risk substantially increased during the recent financial crisis, especially for private borrowers.

Our findings highlight the importance of including borrower-level information. First, loan spreads are heavily influenced by borrower characteristics — including borrower characteristics in the loan spread equations substantially increases the R-squared. Second, there is a drastic shift in sensitivities of loan spreads to borrower characteristics during the crisis period. Studies that use firm fixed effects to control for borrower characteristics are not able to capture this fact. Third, as noted above, the estimated effects of the financial crisis on the difference between foreign and domestic banks change substantially after controlling for borrower characteristics.

References

Bae, K.-H., Kang, J.-K., & Lim, C. W. (2002). The value of durable bank relationships: evidence from Korean banking shocks. *Journal of Financial Economics*, *64*, 181–214.

Beck, T., Demirguc-Kunt, A., & Maksimovic, V. (2004). Bank competition and access to finance: International evidence. *Journal of Money, Credit, and Banking*, *36*, 627–648.

Berger, A. N., DeYoung, R., Genay, H., & Udell, G. F. (2000). Globalization of financial institutions: Evidence from cross-border banking performance. *Brookings-Wharton Papers on Financial Services*, *3*, 23–158.

Berger, Allen N., Makaewn T., & Turk-Ariss, R. (2016). How did foreign bank lending change during the recent financial crisis? Evidence from a very comprehensive dataset. *Working Paper*. Columbia South Carolina: University of South Carolina.

Berger, A. N. & Udell, G. F. (1992). Some evidence on the empirical significance of credit rationing. *Journal of Political Economy*, *100*, 1047–1077.

Berger, A. N. & Udell, G. F. (1995). Relationship lending and lines of credit in small firm finance. *Journal of Business*, *68*, 351–381.

Bruno, V. & Hauswald, R. (2008). The real effect of foreign banks. *Working Paper*. Washington DC: American University.

Carbo-Valverde, S. Rodriguez-Fernandez, F., & Udell, G. F. (2012). Trade credit, the financial crisis, and firm access to finance. *Working Paper*. University of Grenada.

Claessens, S. Demirguc-Kunt, A., & Huizinga, H. (2001). How does foreign entry affect domestic banking markets? *Journal of Banking and Finance*, *25*, 891–911.

Claessens, S. & van Horen, N. (2013). Impact of foreign banks, *Journal of Financial Perspectives*, *1*, 29–42.

Claessens, S. & van Horen, N. (2014). Foreign banks: Trends and impact. *Journal of Money, Credit and Banking*, *46*(1), 295–326.

Claessens, S. & van Horen N. (2015). The impact of the global financial crisis on banking globalization. *IMF Economic Review*, 63(4), 868–918.

De Haas, R. & Van Horen, N. (2012a). International shock transmission after the Lehman brothers collapse: Evidence from syndicated lending, *American Economic Review, Papers & Proceedings*, 102, 231–237.

De Haas, R. & van Horen, N. (2012b). Running for the exit? International bank lending during a financial crisis. *Review of Financial Studies*, *26*, 244–285.

Detragiache, E. & Gupta, P. (2004). Foreign banks in emerging market crises: Evidence from Malaysia. *Working Paper, International Monetary Fund.*

Detragiache, E., Gupta, P., & Tressel, T. (2008). Foreign banks in poor countries: Theory and evidence. *Journal of Finance*, *63*(5), 2123–2160.

Feyen, E., Letelier, R., Love, I., Maimbo, S. M., & Rocha, R. (2014). The impact of funding models and foreign bank ownership on bank credit growth is Central and Eastern Europe different? *World Bank Policy Research Working Paper* No. 6783.

Gao, H., Harford, J., & Li, K. (2013) Determinants of corporate cash policy: Insights from private firms. *Journal of Financial Economics*, 109(3), 623–639.

Gan, J. (2007). The real effects of asset market bubbles: Loan- and firm-level evidence of a lending channel. *Review of Financial Studies*, *20*, 1941–1973.

Giannetti, M. & Laeven, L. (2011). The flight home effect: Evidence from the syndicated loan market during financial crises. *Journal of Financial Economics*, *104*(1): 23–43.

Giannetti, M. & Ongena, S. (2008). Lending by examples: Direct and indirect effects of foreign bank presence in emerging markets. *Journal of International Economics*, 86(1), 167–180.

Gormley, T. A. (2010). The impact of foreign bank entry in emerging markets: Evidence from India, *Journal of Financial Intermediation*, *19*(1), 26–51.

Ivashina, V., & Scharfstein, D. (2010). Bank lending during the financial crisis of 2008. *Journal of Financial Economics*, *97*, 319–338.

Levine, R. (1996). Foreign banks, financial development, and economic growth. *Journal of Economic Literature*, 35, 688–726.

Maksimovic, V., Phillips, G., & Yang, L. (2013). Private and public merger waves. *Journal of Finance*, 68(5), 2177–2217.

Mian, A. (2006). Distance constraints: The limits of foreign lending in poor economies. *Journal of Finance*, *61*, 1465–1505.

Michaely, R. & Roberts, M. R. (2012). Corporate dividend policies: Lessons from private firms. *Review of Financial Studies*, 25(3), 711–746.

Ongena, S., Smith D. C., & Michalsen, D. (2003). Firms and their distressed banks: Lessons from the Norwegian banking crisis. *Journal of Financial Economics*, 67(1), 81–112.

Ongena, S., Peydro, J., & Van Horen, N. (2013). Shocks abroad, pain at home? Bank-firm level evidence on the international transmission of financial shocks. *DNB Working Paper* No. 385.

Peek, J. & Rosengren, E. S. (2000). Collateral damage: Effects of the Japanese bank crisis on real activity in the United States. *The American Economic Review*, *90*, 30–45.

Petersen, M. A. & Rajan, R. G. (1994). The benefits of firm-creditor relationships: Evidence from small business data. *Journal of Finance*, *49*, 3–37.

Popov, A. & Udell, G. (2010). Cross-border banking and the international transmission of financial distress during the crisis of 2007–2008. *Working Paper*. European Central Bank.

Popov, A. & Van Horen, N. (2015) Exporting sovereign stress: Evidence from syndicated bank lending during the euro area sovereign debt crisis. *Review of Finance*, *19*, 1825–1866.

Presbitero, A., Udell G., & Zazzaro A. (2012). The home bias and the credit crunch: A regional perspective, *MoFiR Working Paper* No. 60.

Puri, M., Rocholl, J., & Steffen, S. (2009). The impact of the US financial crisis on global retail lending. *Working Paper*. Duke University.

Santos, J. (2011). Bank loan pricing following the subprime crisis. *Review of Financial Studies*, *24*, 1916–1943.

Schnabl, P. (2010). Financial globalization and the transmission of bank liquidity shocks: evidence from an emerging market, *Journal of Finance*, 67(3), 897–932.

Stiglitz, J. E. & Weiss, A. (1981). Credit rationing in markets with imperfect information. *American Economic Review*, *71*, 393–410.

Banking Activity Trends Following the Financial Crisis: Expansion or Retrenchment?

— CHAPTER 9

- Stijn Claessens
  Board of Governors of the Federal Reserve System, University of Amsterdam, and CEPR
- Neeltje van Horen
  De Nederlandsche Bank (DNB) and CEPR

1. Introduction

In the wake of the global financial crisis, many commentators have posed that global financial integration has gone into reverse. The discussion has mainly focused on the collapse in cross-border bank flows globally (e.g., Milesi-Ferretti & Tille 2011) and the fragmentation of financial markets within the euro zone (e.g., ECB, 2014; IMF, 2015). While the collapse in capital flows and signs of financial fragmentation in certain regions are well documented, the developments in local foreign bank presence, i.e., "brick and mortar" operations, are not, creating some confusion on actual facts. Drawing on our recent paper (Claessens &

The authors would like to thank the conference participants for their comments. This chapter draws heavily on Claessens & van Horen (2015). The database accompanying that paper is available online at http://www.dnb.nl/en/onderzoek-2/databases/bank.jsp. The views expressed in this paper are those of the authors and do not necessarily represent those the Federal Reserve Board, DNB or any of the institutions with which they have been affiliated.

van Horen, 2015), we show that in terms of foreign bank presence, the global banking system has not become more fragmented. Rather, the crisis has accelerated a number of structural transformations, with banks from a larger variety of home countries now active abroad and a system that, while globally less, is becoming regionally more integrated.

It should come as no surprise that the debate surrounding the impact of the crisis on global banking has focused almost entirely on the behavior of (large) European and the U.S. banks. After all, these banks were the main vehicles through which financial systems became more integrated before the crisis (Goldberg, 2009) and the ones most affected by the crisis. The need to restore balance sheets and profitability, meet stiffer capital requirements, and other regulatory changes aimed at strengthening banking systems in the wake of the crisis have incentivized many of these banks to reduce their international operations. But focusing solely on the behavior of European and American banks does not provide a complete picture of the global banking landscape, as many banks from emerging markets and developing countries are important global players as well (van Horen, 2011; Beck, Fuchs, Singer, & Witte, 2014; BIS, 2014; Claessens & van Horen, 2014a). Furthermore, developments in banking systems globally do not necessarily mirror developments in one region, e.g., Europe.

As such, in order to fully grasp how the crisis has affected global banking, it is important to study the behavior of all globally active banks in a large variety of countries, not just banks from advanced countries. This is what Claessens & van Horen (2015) do. Their paper uses an updated version of the bank ownership database of Claessens & van Horen (2014a), which now includes ownership information for 5,498 banks for the period 1995–2013 and covers 138 countries that widely differ in economic and financial development.[1] Importantly, the database covers foreign activities of both banks from advanced as well as emerging economies and is therefore ideally suitable to study how the crisis has affected the foreign activities of all globally active banks.

The paper shows that the crisis has affected foreign bank presence in a number of important ways. First, while the crisis resulted in some

[1] The original database covers the period 1995–2009.

retrenchment globally, as the overall importance of foreign banks in local financial intermediation declined somewhat, this was not a uniform trend. Some host countries experienced a decline in foreign bank presence between 2007 and 2013, but others saw the importance of foreign banks in their markets rise. Furthermore, while at end 2013 bank ownership by OECD home countries still represented 89% of foreign bank assets globally, this was 6 percentage points less than before the crisis, mostly on account of a retrenchment by crisis-affected Western European banks. To the contrary, banks from non-OECD countries continued to increase their presence abroad, mainly in their own geographical region, and more than doubled their presence. As a result, the global banking system encompasses now a larger variety of players and has become regionally more integrated.

These changes were driven by a number of factors. Banks from countries facing systemic crises at home exited (more distant) markets and curtailed their subsidiaries' growth. Furthermore, banks more likely sold smaller, more recent investments, and entered closer and more important trading partners, shunning crisis and euro zone countries. In terms of growth of existing operations, banks with systemic crises at home and more distant foreign banks expanded their foreign assets relatively less, while more recent entrants and banks with a small market share before the crisis grew their balance sheets more. Many of these patterns relate to the growing importance of foreign banks from non-OECD countries. All in all, results show that exiting and limiting expansions of foreign operations versus entering new and expanding existing markets is not only about crisis versus non-crisis home countries. Rather, the shifts and refocusing of strategies of internationally active banks relate to a number of factors previously identified in the literature and dynamics between them.

The remainder of the paper is structured as follows. Section 2 describes the database and provides an overview of how foreign bank ownership has changed in the wake of the crisis. Section 3 examines the key variables related to changes — exit, entry and growth — in foreign bank presence. Section 4 concludes with reviewing some policy issues that are more important in light of these changes.

2. The Global Banking System Before and After the Financial Crisis

2.1. *Data*

To examine how the global financial crisis has affected foreign bank ownership, the database of Claessens and van Horen (2015) is used.[2] The database contains ownership information of 5,498 banks, currently and previously active, in 138 countries.[3] For each year the bank is active it is classified as either domestic- or foreign-owned. A bank is defined as foreign owned when 50% or more of its shares are held by foreigners. In addition, for each foreign bank the home country of its largest foreign shareholder is determined. The data is very comprehensive as it covers more than 90% of bank assets in all countries. It thus provides an almost complete picture of bank ownership around the world for the period 1995–2013. The ownership data are matched to Bankscope for balance sheet information.

2.2. *State of Foreign Banking at the Onset of the Global Financial Crisis*

The period before the global financial crisis was characterized by a sharp increase in foreign bank ownership. With the number of foreign

---

[2] The data were manually collected using many sources. These include but are not limited to (parent) bank websites and annual reports, banking regulatory agency/Central Bank websites, reports on corporate governance, local stock exchanges, SEC's Form F-20, newspaper articles, and country experts. For a detailed description of the database and its construction, see Claessens & van Horen (2015).

[3] While coverage is comprehensive, a few limitations apply. First, as the database only include banks that report financial statements to Bankscope, it mainly covers foreign-owned subsidiaries and not foreign branches, which in general do not report separate balance sheet information. Second, the database only includes host countries with more than five active banks reporting to Bankscope in 2013. In addition, for the advanced countries in the sample, coverage is restricted to the 100 largest banks in each country in terms of 2012 assets, so smaller (typically regional) banks are not included in the database for these countries (which especially reduces the coverage of banks in the United States).

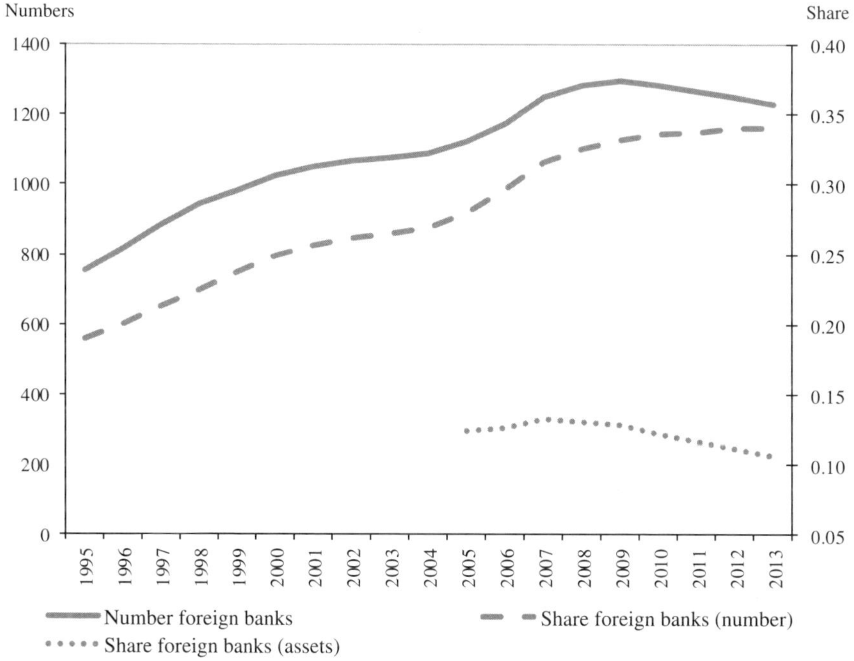

Figure 1. Number and share of foreign banks, 1995–2013.

Note: As the database starts in 1995 the number of foreign banks that exited the market in that year cannot be determined.
Source: Claessens and van Horen (2015).

banks rising from 755 in 1995 to 1,249 in 2007 (Figure 1 and Table 1). As over the same time period the number of domestic banks decreased, reflecting consolidation driven by technological changes and deregulation as well as the occurrence of financial crises, the relative importance of foreign banks increased substantially, from a market share in numbers of 19% in 1995 to 32% in 2007. In terms of assets, and covering a shorter period due to more limited data, the share was 13% in 2007, up slightly from 12.5% in 2005.[4]

[4] Balance sheet information in the current Bankscope database is very limited before 2005, making it not possible to provide reliable estimates of the assets share of foreign banks for earlier periods.

Table 1. Number and assets (US billions) of banks by host country, aggregates by income level and region.

	2007		2013		2007		2013	
	Number	Share	Number	Share	Asset	Share	Asset	Share
All countries								
Domestic	2,702	0.68	2,384	0.66	97,057	0.87	115,216	0.89
Foreign	1,249	0.32	1,229	0.34	14,850	0.13	13,590	0.11
Total	3,951	1	3,613	1	111,907	1	128,806	1
Income groups								
OECD								
Domestic	1,087	0.77	925	0.77	83,817	0.88	81,587	0.91
Foreign	319	0.23	280	0.23	11,385	0.12	8,409	0.09
Total	1,406	1	1,205	1	95,202	1	89,995	1
Non-OECD								
Domestic	1,615	0.63	1,459	0.61	13,240	0.79	33630	0.87
Foreign	930	0.37	949	0.39	3,465	0.21	5181	0.13
Total	2,545	1	2,408	1	16,705	1	38,811	1

Note: OECD includes all core OECD countries, non-OECD includes all other countries. Current OECD countries like Hungary, Czech Republic, Korea, Poland, Slovakia and Slovenia are included in the non-OECD group.
Source: Claessens & van Horen (2015).

Table 2. Number and assets (US billions) of foreign banks by home country, aggregates by income level and region.

	2007		2013		2007		2013	
	Number	Share	Number	Share	Asset	Share	Asset	Share
All countries	1,249	1	1,229	1	14,850	1	13,590	1
Income groups								
OECD	873	0.70	747	0.61	14,116	0.95	12,041	0.89
Non-OECD	376	0.30	482	0.39	734	0.05	1,549	0.11

Notes: OECD includes all core OECD countries, non-OECD includes all other countries. Current OECD countries like Hungary, Czech Republic, Korea, Poland, Slovakia, and Slovenia are included in the non-OECD group. The sum of foreign banks in the different income groups does not completely correspond with the total number of foreign banks at the top of the table. This discrepancy is caused by the fact that when a foreign bank is owned by an international investor no home country has been assigned. In addition, for some foreign owned banks no home country could be determined. Therefore those banks could not be assigned to an income group or region. The same holds for total assets. "Share" reflects the share with respect to the total number of foreign banks or total volume of foreign assets.
Source: Claessens & van Horen (2015).

This growth, however, was much more pronounced in non-OECD compared to OECD countries. As such, at the onset of the global financial crisis, market shares in OECD countries equaled 23% and 12% in terms of numbers and assets respectively, while in non-OECD countries they equaled 37 and 21% (see Table 1).[5] While large foreign bank presence is thus to more a non-OECD country phenomenon, most parent banks are headquartered in OECD countries. Table 2 shows that in 2007, banks from OECD countries accounted for 70% of all foreign-owned banks and 95% of all foreign-controlled assets. However, a substantial number of foreign banks (30%) came from non-OECD countries. While quite substantial in numbers, banks from non-OECD countries

[5] The OECD group only includes the core OECD countries and the non-OECD group includes all other countries. As such, current OECD countries like Hungary, Czech Republic, Korea, Poland, Slovakia, and Slovenia are included in the non-OECD group.

still tend to be (very) small, representing only 5% of all foreign assets as of 2007.

2.3. *The Impact of the Global Financial Crisis*

It will surprise no one that a crisis as severe as the recent one had important implications for foreign bank activity. While some banks, either voluntary or forced, had to retrench from foreign activities, others were able to grasp opportunities to increase their market shares in foreign countries or expand abroad. As a result, as highlighted by Claessens and van Horen (2015), over the period 2007–2013 foreign bank presence has changed in four important ways.

First, the crisis led to some overall retrenchment as the importance of foreign banks in financial intermediation declined globally. Not surprising, the number of new entries declined sharply in the years following the crisis (Figure 2). In 2013, only 19 foreign banks entered, only about one-sixth as many as the peak of 120 in 2007. As the number of

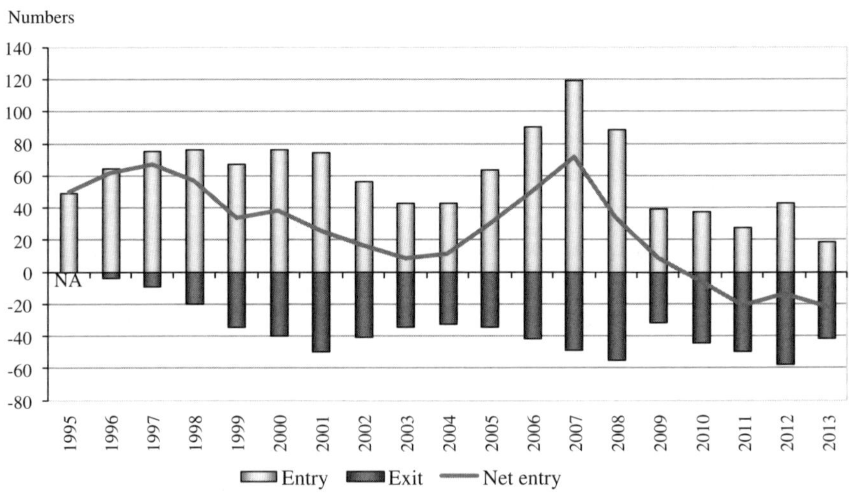

Figure 2. Number of entries and exits of foreign banks, 1995–2013.

Note: As the database starts in 1995 the number of foreign banks that exited the market in that year cannot be determined.
Source: Claessens & van Horen (2015).

exits (that is, a sale to another foreign bank, to a domestic bank, or a complete closure) stayed roughly the same, net entry turned negative in the years 2010–2013, for the first time since 1995 (the year the bank ownership database starts). As a result, the number of active foreign banks declined from 1,249 in 2007 (after peaking at 1,295 in 2009) to 1,229 in 2013 (see Figure 1 and Table 1). As the number of active domestic banks fell even more, from 2,702 in 2007 to 2,384 in 2013, the overall foreign bank share still increased from 32 to 34%. However, since foreign banks' balance sheets grew relatively less than those of domestic banks, the share of total assets controlled by foreign banks globally declined somewhat, from 13% in 2007 to 11% in 2013 (see Table 1).

Second, these aggregate developments did not affect all host countries uniformly. Figure 3 shows the distribution of the change in the

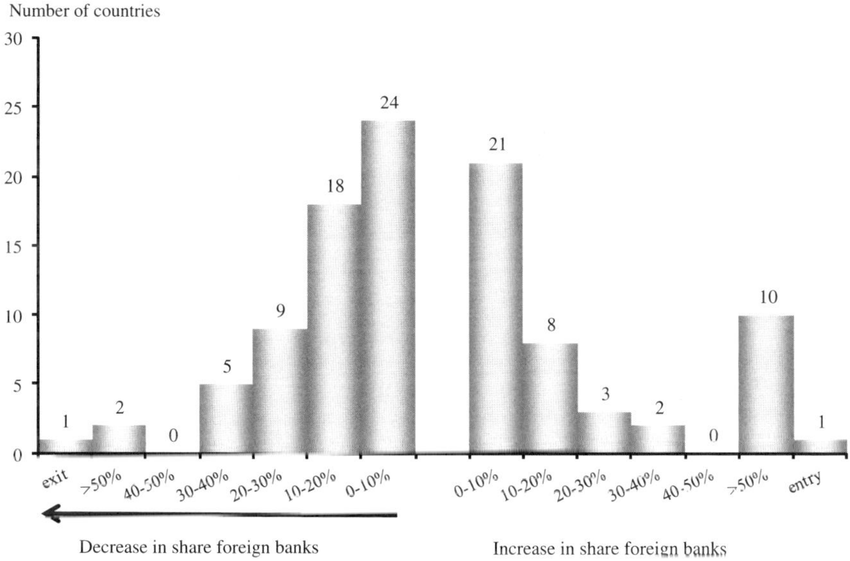

Figure 3. Change share foreign assets, 2007–2013

Notes: Only banks are included that have asset information for both years. Banks that were only active in 2007 or 2013 are also included if asset information is available for the year the bank is active. Countries in which less than 60% of the banks qualify are excluded from the sample altogether.
Source: Claessens & van Horen (2015).

asset share of foreign banks in each host country in which foreign banks were present in 2007. While only from one host country all foreign banks exited over the past five years (Greece), in 58 countries foreign banks' role in financial intermediation decreased, with a median decline of 14% (an average of 16%). Over the same period, however, foreign banks' relative presence increased in 44 countries, with a median increase of 10% (an average of 42%). And in one host country with no foreign bank present in 2007, Oman, a foreign bank entered (due to the acquisition of Oman International Bank by HSBC).

Third, ownership shifted away from OECD towards non-OECD countries' parent banks. Between 2007 and 2013, the number of foreign banks owned by OECD countries decreased substantially from 873 to 747 banks, while at the same time the number of foreign banks owned by non-OECD countries continued to grow, even at an slightly accelerated pace, culminating in a total increase of 106 banks (Figure 4 and Table 2). As a result, banks from non-OECD countries doubled the assets they control, from $734 billion to $1,549 billion. Although still small, non-OECD banks now account for 11% of total foreign bank assets. At the same time, OECD banks' controlled assets declined by some $2 trillion, or a 6 percentage point asset share decline.

Fourth, foreign bank presence became less globalized and more regionalized. While in 2007 on average 56% of foreign bank assets were owned by banks headquartered in the same region as the host country, by 2012 this increased to 60% (Figure 5). This happened in all regions (but less so in Europe where foreign banking traditionally has been highly regional; see also ECB, 2013). Partly this related to the (forced or voluntary) sale of foreign operations by a number of crisis-affected European and American banks to some (well-capitalized) emerging markets' banks that were willing and able to seize investment opportunities within their own geographical region. To name a few: Russia's Sberbank bought the Central and Eastern European subsidiaries of Austria's Volksbank; Chile's Corpbanca bought the Colombian operations of Santander; and HSBC sold its operations in Costa Rica, El Salvador, and Honduras to Banco Davivienda of Colombia. However, it is also the result of some large acquisitions among OECD countries, like that of U.S. Commerce Bank by Canadian TD Bank.

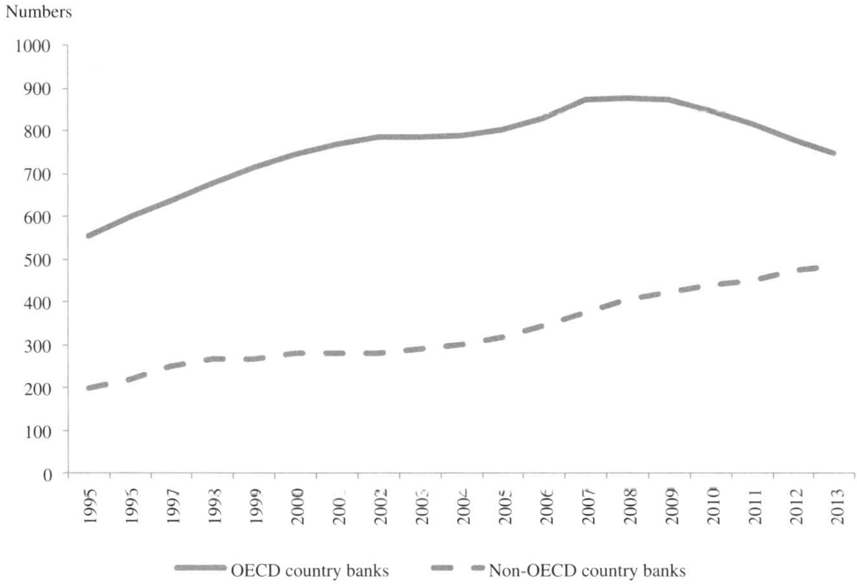

Figure 4. Number of foreign banks from OECD and non-OECD countries, 1995–2013.

Notes: OECD country banks includes foreign banks from all core OECD home countries. Non-OECD country banks includes all foreign banks from other high-income, emerging markets, and developing country home countries. For exact country classification see main text.
Source: Claessens & van Horen (2015).

Summarizing, the recent financial crisis has been associated with important changes in global banking and patterns of foreign bank presence. While not becoming more fragmented, global banking has gone through some important structural transformations with a greater variety of players and a more regional focus.

3. Factors Associated with the Shifts in Global Banking

Analyzing the detailed bank-level information in the bank ownership database, Claessens & van Horen (2015) provide some further insights into what factors at the individual bank, home country, host country

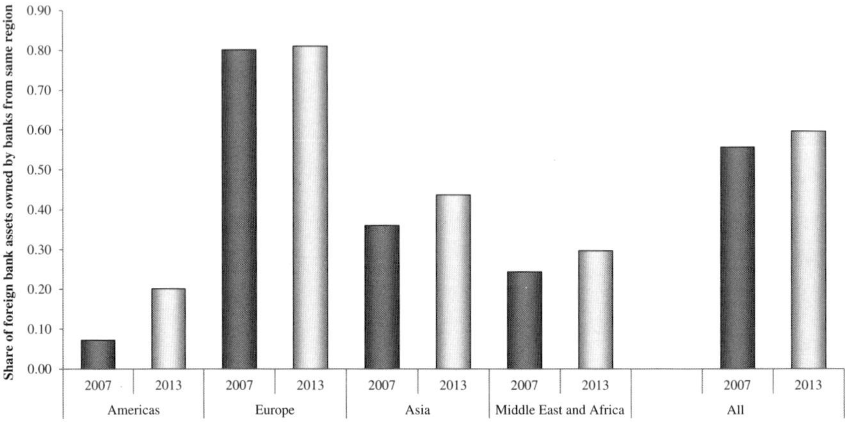

Figure 5. Share foreign banks from within the region, by region before and after the crisis.

Notes: Countries are grouped in four geographical regions irrespective of the income level of the countries. "America" includes Canada, United States and all countries in Latin American and the Caribbean, "Europe" includes all Western and Eastern European countries "Asia" includes all countries in Central, East and South Asia and the Pacific countries including Japan, Australia and New Zealand. "Middle East and Africa" includes all countries in the Middle East and North and Sub-Saharan Africa.
Source: Claessens & van Horen (2015).

and home-host country pair levels were related to the decision of a foreign bank to retrench from a particular banking system in the wake of the crisis, to stay active in it and expand (or not), or to enter in it. We summarize their findings here.

In order to investigate the factors associated with the shifts in global banking the authors create three dependent variables. The first one, *Exit*, is a dummy variable if a bank from a particular home country fully ends operations in a particular host country between 2007 and 2012, and zero when it remains present. Of the total 1,221 foreign banks from 80 home countries that were active in 116 host countries in 2007, 200 had exited by 2012. The second one, *Growth*, equals the (log) change in the assets of a particular foreign bank from a particular home country in a particular host country between 2007 and 2012, calculated for those foreign banks that remain active in the host country. This organic growth measure shows a big variation: while on average, assets grew by 30%, 276 banks experienced negative growth. The third one, *Entry*, is a dummy variable which is one if a foreign bank from a particular home country newly entered a particular host country by 2012, and zero if there was no new investment from a bank from that home country in the host county by 2012. Such new entries occurred between 2007 and 2012 in 178 out of the 10,036 possible home–host country pairs.

Table 3 presents the main regression results in summary form, using multivariate regressions, without and with interactions with bilateral

Table 3. Factors associated with changes in foreign bank presence.

	Exit	Exit	Growth	Growth	Entry	Entry
Asset growth host			+	+		
Home crisis	NS	NS	NS	NS	–	–
Home in euro zone	+	+	NS	NS	–	–
Host crisis	NS	NS	NS	NS	–	–
Host in euro zone	NS	NS	+	+	–	–
Foreign market share — Same country	NS	NS	NS	NS	+	+
Foreign market share — Other country	NS	NS	NS	NS	+	+
Market share	–	–	–	–		
Young	+	+	+	+		
Distance	NS	NS	–	–	–	–
Trade	–	NS	–	NS	+	+
Trade growth	NS	NS	+	NS	+	NS
Distance* Home crisis		NS		NS		+
Trade* Home crisis		–		NS		NS
Trade growth* Home crisis		NS		NS		+

Notes. Regression results, with + (–) statistically significant positive (negative), and NS not statistically significant. Based on multivariate regressions, without and with interactions. Results reported in Claessens & van Horen (2015).

variables.[6] It shows that banks from a particular home country are more likely to completely pull out when the country is experiencing a banking crisis and when it is from a euro zone country.[7] A systemic crisis in the host country does not significantly affect exit, which could reflect that on one hand, foreign banks support their subsidiaries when the host country is in crisis (and the home country is not), and on the other hand, that a host systemic crisis makes for less profitable opportunities and therefore increases a parent's desire to exit the market. Overall, these two effects seem to balance each other out. Competition from other foreign banks, proxied by foreign bank presence from the same or other home countries, does not play a significant role in a bank's decision to exit a market. Individual bank characteristics do matter, however, as banks with smaller market shares and more recently established ones are more likely to exit. Furthermore, banks from home countries that experienced a crisis especially withdrew from more distant markets and less important trading partners.

Foreign banks' asset growth importantly relates to the overall growth in host country banking assets, not surprising as general credit growth, including that of foreign banks, will to a large extent be driven by local host country factors, including overall economic growth. Furthermore, asset growth tends to be lower if the home country experiences a crisis, maybe as home banks were less able (or willing) to support their subsidiaries. And banks with a smaller market share and younger, which are often banks from non-OECD countries, experience higher asset growth. Distance has an (somewhat) adverse impact on asset growth of individual foreign banks, consistent with banks having greater difficulty managing far-fetched subsidiaries. Trade growth and asset growth are positively correlated, in line with foreign banks facilitating trade (Claessens, Hassib, & van Horen, 2015).

As regard to entry, excluding banks from two crisis-affected countries that expanded much (Russian Sberbank, which bought the Eastern

---

[6] Probit regressions are used for the *Exit* and *Entry* variables and OLS for the *Growth* variable.

[7] Note that all euro zone home countries experienced a banking crisis during the sample period, so the parameter captures an additional effect for these countries.

European subsidiaries of Austrian Volksbank, and the pan-African expansion of Nigerian United Bank for Africa), banks from crisis-affected countries less likely enter other markets (but statistically insignificant). Not surprisingly, entry is less likely in euro zone host countries, and more likely when the foreign market share from the same home country is already high, perhaps as it increases information about opportunities. Entry is importantly less likely in far-away countries, consistent with the literature that banks, notably from non-OECD countries responsible for the majority of entries over this period, tend to invest in their own geographical region. Bilateral trade and growth in trade also positively correlate with entry, presumably due to greater familiarity and economic opportunities. Overall, distance between home and host, trade, and trade growth explain much of entry, albeit less so for crisis countries.

Claessens & van Horen (2015) also show that the importance of these factors vary by the home country of the foreign bank. In terms of exit, the group of OECD home countries drive results. This is not surprising, given that most non-OECD banks were not selling their subsidiaries. Interestingly, foreign banks from euro zone home countries pull back less from euro zone host countries, i.e., foreign banks have a somewhat stabilizing influence within the euro zone. In terms of asset growth, banks from non-OECD home countries importantly drive developments. Also, competition faced from foreign banks of the same country and being at a greater distance matter more for non-OECD home countries, suggesting that prior familiarity is more important for these banks. For the decision to enter, trade matters similarly across OECD, non-OECD and euro zone home countries, and all home countries shy away from entering euro zone and remote host countries. A systemic crisis in the host country deters banks from non-OECD home countries, but not the other two groups of banks. And only banks from non-OECD countries more likely enter a country when there is a larger presence of banks from their own country. All in all, entry decisions of non-OECD banks can be better explained than those of OECD and euro zone banks.

Together, these analyses suggest that, under pressure to consolidate, foreign banks from OECD countries pulled out of countries with whom they were less connected, where they had a small presence, and in which they had only recently invested (behavior very similar to how global banks reallocate their cross-border lending after a crisis).[8] Furthermore, while, understandably, most banks shied away from starting new operations in the euro zone, foreign banks from OECD countries and especially from within the euro zone grew their balance sheet relatively fast compared to domestic banks in euro zone host countries, and as such seem to have acted as a stabilizing force in the euro zone. At the same time, non-OECD banks, with only limited desire to exit in the first place, exited in less systematic ways. They also grew their balance sheets faster, in part as their operations were (still) small, and were more willing to enter new markets, provided markets were closer, had more trade links prior to entry, were not in a crisis or in the euro zone, and already had some banks present from the same home country. These analyses confirm many of the trends noted in the raw statistics and highlighted earlier.

4. Conclusions

The newly collected data by Claessens and van Horen (2015) show that as a result of the recent crises, banking in terms of foreign bank presence has become somewhat less global, but not more fragmented. Rather, reflective of the global financial and sovereign debt crises affecting especially banks from advanced countries and the increasing international expansion of banks from emerging markets and developing countries, the global banking system has gone through some important transformations with a greater variety of players and a more regional focus. While, as their banking systems restructure and economies recover, the trend of less internationalization by banks from and in advanced countries could halt and possibly reverse itself, the increased importance of emerging markets and developing countries in foreign banking and the associated regionalization are likely to continue.

---

[8] De Haas & van Horen (2013) show that after the collapse of Lehman Brothers, banks reduced cross-border lending less to markets that were geographically close; where they were more experienced; where they operated a subsidiary; and where they were integrated into a network of domestic co-lenders.

This transformation offers many opportunities and benefits. It also poses though a number of challenges. For one, in terms of monitoring developments in global banking, the increased variety of banks makes it more imperative to expand international banking data coverage to key emerging markets and developing countries. This will allow, among others, academics and policy makers to examine whether there is indeed a general retrenchment in cross-border lending as often thought, or whether new players are filling the gap left by retreating banks. Second, it will be important that the newly emerging foreign bank exporting countries adequately perform their role as home regulator and supervisor of foreign affiliates, including by making sure that their parent banks are adequately capitalized and weak banks are quickly restructured and resolved. Third, with banking becoming more regional, it is important to improve the understanding of not only the drivers of regionalization, but also its pros and cons. A more regionalized global banking system could be more prone to shocks, as diversification will be more limited. Also, regionalization may not allow for the best banking technology and know-how to be employed in every market. On the other hand, international coordination, including in supervision, could become easier to achieve. *A priori*, it is thus not clear to what extent (and under what conditions) the benefits of regionalization outweigh the costs, calling for close monitoring and more research.

References

Bank of International Settlements (BIS) (2014). EME banking systems and regional financial integration. *CGFS Paper* No. 51.

Beck, T., Fuchs M., Singer D., & Witte, M. (2014). Making cross-border banking work for Africa, The World Bank Working Paper No. 89202. Available at: http://documents.worldbank.org/curated/en/2014/01/19761778/making-cross-border-banking work africa.

Claessens, S., Hassib O., & van Horen, N. (2015). The impact of foreign banks on trade. Mimeo: Federal Reserve Board.

Claessens, S. & van Horen, N. (2013). Impact of foreign banks. *Journal of Financial Perspectives*, *1*(1), 1–14.

Claessens, S. & van Horen, N. (2014a). Foreign banks: Trends and impact. *Journal of Money Credit and Banking*, 46(1), 295–326.

Claessens, S. & van Horen, N. (2014b). Location decisions of foreign banks and competitor remoteness. *Journal of Money Credit and Banking*, 46(1), 145–170.

Claessens, S. & van Horen, N. (2015). The impact of the global financial crisis on banking globalization. *IMF Economic Review*, 63(4), 868–918.

De Haas, R. & van Horen, N. (2013). Running for the exit? International bank lending during a financial crisis. *Review of Financial Studies*, 26(1), 244–285.

European Central Bank (ECB) (November, 2013). Banking structures report. Frankfurt.

European Central Bank (ECB) (April, 2014). Financial integration in Europe. Frankfurt.

Goldberg, L. (2009). Understanding banking sector globalization. *International Monetary Fund Staff Papers*, 56(1), 171–197.

International Monetary Fund (IMF) (2015). International banking after the crisis: Increasingly local and safer? *Global Financial Stability Report*. Washington, D.C.

Milesi-Ferretti, G.-M. & Tille, C. (2011). The great retrenchment: International Capital Flows During the Global Financial Crisis. *Economic Policy*, *26*(66), 285–342.

Van Horen, N. (2011). The changing role of emerging market banks. In T. Beck (Ed.), *The Future of Banking*. CEPR/VoxEU-eBook, pp. 79–83. Available at: http://www.voxeu.org/epubs/cepr-reports/future-banking.

Global Banking: Old and New Lessons from Emerging Europe

— CHAPTER 10

▪ Ralph De Haas
European Bank for Reconstruction and Development (EBRD) and Tilburg University

1. Introduction

What are the benefits and costs of cross-border banking and how has the balance between the two shifted in the aftermath of the global financial crisis? This question is not only of academic interest but also relevant for policymakers in host countries that have opened up their banking sectors to foreign strategic investors. Nowhere has banking integration advanced more than in Emerging Europe. After the fall of the Berlin Wall, many Western European banks bought former state banks and opened new affiliates, both branches and subsidiaries. Banks with saturated home markets were particularly attracted to the region due to its scope for further financial deepening at relatively high margins. As a result, between 67 and 100% of all banking assets in many emerging European countries are nowadays in foreign hands.

Ralph De Haas is Director of Research at the European Bank for Reconstruction and Development (EBRD) and a part-time associate professor of finance at Tilburg University in London.

The first part of this chapter briefly revises the literature on global banking while distinguishing between contributions from before the global financial crisis and new evidence that emerged following the crisis. The second part then analyzes in more detail the recent retrenchment of global banks from emerging Europe and its impact on local firms and households.

2. Global Banking: What We Knew Before the Great Recession

Academic and policy discussions about the economic impact of global banks on emerging markets typically focus on either the efficiency or the stability of financial intermediation. As regards the former, foreign banks often introduce superior lending technologies and marketing know-how in emerging markets (Grubel, 1977).[1] Evidence from emerging Europe, where commercial banks were still largely absent at the start of the 1990s, suggests that local banking systems have reaped substantial efficiency gains due to foreign-bank entry.[2] Foreign banks are not only efficient themselves but also generate positive spillovers to domestic banks which may, for instance, copy the risk management methodologies of new foreign competitors. Moreover, new foreign entrants are typically not linked to local underperforming enterprises and can therefore harden "soft budget constraints" for such inefficient firms, thus improving the efficiency of the credit-allocation process.

An important issue is whether this higher efficiency comes at the cost of a narrower client base. Foreign banks may simply be more efficient because they cherry-pick the best customers and leave the more difficult clients — such as opaque small and medium-sized enterprises (SMEs) — to domestic banks. Domestic lenders may be better positioned to collect and use soft information about such opaque clients

[1] In developed countries, foreign banks are generally less efficient than domestic banks as the advantages of incumbent banks tend to dominate those of new entrants (Claessens, Demirgüç-Kunt, & Huizinga, 2001).

[2] See Bonin, Hasan, & Wachtel (2005) and Fries & Taci (2005).

(Berger & Udell, 1995) whereas foreign banks rely more on standardised lending technologies. Some evidence suggests indeed that foreign banks are associated with a relative decline in SME lending (Detragiache, Tressel, & Gupta, 2008; Gormley, 2010; Beck & Martinez Peria, 2010). Yet, more recent findings indicate that foreign banks may actually find ways to effectively lend to SMEs (Beck, Ioannidou, & Schäffer, 2012) either by using techniques that rely on hard information, such as credit scoring, or by using relationship lending (Beck, Degryse, De Haas, & van Horen, 2014). As a result, foreign banks may increase SME lending in the medium term as they adopt these new lending technologies (De la Torre, Martinez Peria, & Schmukler, 2010). For emerging Europe, the evidence indeed suggests that foreign bank entry has not led to a reduced availability of small business lending (De Haas, Ferreira, & Taci, 2006; De Haas & Naaborg, 2006; Giannetti & Ongena, 2008).

Even if foreign bank entry is associated with more (and more efficiently delivered) credit, this advantage may be (partly) offset if lending by global banks is particularly volatile and contributes to economic instability. Theory predicts that multinational banks reallocate capital to countries where bank capital is in short supply (for example, those experiencing a banking crisis) and away from countries where investment opportunities are scarce, such as countries in a downturn (Morgan, Rime, & Strahan, 2004; Kalemli-Ozcan, Papaioannou, & Perri, 2013). Such cross-border capital movements can cause instability in countries that experience a reduction in bank capital. The empirical evidence here focuses on three separate impacts banking integration may have on local financial stability.

First, there is abundant evidence that global banks stabilize aggregate lending during local bouts of financial turmoil.[3] Compared with stand-alone domestic banks, global bank subsidiaries tend to have access to supportive parent banks that provide liquidity and capital if and when needed. De Haas & van Lelyveld (2006) find such a

[3] See Dages, Goldberg, & Kinney (2000), Crystal, Dages, & Goldberg (2002), Peek & Rosengren (2000b), Goldberg (2001), Martinez Peria, Powell, & Vladkova Hollar (2002), and Cull & Martinez Peria (2007).

stabilising role for global bank subsidiaries in emerging Europe and De Haas & van Lelyveld (2010) for a broader set of countries.

Second, the entry of global banks may expose a country to foreign shocks. Parent banks reallocate capital across borders and therefore capital may be withdrawn from country *A* when it is needed in country *B*. Peek & Rosengren (1997, 2000a) show how the drop in Japanese stock prices starting in 1990, combined with binding capital requirements, led Japanese bank branches in the United States to reduce credit. Van Rijckeghem & Weder (2001) find banks that are exposed to a financial shock in either their home country or another country reduce credit in their (other) host countries. Schnabl (2012) shows how the 1998 Russian crisis spilled over to Peru, as banks, including foreign-owned ones, saw their foreign funding dry up and had to cut back lending.

While foreign bank subsidiaries can transmit foreign shocks, it is important to keep in mind that lending by such local brick-and-mortar affiliates is typically less volatile than *cross-border* lending by foreign banks (García Herrero & Martinez Peria, 2007). Peek & Rosengren (2000) find that cross-border lending to Latin America did in some cases diminish during economic slowdowns, whereas local lending by foreign banks was much more stable.[4]

Third, foreign bank ownership may also affect the sensitivity of the aggregate credit supply to the business cycle. Because multinational banks trade off lending opportunities across countries, their subsidiaries tend to be more sensitive to the local business cycle than domestic banks (Morgan & Strahan, 2004). However, if the population of foreign banks in a country is sufficiently diverse in terms of home countries, this diversity may make aggregate lending more stable. In line with this, Arena, Reinhart, & Vázquez (2007) find on the basis of data from 20 emerging markets that foreign banks have contributed somewhat to overall bank lending stability in these countries.

To sum up, the empirical evidence that was available before the 2008–2009 crisis provides four main findings. First, the evidence suggests that global banking can improve the availability of credit in

[4] See De Haas & van Horen (2012, 2013) for evidence on the rapid decline in cross-border lending during the 2008–09 crisis, in particular by distant and relatively inexperienced international lenders.

emerging markets and make the delivery of credit more efficient, although small firms may benefit less — at least in the short term. Second, the presence of global banks may exacerbate business and credit cycles, particularly if parent banks are mostly from the same home country or region. Third, the presence of global banks tends to reduce the economic impact of local financial crises. Fourth, cross-border banking integration tends to expose host countries to foreign shocks.

3. Global Banking: New Evidence from the Great Recession and Its Aftermath

The Lehman Brothers bankruptcy on 15 September, 2008 triggered a significant amount of research into how large, internationally active banks transmitted this massive shock across borders. Many of these banks were either directly exposed to the subprime market or indirectly affected by the U.S. dollar illiquidity. It consequently became more difficult for parent banks to support foreign subsidiary networks with capital and liquidity. Cetorelli & Goldberg (2012) show, for instance, that U.S. banks with high pre-crisis exposure to asset-backed commercial paper became more constrained when off-balance sheet became on-balance sheet commitments. This affected foreign affiliates as funds were reallocated towards the parent (although this effect was mitigated for large affiliates).

Likewise, Popov & Udell (2012) and Ongena, Peydró-Alcalde, & van Horen (2015) show how Western banks propagated the crisis eastwards by reducing the credit supply to both existing and potential borrowers in emerging Europe. De Haas, Korniyenko, Pivovarsky, & Tsankova (2015) find that global bank subsidiaries in emerging Europe reduced lending earlier and faster than domestic banks. Global banks that took part in the Vienna Initiative, a public–private coordination mechanism to guarantee macroeconomic stability in emerging Europe, were somewhat more stable lenders.[5] This stabilising effect of the

[5] The Vienna Initiative was launched in January 2009 as a coordination platform for multinational banks, their home and host country supervisors, fiscal authorities, the IMF, and development institutions. The goal was to safeguard a continued

Vienna Initiative is confirmed by Cetorelli & Goldberg (2011) on the basis of aggregate data from the Bank for International Settlements (BIS). They find that multinational banks transmitted the crisis to emerging markets via a reduction in cross-border lending and local subsidiary lending. Importantly, stand-alone domestic banks, many of which had borrowed heavily in the international syndicated loan and bond markets before the crisis, were forced to contract credit as well.

A common finding of many recent empirical papers is the importance of banks' pre-crisis funding structure for their subsequent credit stability during the Great Recession. In particular, it has become clear that banks that relied more on short-term wholesale funding reduced domestic credit more (Ivashina & Scharfstein, 2010), were more often financially distressed (Cihák & Poghosyan, 2009) and experienced sharper stock-price declines when Lehman Brothers collapsed (Raddatz, 2010) and during the crisis in general (Beltratti & Stulz, 2012). Short-term wholesale funding made banks vulnerable to sudden liquidity shortages during which they could not roll over debt. De Haas & Van Lelyveld (2014) analyze an international sample of banks and find that during the recent crisis multinational bank subsidiaries had to curtail credit growth about twice as much as stand-alone domestic banks. Subsidiaries of parent banks that used more wholesale funding had to reduce credit the most.

4. Global Banking, the Great Recession and Firms and Households in Emerging Europe

How has the rapid cross-border deleveraging by global banks in Emerging Europe affected local firms and households?[6] To answer this question, it is instructive to first gain a better understanding of the extensive branch footprint of global banks in this region. Figure 1

---

commitment of parent banks to their subsidiaries. Multinational banks signed country-specific commitment letters in which they pledged to maintain exposures and to provide subsidiaries with adequate funding.

[6] This section draws on Chapter 2 of the EBRD Transition Report 2015–2016 on *Rebalancing Finance*.

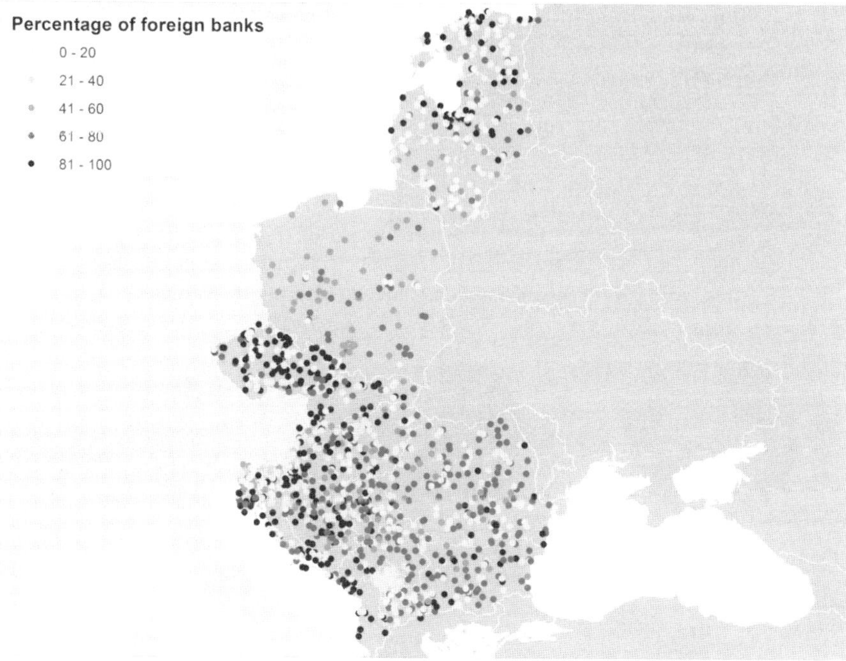

Figure 1. Local presence of foreign banks across emerging Europe.
Source: EBRD Banking Environment and Performance Survey II (BEPS II).

shows detailed data on the local presence of global bank branches as taken from the 2nd Banking Environment and Performance Survey (BEPS II) undertaken by the EBRD and Tilburg University in 2012.

As part of this survey, data on bank branch networks were collected and over 600 bank CEOs were interviewed face-to-face. The map shows how global banks are now operating dense branch networks throughout much of emerging Europe. Darker dots indicate localities (villages, towns, and cities) with a higher percentage of branches that are owned by foreign banks. It is striking how dominant and widespread global banks have become. These banks are not just lending to large blue chip corporates in the main cities, but are active throughout the countries they entered and have become an important source of credit for many small businesses and households. In some countries, such as the Czech Republic, many localities have foreign-bank branches only. This means

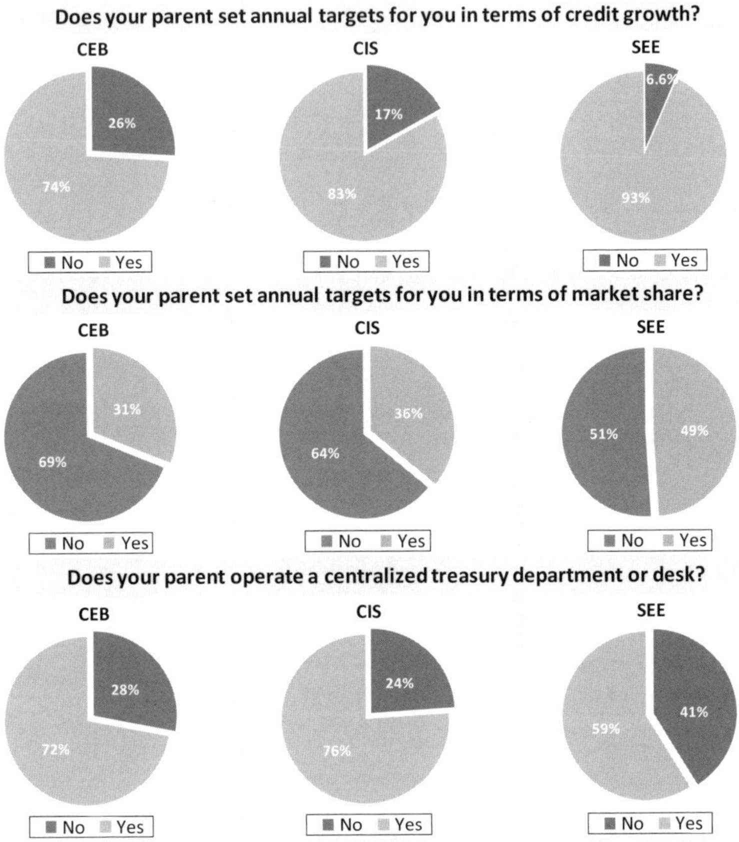

Figure 2. Impact of parent banks on their emerging European subsidiaries.
Source: EBRD BEPS II Survey.

that small businesses and households that want to open a bank account or apply for a loan have become completely dependent on the branches of large, internationally active banks.

These local branch networks are not only owned by global banks, they are also deeply financially integrated into these financial institutions. Many foreign parent banks take a very active approach to steering their local subsidiaries. The pie charts in Figure 2 are based on interviews with bank CEOs as part of the aforementioned BEPS II survey. They show that across Central and Eastern Europe and the Baltics (CEB), the Commonwealth of Independent States (CIS), and South-Eastern Europe (SEE), the vast majority of CEOs of foreign-bank subsidiaries mention that their parent banks set annual credit-growth targets for them. Interestingly, Figure 2 also shows that these powerful parents do not simply set nominal credit growth targets but in many cases — in particular in SEE — also instruct their subsidiaries to reach specific market shares. Moreover, they subsequently provide subsidiaries with the funding, often in a foreign currency (FX), to help them achieve these market shares.

Many countries, in particular in South-Eastern Europe, therefore ended up in a situation, where various subsidiaries of foreign-owned banks were for several years in intense competition for local market shares, in particular in the household segment (mortgages and consumer loans). Parent banks were steering their local subsidiaries to reach certain market shares while backing them up with sufficient intra-bank funding. It will be clear that these dynamics contributed to unsustainable credit booms in the years before the global financial crisis, in particular in countries were regulators, for various reasons, where relatively powerless when trying to stem these cross-border financial inflows.

5. Adjusting Banking Sectors in the Wake of the Lehman Brothers Collapse

Figure 3 depicts a number correlation coefficients (the black bars) that indicate the strength of the relationship between, on the one hand, various characteristics of banking systems and, on the other hand, the size of such banking systems across Emerging Europe. It shows that before the crisis, countries with a higher percentage of foreign banks, greater dependence on cross-border bank funding (excluding funding from parent banks), greater use of wholesale funding (as opposed to deposit funding) and fewer non-performing loans managed to build up the largest banking sectors.

Together, these characteristics describe the economic model that emerging Europe used prior to the financial crisis to rapidly develop its banking sectors. But was this model unique to emerging Europe? Data

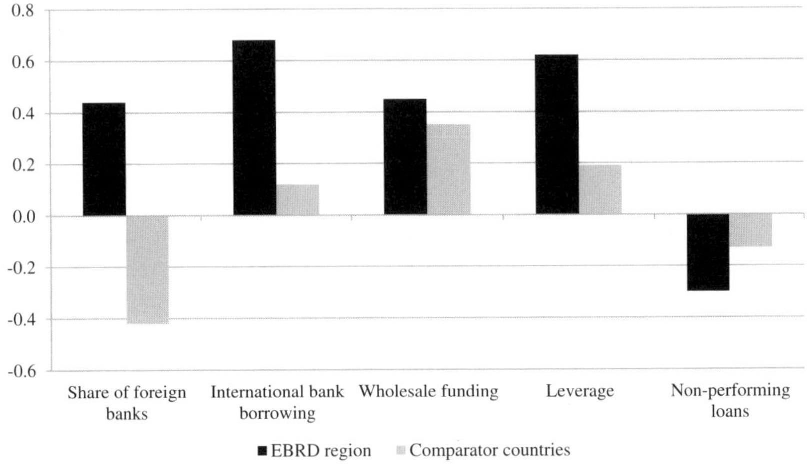

Figure 3. Banking integration, bank funding and the size of the banking system.

Notes: This chart shows the correlation between the size of the banking sector (measured as the ratio of private-sector credit to GDP) and the respective variables. "Share of foreign banks" means assets held by foreign banks as a percentage of total bank assets; "international bank borrowing" means the ratio of cross-border borrowing to private-sector credit; "wholesale funding" means the ratio of total loans to total deposits held by banks; "leverage" is the ratio of total assets to total equity held by banks. Non-performing loans are measured as a percentage of total loans (albeit national definitions of non-performing loans may vary). Data for all variables relate to 2005. "EBRD region" means all countries in which the EBRD invests, while the "comparator countries" are a group of 65 countries that have banking sectors between the minimum and maximum sizes observed in the EBRD region.

Source: Claessens & van Horen (2014), Bankscope, BIS Consolidated Banking Statistics, World Development Indicators, CEIC Data and authors' calculations.

for a group of comparator countries with banking systems of a similar size show that in these comparator countries, the link between banking-sector development on the one hand and international financial integration and wholesale funding on the other is less strong. The correlation with bank leverage is also much weaker (see the grey bars in Figure 3). Thus, the growth model employed by emerging Europe's banking sectors appears to have been fairly distinctive. Much more than in other regions, emerging Europe relied on cross-border banking integration, wholesale funding and high leverage multiples. These were, unfortunately, the very margins along which those banking systems were forced to adjust significantly during the recent financial and eurozone crises.

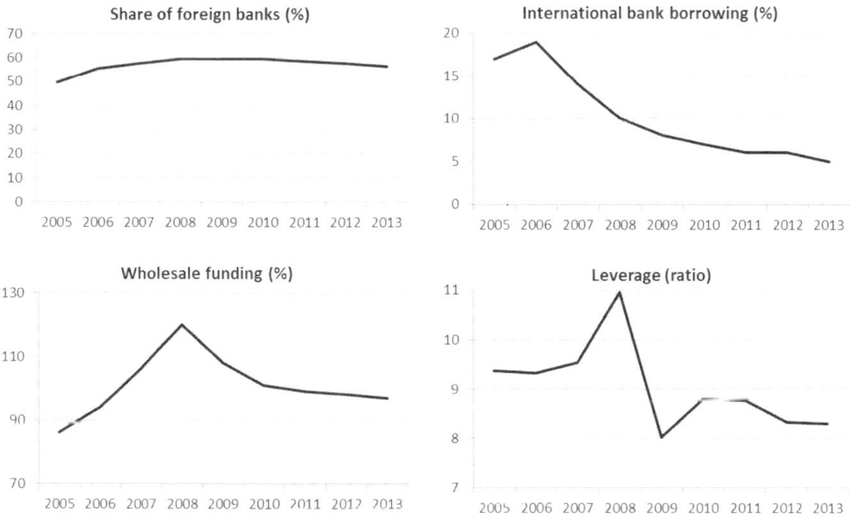

Figure 4. Banking-sector adjustment across emerging Europe.

Note: Panel A shows assets held by foreign banks as a percentage of total bank assets in each country, averaged over countries in emerging Europe. Panel B shows cross-border borrowing by banks as a percentage of private-sector credit in each country, averaged over the countries of emerging Europe. Panel C shows total loans as a percentage of total deposits held by banks in each country, averaged over the countries of emerging Europe. Panel D shows total assets as a share of total equity held by banks in each country, averaged over the countries of emerging Europe.

Source: Bankscope, Claessens & van Horen (2014), BIS Consolidated Banking Statistics, World Development Indicators, CEIC Data and authors' calculations.

The first panel of Figure 4 indicates that, in terms of foreign bank ownership, adjustments during the recent crisis period have been relatively limited. This is in line with earlier evidence that suggests that foreign direct investment is a relatively stable source of cross-border investment. Foreign bank ownership peaked in 2010, after which a gradual decline set in as some foreign banks exited specific countries by selling to domestic investors.

The second panel of Figure 4 shows a very rapid decline in cross-border lending by BIS-reporting banks to banks in emerging Europe. This cross-border deleveraging began as early as 2006 in countries such as Bulgaria, Croatia, Hungary, and the Baltic states, accelerated after the collapse of Lehman Brothers and continues today in the wake of the eurozone debt crisis.

The third panel shows that, after peaking in 2008, banks' reliance on wholesale funding (as opposed to deposit funding) has fallen significantly. The average ratio of total loans to customer deposits declined from 120% in 2008 to 97% in 2013. In particular, banks that had rapidly expanded their loan portfolios on the basis of a very small deposit base had to reduce their lending quickly.

The fourth panel shows that banks have also been adjusting their leverage. Before the crisis, many banks operated with high asset-to-equity ratios (termed "leverage multiples"). The fourth panel shows the procyclical behavior of this leverage multiple across emerging Europe. It peaked just before the collapse of Lehman Brothers and has been declining ever since as banks have strengthened their equity bases while shedding or writing off non-performing assets.

6. Adjustments in Banking Models: Impacts on Small Business Borrowers and Households

How did these unexpected and drastic funding adjustments in banking systems that were dominated by large, internationally active banks affect local businesses, and households? To gauge the extent to which firms in emerging Europe experienced more problems in accessing new bank credit, this section draws on the Business Environment and Enterprise Performance Survey (BEEPS) conducted by the EBRD and the World Bank. The BEEPS involves face-to-face interviews with the owners or main managers of a representative sample of firms and seeks to determine the extent to which various features of the business environment (including access to finance) represent obstacles to firms' operations. This section uses three rounds of the survey — BEEPS III, which was conducted in 2005 during the credit boom that preceded the global financial crisis (involving 7,053 firms); BEEPS IV, which was carried out in 2008–2009 at the time of the crisis (involving 7,047 firms); and BEEPS V, which was conducted in 2013–2014 in the aftermath of the crisis (involving 20,321 firms).

In order to gain a real understanding of SMEs' ability to access bank loans, it is important to properly disentangle demand for and the supply of bank credit. Both can cause bank lending to fall, so a decline in lending does not necessarily mean that a lack of bank credit is hindering firms' growth. By combining answers to various survey questions, one can distinguish between firms with and without demand for credit, before dividing the first group into firms that are credit-constrained and those that are not. Credit-constrained firms are those that are in need of (additional) credit, but are either discouraged from applying for a bank loan or are rejected when they do. Aggregating individual firms' responses to these questions can yield useful insights into whether a decline in lending in a given country at a particular point in time mainly reflects reduced demand for credit or a fall in the supply of new lending.

Figure 5 shows that, there has been a marked increase in the percentage of credit-constrained firms — that is to say, firms that need additional credit but are either rejected when they apply for a bank loan or feel discouraged from applying for such a loan. In the most recent survey, 51% of all firms that needed credit reported that they had

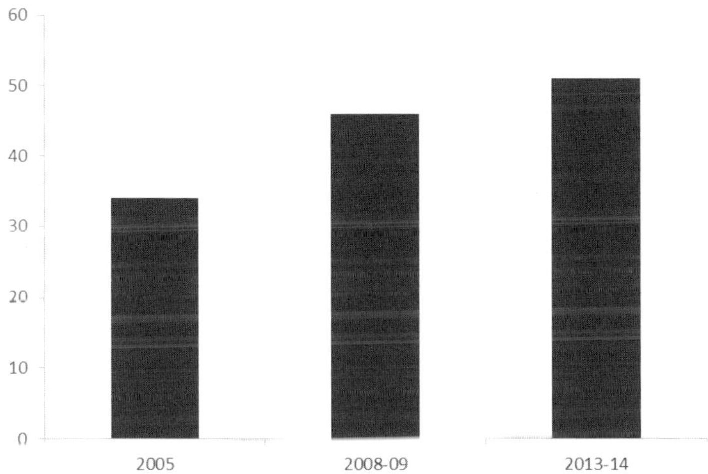

Figure 5. Credit-constrained firms as a percentage of firms that need a loan.

trouble accessing it. This figure was significantly lower in 2005 (34%) and 2008–2009 (46%), indicating that credit conditions for SMEs have tightened further in the wake of the global financial crisis. This reflects the more or less seamless transition from the global financial crisis to the eurozone debt crisis, which had a further negative impact on the balance sheets of many European banks operating affiliate networks across emerging Europe.

Table 1 analyses how the various forms of banking-sector rebalancing have affected credit constraints at the firm level. In the reported regression estimates, the dependent variable is the probability that a firm was credit-constrained in 2013–2014. The explanatory variables are the country-level variables shown in Figure 3, plus the percentage of credit-constrained firms in 2005 (which is calculated at country level). That last variable absorbs unobserved cross-country variation affecting firms' ability to access credit. The regression framework also controls for a battery of (unreported) firm-level characteristics.

The results in columns 2–5 of Table 1 indicate that the probability of a firm being credit-constrained in 2013–2014 was substantially higher in countries where, in the previous five years, banks had to adjust their international and wholesale borrowing more, where they had to deleverage more, and where non-performing loans increased the most. A direct comparison of these variables indicates that changes in cross-border and wholesale funding are particularly strongly associated with increases in credit constraints (see column 6). These results help to explain why there exists strong cross-country variation in the tightening of credit conditions for SMEs. For example, while in 2005 the percentage of credit-constrained firms was about 35% in Georgia, Bulgaria and Kazakhstan, it remained unchanged in Georgia but increased sharply in the other two countries. In line with the results in Table 1, cross-border bank lending to Georgia declined by only 15%, while cross-border lending to Bulgaria and Kazakhstan fell by 70% and 80%, respectively.

The strong deleveraging, in particular by subsidiaries of global banks, has not only negatively impacted the ability of small businesses to access credit but has also affected many households in the region. To gain a better insight into these household-level impacts, this section uses data from the Life in Transition Survey (LiTS) II, which was conducted

Table 1. Banking-sector adjustment and firm-level constraints in 2013–2014.

Dependent Variable: Credit-Constrained Dummy (2013–2014)	(1)	(2)	(3)	(4)	(5)	(6)
Change in share of foreign banks (2007–2012)	0.038					0.018
	(0.300)					(0.599)
Change in international bank borrowing (2007–2012)		–0.255*				–0.313**
		(0.090)				(0.029)
Change in wholesale funding (2007–2012)			–0.475***			–0.439*
			(0.003)			(0.063)
Change in leverage (2007–2012)				–0.549**		–0.125
				(0.049)		(0.714)
Change in non-performing loans (2007–2012)					0.031**	0.004
					(0.050)	(0.884)
Percentage of credit-constrained firms in 2005	1.806**	1.816***	1.533***	2.271***	1.662***	1.992***
	(0.020)	(0.000)	(0.003)	(0.003)	(0.004)	(0.001)
Number of observations	6,285	6,285	6,285	6,285	6,296	6,177
Firm-level covariates	Yes	Yes	Yes	Yes	Yes	Yes
Locality-level covariates	Yes	Yes	Yes	Yes	Yes	Yes
Adjusted R^2	0.076	0.080	0.083	0.080	0.076	0.088

Note: This table reports the results of profit regressions explaining the probability of a firm surveyed as part of the 2013–2014 BEEPS survey indicating that it was credit-constrained. Observations are weighted on the basis of the number of firms in the country that participated in the survey. Standard errors are clustered by country. *P*-values are reported in parentheses: * = $p < 0.10$; ** = $p < 0.05$; *** = $p < 0.01$.
Source: BEEPS III and V, BIS, Claessens & van Horen (2014), Bankscope and EBRD (data on non-performing loans).

by the European Bank for Reconstruction and Development and the World Bank in late 2010. As part of this survey, almost 39,000 households in 34 countries were interviewed to assess public attitudes, well-being and the impacts of economic and political change. The LiTS II survey provides vivid evidence of how people's lives have been affected by the global economic crisis and its aftermath. The survey data show that many households directly felt the impact of the crisis. For instance, in about 20% of all households at least one person lost his or her job, 2% of the households had to close their family business, almost 40% of the households saw their income from wages reduced, and 16% of all households had to cope with a reduction in the remittances they received from abroad. Importantly, compared with their western counterparts, households in Emerging Europe suffered far more job losses, wage reductions and reductions in remittances. For example, the proportion of households which reported a job loss between late 2008 and late 2010 was twice as high (20%) as in Western Europe. As a result of these shocks, many households had to adjust their consumption and investment behavior. While only 11% of households in western comparator countries had to reduce staple food consumption as a result of the crisis, this was 38% in emerging Europe. In the western countries, only 4% reported postponing or skipping medical treatment; in emerging Europe, almost 13% did so. The percentage of households reporting delays in paying utility bills was also more than twice as high in Emerging Europe. One stark finding from the LiTS II survey is that households with FX-denominated mortgages had to reduce consumption considerably more in response to negative income shocks when compared with similar households without such debt.[7] This held particularly true for those households living in countries that experienced a substantial (>2%) depreciation or devaluation of the local currency vis-à-vis the euro during the crisis. The accumulation of this FX debt before the onset of the global financial crisis had made many households vulnerable to external shocks.

---

[7] Before the crisis, 42% of all mortgages in Eastern Europe were denominated in a FX. In contrast, in the western comparator countries FX mortgages were virtually absent.

Evidence from Ukraine — one of the countries with such a pre-crisis built up of FX household debt (albeit from low levels) and a large currency devaluation during the crisis — suggests that crisis exposure may also have longer-term impacts as it affects households' economic and political preferences (De Haas, Djourelova, & Nikolova, 2015). Households that were hit hardest by the crisis (that is, those that had to reduce their consumption the most) became significantly more negatively disposed towards market-based economic systems and democratic institutions. Importantly, the data for Ukraine show that the dependence on wholesale funding of bank branches in a locality is a good instrument to predict how hard households were hit by the crisis. In other words, the transmission of the crisis through wholesale-funded banks impacted household consumption and moved households' social preferences in the direction of more state-led and autocratic regimes. This implies that economic volatility caused or amplified by banking integration can quickly undermine public support for market-based institutions. If persistent, such changing preferences might even lead to reform reversals by driving countries toward less liberal economic systems.

7. Conclusions

The post-crisis literature on global banking has resulted in at least two key insights. First, the crisis underlined the importance of funding structures for banking stability. In particular, it became clear that an excessive use of short-term wholesale funding exposes banks to the bouts of illiquidity that characterize these markets. Before the crisis, policymakers, and academics had focused mainly on the potentially adverse effects of depositor runs, largely ignoring the risks in the increasingly important wholesale markets. During the crisis it became clear that, relative to "flighty" wholesale funding, (insured) deposits actually turned out to be quite "sticky".

A dependence on wholesale funding may hurt lending stability particularly when a bank's assets and liabilities are denominated in different currencies. When banks carry substantial currency mismatches on their balance sheets, they become heavily exposed to temporary breakdowns in FX swap markets. During the recent crisis, this affected both domestic and globalized banks. In pre-crisis emerging Europe, many domestic banks had borrowed in local currency wholesale markets and, after swapping these funds into euros, turned them into euro loans. During the crisis this became more and more difficult. Likewise, global banks with U.S. branches found it increasingly problematic to swap euros into U.S. dollars and therefore experienced difficulties in supporting these branches with funding through their internal capital markets (Ivashina, Scharfstein, & Stein, 2015).

The Latin American experience has shown that deep financial integration through a large-scale presence of foreign banks may go hand in hand with financial stability if sufficient local deposit and wholesale funding is available. Kamil & Rai (2012) show that crisis transmission to Latin America was less severe in countries where foreign banks were lending through subsidiaries rather than across borders. Subsidiaries that were funded locally instead of through the international wholesale markets or through their parent banks were particularly stable credit sources. Some (but not all) multinational bank subsidiaries, particularly in emerging Europe, may have to adjust their funding models in this direction. These subsidiaries will increasingly have to stand on their own financial feet by raising local customer deposits and topping these up with wholesale funding if and when required. This will be easier for and more relevant to subsidiaries that target retail rather than corporate clients. In many countries in emerging Europe banks are already making real progress with adjusting their funding structures.

An increased focus on local funding will also be a more realistic option in countries with more conducive macroeconomic frameworks, including flexible exchange rate regimes and inflation targeting, that facilitate the development of local currency markets and a local currency deposit base. This in turn reduces the need for banks, both foreign and domestic, to borrow and lend in FX (Brown & De Haas, 2012; Brown, De Haas, & Sokolov, 2013).

Second, while the Japanese experience of the 1990s had already shown (or perhaps forewarned) that global banks may pass on shocks from home to host countries, what remained under-appreciated until recently is how large these effects can be if foreign bank affiliates are of systemic importance. Nowhere has this been more evident than in emerging Europe where one or several of the top three banks are in foreign hands in many countries. It was this combination of foreign ownership and systemic importance that threatened financial stability in the region and necessitated the *ad hoc* establishment of the Vienna Initiative.

The recent European experience underlines the need to further reassess and possibly even adjust the role multinational banks play in many emerging markets. The evidence suggests that multinational banks often play a positive role in these economies as they give households and firms access to more and more efficiently delivered financial services. A key issue that nevertheless remains high on the policy and research agenda is how to reap these benefits of banking integration while minimizing "collateral damage" in the form of an increased exposure to foreign shocks. One part of the answer lies in a gradual rebalancing of the funding structure of some of the more highly leveraged multinational bank subsidiaries towards a greater focus on local funding sources. This will reduce subsidiaries' need to borrow abroad, either from external financial markets or through their parent's internal capital market, thus limiting their role as conduits for financial shocks. The question remains what is the optimal mix of local and foreign funding, bearing in mind that a complete reliance on local funding would entail costs to local economies in the form of less (and more expensive) borrowing opportunities for local firms.

References

Arena, M., Reinhart, C., & Vázquez, F. (2007). The lending channel in emerging economies: Are foreign banks different? *IMF Working Paper* No. 07. Washington D.C.: International Monetary Fund.

Beck, T., Degryse, H., De Haas, R., & van Horen, N. (2014). When arm's length is too far. Relationship banking over the business cycle. *EBRD Working Paper* No. 169. London: European Bank for Reconstruction and Development.

Beck, T., Ioannidou, V., & Schäfer, L. (2012). Foreigners vs. natives: Bank lending technologies and loan pricing. *Center Discussion Paper* No. 55. Tilburg University.

Beck, T., & Martinez Peria, M. S. (2010). Foreign bank participation and outreach: Evidence from Mexico. *Journal of Financial Intermediation*, *19*(1), 52–73.

Beltratti, A. & Stulz, R. M. (2012). The credit crisis around the globe: Why did some banks perform better? *Journal of Financial Economics*, *105*(1), 1–17.

Berger, A. N. & Udell, G. F. (1995). Relationship lending and lines of credit in small business finance. *Journal of Business*, *68*, 351–382.

Bonin, J. P., Hasan, I., & Wachtel, P. (2005). Bank performance, efficiency and ownership in transition economies. *Journal of Banking & Finance*, *29*(1), 31–53.

Brown, M. & De Haas, R. (2012). Foreign currency lending in emerging Europe: Bank-level evidence. *Economic Policy*, *27*(69), 59–98.

Brown, M., De Haas, R., & Sokolov, V. (2013). Regional inflation and financial dollarization. *EBRD Working Paper* No. 163. European Bank for Reconstruction and Development.

Cetorelli, N. & Goldberg, L. (2011). Global banks and international shock transmission: Evidence from the crisis. *IMF Economic Review*, *59*, 41–76.

Cetorelli, N. & Goldberg, L. (2012). Liquidity management of US global banks: Internal capital markets in the great recession. *Journal of International Economics*, *88*(2), 299–311.

Cihák, M. & Poghosyan, T. (2009). Distress in European banks: An analysis based on a new data set. *IMF Working Paper* No. WP/09/9. Washington D.C.: International Monetary Fund.

Claessens, S., Demirgüç-Kunt, A., & Huizinga, H. (2001). How does foreign entry affect domestic banking markets? *Journal of Banking & Finance*, *25*, 891–911.

Claessens, S. & van Horen, N. (2014). Foreign banks: Trends, impact and financial stability. *Journal of Money, Credit and Banking*, *46*(1), 295–326.

Crystal, J. S., Dages, B. G., & Goldberg, L. S. (2002). Has foreign bank entry led to sounder banks in Latin America? *Current Issues in Economics and Finance*, *8*(1), 1–6.

Cull, R., & Martinez Peria, M. S. (2007). Foreign bank participation and crises in developing countries. *World Bank Policy Research Working Paper* No. 4128. Washington D.C.: World Bank.

Dages, B. G., Goldberg, L. S., & Kinney, D. (2000). Foreign and domestic bank participation in emerging markets: Lessons from Mexico and Argentina. *Federal Reserve Bank of New York Economic Policy Review*, September, 17–36.

De Haas, R., Djourelova, M., & Nikolova, E. (2015). The great recession and social preferences: Evidence from Ukraine. *Journal of Comparative Economics*, *44*(1), 92–107.

De Haas, R., Ferreira, D., & Taci, A. (2010). What determines the composition of banks Loan Portfolios? Evidence from transition countries. *Journal of Banking & Finance*, *34*, 388–398.

De Haas, R., Korniyenko, Y., Pivovarsky, A., & Tsankova, T. (2015), "Taming the Herd? Foreign Banks, the Vienna Initiative and Crisis Transmission. *Journal of Financial Intermediation*, *24*(3), 325–355.

De Haas R. & Naaborg, I. (2006). Foreign banks in transition countries: To whom do they lend and how are they financed? *Financial Markets, Institutions & Instruments*, *15*(4), 159–199.

De Haas R. & Van Horen, N. (2012). International shock transmission after the Lehman Brothers collapse. Evidence from syndicated lending. *American Economic Review Papers & Proceedings*, *102*(3), 231–237.

De Haas, R. & Van Horen, N. (2013). Running for the Exit? International bank lending during a financial crisis. *Review of Financial Studies*, *26*(1), 244–285.

De Haas, R. & Van Lelyveld, I. (2006). Foreign banks and credit stability in Central and Eastern Europe. A panel data analysis. *Journal of Banking & Finance*, *30*, 1927–1952.

De Haas, R., & Van Lelyveld, I. (2010). Internal capital markets and lending by multinational bank subsidiaries. *Journal of Financial Intermediation*, *19*(1), 1–25.

De Haas, R., & Van Lelyveld, I. (2014). Multinational banks and the global financial crisis: Weathering the perfect storm? *Journal of Money, Credit, and Banking*, *46*(1), 333–364.

De la Torre, A., Martínez Pería, M.S., & Schmukler, S. L. (2010). Bank involvement with SMEs: Beyond relationship lending. *Journal of Banking & Finance*, *34*(9), 2280–2293.

Detragiache, E., Tressel, T., & Gupta P. (2008). Foreign banks in poor countries: Theory and evidence. *Journal of Finance*, *63*(5), 2123–2160.

Fries, S. & Taci, A. (2005). Cost efficiency of banks in transition: Evidence from 289 banks in 15 post-communist countries. *Journal of Banking & Finance*, *29*(1), 55–81.

García Herrero, A. & Martínez Pería, M. S. (2007). The mix of international banks' foreign claims: Determinants and implications. *Journal of Banking & Finance*, *31*(6), 1613–1631.

Giannetti, M. & Ongena, S. (2008). Lending by example: Direct and indirect effects of foreign banks in emerging markets. *Journal of International Economics*, *86*, 167–180.

Goldberg, L. S. (2001). When is U.S. bank lending to emerging markets volatile? *NBER Working Paper* No. 8209. Cambridge, MA.: National Bureau of Economic Research.

Gormley, T. A. (2010). The impact of foreign bank entry in emerging markets: Evidence from India. *Journal of Financial Intermediation*, *19*(1), 26–51.

Grubel H. G. (1977). A theory of multinational banking. *Banca Nazionale del Lavoro Quarterly Review*, *123*, 349–363.

Ivashina, V. & Scharfstein D. S. (2010). "Bank Lending During the Financial Crisis of 2008." *Journal of Financial Economics*, 97, 319–38.

Ivashina, V., Scharfstein, D. S., & Stein, J. C. (2015). Dollar funding and the lending behavior of global banks. *Quarterly Journal of Economics*, *130*(3), 1241–1281.

Kalemli-Ozcan, S., Papaioannou, E., & Perri, F. (2013). Global banks and crisis transmission. *Journal of International Economics*, *89*(2), 495–510.

Kamil, H. & Rai, K. (2012). The global credit crunch and foreign banks' lending to emerging markets: Why did Latin America fare better? *IMF Working Paper* No. 10/102. Washington D.C.: International Monetary Fund.

Martinez Peria, S., Powell, A., & Vladkova Hollar, I. (2002). Banking on foreigners: The behavior of international bank lending to Latin America, 1985–2000. *World Bank Working Paper* No. 2893. Washington D.C.: World Bank.

Morgan, D., Rime, B., & Strahan, P. E. (2004). Bank integration and state business volatility. *Quarterly Journal of Economics*, *119*(4), 1555–1585.

Morgan, D. & Strahan, P. E. (2004). Foreign bank entry and business volatility: Evidence from U.S. states and other countries. In L. A., Ahumada, & J. R. Fuentes Eds.), *Banking Market Structure and Monetary Policy* (pp. 241–269). Santiago: Central Bank of Chile.

Ongena, S., Peydro, J. L., & van Horen, N. (2015). Shocks abroad, pain at home? Bank-firm level evidence on the international transmission of financial shocks. *IMF Economic Review*, *63*(4), 698–750.

Peek, J. & Rosengren, E. S. (1997). The international transmission of financial shocks: The case of Japan. *American Economic Review*, *87*, 495–505.

Peek, J. & Rosengren, E. S. (2000a). Implications of the globalization of the banking sector: The Latin American experience. *New England Economic Review*, September/October, 45–63.

Peek, J. & Rosengren E. S. (2000b). Collateral damage: Effects of the Japanese bank crisis on the United States. *American Economic Review* *90*(1), 30–45.

Popov, A. & Udell, G. (2012). Cross-Border banking, credit access, and the financial crisis. *Journal of International Economics*, *87*, 147–161.

Raddatz, C. (2010). When the rivers run dry. Liquidity and the use of wholesale funds in the transmission of the U.S. subprime crisis. *Policy Research Working Paper* No. 5203. Washington D.C.: World Bank.

Schnabl, P. (2012). Financial globalization and the transmission of bank liquidity shocks: Evidence from an emerging market. *Journal of Finance*, 67(3), 897–932.

Van Rijckeghem, C. & Weder, B. (2001). Sources of contagion: Finance or trade? *Journal of International Economics*, *54*, 293–308.

Banks' Love Story with Sovereign Debt: Causes, Consequences, and Policy

— CHAPTER 11

■ Alexander Popov
European Central Bank

1. Introduction

The special relationship between banks and the state permeates the history of western civilization. For example, after the Glorious Revolution of 1688, the English government granted a monopoly charter to the country's first banking corporation, the Bank of England, in exchange for a series of loans to the government. Calomiris & Haber (2014) consider this an early example of modern banking defined as a "[...] partnership between the government and a group of bankers, a partnership that is shaped by the institutions that govern the distribution of power in the political system." However, governments and banks go way further back than that. Budin (2004) reports that the Temple of Athena[1] loaned money

Alexander Popov is a research economist at the ECB. The opinions expressed herein are those of the author and do not necessarily reflect those of the ECB or the Eurosystem.

[1] In the pre-Christian era, temples often served as wealth depositories and loan providers (see Gilbart, 1911). The word "bank" reflects the origins of banking in temples. In the New Testament, Christ drove the money changers out of the temple in Jerusalem, in the process overturning their tables. In Greece, bankers were known as *trapezitai*, a name derived from the tables at which they sat. The English word *bank* comes from the Italian *banca*, for bench or counter.

to the state of Athens between 433 and 427 BC at 6% interest — a rather generous arrangement, given that interest rates of around 30% were levied on loans to the likes of merchants and shipmasters.

The relationship between banks and sovereigns has become particularly complicated in recent decades. Governments monitor and regulate banks' behavior in order to minimize the cost of potential bank failures to the taxpayer, while at the same time often looking to banks as a source of finance. Banks' activities have become increasingly multinational, but even the most global banks retain their close connections with depositors and especially with state officials in their primary domestic market. Finally, the Basle Accord has singled out sovereign debt issued in domestic currency as the primary zero-risk asset, a recognition not extended to loans to governments or to sovereign debt issued in foreign currency. The result has been an even tighter grip between banks and sovereigns as evidenced by banks' rapidly increasing holdings of domestic sovereign bonds during the sovereign debt crisis in the euro area.

There are compelling reasons for why banks choose to hold domestic sovereign debt on their balance sheets. Government bond markets are among the most liquid in the world, making sovereign bonds an excellent storage technology. Moreover, governments — especially in industrialized economies — are historically considerably less likely to fail than private entities, elevating sovereign bonds to the status of that elusive economic concept, the "risk-free asset". However, some of the reasons for why banks' holdings of domestic sovereign bonds have exploded in recent years are less innocuous. The "risk-shifting" channel implies that banks in countries under fiscal stress load up on domestic sovereign bonds because they are bankrupt anyway if the government defaults. The "carry-trade" channel implies that banks use cheap wholesale funding to load up on high-yield sovereign debt, hoping to pocket the spread, and sometimes domestic sovereign debt is the most high-risk high-return one. Last but not least, the "moral suasion" channel implies that governments gently coerce domestic banks to increase their holdings of domestic sovereign bonds when other investors are unwilling to keep buying it, so as to keep the costs of refinancing public debt low.

Recognizing that banks may have the wrong incentives to accumulate sovereign debt, and that by doing so, they may be increasing the cost to governments of safeguarding the banking sector, policy makers in Europe have been busy trying to sever the link between banks and sovereigns by establishing the Banking Union. In particular, the Single Supervisory Mechanism (SSM), housed at the European Central Bank (ECB), has the task of overseeing the largest and most systemically important euro area banks. On the regulatory front, changes to the preferential treatment of domestic sovereign debt are being discussed. Finally, the ECB has spent large resources in arresting the negative consequences of the bank–sovereign nexus during crisis times.

In this chapter, I review the evidence on banks' incentives to increase their holdings of domestic sovereign debt before the introduction of the SSM. I then evaluate the consequences of high levels of balance sheet exposure to impaired sovereign debt at times of crisis. Finally, I discuss the effect of monetary policy and conclude with some policy implications.

2. Banks' Love Story with Sovereign Debt: Causes

The question whether banks' holdings of domestic sovereign debt have become excessive became particularly burning in the aftermath of the global financial crisis when over the span of four and a half years, between September 2008 and March 2013, the holdings of domestic sovereign bonds, as a share of total assets, for euro area banks more than doubled (Figure 1). The figure also makes the point that it is in particular banks' propensity to hold *domestic* sovereign debt that has increased, as their holdings of *foreign* sovereign debt have stayed more or less constant over the sample period.

This development was not uniform across euro area member states. Indeed, it was largely driven by banks in countries under fiscal stress, namely Greece, Ireland, Italy, Portugal, and Spain (hereafter "stressed countries"), for which the holdings of domestic sovereign bonds, as a share of total assets, almost tripled during this period. In comparison, holdings of domestic sovereign bonds, as a share of total assets, for banks in Austria, Belgium, Finland, France, Germany, and the Netherlands ("non-stressed countries") increased by a factor of less than two (Figure 2).

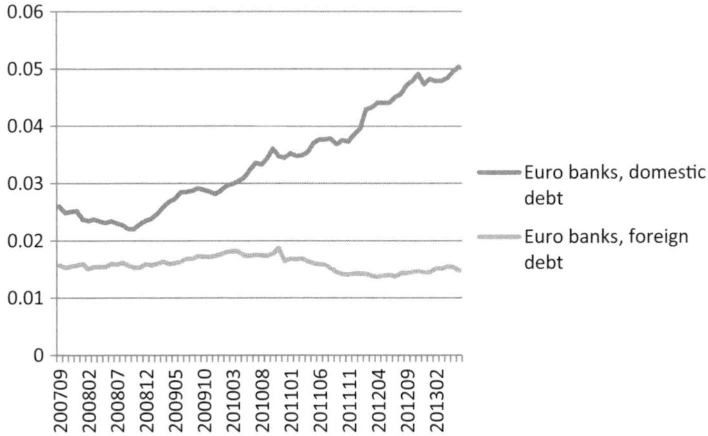

Figure 1. Domestic and foreign sovereign securities holdings: All euro area banks.

Note: Average holdings of domestic and foreign sovereign securities, divided by total assets, for 207 banks in 11 euro area countries (Austria, Belgium, Finland, France, Germany, Greece, Ireland, Italy, the Netherlands, Portugal, and Spain), for the period September 2009 to February 2013.
Source: ECB's Individual Balance Sheet Statistics.

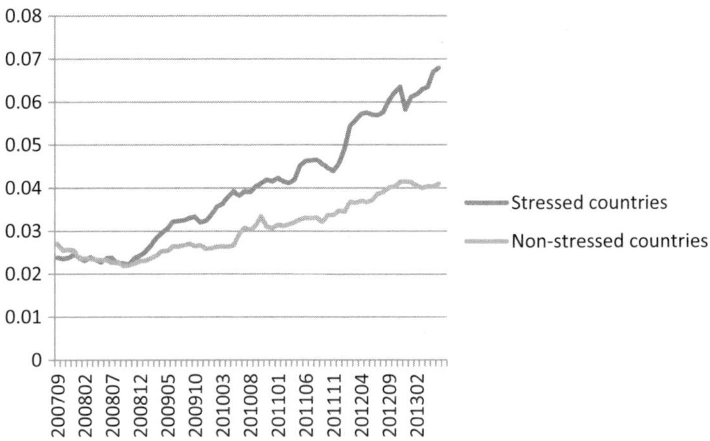

Figure 2. Domestic sovereign security holdings: Stressed versus non-stressed countries.

Note: Average holdings of domestic sovereign securities, divided by total assets, for 207 banks in five stressed (Greece, Ireland, Italy, Portugal, and Spain) and six non-stressed (Austria, Belgium, Finland, France, Germany, and the Netherlands), for the period September 2009–February 2013.
Source: ECB's individual balance sheet statistics.

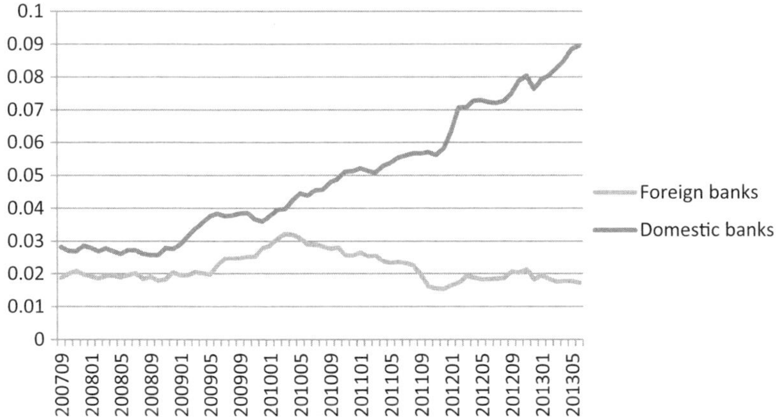

Figure 3. Domestic sovereign security holdings: Domestic versus foreign banks in stressed countries.

Note: Average holdings of domestic sovereign securities, divided by total assets, for 47 domestic banks in 13 foreign banks in five stressed euro area countries (Greece, Ireland, Italy, Portugal, and Spain), for the period September 2009–February 2013.
Source: ECB's individual balance sheet statistics.

The most crucial fact is illustrated in Figure 3. The Figure shows that while initially both domestic and foreign banks in stressed countries were increasing their holdings of domestic sovereign debt, after the start of the sovereign debt crisis in May 2010, domestic banks as a group continued to increase their holdings at an ever higher pace — with their holdings of domestic sovereign bonds, as a share of total assets, *quadrupling* between September 2008 and December 2012 — while foreign banks' holdings of domestic sovereign debt (i.e., holdings of Italian sovereign bonds by affiliates of euro area non-Italian banks in Italy), at the end of 2012 were roughly at the same level as at the beginning of the global financial crisis.

What are the underlying reasons for this tectonic shift in the propensity of domestic banks to hold domestic sovereign debt which started in the fall of 2008? There are a number of reasons related to regulatory compliance and to banks' own incentives. Starting with the simplest one, banks hold a large amount of high-quality low-risk assets in order to satisfy liquidity needs and regulatory pressure to maintain adequate levels of capital. For that reason, during the 2000s, banks accumulated large quantities of privately issued AAA-rated securities. However, after Lehman Brothers filed for bankruptcy in September 2008, privately issued debt securities as a class lost their appeal. As banks scrambled to replenish their capital and to rebuild their portfolio of liquid assets, they turned increasingly to sovereign bonds. This double "flight to safety" and "flight to liquidity" was facilitated by the preferential treatment of this class of assets under the Capital Requirements Directive (CRD) which gives sovereign debt securities issued in domestic currency a zero-risk weight and exempts them from the limit on large exposures. Already at the time many observers were worried that by giving banks incentives to invest in one particular class of assets, regulatory rules were sowing the seeds of the next crisis.[2]

Second, domestic banks may be shifting risk. In good states of the world (i.e., in states of the world without sovereign default), holding domestic sovereign debt may be tremendously profitable. In bad states of the world, when the government is in default, even the safest banks will collapse as explicit and implicit guarantees are being withdrawn. Hence, banks have an incentive to acquire a riskier asset portfolio when their sovereign is close to default (Livshitz & Schoors, 2009; Broner, Erce, Martin, & Ventura, 2014). There could be an added collective moral hazard motive (Farhi & Tirole, 2012) whereby banks with little exposure to their sovereigns may wish to increase their exposures and link better their fate to that of the domestic sovereign.

Third, banks may engage in a carry-trade-type behavior whereby they use their access to cheap wholesale funding to build large sovereign bonds positions. Such strategy can be supremely profitable if the issuing country is facing elevated fiscal stress, leading investors to demand ever higher yields to keep funding the government, while at the same time sovereign default is a close-to-zero-probability event due to explicit or implicit collective insurance mechanisms. Acharya & Steffen (2015)

---

[2] *"By 2016, the conditions for a new systemic crisis — this time sovereign — might be in place. What is unique is that, while defaults on sovereign debt occurred before Basel I and II, this time regulatory authorities are actively encouraging banks to take refuge in government debt. So why is the Basel Committee insisting on calling local currency-denominated sovereign debt risk-free? I don't know."* (M. Pomerleano, *Financial Times*, February 3, 2010).

show that during the acute phase of the euro area sovereign debt crisis, banks' stock prices were positively correlated with their exposures to impaired sovereign debt, suggesting that they were likely engaging in such behavior.

The three channels just discussed are similar in that they capture characteristics of the regulatory environment or of the underlying asset which give incentives to banks to keep buying sovereign bonds even at times of crisis. However, there is a fourth channel which goes by the name "moral suasion", and it is rather more onerous because it is seemingly incentive-free. It is a channel whereby governments appeal to a higher objective, such as "patriotic duty", in order to push citizens, private investors, or, in this case, banks to engage in a behavior which is not necessarily profit maximizing from their point of view. This mechanism has a long history in countries with weak institutions, but also in industrialized economies. Romans (1966) argues that moral suasion is the cornerstone of British monetary policy, and it works well because — unlike in the United States — the British banking sector is traditionally dominated by few banks. Horvitz & Ward (1987) describe how in order to limit the outflow of dollars from the U.S., during the 1960s the Federal Reserve demanded that domestic banks reduced their foreign lending, warning that banks could not expect the increase in their loan portfolio to be considered an adequate reason for the extension of Federal Reserve credit through the discount window. Moral suasion has often been applied in the case of sovereign bonds, too, with the U.S. government running campaigns with slogans such as "Buy a liberty bond — defend your country with dollars!" and "Save your child from autocracy and poverty — buy war savings stamps!" during WWI and WWII. But was moral suasion part of the reason for the unprecedented increase in domestic sovereign bond holdings by domestic banks in stressed countries during the recent sovereign debt crisis? While many observers certainly believed so,[3] there is no "smoking gun" in the shape of a Wikileaks file documenting a conversation between a finance minister

[3] "[...] sovereign credit risk may alter swiftly as it did in 2008–2009 due to [...] moral suasion of the financial sector ('financial repression') to hold sovereign debt." (Viral Acharya, "Banking Union in Europe and other reforms," *VOXEU*, 16 October 2012.

and a bank CEO demanding participation in an upcoming government bond auction.

In a recent paper, Ongena, Popov, & van Horen (2015) take a step towards identifying if and when governments "morally sway" banks to purchase sovereign bonds. We employ a novel identification strategy which rests on three facts. First, cyclical needs notwithstanding — the main determinant of newly issued sovereign debt is the amount of maturing sovereign debt. Second, the amount of retiring government debt is strappingly pre-determined, because it is the outcome of choices typically made years ago, often by previous governments. As a result, the government's need today to refinance maturing debt fluctuates wildly month-on-month. Third, domestic banks are more likely to be "morally swayed" than foreign banks, through explicit and implicit threats to those banks that decide not to cooperate (Romans, 1966; Reinhart & Sbrancia, 2015).

Employing the ECB's Integrated Balance Sheet Statistics dataset, which contains detailed end-of-month information on net flows and holdings of domestic sovereign debt securities for a large sample of domestic and foreign banks active in stressed euro zone countries, we assess the differences in net purchases of domestic sovereign debt between high-need and low-need months, for domestic banks (the treatment group) relative to foreign banks (the control group). We define a "high-need" month to be a month in which the total amount of new debt auctioned by the domestic government is above the country-specific median for the applicable sample period because of a high refinancing need stemming from a large amount of maturing debt. We focus on Greece, Ireland, and Portugal during the period May 2010–August 2012 and on Italy and Spain during the period August 2011–August 2012. This is the period during which the ECB's Securities Markets Program was in place for the countries in question, coinciding with the acute phase of their sovereign problems. Our hypothesis is that if the moral suasion channel is operational, domestic banks will be more likely than foreign banks to increase their holdings of domestic sovereign bonds during high-need months, while there should be no differences in behavior between the two classes of banks during low-need months.

Our analysis confirms that during the height of the sovereign debt crisis, domestic banks were substantially more likely to purchase domestically-issued sovereign debt than foreign banks in high-need months. This effect is not only statistically significant but also economically relevant, i.e., it amounts to about half of the within-sample standard deviation of monthly purchases. It is also robust across different proxies for sovereign debt holdings and across many different specifications. Finally, it is strongest for state-owned and supported banks and in particular for those with low initial holdings of domestic sovereign banks. This indicates that the government may strategically pick the banks it chooses to sway (i.e., those whose balance sheets are not already saturated with domestic sovereign debt). Importantly, our month-on-month identification strategy enables us to control for both unobservable time-invariant and observable time-varying bank characteristics that can impact the decision of a bank to buy sovereign bonds in a particular month through the channels of regulatory compliance, risk shifting, and carry trade. Moreover, the effect still obtains when we use the amount of *maturing* government debt to extract the exogenous component of the amount of *auctioned* government debt.

In sum, our estimates strongly and consistently suggest that during the sovereign debt crisis. In Europe, domestic banks acted in the best interest of their government, propping up the government's financial needs at times when these needs were particularly high. Of course, it is highly unlikely that banks are voiceless "victims" in this process, being forced by a desperate government to act against their will. A more reasonable interpretation of our results is that banks and sovereigns are locked in a partnership of mutual understanding, in which favors are exchanged over a long horizon, to the ensuing benefit of both parties.

3. Banks' Love Story with Sovereign Debt: Consequences

I have argued in the previous section that euro area banks seem to be holding amounts of domestically-issued sovereign bonds that are in excess of what is implied by fundamental considerations. But where is the inefficiency in that? Excessive sovereign bond holdings would be problematic if, for example, they led to a crowding out of private investment. If banks increased their holdings of sovereign debt with no effect on lending to the real sector, policy makers would have one less reason to worry about (even though they might still have to worry about financial stability).

In a recent paper, Popov & van Horen (2015) analyse the effect of banks' balance sheet exposure to impaired sovereign debt on syndicated lending to both domestic and foreign corporate borrowers. We do so for a sample of 34 banks domiciled in 11 non-stressed European countries, for which we have exact exposures to GIIPS sovereign debt. The reason we focus on non-stressed countries is that banks in a recessionary environment may be reducing lending for other reasons, too (such as depositors withdrawing their savings to smooth the shocks to their labor income), making identification problematic. We also study changes in the geographic composition of banks' loan portfolios, trying to determine if a potential reduction in lending is also associated with a flight home effect, whereby the negative consequences of banks' excessive exposures to the impaired sovereigns would be negligible for domestic borrowers.

Our empirical analysis uncovers a direct link between deteriorating creditworthiness of (foreign) sovereign debt and lending by banks holding this debt on their balance sheet. When using our preferred econometric specification with bank and borrower country X quarter fixed effects, we find that after 2010:Q3, banks with substantial holdings of GIIPS sovereign debt reduced syndicated lending by 21.3% relative to banks with marginal or zero holdings. This indicates that exposure to GIIPS sovereign debt mooted the observed recovery in syndicated lending in the wake of the global financial crisis. Figure 4 illustrates this result. It plots the evolution of total syndicated lending by our sample of 34 European banks from non-GIIPS countries over our sample period 2009:Q3 to 2011:Q4. The figure shows that up until 2010:Q3, there were no significant differences in the rate of change of syndicated lending by the group of affected and the group of non-affected banks. After the crisis intensified with the Greek government securing a €110 billion bailout loan from the EU and the IMF in mid-2010,[4] loan growth by non-GIIPS European banks exposed to GIIPS sovereign debt has been

[4] This was followed by a €85 billion rescue package for Ireland in November 2010 and by a €78 billion rescue package for Portugal in May 2011.

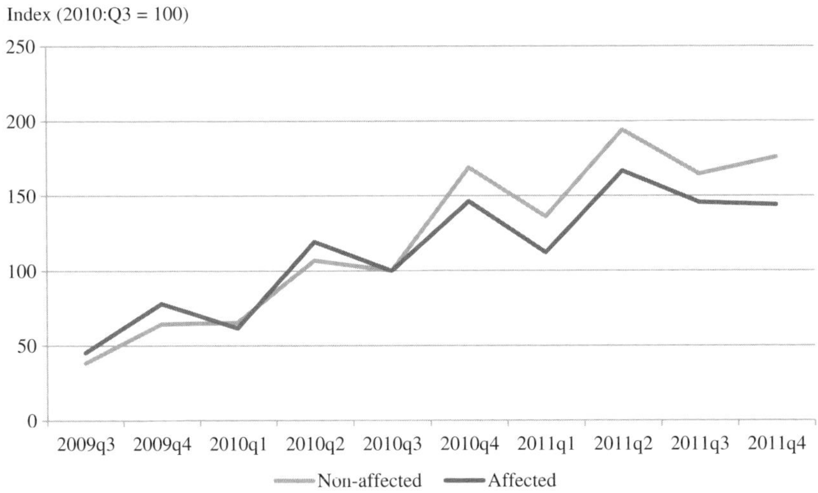

Figure 4. Syndicated lending to the corporate sector, affected versus non-affected banks.

Notes: The Figure shows the evolution of total syndicated lending by our sample 34 European banks over the period 2009:Q3 to 2011:Q4. It depicts total volume (in euros) of syndicated loans issued in each quarter for the two groups of banks indexed to be 100 at 2010:Q3. Only loans to non-financial corporates are included. *Non-affected* contains the group of banks whose exposure to GIIPS debt was below the median level and *Affected* contains the group of banks whose exposure was above the median level.
Source: Dealogic.

substantially lower than lending by non-GIIPS European banks not exposed to GIIPS sovereign debt. We also provide evidence that banks cut syndicated lending relatively more to foreign corporates, with the exception of U.S. borrowers, implying that the decline in lending was also accompanied by an increase in home bias.

Evidence to the same end abounds from studies using different methodologies and different data sets. Correa, Sapriza, & Zlate (2012) show that the branches of European banks in the U.S. experienced a run on their deposits and reduced their lending to U.S. entities. Ivashina, Scharfstein, & Stein (2012) show that money-market funds sharply withdrew funding for euro area banks when the sovereign debt crisis started, leading to a decline in dollar lending relative to euro lending. Bofondi, Carpinelli, & Sette (2014) show that relative to foreign banks in Italy, domestic banks reduce credit and increase loan spreads at the height of the crisis. De Marco (2013) shows that aggregate lending declined for banks with balance sheet exposure to impaired foreign debt. Gennaioli, Martin, and Rossi (2014) show that banks with substantial sovereign exposures reduce lending when the issuing government is close to default. Becker and Ivashina (2015) show that large firms borrowing from exposed banks are more likely to issue corporate bonds and less likely to make use bank loans.

The conclusion that emerges from these empirical studies is that large amounts of sovereign bonds on banks' balance sheets have a substantial negative effect on their credit supply. The natural question that emerges is, what can policy do once sovereign risk materializes?

4. Banks' Love Story with Sovereign Debt: Policy

The inconvenience of learning from one's mistakes is that you have to make them first. The Federal Reserve responded timidly to the banking panics and failures during 1929–1933, as well as to large declines in the price level and output, given the tools at its disposal (Carson & Wheelock, 2012). Some scholars have charged that through a dramatic decline in the money stock and the failure of a third of U.S. banks, the Fed's failure to serve effectively as a lender of last resort turned what would have been a severe economic contraction into what came to be known as the "Great Depression" (Friedman & Schwartz, 1971).

Having learned that lesson, central banks around the world responded forcefully to the global financial crisis that started in 2008. The same goes for the sovereign debt crisis which erupted in the euro area in the spring of 2010, and which prompted the ECB to adopt a number of unprecedented conventional and unconventional measures to stem the decline in economic activity. Among other policies, the ECB injected unprecedented amounts of liquidity into the euro area banking system; it bought around €250 billion of impaired sovereign debt in secondary markets through the Securities Markets Program; it committed to buying unlimited amounts of sovereign bonds, under strict conditionality, through the Outright Monetary Transactions (OMT) program; and it embarked on its own version of Quantitative Easing through the Assets Purchases Program. In addition, the Banking Union in Europe has been set up, with unified supervision of the euro area's largest banks becoming the prerogative of the ECB-housed SSM in November 2014.

Evidence suggests that some of these programs have been successful in bringing down sovereign bond yields from euro area record high levels between 2010 and 2012 (e.g., Altavilla, Giannone, & Lenza, 2014; Ghysels, Idier, Manganelli, & Vergote, 2014; Eser & Schwaab, 2015). This should reduce borrowing costs as investors now perceive banks loaded with large balance sheet exposures to impaired sovereigns as less risky and start demanding lower returns to keep funding the banks. But is the reduction of borrowing costs mirrored by an increase in bank lending?

In a recent paper, Ferrando, Popov, and Udell (2015) evaluate the effect of the OMT program on access to finance by small businesses in the euro area. In terms of scale, the OMT Program, announced in August 2012, has arguably been the most ambitious unconventional policy employed in the euro area since its inception,[5] as well as one of the most successful ones, with bond yields on sovereign debt issued by stressed countries declining immediately, sharply, and permanently. It was expected at the time that due to their high dependence on bank funding, small and medium enterprises (SMEs) might be among the biggest beneficiaries of the program. At the same time, because SMEs comprise up to 99% of firms in Europe, provide two out of three private sector jobs, and contribute more than half of total business-provided value added, the benefits from using monetary policy tools aimed at reducing sovereign pressures on bank balance sheets could be large in the aggregate. However, there has been no systematic cross-country test of this hypothesis.

We first analyse the experience of SMEs during the acute phase of the sovereign debt crisis. We employ a difference-in-differences methodology whereby we trace changes in credit access by firms in stressed countries versus firms in non-stressed countries, before and after the crisis. We find that the sovereign debt crisis resulted in a strong supply-driven reduction

[5] Under the OMT Program, the ECB committed to purchasing in secondary markets — and under a number of strict conditions — *unlimited* amounts of government debt issued by eligible euro area governments.

in access to finance for SMEs across, mostly due to quantity and to price rationing by banks. More transparent and creditworthy firms experienced a relatively larger decline in credit access, suggesting that the overall reduction in the credit supply was not part of a "flight to quality" in lending. Firms in stressed countries made up for the reduction in bank credit by resorting to issuing debt securities, likely driving the overall cost of finance up. Our findings imply that bank credit is difficult to replace as a source of funding for European corporates.

We next turn to the effect of the OMT announcement. We find that bank lending improved immediately after the OMT announcement in that credit rationing and rates of discouragement for firms in stressed countries declined. This improvement in credit supply was more pronounced for more creditworthy firms, suggesting favorable distributional consequences of unconventional monetary policy. In addition, firms in stressed countries were less likely to use government-subsidized loans, as well as to resort to more expensive sources of external finance, such as debt securities and trade credit. Once again, the importance of affordable bank credit to the European corporate sector becomes readily apparent. Figure 5 depicts this evolution of SMEs' credit constraints between 2009 and 2013.

While a number of demand-side effects clearly played a role at all stages of the sovereign debt crisis (for instance, by affecting final customers' demand for goods and services), we go to great lengths to identify the casual impact of the crisis through the channel of the supply of external finance. First, we employ an exhaustive set of fixed effects, notably country-sector-time interactions, in order to net out the effect of common demand shocks (e.g., to changes in the willingness of households in Spain to purchase residential property). Second, we show that the trends in credit access that we observe during the sovereign debt crisis do not exist before the spring in 2010, suggesting that differences in lending practices across stressed and non-stressed countries are specific to the period of the crisis. Finally, we isolate the subset of the most creditworthy corporate borrowers, specifically, firms with the highest credit history, collateral quality, and growth opportunities. We show that even in this class of firms, those in stressed countries are more likely

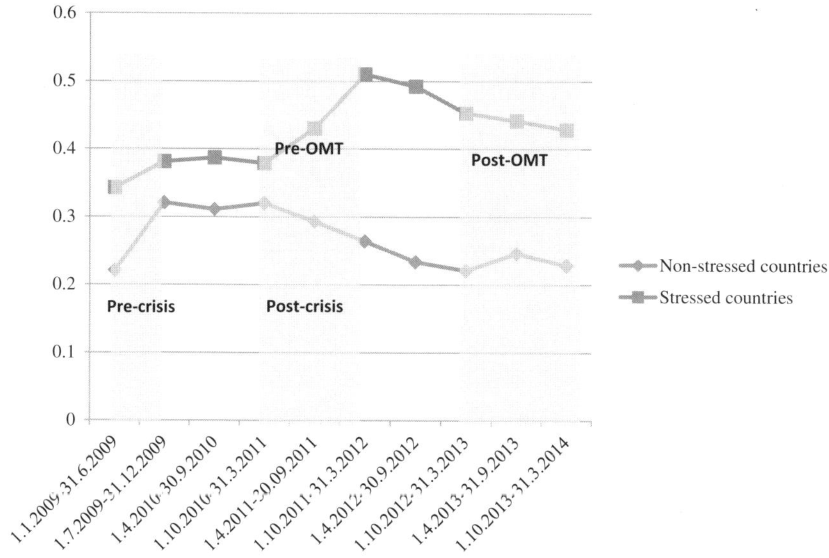

Figure 5. Credit constrained firms: stressed versus non-stressed countries.

Notes: The Figure summarizes weighted averages of credit constrained firms over the sample period. 'Credit constrained' is a dummy variable equal to one if the firm declared a positive demand for bank financing in the past six months, but it did not apply because of possible rejection, it applied and its loan application was rejected, it applied and got less than 75% of the requested amount, or it refused the loan because the cost was too high. 'Stressed countries' are Greece, Ireland, Italy, Portugal, and Spain. 'Non-stressed countries' are Austria, Belgium, Finland, France, Germany, and the Netherlands.

to be credit constrained during the sovereign debt crisis than those in non-stressed countries.

Our empirical analysis has a number of implications. First, it underscores the importance of using survey data on discouraged corporate borrowers in the analysis of credit access as such borrowers are observationally equivalent to rejected ones and constitute a substantial share of credit constrained firms. Second, it points to the fact that in addition to increased pressures on fiscal policy, sovereign stress has an indirect economic cost through a reduction in lending to the corporate sector. Third, non-conventional monetary policy (in this case, the OMT Program) can have a positive effect on credit access. Nevertheless, we also find that a year and a half after the OMT announcement, firms in stressed countries were once again considerably more likely to be discouraged from applying for a bank loan. This signals the need for a multi-dimensional approach to supporting the monetary transmission mechanism, both through alleviating pressures on banks' balance sheets and through restoring the corporate sector's confidence in the banks' intermediation function. It also points to the fact that monetary policy alone cannot be expected to address structural weaknesses in an individual country's economy or banking sector.

5. Conclusion

I have argued that the increased propensity of (mostly European) banks to hold domestic sovereign bonds appears to be to some extent the natural manifestation of a long-standing special relationship between banks and sovereigns; that this development can have negative consequences for the real economy in some states of the world, such as crowding out of private investment; and that monetary policy has proved to be able to temporarily alleviate the negative effect of sovereign stress through the bank lending channel, but that its ability to do so in the short run should not be viewed as a substitute for policies that would go to the heart of the bank–sovereign embrace.

A number of recent and ongoing policy developments strive to fit that description. The Banking Union — and in particular, unified supervision under the SSM since November 2014 — is supposed to sever the often cosy relation between national supervisors and domestic banks, potentially ending the "deadly embrace" between banks and sovereigns. Second, regulators are currently debating potential changes to the regulatory treatment of sovereign debt, and in particular to its zero-risk status and to its exemption from the limit on large exposures. How far-reaching this reform will be is, however, unclear. Third, even in the absence of supranational reform, various regulators (e.g., the FSA in Sweden) are already asking banks to add risk weights to government bonds. Such and other reforms to the current regime will hopefully address some of the issued I touched upon in this article, and their effect will be studied intensely for years to come.

References

Acharya, V. & Steffen, S. (2015). The "greatest" carry trade ever? Understanding Eurozone bank risks. *Journal of Financial Economics*, 115(2), 215–236.

Altavilla, C., Giannone, D., & Lenza, M. (2014). The financial and the macroeconomic effects of the OMT announcements. *CSEF Working Paper* No. 352.

Becker, B. & Ivashina, V. (2015). *Financial repression in the European sovereign debt crisis*. Mimeo, Harvard Business School.

Bofondi, M., Carpinelli, L., & Sette, E. (2014). Credit supply during a sovereign crisis. *Bank of Italy Working Paper* No. 909.

Broner, F., Erce, A., Martin, A., & Ventura, J. (2014). Sovereign debt markets in turbulent times: Creditor discrimination and crowing-out effects. *Journal of Monetary Economics*, *61*, 114–142.

Budin, S. (2004). *The ancient Greeks: New perspectives (understanding ancient civilizations)*. Santa Barbara: ABC-Clio.

Calomiris, C. & Haber, S. (2014). *Fragile by design: The political origins of banking crises and scarce credit*. Princeton NJ: Princeton University Press.

Carson, M. & Wheelock, D. (2012). The lender of last resort: Lessons from the Fed's first 100 years. *Federal Reserve Bank of St. Louis Working Paper* 2012–056.

Correa, R., Sapriza, H., & Zlate, A. (2012). Liquidity shocks, dollar funding costs, and the bank lending channel during the European sovereign crisis. *Board of Governors of the Federal Reserve System International Finance Discussion Paper* No. 1059.

De Marco, F. (2013). Bank lending and the sovereign debt crisis. *Boston College Working Paper*.

Eser, F. & Schwaab, B. (2015). Evaluating the impact of unconventional monetary policy measures: Empirical evidence from the ECB's Securities Markets Program. *Journal of Financial Economics*, 119(1), 147–167.

Farhi, E. & Tirole, J. (2012). Collective moral hazard, maturity mismatch, and systemic bailouts. *American Economic Review*, *102*, 60–93.

Ferrando, A., Popov, A., & Udell, G. (2015). Sovereign stress, unconventional monetary policy, and SMEs' access to finance. *ECB Working Paper* No. 1820.

Friedman, M. & Schwartz, A. (1971). *A monetary history of the United States, 1867–1960*. Princeton, NJ: Princeton University Press.

Gennaioli, N., Martin, A., & Rossi, S. (2014). Banks, government bonds and defaults. What do the data say? Working Paper No. 14/120. International Monetary Fund.

Ghysels, E., Idier, J., Manganelli, S., & Vergote, O. (2014). A high frequency assessment of the ECB Securities Markets Programme. *European Central Bank Working Paper* No. 1642.

Gilbart, J. (1911). *The history, principles, and practice of banking*. London: G. Bell and Sons.

Horvitz, P. & Ward, R. (1987). *Monetary policy and the financial system.* Englewood Cliffs, NJ: Prentice Hall.

Ivashina, V., Scharfstein, D., & Stein, J. (2012). Dollar funding and the lending behavior of global banks. *Harvard Business School Working Paper* No. 13–059.

Livshitz, I. & Schoors, K. (2009). Sovereign default and banking. Mimeo, University of Western Ontario.

Ongena, S., Popov, A., & van Horen, N. (2015). The invisible hand of the government: Moral suasion during the European sovereign debt crisis. *De Nederlandsche Bank Working Paper* No. 505.

Popov, A. & van Horen, N. (2015). Exporting sovereign stress: Evidence from syndicated bank lending during the euro area sovereign debt crisis. *Review of Finance*, *19*, 1825–1866.

Reinhart, C. & Sbrancia, M. B. (2015). The liquidation of government debt. *IMF Working Paper* WP/15/7.

Romans, J. (1966). Moral suasion as an instrument of economic policy. *American Economic Review*, *56*, 1220–1226.

Part IV
Implications for Supervision and Regulation

Patterns in International Banking and Their Implications for Prudential Policies

— Chapter 12

▪ Ingo Fender and Patrick McGuire
BIS

1. Introduction

This chapter was prepared for the session entitled "Implications for regulation and supervision". With a session title like this, the temptation for conference organisers is always to ask the BIS participant to cover the various versions of the Basel Accord and how they have developed into the post-crisis Basel III framework. This was thankfully not the case this time around, which is why this chapter takes a different approach. Instead of talking about Basel-based regulation per se, it covers something else that the BIS is known for — namely, the *International Banking Statistics* (IBS). Specifically, the IBS are employed to identify

Ingo Fender is Head of Financial Systems and Regulations, Monetary and Economic Department and Patrick McGuire is Head of the International Data Hub, Monetary and Economics Department. Both at the Bank for International Settlements (BIS). The views expressed in this chapter are those of the authors and do not necessarily reflect those of the BIS. We gratefully acknowledge expert research assistance by Jhuvesh Sobrun.

key "patterns" in international banking that are then used to derive broad-based implications for regulators and supervisors.

Against this background, the paper proceeds as follows. Section 2 provides a short overview of the BIS IBS and how they can be used to track developments in international banking. Section 3 identifies six key patterns in international banking on the basis of the IBS. Patterns one and two state that international banking is centred on hubs (hosts) and that different (home) banking systems have very different degrees of international orientation. Patterns three and four relate to differences in bank structure and roll-over risks, respectively. Patterns five and six, then, point to a regionalization trend in banks' international activities and highlight changes in the mix of bank and bond finance. Section 4, finally, derives broad prudential regulations based on these patterns.

2. The BIS IBS: A Quick Refresher

The BIS IBS are an established statistical reporting framework tracking the international activities of more than 7,000 banking entities located in about 40 countries.[1] They consist of two complementary datasets, each of which comes in two versions. These are (i) the locational banking statistics (LBS) by residency; (ii) the locational statistics by nationality; (iii) the consolidated banking statistics (CBS), immediate borrower (IB) basis; and the (iv) CBS, ultimate risk (UR) basis (i.e., adjusted for risk-transfers). The statistics were established by central banks and the BIS at different times and with different objectives in mind.[2]

The first two sets, collectively referred to as the LBS, cover banks' international financial assets and liabilities based on the residence of the

[1] For details, see for example Committee on the Global Financial System — CGFS (2012).

[2] The locational statistics were originally established in the 1960s to track the growth in U.S. dollar deposits outside the United States, and are a key source of information on the currency and geographical composition of banks' international balance sheets. The consolidated statistics were established in the early 1980s after debt crises in developing countries highlighted the need for information on banks' exposures to country risk.

reporting entity. The locational by residency statistics provide information about the residence of the reporting banks' counterparties (e.g., claims of banks in the UK on Germany), while the locational by nationality data provide information about the nationality of ownership of the reporting banks (e.g., Swiss banks in the United Kingdom). The other two data sets, collectively forming the CBS, cover reporting banks' worldwide consolidated foreign claims on counterparties in individual countries, both on an IB and UR basis. Foreign claims comprise cross-border claims booked in all offices on borrowers in a particular counterparty country plus any claims extended locally by banks' offices located in the counterparty country.

The available breakdowns differ across the various sets of statistics, as summarized in Table 1, with additional information on domestic positions as well as more granular breakdowns currently being phased in (see CGFS (2012); Avdjiev, McGuire, & Wooldridge (2015)). Details for global aggregates and individual reporting countries are published quarterly by the BIS, according to the confidentiality restrictions specified individually by each reporting country.

How can the IBS be used to track information regarding developments in international banking? Figure 1 provides an example, based on foreign claims captured in the CBS (IB basis). Foreign claims, which are defined as cross-border claims plus local claims in both local and foreign currencies, captures both banks' true cross-border lending activities as well as lending done by foreign affiliates from a given national banking sector across various host jurisdictions. Figure 1 depicts these outstanding foreign claims positions scaled by world GDP, and offers three broad take-aways.

First, measured by this metric, international banking expanded significantly in the run-up to the global financial crisis (Figure 1). After peaking in early 2008, outstanding positions then contracted and have yet to show a broad-based recovery — despite some signs of a stabilization at least in U.S. dollar-denominated terms. Second, much of the observed expansion and subsequent contraction in international banking was due to European banks (right-hand panel), whose balance sheets drove the expansion in the run-up to the crisis in 2008, and later

Table 1. The BIS LBS and CBS compared.

	Locational Statistics		Consolidated Statistics	
Reporting unit	Banking offices resident in the reporting country (host country)		Banks headquartered in the reporting country (home country)	
Reporting countries	44		30	
Reporting basis	Unconsolidated data, including inter-office positions		Worldwide consolidated data, excluding inter-office positions	
Reported positions	Claims and liabilities, excluding positions in local currencies vis-à-vis residents of the reporting country		Claims and other potential exposures, excluding positions vis-à-vis residents of the reporting country	
Measures	Amounts outstanding at quarter-end and exchange rate adjusted changes in amounts outstanding		Amounts outstanding at quarter-end	
Reported breakdowns:	Locational by residency of banking office[a]	Locational by nationality of banking office[a]	Consolidated on an IB basis	Consolidated on an UR basis
1. Claims	cross-border in all currencies, local in foreign currencies	cross-border in all currencies, local in foreign currencies	International, local in local currencies	Cross-border, local in all currencies
2. Vis-à-vis country	>200 countries	n/a	>200 countries	>200 countries
3. Currencies	Domestic, USD, EUR, JPY, GBP, CHF	Domestic, USD, EUR, JPY	n/a	n/a

4. Sector	Non-banks, banks	Non-banks, banks, of which related offices, official monetary authorities	Banks, non-bank private, public	Banks, non-bank private, public
5. Type of instrument	Loans and deposits, debt securities, other financial instruments	n/a	n/a	n/a
6. Maturity	n/a	n/a	$\leq$1yr, >1yr $\leq$2yr, >2 year (remaining maturity)	n/a

Note: [a]The nationality statistics are compiled by regrouping the same locational data into categories based on the control or ownership of the banking offices in question. Both locational data sets are on an immediate counterparty basis.

Source: CGFS (2012).

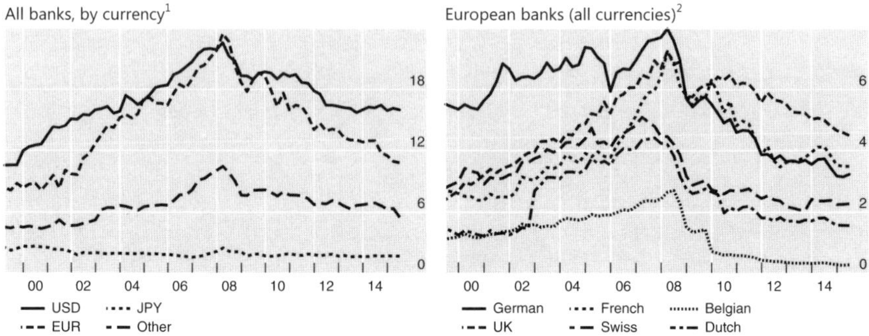

Figure 1. Foreign claims scaled by world GDP (in per cent).

Notes: [1]Estimated totals for 19 banking systems. [2]Foreign claims excluding claims on residents of the home country booked by banks' foreign offices.
Sources: IMF; BIS consolidated statistics (IB basis); BIS locational statistics by nationality; BIS calculations.

contracted significantly in its wake and again during the subsequent European sovereign risk crisis.

Finally, reflecting in part the contraction in European banks' activities, international banking remains largely a U.S. dollar-based business (Figure 1, left-hand panel). As of early 2015, U.S. dollar-denominated foreign claims totalled some $13 trillion — almost half of global foreign claims. At the same time, these large amounts were not necessarily transacted by U.S. banks. Indeed, over the 2002–2014 period, the U.S. bank share in U.S. dollar business was around 25–30%. That is, the majority of U.S. dollar lending was done by banks headquartered outside United States.

3. Six Patterns in International Banking

Having set the scene with the above example, this section uses IBS data to identify six key patterns in international banking. The analysis draws on previous BIS research as well as the established academic literature, combining both the consolidated (i.e., headquarter-based) and locational (residency-based) perspectives provided by the BIS data.

3.1. *International Banking is Centered on "Hubs"*

The analysis starts with the BIS LBS by residency, which track the cross-border claims and liabilities of banks located in a particular reporting country (ignoring the nationality of the reporting banks in each location). These statistics follow balance of payments compilation methodologies, and provide a sense of how concentrated international banking is geographically while highlighting (country-to-country) balance sheet interlinkages.

For this purpose, Figure 2 provides familiar network charts of geographical interlinkages of banks' cross-border claims and liabilities positions separately for their U.S. dollar and euro-denominated positions (see Fender & McGuire (2010b)). The nodes in each panel depict reporting countries/regions where banks' offices are located. The size of

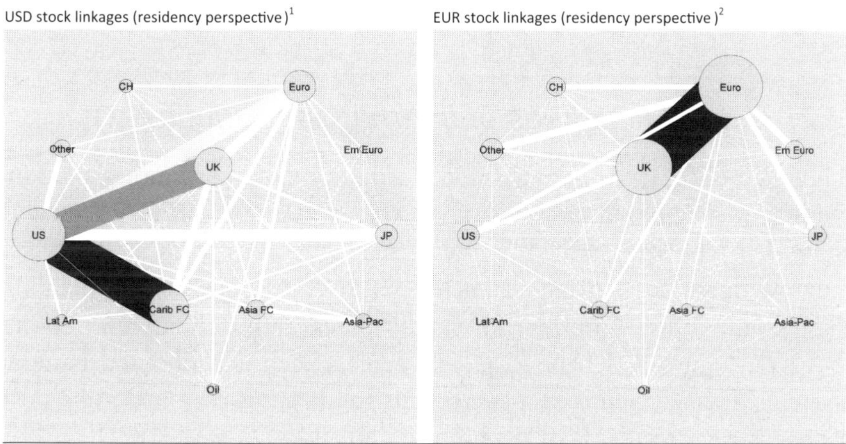

Figure 2. Geographic linkages in the international banking system: Cross-border claims and liabilities in U.S. dollar trillion.

Notes: The size of each circle is proportional to the stock of cross-border claims and liabilities of reporting banks located in the particular geographical region. Some regions include non-reporting countries. The thickness of a line between regions A and B is proportional to the sum of claims of banks in A on all residents of B, liabilities of banks in A to non-banks in B, claims of banks in B on all residents of A and liabilities of banks in B to non-banks in A. 2010-Q1 data.

Source: Fender & McGuire (2010b), based on BIS LBS by residency; BIS calculations.

the nodes is proportional to the share (in the global total) of cross-border bank assets and liabilities booked by banks located in that country node. The thickness of the lines, in turn, is a measure of the size of cross-border claims and liabilities positions with counterparties in other countries/regions.

What we see is that cross-border banking is very concentrated in just a few locations. Specifically, a large chunk of the world's cross-border banking business is booked by banks located in, or against a counterparty in, London, New York and some other key banking hubs (including the Caribbean Offshore centres, particularly for U.S. dollar business). However, the cross-border positions booked in these locations can be (and often are) largely driven by foreign banks (i.e., affiliates of foreign-headquartered institutions). For example, UK-headquartered banks accounted for less than a third of all total cross-border positions booked by banks located in the United Kingdom in 2010. That is, bank location says little about bank nationality, and vice-versa.

3.2. *Differing Degrees of International Orientation*

Having looked at the patterns in the geography of international banking with residency-based data, just how large are these positions to the *consolidated* reporting banks? To get a sense, we turn to the CBS, which align with the accounting perimeter of banks' balance sheets (including their home offices and their foreign affiliates) rather than with national borders. Figure 3 (left-hand panel) depicts each consolidated banking systems' foreign claims as a share of its total claims (i.e., including positions vis-à-vis residents of the home country) — a measure of the degree of international orientation in banks' consolidated balance sheets.

Starting with the high bars on the left, banks headquartered in Singapore, Sweden, Switzerland and the United Kingdom stand out as having very internationally-oriented balance sheets, with foreign claims accounting for more than half of their total claims at end-March 2015. At the other end of the spectrum, banks from Korea and Turkey stand out as being essentially domestic. Italian, Japanese and U.S. banks, in turn, are also largely domestically oriented, with foreign claims accounting for less than 25% of their worldwide claims.

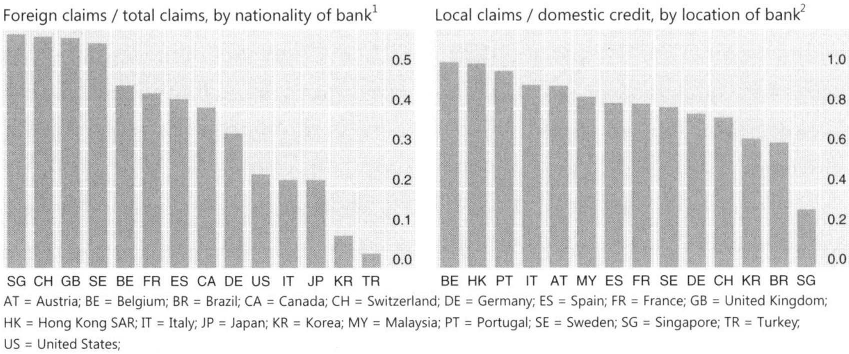

Figure 3. International banking business: At end-March 2015, as a ratio.

Notes: [1]Consolidated claims of CBS reporting banks on an immediate counterparty basis. Foreign claims refer to claims on borrowers outside of banks' home country. Total claims comprise foreign claims plus domestic claims. [2]Local claims on non bank borrowers as a ratio of domestic credit to non-bank borrowers. Local claims refer to claims of LBS reporting banks located in the specified country on residents. Domestic credit refers to credit extended by all deposit-taking institutions located in the specified country to residents.
Source: Avdjiev, McGuire, & Wooldridge (2015), based on BIS CBS; BIS LBS; ECB; IMF International Financial Statistics; national data.

Why does this matter? One reason is that banks with large domestic operations may be less vulnerable to economic or financial difficulties in foreign countries. At the same time, their portfolios may be less diversified, which can affect shock transmission (e.g., Buch, Carstensen, & Schertler (2010)). Similarly, internationally oriented banks are known to have acted as both shock transmitters and shock absorbers in the past (e.g., Cetorelli & Goldberg (2011)).

As an aside, the right-hand panel compares reporting banks' local claims on non-bank borrowers in a given country, as captured in the recently enhanced LBS statistics, to domestic bank credit.[3] This provides a sense of the coverage of the BIS IBS relative to the IMF's domestic debt figures. For most countries, the ratio is below but close to one. In a few

[3]The LBS were recently enhanced to include reporting banks' domestic positions, that is, positions in local currencies vis-à-vis residents of the reporting country. See Avdjiev, McGuire, & Wooldridge (2015) for a discussion of the enhancements to both the LBS and CBS.

cases, however, the ratio exceeds one, because the locational IBS data include some assets not included in IMF domestic debt numbers. In other cases, such as Brazil and Singapore, the ratio is much less than one because the BIS data exclude the assets of banks with little international business. That is, differences across reporting countries in the compilation of the LBS statistics, on which the right-hand panel is based, have a bearing for the interpretation of the data.

3.3. *Differences in Bank Structure*

Yet another perspective is provided by focusing on differences in the booking location of foreign assets and liabilities across different national banking systems. Figure 4 provides such information, highlighting notable differences.

Focusing on foreign assets (left-hand panel), German and Japanese banks emerge as being characterized by a relatively centralized pattern of international activities. That is, a lot of foreign assets are booked via their home offices (lower areas). At the same time, the two banking

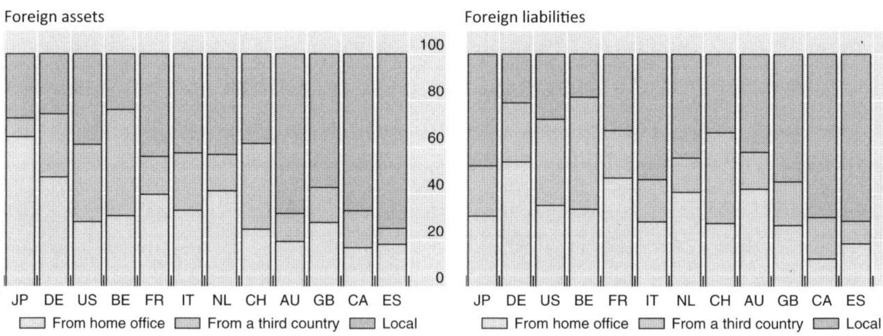

Banks domiciled in: AU = Australia; BE = Belgium; CA = Canada; CH = Switzerland; DE = Germany; ES = Spain; FR = France; GB = United Kingdom; IT = Italy; JP = Japan; NL = Netherlands; US = United States.

Figure 4. Foreign assets and liabilities at end-2013, by booking location[a]: In per cent.

Notes: [a]Cross border, from home office = cross-border positions booked by the lending bank's home office plus estimated cross-border funding of positive net positions vis-à-vis residents of the home country; Cross border, from a third country = cross-border positions booked outside the lending bank's home country; Local = positions booked where the borrower resides.
Sources: BIS CBS (UR and IB basis); BIS LBS by nationality.

systems differ in terms of their reliance on hubs (see Section 3.1 above) for parts of their international activities, with London being an important hub for German banks (center area).

Spanish banks and those from Canada, in turn, are at the other end of the spectrum, reflecting much more locally managed and funded foreign activities (upper areas). Spanish banks, for example, are known to have large presence in Latin America, based on independently operated local subsidiaries (e.g., CGFS (2014a)).

A key implication is that different bank structures will matter in terms of location of the decision making unit and the corresponding importance of internal capital markets (see Appendix). As a result, different bank structures will perform differently in terms of shock transmission and absorption, as suggested by the empirical literature (see Cetorelli & Goldberg (2011, 2012); Ongena, Tümer-Alkan, & Westernhagen (2015)). Local claims booked by banks' foreign affiliates, particularly if funded by local liabilities in local currencies, tended to be more stable than their cross-border claims during the crisis, especially vis-à-vis counterparties in emerging markets (McCauley, McGuire, & von Peter (2012). Thus, those banking systems with a higher share of such positions in their total foreign claims (e.g. Spanish banks) reported much smaller contractions in total claims during the financial crisis.

3.4. *Reduced Maturity Mismatches?*

Foreign currency funding risk turned out to be a major factor in the early stages of the global financial crisis. System-wide problems developed when a large number of financial institutions found themselves in need of U.S. dollars that they had incorrectly assumed could always be obtained directly, via interbank or other such whole sale borrowing, or indirectly via the foreign exchange (FX) swap market.[4] Gauging the extent of cross-currency funding in the system requires data not only on the remaining maturity of assets and liabilities denominated in

[4] See McGuire & von Peter (2012) and Fender & McGuire (2010a) for a more detailed analysis of this U.S. dollar shortage and its origins.

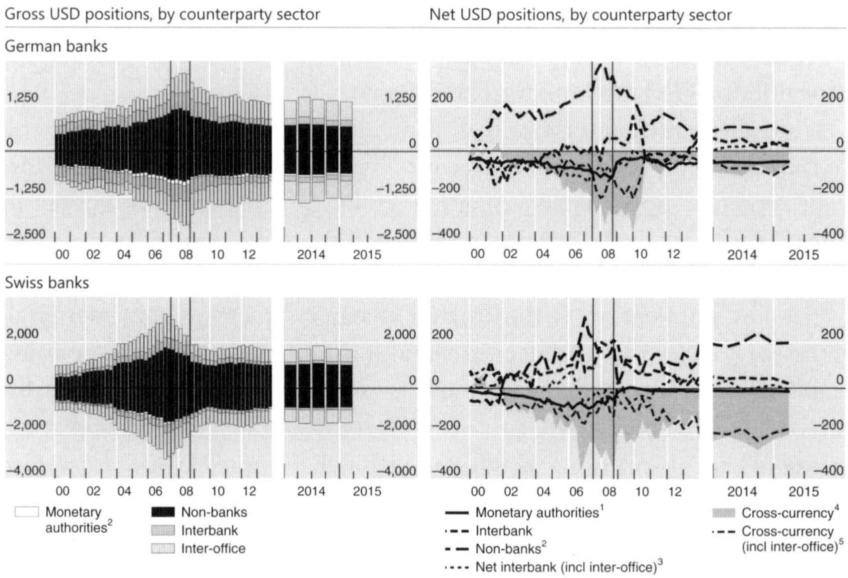

Figure 5. U.S. dollar-denominated foreign positions.

Notes: The vertical lines indicate the 2007 beginning of the global financial crisis and the 2008 collapse of Lehman Brothers. [1]Cross-border positions in all currencies and local positions in foreign currencies vis-à-vis official monetary authorities. [2]Net position vis-à-vis non-banks estimated as the sum of net international claims on non-banks and net local claims on US residents (vis-à-vis all sectors) booked by the US offices of the reporting bank. The "interbank" line tracks the reported positions vis-à-vis unaffiliated banks only. [3]The dashed "interbank" line is an alternative measure of net interbank positions calculated without stripping out inter-office positions. The corresponding alternative estimate of cross-currency positions is also given. [4]Implied cross-currency funding (ie FX swaps) which equates gross US dollar assets and liabilities. [5]Implied reliance on FX swaps which corresponds to the alternative estimate of interbank positions calculated without stripping out inter-office positions.
Sources: BIS CBS (IB basis); BIS LBS by nationality; BIS calculations.

a particular currency, but also information on how and under which conditions these positions translate into measures of short-term funding (or "rollover") needs in that currency.

Such detailed information is difficult to come by, but the BIS IBS can be used to derive a reasonable proxy. Figure 5 develops the relevant information for the consolidated German and Swiss banking sectors (Graphs for UK banks would look broadly similar). It starts with

German and Swiss banks' U.S. dollar book (left-hand panels), highlighting the growth in gross assets and liabilities going into the crisis as well as their subsequent contraction.

It then (right-hand panels) turns to net positions, i.e., claims minus liabilities, differentiated by different counterparty types. The idea is to capture the net amount of short-term U.S. dollar funding that banks must roll over, either via direct interbank borrowing or the FX swap market. For this purpose, banks' claims on non-banks (i.e., their retail and wholesale lending, and holdings of securities) are thought to be their *desired* U.S. dollar-denominated investment portfolio. These exposures are of varying maturities, but, on average, are likely to be longer-term than the funding that supports them (see Table 2).

Now, if *liabilities* to non-banks are all assumed to be long-term, then a lower bound estimate of these banks' overall U.S. dollar funding gap is net interbank borrowing (if positive) plus net borrowing from the FX swap market, which is backed out from the balance sheet identity (gray area in the right-hand panels). To this, any net U.S. dollar borrowing from official monetary authorities would be added (see Table 2). An upper bound estimate would then be given simply by adding gross liabilities vis-à-vis-banks to the lower bound measure, under the assumption that these are short-term liabilities.

Overall, the Graph suggests that these roll-over risks have come down substantially after the crisis — having peaked at a U.S. dollar funding gap for the combined European banking sector of somewhere between $1.1 and 2.3 trillion U.S. dollars in mid-2007, according to BIS estimates (McGuire & von Peter, 2012).

Table 2. Stylised bank balance sheet.

Assets	Liabilities
Claims on non-banks (assumed long-term)	Liabilities vis-à-vis non-banks (short- or long-term)
	Net interbank borrowing (short-term)
	Net borrowing from monetary authorities (short-term)
	Net borrowing via the FX swap market (short-term)

Note: U.S. dollar book (assets and liabilities denominated in U.S. dollars).

3.5. *A Regionalisation Trend*

Another pattern that can be gleaned from the BIS IBS data is that the international expansion of EME banks (i.e., banks headquartered in emerging market economies) has gained considerable momentum since the 2008–2009 financial crisis. This is evident in all EME regions, but particularly in the Asia-Pacific region (Figure 6, left-hand panel). Intra-regional bank lending, in particular, has grown strongly in recent years, offsetting in part a retrenchment by euro area institutions (right-hand panel).[5] But expansion strategies demonstrate a strong regional orientation also outside the area of bank lending, with cross-border merger and acquisition activity among EME banks, for example, predominantly taking place within the same region (see CGFS (2014a)).

The trend towards regional banking described above presents EME authorities with a number of potential benefits, some of which

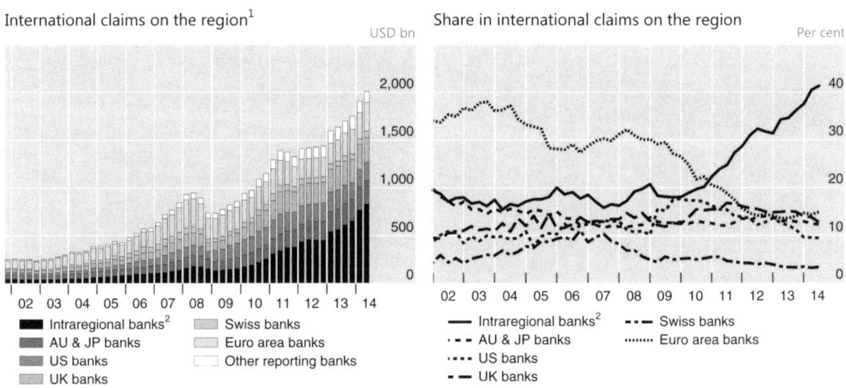

Figure 6. Bank claims on emerging Asia-Pacific.

Notes: [1]Sum of all cross-border claims and locally extended claims in foreign currency. [2]Intraregional share is the sum of international claims on the emerging Asia-Pacific region of banks headquartered in Chinese Taipei, Hong Kong SAR, India, Singapore and the offices of banks located in the region that have a parent institution from a non-BIS reporting country (assuming these are headquartered in Asia).
Source: CGFS (2014a), based on BIS CBS (IB basis).

[5]See McGuire & van Rixtel (2012) for discussion of how the IBS help in tracking regional banking in Asia-Pacific.

resemble, although in a new guise, those that arose during the earlier process of financial integration of EMEs with advanced economies — allocative efficiency, market deepening and regional risk-sharing (see, e.g., Berger, Buch, DeLong, & DeYoung (2004)). Yet, these potential benefits will have to be traded off against potential costs. The flip side of diversification benefits, for example, is greater potential for spillovers at the institutional and system levels (see discussion under Sections 3.2 and 3.3), particularly for EMEs where foreign bank operations account for a relatively large share of host system assets.

3.6. *The Changing Mix of Bank and Bond Finance*

The final pattern to be highlighted in this chapter is one of disintermediation. Recall Figure 1 above, which indicated that international banking has failed to truly recover from the financial crisis. Figure 7 provides a longer-term perspective, based on year-on-year growth rates in international claims across all banking systems covered by the BIS IBS. Based on this metric, international banking is subject to a pattern of pronounced run-ups in growth rates that are followed by subsequent contractions. These, in turn, tend to coincide with periods of more broadly-based

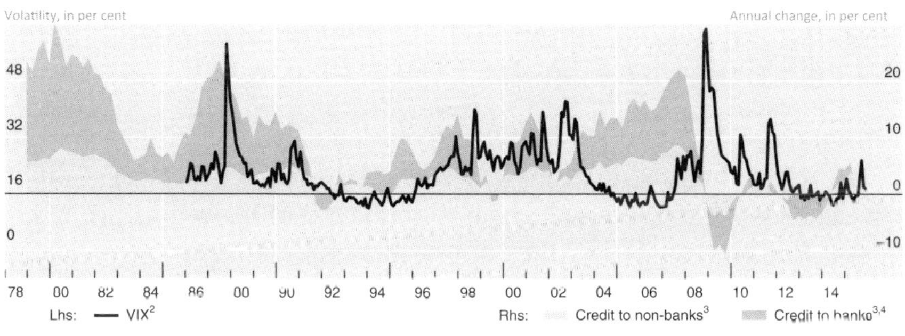

Figure 7. Year-on-year rate of growth in international bank claims.[1]

Notes: [1]LBS reporting banks' cross border claims plus local claims in foreign currencies. [2]VIX refers to the Chicago Board Options Exchange Market Volatility Index. It measures the implied volatility of S&P 500 index options. [3]Contribution to the annual percentage change in credit to all sectors. [4]Including intragroup transactions.
Sources: CGFS (2011), based on Bloomberg data and the BIS LBS.

de-risking, as suggested by abrupt adjustments in market-based measures of risk appetite, such as the VIX index (CGFS (2011) and Domanski, Fender, & McGuire (2011)). The global financial crisis marks the most recent and most violent of these contractions, and post-crisis growth in international bank credit has remained well below its longer-term average.

What does this imply? Mainly that watching banks alone may be misleading. In fact, while international bank lending has been sluggish, bond issuance, particularly U.S. dollar-denominated bonds, by non-bank borrowers, particular in emerging economies, has grown substantially (Chui, Fender, & Sushko (2015); McCauley, McGuire, & Sushko, 2015). As a result, U.S. dollar credit to non-residents has risen to more than $9 trillion, of which about $3 trillion is to EME non-banks (BIS (2015)). That is, the bank-/bond-funding mix is changing, at least for now, and with it transmission channels for international spillovers will change too (Shin, 2014).

4. Prudential Implications?

So far, we have looked at patterns, but what are the implications? In what follows, we will take the various patterns in pairs, discussing their relevant implications in turn.

4.1. *No One-Size-Fits-All!*

Patterns one and two state that international banking is centered on hubs (hosts) and that different (home) banking systems have very different degrees of international orientation. These observations are linked in that foreign banks of various (home) nationalities systems congregate in a few key hub locations. This puts a premium on supervisory activity in those host jurisdictions.

Because the large-scale presence of foreign banks can have a material impact on financial stability in host jurisdictions, supervisors need to understand how these banks are organized and operate within their borders. Each entity (i.e., branches, subsidiaries, and joint ventures) can present unique supervisory challenges and different degrees of reliance on the home supervisory authority. This, in turn, requires tailored approaches for supervisory cooperation between home and host jurisdictions (see Section 4.3) that take different degrees of internationalisation and portfolio diversification into account, for example via supervisory stress tests and corresponding pillar 2 requirements focused on the local (and not only the consolidated) entity level. In short, there is no "one-size-fits-all". In addition, coordination issues may also arise between bank supervisors and prudential authorities in the area of securities markets. Or between banking supervisors, resolution authorities and macro-prudential authorities. This includes cooperation on thorny institutional issues, such as cross-border resolution frameworks, and the question of how reforms in these other areas may affect banking supervision.

4.2. *Funding Patterns*

Next are patterns three and four, which relate to bank structure and roll-over risks, respectively. The common element in both of these observations is that different bank business models can give rise to unique funding patterns and corresponding supervisory challenges. Different bank structures, for example, imply differences in the importance of internal capital markets across banks and banking systems. More centralised structures, in turn, point in the direction of more centralized decision making — a feature that can lead to banks' local operations spreading funding stresses from other geographical regions to that of the home or host jurisdiction.

The risks arising from such spillovers through parent bank–subsidiary relationships have prompted policymakers in various host jurisdictions to require that the local operations of foreign banks be more self-sufficient. Yet, such measures (which sometimes entail full legal subsidiarization) come with important trade-offs (CGFS, 2014a). For instance, even if justified by systemic risk considerations, subsidiarization may hinder the movement of funds among affiliates within the same holding company, while at the same time raising the affiliate's operational costs. Any systemic risk benefits will thus have to be traded off against the risk of deterring foreign bank expansion.

Another example for such regulatory policy trade-offs is requirements for banks to fulfil certain minimum criteria with regard to key balance sheet metrics, such as holding a minimum amount of local deposits (in the form of maximum lending/deposit ratios), as is done in a number of EME banking systems. Such measures may not be feasible in host countries where the domestic deposit base is narrow, due to the effect of intensified competition for deposits on domestic banks' profitability and possible longer-run implications for the stability of retail funding (CGFS, 2014a).

Cross-currency funding mismatches, like those described in Section 3.4 above, raise issues of their own — in particular for the central banks issuing the major reserve currencies for which such mismatches are most likely to arise. A key point is that, in a crisis context (e.g., in case of a freezing-up of interbank markets in major funding currencies, as during 2007–2008), central banks may be required to supply official liquidity in major currencies in an elastic manner to fill "funding gaps" on foreign banks' balance sheets and avoid a disorderly deleveraging (see also the Appendix). Only the currency-issuing central banks have this ability and, consequently, may have to serve as lenders of last resort (Domanski *et al.*, 2011). This is why, during the recent crisis, major central banks opted for a network of ad-hoc swap lines among themselves to supply and on-distribute the necessary U.S. dollar liquidity in a flexible manner. Despite this success, moral hazard concerns imply that such arrangements are likely to remain limited in scope (CGFS, 2011), placing additional emphasis on preventive measures against excessive maturity transformation (such as the Liquidity Coverage Ratio under Basel III) and rules that enhance the resilience of financial institutions more generally (such as the new, higher Basel III capital ratios (Basel Committee on Banking Supervision — BCBS, 2011).

4.3. *New Players/New Targets*

Finally, patterns five and six. The key implication of increased regionalization in prudential terms is that home/host issues are arising for new country pairs. And, increasingly, both countries in the pair are emerging market economies. In addition, in many cases, the target jurisdiction will be a so-called frontier market.

One issue is supervisory capacity. Authorities in frontier markets will have much less experience with international banking than their peers from home economies. They may also face tighter resource constraints, placing a particular onus on effective supervision by home authorities. In this context, concrete risk management guidance for regionally expanding banks is an obvious item for supervisors' list of priorities, including monitoring balance sheet capacity and foreign currency funding (see above). Risk management frameworks need to account for international shocks and linkages between banking systems, and supervisory stress tests need to be designed with such linkages in mind.

Another issue is tools for supervisory cooperation. In this area, supervisory colleges tend to be the instrument of choice, even though modalities continue to differ across jurisdictions.[6] Among the constraints are asymmetries in regulatory powers between country authorities, which can drive a wedge between the ability and willingness to cooperate. In this context, bigger supervisory colleges often lack sufficient focus on regional issues and certain types of sensitive information are difficult to share in a college context. As a result, deepened bilateral relations among supervisors as well as memoranda of understanding (MoUs) are important complements of the college-based approach to cooperation (CGFS, 2014a, 2014b).

Changes in the bank-/bond-funding mix, finally, imply that different players will be key to shaping international spillovers going forward. There are signs, for example, that the composition of bond market investors is changing as markets are growing — with price-sensitive investors becoming more important (witness the $3 trillion of flows into bond funds in 2009–2014). Prudential attention, therefore, may have to shift from banks to players such as asset managers and other so-called shadow banks, where regulatory initiatives have so far lagged those in the area of banking (BIS, 2015).

[6] For guidance in this area, see BCBS (2014).

References

Avdjiev, S., McGuire, P., & Wooldridge, P. (2015) Enhanced data to analyse international banking. *BIS Quarterly Review*, September. Available at: http://www.bis.org/publ/qtrpdf/r_qt1509f.htm.

Bank for International Settlements (2015). 85th *annual report*. June, Basel.

Basel Committee on Banking Supervision (2011). Basel III: A global regulatory framework for more resilient banks and banking systems, revised version, June.

Basel Committee on Banking Supervision (2014). Principles for effective supervisory colleges. June, Basel.

Berger, A., Buch, C., DeLong, G., & DeYoung, R. (2004). Exporting financial institutions management via foreign direct investment mergers and acquisitions. *Journal of International Money and Finance*, *23*, 333–366.

Buch, C., Carstensen, K., & Schertler, A. (2010). Macroeconomic shocks and banks' foreign assets. *Journal of Money, Credit and Banking*, *42*(1), 171–188.

Cetorelli, N., & Goldberg, L. (2011). Global banks and international shock transmission: Evidence from the crisis. *IMF Economic Review*, *59*(1), 41–76.

Cetorelli, N, & Goldberg, L. (2012). Liquidity management of U.S. global banks: Internal capital markets in the great recession. *Journal of International Economics*, *88*(2), 299–311.

CGFS (2011). Global liquidity — concept, measurement and policy implications. *CGFS papers* No. 45, Basel.

CGFS (2012). Improving the BIS international banking statistics. *CGFS papers* No. 47, Basel.

CGFS (2014a). EME banking systems and regional financial integration. *CGFS papers* No. 51, Basel.

CGFS (2014b). Workshops on EME banking systems and regional financial integration. *CGFS papers* No. 51a, Basel.

Chui, M., Fender, I., & Sushko, V. (2014). Risks related to EME corporate balance sheets: The role of leverage and currency mismatch. *BIS Quarterly Review*, September, 35-47.

Domanski, D., Fender, I. & McGuire, P. (2011). Assessing global liquidity. *BIS Quarterly Review*, December. Available at: http://www.bis.org/publ/qtrpdf/r_qt1112g.pdf.

Fender, I. & McGuire, P. (2010a). European banks' US dollar funding pressures. *BIS Quarterly Review*, June. Available at: http://www.bis.org/publ/qtrpdf/r_qt1006h.pdf

Fender, I. & McGuire, P. (2010b). Bank structure, funding risk and the transmission of shocks across countries: Concepts and measurement. *BIS Quarterly Review*, September. Available at: http://www.bis.org/publ/qtrpdf/r_qt1009h.htm.

McCauley, R., McGuire, P. & Sushko, V. (2015). Global dollar credit: Links to US monetary policy and leverage. *Economic Policy*, April, 2015. Also published as *BIS Working Paper* No 483.

McCauley, R., McGuire, P. & von Peter, G. (2012). After the global financial crisis: From international to multinational banking. *Journal of Economics and Business*, *64*(1), 7–23; based on The architecture of global banking: From international to multinational? *BIS Quarterly Review*, March.

McGuire, P. & van Rixtel, A. (2012). Shifting credit patterns in emerging Asia. *BIS Quarterly Review*, December.

McGuire, P. & von Peter, G. (2012). The US dollar shortage in global banking and the international policy response. *International Finance*, June 2012; based on *BIS Working Paper* No. 291 (October 2009) and The US dollar shortage in global banking. *BIS Quarterly Review*, March 2009.

Ongena, S, Tümer-Alkan, G., & Westernhagen, N. (2015). Do exposures to sagging real estate, subprime or conduits abroad lead to contraction and flight to quality in bank lending at home?", *Deutsche Bundesbank Discussion Papers* No. 09/2015, Frankfurt.

Shin, H. (2014). Financial stability risks: Old and new. *Speech delivered at the Brookings Institution*, 4 December, Washington DC.

Appendix A: Why Bank Structure Matters[7]

Large, international banks tend to have offices in many different countries. A key implication of this geographically diverse setup is that interlinkages between individual office locations can matter for how shocks are transmitted from one location (country) to another. In terms of funding risk, *only if* resources available at one office location can immediately be used elsewhere (i.e., if banks' internal transfers of funds are perfectly frictionless) will group-level consolidated data provide an adequate picture of any vulnerabilities. And *even if* internal funds

[7] See Fender & McGuire (2010b) for a more detailed discussion.

transfers are frictionless, knowledge about banks' local balance sheet positions — and how they compare across locations — can convey important information for policymakers on *where* balance sheet adjustments might actually take place in response to any adverse shocks. In turn, this can shed some light on the identity of the borrowers which might ultimately be affected.

To see why this is the case, consider how a hypothetical European bank (TRUST Ltd.), might set up its global operations (Figure A.1). At the group level, the bank is assumed to have $100 billion in exposures to non-banks in a particular economy, say Korea. Suppose that $40 billion of this is booked by TRUST Ltd's home office in the euro area, while $20 billion is booked by each of its local offices in New York, London, and Korea. That is, four different offices of the same global entity lend to non-banks in Korea.

What does this imply? With such a geographically dispersed structure, the *stability* of the credit provided by TRUST Ltd. to its Korean non-bank customers (meaning its willingness or ability to continue to roll over said funds) is inherently tied to the funding structures in each of TRUST's subsidiaries, and these structures are likely to be different. In the example in Figure A.1, the liabilities booked in the euro area

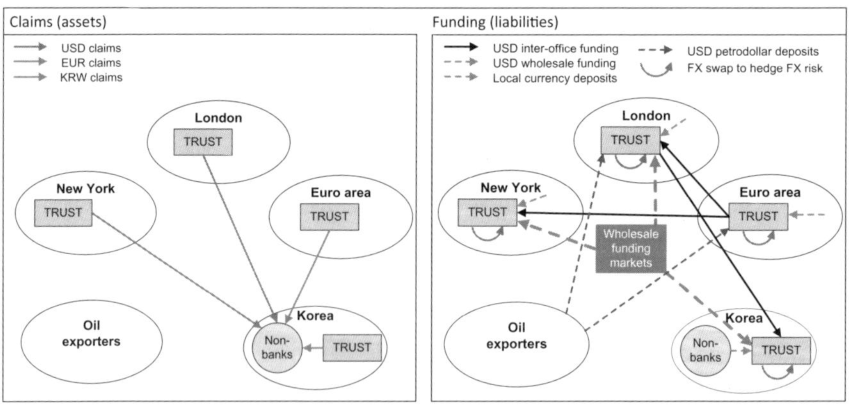

Figure A.1. The structure of TRUST Ltd's global operations.

Note: The ovals depict countries/regions, while the boxes depict offices of TRUST Ltd in each country.

(home) office could be domestic currency deposits which are lent cross-border to non-banks in Korea, or sent to affiliates elsewhere (solid arrows, right-hand panel). At the same time, the lending from the London office could be supported by a combination of wholesale dollar borrowing, petrodollar (or Asian surplus) deposits and the proceeds from swapping interoffice funding in euros with dollars in the foreign exchange (FX) swap market. The positions booked by the New York office, in turn, could be funded with wholesale borrowing and commercial paper issuance, and those booked in Korea could be supported by local currency deposits and interoffice transfers of funds. That is, four different liability structures support the four components on the claim side discussed above.

As a result, when viewed from outside the bank using group-level (globally consolidated) data, stresses at the office location level can be masked, possibly generating a misleading picture of the overall degree of funding risk. Working through a concrete example from the recent crisis helps to clarify this point. Before the crisis, offices of foreign banks (i.e., those headquartered outside the country) in Korea often borrowed U.S. dollars offshore and from their affiliated offices at home, in London or in other financial centres. These dollar funds were then swapped into local currency and invested in local assets in the host country. As a result, the offices of foreign banks located in Korea were net demanders of dollars from offshore wholesale markets and from home offices, and — if their balance sheets were hedged — net providers of dollars to the FX swap market in exchange for local currency. (In terms of Figure A.1, this would amount to TRUST's local office in Korea receiving funds from London and/or the head office, to then swap these into won.) At the same time, these same banks' offices in London, New York and in the home countries were, for example, funding purchases of U.S. dollar securities by borrowing dollars wholesale and by swapping domestic currency deposits into dollars.

In short, in some office locations, these banks were dollar providers to the FX swap market, while in others (e.g., home countries, London) they were U.S. dollar borrowers. In principle, at the group level, banks could thus be net zero in dollar FX swaps. But there would still be potentially significant dollar funding risks across the different office locations. Netting across offices using group level data effectively assumes that the resources in one office can immediately be used elsewhere (i.e., perfectly frictionless internal transfers of funds) — a rather strong assumption.

To see this, consider the following. At the height of the crisis, European banks faced problems borrowing dollars in their home and London offices. What to do? In principle, the Korean office could simply send the dollars it had obtained earlier to cover (part of) the needs of the London office. Yet, in practice, the extent to which this is possible depends on a variety of factors. Think for a second about how the phone conversation between the office manager in London and his colleague in Korea at the height of the crisis might have played out: Our hypothetical Mr. London says, "*We can't roll over our FX swaps! We need dollars to pay back the contracts coming due next Monday! Please send us those dollar funds that you've been borrowing offshore!*" The answer from Ms. Seoul: "*Uh...well...to do that, I have to dump all the local-currency bonds sitting on my balance sheet to unwind the FX swaps used to finance them! And prices of these bonds here are dropping, because all the other foreign banks are doing the same thing!*" That is, depending on the decisions made at head office,[8] locally mismatched positions (even when matched at the consolidated level) can serve as a source of important spillover effects across countries, particularly in an environment where many banks are trying to do the same thing. And, when more than one location is involved, adjustments made in one of these may have implications for the others.

More broadly, frictions in banks' internal funds transfers can include the following. First, host countries' local capital and liquidity

---

[8] See Cetorelli & Goldberg (2011) on the role of internal capital markets in international shock transmission. Here, the real tension is in the ownership structure. When the foreign entity is a branch, the parent may have complete control. Yet, when the foreign entity is a partially owned subsidiary, with its own history, corporate culture and management, it is less clear how much access there is to the subsidiary's funding resources.

requirements may restrict a local office's ability to make significant balance sheet adjustments to support affiliates elsewhere. Second, to the extent that funds transfers involve correspondent banks, these relationships may be disrupted in times of stress. And third, ownership structure may play a role as well — only if the foreign entity is a branch, the parent is likely to have complete control.

Supervision and Regulation: Effects of Global Financial Crisis on Japan and Asia

— CHAPTER 13

■ Takatoshi Ito
Columbia University

1. Asian Financial Crisis vs. Global Financial Crisis

Japan and most Asian countries escaped the large negative impacts of Global Financial Crisis (GFC) on their financial systems. No large financial institutions in Japan or emerging and developing Asia failed during GFC as a result of spillovers from the U.S. or Europe. Unlike the U.S. and Europe, dollar liquidity shortage among financial institutions was limited to a few instances, with a notable exception of Korea. Moreover, as European banks withdrew from Asia by selling their operations and loan portfolios. Japanese and Asian banks bought them from European banks. On balance, Asian banks emerged relatively stronger after the GFC. However, the real side of Asian economies, including Japan, suffered severely through the trade channel. For Asia,

Takatoshi Ito is Professor of International and Public Affairs at Columbia University.

damages to the financial systems and the real side during the crisis of 1997–1998 were much worse than those during the GFC.

Why did the Asian financial sector not suffer in the GFC? First, the Asian countries learned the lesson from the Asian currency crisis, a decade earlier, on the importance of maintaining the banking system strong through proper macro prudential policy. In the wake of the Asian currency crisis, the Asian supervisory authorities became more independent from the government and improved in their analysis. The authorities have warned, and regulated, individual banks for the danger of dollar-denominated, short-term external liabilities. Some countries had adopted Basle II before the GFC, and became much more careful on what kind of risk is associated with foreign assets they purchase. The monetary authorities have accumulated foreign reserves, beyond a sufficient amount by any standard, such as the amount of total external short-term liability. Although depreciation of the currencies occurred, it was mostly manageable in most of Asian countries.

Second, in Japan, the Financial Services Agencies (J-FSA) had established credibility in requiring banks to hold sufficient capital and to avoid any financial products that banks cannot understand. Only two of the Japanese financial institutions had any subprime-related CDOs. J-FSA, established in 1998, is a single, integrated regulator, with strong power backed by legislature including a resolution power. The success of J-FSA can be contrasted to a failure of UK FSA that was blamed for banking failures in London.

As many countries are moving to a model where the central bank is a main bank regulator, J-FSA has become more of an exception. However, the good performance of Japanese financial system, at least in relative to the U.S. and Europe, should lend support to a view that a single, integrated regulator makes a better supervisory framework.

Although the emerging Asia escaped financial problems during GFC, the same degree of resilience is not guaranteed in the future. China will be moving toward domestic financial deregulation and capital account liberalization. Whether China can complete liberalization without major financial turbulences, if not a crisis, remains to be seen.

2. Lessons Learned from the Crises in the Late 1990s

For almost all East and Southeast Asian economies, economic down turn in the wake of the Asian currency crisis, 1997–1998, was deeper than that of the GFC of 2008–2009. Indonesia and Thailand experienced GDP contracting by more than 10%, and Korea, Malaysia and Hong Kong by more than 5% in 1998. They experienced much smaller contraction in 2009. Also, the financial turmoil in 1997–1998 in Asia was unprecedented in the region. Many banks and non-bank financial institutions failed, and some of them liquidated, some merged, and some nationalized.

Bank restructuring was one of the important pillars of a recovery plan. In many Asian countries, the supervisory power was given to and enhanced at the central bank. Almost all central bank realized that the fixed exchange rate was a regime in the past; moved to managed float and regulated the banks with a keen realization that capital flows can be volatile.

The bank supervision framework that was built in Asia contributed to relatively minor damage from GFC. Even before GFC, Asian countries were eager to adopt Basle II, and employed many precautionary measure that are now regarded as macro-Prudential regulations.

Since double mismatch — maturity mismatch and currency mismatch — was a single most problem for Asian banks back in 1997, regulatory measures against restricting short-term, foreign-currency denominated debts were popular in Asia. Also, the foreign reserves were intentionally piled up after 2000. This also contributed to building resilience against sudden capital outflows in the wake of GFC.

3. Japan's FSA

The credibility of Ministry of Finance as the financial regulator was completely shuttered in the banking crisis of 1997–1998, which by coincidence was at the same time with Asian financial crisis. Four large financial institutions — three banks in top 20 and one securities firm among the big 4 — failed in the period of 13 months. Surviving Japanese banks were also shut out from foreign businesses as foreign banks questioned the viability of Japanese banks. Japan needed quickly inject public assistance — which was done in two rounds — to banks' capital and revamp the supervisory framework. The cozy relationship between the regulator and the regulated was blamed for the failure in preventing a major banking crisis.

The Japanese government, with strong pressure from the legislature and the public opinion, decided to carve out the financial supervisory power from the Ministry of Finance and created FSA (originally, Financial Supervisory Agency; later renamed as Financial Services Agency; but the same acronym) as a single, integrated regulator. It regulates all financial institutions and all financial products. It is in charge of both micro- and macro-prudential policy in Japan. There is no overlapping or underlapping problem of supervision, which was a part of the reasons why regulations and supervision failed to prevent banks from extending subprime loans in the U.S. and distributing and marketing CDOs in the U.S. and Europe.

The J-FSA has a power to orchestrate an orderly resolution of (near) insolvent bank, in cooperation with Prime Minister and Japan's Deposit Insurance Corporation (JDIC). Article 102–1, items 1, 2, and 3, of the JDIC Act defines how a bank can be closed, merged or nationalized under different circumstances — see Hoshi and Ito (2004). The financial emergency meeting that triggers this clause is chaired by Prime Minister. This was tested in 2003, when Resona Bank was *de facto* nationalized after deemed insufficiently capitalized. In the same year, the Ashikaga Bank was determined to be insolvent and failed (and later sold to the investors). These decisive actions of orderly resolution put to an end to the banking fragility that had continued for a decade, and banks raised capital by various measures.

The J-FSA is also endowed with the power to bail in creditors in JDIC Act, Article 126–2. Hence, this is in accordance with discussions in Financial Stability Board (FSB). This article has not been tested in Japan.

J-FSA and the Bank of Japan cooperate in on-site visits and micro prudential regulation. J-FSA, and not the Bank of Japan, has a sanction power. When new financial products are created, it is automatically under the jurisdiction of J-FSA. A prevailing view in Japan is that J-FSA is functioning well in designing and implementing rules and regulations and independent from political pressure or meddling.

Globally, the FSA model as a single, integrated financial regulator, like Japan is a minority. Reviewing the history of the Japanese FSA, an advantage of having a single integrated regulators seems to be compelling. When a central bank is in charge of financial supervision, the regulated is often limited to banks. Brokerage firms, insurance firms, non-banks that offer financial products are outside the central bank's supervision. This creates a room for future crisis originating from a non-bank sector or shadow banking.

Then should Asian countries switched to the FSA model? Critics of the FSA model may argue that the FSA model would say that if the FSA is a part of the government, like in Japan, the regulator may be subject to political pressure. However, the central bank may be subject to political pressure too. The central bank may suffer from the conflict of interest between the monetary policy wing and the supervision wing, if the interest rate hike may weaken some particular banks. So, there is no perfect solution and Asian emerging market countries have to struggle to find the best framework for themselves.

References

Hoshi, T. & Ito, T. (2004). Financial regulation in Japan: A sixth year review of the Financial Services Agency, *Journal of Financial Stability*, *1*(2), 229–243.

The Future of Large, Internationally Active Banks: Implications for Supervision and Regulation

— CHAPTER 14

▪ Anil K. Kashyap
University of Chicago

1. Introduction

To reach some implications for supervision and regulation I will focus on three questions. First, I will reflect on competing views about the origins of the crisis. Next, I will selectively review the progress that has been made addressing these known vulnerabilities. I will close with a few suggestions that might make the system more robust. In the interest of time, I will mostly focus on the U.S.

2. Crisis Diagnosis

There are broadly three different views of the critical factors that were responsible for the global financial crisis. One is that it was all about

Anil Kashyap is the Edward Eagle Brown Professor of Economics and Finance at the University of Chicago Booth School of Business. These are remarks presented at the Chicago Federal Reserve Bank of Chicago's International Banking Conference; November 5, 2015.

excessive leverage. I find it helpful to differentiate two types of potential leverage problems. One of these supposes that some entities operating with thin capital levels had underestimated the risks they were exposed to. In this case, it was not that they were necessarily counting on getting bailed out or consciously trying to operate with excessive leverage. It just turned out that they were seriously undercapitalized once the crisis became evident.

An alternative, that was often referred while Dodd–Frank legislation was being discussed, is that many firms were taking excessive risks and planning on getting bailed out if their bets turned out badly. In other words, there was a huge moral hazard problem.

I am skeptical of the moral hazard story actually. Jimmy Cayne and Dick Fuld, the CEOs of Bear Stearns and Lehman Brothers respectively, personally lost hundreds of millions of dollars of their own wealth. Economists often write down models where you have an entrepreneur who owns and operates a business. That simplification is rarely accurate for modern corporations except for Bear Stearns and Lehman! The managements at these firms really did have huge pensions that were at risk and a substantial part of their own wealth that was blown up when the firms failed.

If the lesson from the crisis is you have to first lose a billion dollars of your own money before you get bailed out, I do not think many people are going to find that attractive. So I am not sympathetic to that view.

What I am quite sympathetic to is the view that there was excessive opaque liquidity creation that was going on outside of the channels that we understood well. This is the third story of the crisis.

Let me briefly remind you of the six runs that happened in the crisis. I bother to list each of them as a way of concretely illustrating some problems that are (ex-post) understood. It seems like a minimum way to judge progress by asking whether we can avoid these same problems in the future. The first run came in the asset-backed commercial paper market in the fall of 2007. The Federal Reserve Board staff was on that almost instantly. If you read Ben Bernanke's memoir (Bernanke (2015)) he has a long section on the collapse of the ABCP market and how concerned they were. There was a $400 billion funding source that evaporated in basically five months.

The next three runs were peculiar to Bear Stearns and Lehman (and other non-bank broker–dealers). It is instructive to realize that when Bear Stearns failed the concern inside the Federal Reserve was all about what would happen to the tri-party repo market if Bear went under. Bernanke's book also has a long discussion confirming this concern. He is just one of several Fed officials who have now said the reason we had to save Bear was because had that firm failed, the tri-party repo market would have shut down and that in the following week Merrill, Lehman, Goldman and Morgan Stanley would have all been gone (because they were all highly dependent on that market for their funding). We do know that they were all rolling over 10s of billions of dollars of funding each day.

I find the officials account and rationale pretty compelling. For instance, Bear was so tainted that, on its last day of life, could not repo its Treasury securities. Then there are two other vulnerabilities that Darrell Duffie (Duffie, 2010) has talked a lot about, which were the hidden ways in which broker dealers received funding through their clients. One was by failing to post as much collateral as they would need to on derivatives transactions. This deficit means that when you get concerned about the viability of your counterparty and step back, they then have to close out the position. They do not have the full margin in place so closing out requires them to come up with margin quickly and that bleeds out some funding.

The prime brokerage arrangements are another vulnerability. Darrell points out that Morgan Stanley lost $80 billion dollars of funding in the week after Lehman. How? Because their clients stopped wanting to transact with them. As a result, they were forced to come up with funding that they had been receiving by lending their clients securities, and that drain put intense pressure on Morgan Stanley, and to some extent Goldman Sachs as well.

The fifth run was the money market mutual funds. This is well-studied and I will talk in detail about this in a moment.

Then finally there was the run on Target2, which is the payment system inside the Eurosystem. In this case the cause was that many counterparties wanted to reduce their exposure to peripheral country banks. As an interesting side note in history, the people that designed the Euro payment system studied the Great Depression. And in the Great Depression one of the things that happened, as hopefully you know, is that France and the U.S. hoarded their gold supplies. The way that the 1930s payment system should have re-equilibrated was with gold flowing away from France and the U.S., which would have then increased the money supply in countries to which the gold would have flowed. That would have helped prevent deflation. When France and the U.S. hoarded gold, the other countries had to essentially deflate faster than the U.S. and France to prevent gold outflows, and that was one of the big transmission channels of the Great Depression.

The designers of the payment system in the euro area anticipated the possibility that if banks in some country got into trouble banks in another country might try to cut off lending to them. So Target2 does not permit that. Instead the euro area payment system works with national central banks as counterparties with each other and the domestic banks in each country exposed only to their own central banks. And so the Greek banks can keep getting credit even if it turns out that the counterparties in another country (say Germany) do not want to fund them. In the interim, say the Bundesbank and the National Bank of Greece run up a big payment imbalance, where the Greeks owe the Germans money.

This deficit is just accounting entry in normal times with no significance. But in the event of an exit, there would be a hole that would have to be filled and there have been times over the last couple of years when those balances got quite large. So these are the six runs.

3. Implications for Regulation

Now, the immediate thing to notice is none of this is about the topic of this conference. These are all examples of shadow banking — except maybe the Target payment system. So the rest of my remarks are going to be largely focusing on shadow banking.

One big problem with shadow banking is it arises as mostly because of regulatory arbitrage. Given that national regulations are so different to start with, the way you arbitrage them differs in each jurisdiction. So we do not have a single method for regulatory arbitrage because you have to know what the rules are in Canada to recognize what is going on there, and they are different than what is happening in the U.K. and or the U.S. and so on.

So that makes it very, very difficult to monitor and control risks in the shadow banking system. One of the things that Governor Tarullo said in his keynote address that I completely agree with is you can not paint with just a broad brush and say shadow banking is one thing. It is a very different set of things in different countries.

Some people will argue that in the end, when the shadow banking system collapses the debris always blows back into the banking system. So, if you just have big enough capital buffers in the banking system that might be enough to control it. I am skeptical of this view.

We have almost ran that experiment in the United States; I mean we did not have many large banks that failed in the U.S. (except for perhaps Washington Mutual) and yet the U.S. economy burned down as the shadow banking system imploded. And so I think this idea that you can just ring fence the banking system to create a bunch of utility banks that are so safe that even if the casino catches on fire, it would not spread, is pretty doubtful.

What has been the regulatory response to those six runs? Well, asset-backed commercial paper for better or worse is largely gone, so we do not really have to worry about that. Regarding repo — I think there is kind of a mixed report card. The Federal Reserve Bank of New York has spent a lot of energy, trying to clamp down on the amount of intra-day credit that is extended by the clearing banks in the tri-party repo market. At the same time, there are still some challenges that remain.

One alternative to repo markets is to increase the use of centralized clearing. That brings other challenges. Can you have a money market fund be a clearing member? Probably not. What happens if the centralized counterparty itself needs liquidity support? What happens if a clearing bank fails? All of those questions suggest that trying to move away from the repo structure that we had before the crisis is not as easily dealt with as you might think. For just straight clearing of derivatives, what happens if a CCP fails? Probably a very remote possibility but as far as I can tell, nobody in U.S. is working on this.

Prime brokerage is still a real problem. It is just too tempting to lend the securities of your customers and get your funding that way. And so as a result, if concerns surface about the viability of any big broker, some clients will run away from that broker. The funding loss in that case will be big and there's no amount of capital that's going to solve that; if you are going to lose $80 billion of funding in a week, I doubt we are not going to mandate that you have an extra $80 billion in capital to deal with that contingency.

I view the money market reforms as still incomplete. I will offer a little case study on that, because I think it can show the challenges that lie ahead in enacting further reforms.

Finally, what about Target2? If you get rid of the redenomination risks, that problem goes away. I do not see those risks disappearing until the Greek economy is finally back on its feet. So I do not think we can finish that story yet.

Reigning in shadow banking will be hard. We now have thousands of MBAs and PhDs who spend all their time trying to figure out how to get around both old and new rules. So the regulators are always passing rules and then trying to figure out what the private sector is doing to evade them. Once you figure that out, you try and clamp down on that and by then they have figured out another strategy. I think it is a very big problem, but we have to try to do something about it.

The U.S. is probably the worst case, because we have this insane crazy quilt fragmentation in our regulatory system. If the global financial crisis is not enough to get us to consolidate regulation, nothing ever will. The fact that the fragmentation remains contributes to some of the problem.

So let us just look at money market mutual reform to get kind of a gloomy assessment of how hard this will be. There was a run on the money funds in the week right after Lehman failed. The possibility of a run was well understood, and the run itself was highly visible. It frustrates most observers outside the U.S. that this problem was not attended to well before the crisis.

So you might have thought that afterwards we would at least finally fix the problem. The economics here is simple. A money market fund is a bank with no capital. The lack of capital is rationalized on the grounds that the funds can only invest in "really safe" assets. Safety, however, is couched in terms of default risk. Unfortunately many of the assets are terribly illiquid. Who can give you a price for 32-day commercial paper? No one knows what the price is because there is no active market for this kind of security.

The accounting rules allow the funds to mark down prices for assets which never trade and say we're just fine. Of course, then comes the day when you need to get the money and you discover you cannot sell many of the underlying assets or can only sell at a very deep discount. So I think any reasonable attempt to deal with this problem would have to put on some capital requirements. If you have been following this case, you will know that did not happen.

Instead, the industry was able to say that imposing capital requirements would have led to the end of the industry. Ironically, saying that the industry would not be viable is considered compelling. No one asks why an industry exists which cannot capitalize itself. The answer is, of course, because the industry was created as a form of regulatory arbitrage. This industry allowed people to receive interest payments that would have violated interest ceilings that banks used to face. So the whole industry developed around avoiding those rules and the regulators just got tired of fighting about this at some point. So we are left hoping that floating net asset values will prevent future runs.

I think the best lesson from this is that the Financial Stability Oversight Council (FSOC) has been tested once and it failed miserably. Everybody else except the primary regulator (the SEC) wanted to do something about this. The primary regulator did not want to do something about it and the FSOC wound up with a relatively weak remedy. Let us hope that this does not blow up on us.

4. Recommendations

All right, so that is my gloomy assessment. What can be done? I offer three modest suggestions. The first is everybody should read Kohn (2014). Besides being a former Vice Chair of the Fed, Don also serves on the U.K. Financial Policy Committee, which was formed as the British answer to preventing another crisis. He offered a long and thoughtful discussion of what he learned thinking about how participating in the FPC has taught him about the appropriate structure of the FSOC and the FSOC's responsibilities.

One of the things he points out is a huge problem in the United States is the fact that some of the regulators say paying attention to financial stability is not my job. Bernanke (2015) offers a number of big differences of opinion between the Fed and the FDIC about what to do at various points during the crisis. In essence, the FDIC would always, in the end, default to saying that our statutory obligation is to minimize the taxpayer cost of all its immediate decisions. It does not matter if I throw the economy under the bus and back it up two times over the economy, that is all okay, as long as I minimize cost. Well, sometimes in these disputes the Fed prevailed, but other times it did not.

The SEC is another problem. The SEC was supposed to be supervising the broker dealers. They failed in this task. Recall that Christopher Cox (the then chair of the SEC) said two days before Bear failed that he had good confidence in them. He was not even on the conference call when they made the decision to save Bear. That is how valuable his information was.

So I think we should start by saying that there ought to be a systemic risk overlay for every regulator in the United States, so that nobody can hide behind the excuse that my mandate does not involve worrying about systemic threats. I do not know if that would change behavior but it would be a first step.

I think we should also insist that the FSOC has somebody that spends all their time thinking about financial stability. The Secretary of the Treasury is just too busy. Tim Geithner was more interested in this than his successor, but it would be better to make sure someone is always charged with worrying about these problems. I think there would be strong incentives from knowing that you are going to be the person mentioned as being asleep in every economics textbook if another crisis occurs. Right now the responsibility is too diffused.

I also believe you should arm the reformed FSOC with a dedicated independent staff by spinning out the Office of Financial Research from the Treasury.

Finally, I would love to see a Basel committee on shadow banking. It wll take years to implement, but part of the reason why we are clamping down so hard on the banks is because we have the machinery to do it. Everybody knows where to go, you have this regulatory structure in place and many committees are working hard. And so, it is natural to focus your attention there.

If you actually had a super structure that was all about shadow banking, it would be a mongrel beast. In some countries you would have the insurance people coming, in other cases you would have securities markets regulators and you probably also have some bank supervisors too. These are not groups that normally meet and coordinate their actions, so it will take time to get them working well. I fear, however, that without the bureaucracy in place we will never get started on this. I realize that the Financial Stability Board is doing a bit, but we need more effort on this.

References

Bernanke, Ben S. (2015). *The courage to act: The memoir of a crisis and its aftermath*, New York: Norton.

Duffie, D. (2010). *How big banks fail: And what to do about it*, Princeton: Princeton University Press.

Kohn, D. S. (2014). Institutions for macroprudential regulation: The UK and the U.S. *Speech at the Kennedy School of Government*, April 17, 2014.

Part V
Risk Management

At a Crossroad? Regulatory Capital and Operational Risk

— Chapter 15

▪ Dietmar Serbee and Michael Alix
PricewaterhouseCoopers

1. Introduction

Basing operational risk regulatory capital requirements on banks' internal measurements seemed perfectly logical. Under the Advanced Measurement Approach (AMA) established by the *Basel II capital accord of 2003*, large financial institutions were required to measure their operational risk regulatory capital using advanced models that were sensitive to the quality of risk management and tailored to the institution's risk profile. As the adage goes, what gets measured, gets done; therefore, the approach was expected to result both in improved operational risk management and lower capital levels. Yet, 12 years on, the effort to link operational risk regulatory capital to operational risk management via the AMA seems to have reached an impasse. Financial institutions and regulators are indeed frustrated. What happened, and what is a possible path forward?

Financial institutions originally faced two main challenges in fully implementing the AMA envisioned by the Basel Committee: a data

This article originally appeared in the Q2 2015 edition of *Banking Perspective*, the quarterly journal of The Clearing House (theclearinghouse.org/publications/banking-perspective). It is reprinted with permission with minor alternations in referencing style.

challenge and a modeling challenge. On the one hand, the AMA requires data inputs (internal and external loss event data, scenario analysis, as well as business environment indicators and internal control factors) which financial institutions needed to collect in a comprehensive way. On the other hand, the Basel Committee provided only high-level guidance on AMA-compliant regulatory capital models, leaving the door open to a lengthy discovery process which showed that building such models was more resource-intensive, assumption-laden, and complex than originally assumed.

As banks were enhancing capabilities on both fronts, the aftermath of the financial crisis added a third challenge regarding the AMA's credibility. Its qualitative components failed to help institutions anticipate the operational risk failures that contributed to the crisis or occurred in its wake — e.g., issues with mortgage underwriting practices or with the collection of non-performing loans. Meanwhile operational risk regulatory capital proved insufficient to cover unprecedented government agency fines and settlements. To boot, once realized, these historical losses left many financial institutions with modeled operational risk capital figures which, they claim, are outsized relative to their true risk profile going forward.

Statistical loss distribution approaches, which are the predominant AMA mechanism in the U.S., carry much of the blame for this impasse. Their reliance on historical-event data makes them by definition backward-looking. Once a significant loss enters into an institution's data set, theoretical capital numbers could rise significantly and permanently unless institutions are allowed to somehow mitigate the impact of such loss events on their regulatory capital calculations. Many banks argue that, without adjustments, the burden of expensive, past losses lingers on in their capital numbers long after the causes of those losses have been remediated. Moreover, there seems to be little they can do to directly manage their AMA operational risk regulatory capital number, e.g., by investing in governance, infrastructure, or controls, or leaving a risky business entirely. This could create pernicious incentives and discourage investments intended to strengthen control environments.

Regulators, for their part, have been very cautious about adjustments to model inputs, likely for two reasons. First, fixing a set of specific control issues to address the causes of past losses doesn't mean that there won't be new losses elsewhere. For example, addressing equity research analyst conflicts years ago did not prevent more recent compliance failures in mortgage foreclosures. Thus, to regulators, maintaining substantial regulatory capital buffers for operational risk could be a way to strengthen the industry's resilience to the unexpected source of the next crisis.

Second, loss distribution-based models require many assumptions and choices with respect to modeling approach. Disparate practices are common when it comes to model data inputs, assumptions, and modeling choices generally. Such variations matter greatly because similar data sets can be modeled in very different ways and yield significantly different regulatory capital figures. This decreases comparability and transparency of calculated regulatory capital across institutions, and invites caution — particularly if the models suggest a decrease in required operational risk regulatory capital.

Incidentally, many bank management teams are skeptical of loss distribution-derived capital figures as well: the model outputs do not resonate because the input data is inconsistent and modeling choices are often not driven by practical management needs. Unlike for, say, credit models, there often seems to be no clean narrative to describe what is happening in operational risk models. As a result, many operational risk managers will admit that their institutions have benefited more from gathering and analyzing capital model inputs (such as loss event data, or operational risk and control self-assessments) than from modeling them. The inputs give management better insight into the bank's current risk exposures, which allows for better risk management.

For all these reasons, it is tempting to think that fixing the AMA — or replacing it with another approach entirely — could possibly save the linkage that the Basel Committee intended between operational risk regulatory capital and the quality of operational risk management. In fact, in October 2014 the Basel Committee proposed a New Standardized Approach to replace Basel II's original (and computationally simple) Standardized Approach and Basic Indicator Approach. The New Standardized Approach achieves greater comparability among firms. It is also far less computationally intensive and more transparent because its inputs are readily available for most banks today (see PwC's regulatory brief: *Operational Risk Capital: Nowhere to Hide*). If admitted for use in the U.S., a version of this New Standardized Approach could become an alternative to the AMA, even for large U.S. institutions, as long as it enables institutions to more directly link improvements in the control environment to their capital numbers.

Indeed, the New Standardized Approach is more likely than not to become part of the U.S. regulatory framework. After all, U.S. regulators have signaled their general unease with internal capital models and have been moving in the direction of greater comparability in the context of credit and market risk as well. At a minimum, the New Standardized Approach will serve as a calibration tool, or even establish an easily observable "floor" for operational risk regulatory capital within individual institutions.

And therein lies the problem: most institutions would actually experience an increase in operational risk regulatory capital under the New Standardized Approach, at least as currently proposed. Figure 1 shows that for a sample of 29 of the largest global banks, operational risk capital would be considerably higher under the New Standardized Approach than under Basel II's Basic Indicator Approach. (*A meaningful direct comparison between the New Standardized Approach and Basel II's AMA is not yet possible, given the scarcity of public information on AMA-derived capital requirements for individual institutions. The graphic is based on the banks' public information as of*

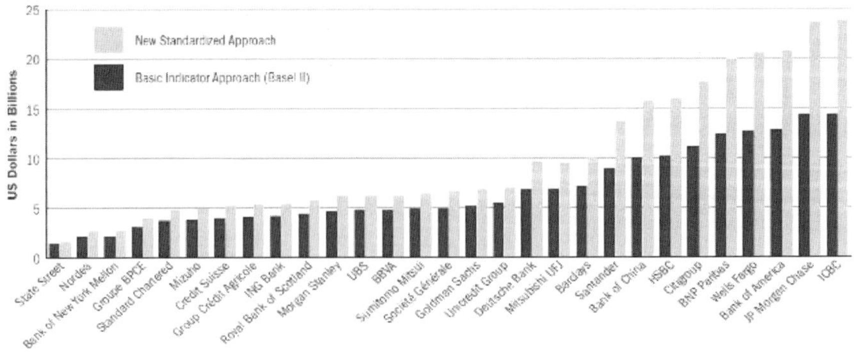

Figure 1. Operational risk regulatory capital: Upward pressure

December 31, 2014 (with the exceptions of Mizuho, Sumitomo Mitsui, Unicredit Group, and Mitsubishi UFJ, which are based on data as of March 31, 2014).)

Since the AMA is based on internal models that are presumably more precise than the Basic Indicator Approach (and calibrated to produce lower capital numbers), it is reasonable to assume that the New Standardized Approach is likely to place upward pressure on capital for AMA institutions as well. In addition, the New Standardized Approach, as proposed, still does not reward banks for improving their control environment, all other things equal. For banks this could mean double jeopardy: higher capital, and still no way of aligning capital with their real operational risk profile.

Regardless of the path taken by regulators, this impasse should not distract the industry from pressing forward with efforts to better measure and manage operational risks. This will require three important shifts in focus by financial institutions.

First, regulators may require banks to hold operational risk regulatory capital that exceeds a bank's own internal calculations. Too often, arguing that regulatory capital should be lower has proven to be a time consuming battle that distracts from the real prize of better long-term management outcomes. In other words, the primary benefit of good operational risk measurement is not lower regulatory capital requirements, but an improved understanding of risk exposures and management. To improve returns on regulatory capital, firms will be better off by redeploying their analytic resources toward better identifying and managing risks, thereby reducing future operational losses. Differentiation among firms' operational risk management prowess will come in the form of better long-term performance.

Second, banks should continue to improve operational risk analytics and gain further insight into the behavior of operational risks under stress. In doing so, institutions should emphasize forward-looking tools such as scenario development, analysis of the underlying factors that drive operational risk exposures, and careful consideration of how much predictive information their backward-looking data truly possess. The industry is doing promising work in factor-based models, which quantify operational risk at the process and product level based on underlying risk drivers. Such models do not fit into the current regulatory capital framework, although they could yield considerable benefits from a management perspective. They are intended to be highly sensitive to increases and decreases in the level of risk of the business, and enable a more granular alignment of risk and performance measures than is typically possible with loss distribution-derived models. A misguided focus on regulatory capital could hamper investments to drive progress in this area.

Third, banks should leverage their new insights, and direct more operational risk resources to help inform business decisions. Too often, the emphasis on operational regulatory capital requirements and on the production of inputs to capital models has left operational risk managers with little time to mine their data for insights that are true value-adds to the business. In many banks, operational risk managers need to shift their attention to engaging business leaders into strategic conversations regarding the operational risks to which they are exposed, and how to manage and effectively mitigate that risk. Such a shift is cultural in nature. It may take time, and will require operational risk managers to enhance their current skill sets, but it should help firms position themselves favorably in light of regulators' heightened expectations with respect to risk management.

The current regulatory framework in the U.S. has drawn the immediate attention of many banks to the misalignment between their operational risk regulatory capital and their true risk profile. A perfect solution is not on the horizon, and far-reaching changes are needed in the regulatory regime to eventually achieve an equilibrium banks and regulators can live with. For the time being, banks that strategically focus their operational risk management efforts on better long-term management of outcomes will have a competitive advantage over peers who continue to focus solely on achieving lower regulatory capital levels.

The Transmission of Bank Default Risk During the Global Financial Crisis

— CHAPTER 16

- Deniz Anginer
  Virginia Tech and World Bank
- Eugenio Cerutti
  International Monetary Fund
- Maria Soledad Martinez Peria
  International Monetary Fund

1. Introduction

Foreign banks have markedly increased their participation in emerging markets in recent decades, raising questions about their potentially stabilizing or destabilizing role during times of financial distress.

Pedro Juarros provided excellent research assistance. This chapter's findings, interpretations, and conclusions are entirely those of the authors and do not necessarily represent the views of the World Bank, the International Monetary Fund, their Executive Directors, or the countries they represent. Anginer is Assistant Professor of Finance at the Department of Finance, Pamplin College of Business, Virginia Tech. Prior to that he was Financial Economist in the Development Research Group at the World Bank. Cerutti is currently the Assistant to the Director at the Research Department of the IMF. Martinez Peria is Division Chief of the Macro Financial Division in the IMF Research Department and is currently on leave from her position as Research Manager, Finance and Private Sector Development, Development Research Group at the World Bank.

The recent global financial crisis offered a unique event to analyze the role that foreign banks can play in the transmission of shocks.

A significant literature, including studies before the crisis, offers evidence consistent with the notion that foreign banks can indeed transmit shocks. Most of these studies focus on how shocks to parent banks lead foreign bank subsidiaries to reduce the loans they make. For example, Peek & Rosengren (2000) analyze the behavior of Japanese banks operating in the U.S. during the 1990s Japanese crisis. Schnabl (2012) studies the lending behavior of foreign bank affiliates in Peru in the aftermath of the 1998 Russian crisis. In the context of the recent global financial crisis, Claessens & van Horen (2013), Choi, Martinez Peria, & Gutierrez (2013), and De Haas & van Horen (2013), among others, show that foreign bank lending across countries declined more than domestic bank lending during the period 2008–2009.

An unexplored but potentially important channel for how foreign banks can transmit shocks to their hosts relates to the correlation in default risk between global banks and their subsidiaries. This is an important channel because default risk — i.e., the likelihood that a bank fails and is not be able to meet its debt obligations — is arguably the ultimate risk that matters for banking stability and the risk that supervisors are likely to care about the most. Default risk negatively affects bank creditors and borrowers, since a bank that fails cannot pay depositors or honor its loan commitments. Similarly, bank failures can have significant implications for governments that have to shoulder the cost of paying insured depositors if a bank fails or of recapitalizing the bank if it is deemed too large to fail.

There are multiple reasons why the correlation between the default risk of parent banks and their foreign subsidiaries could be positive. First, because global banks have internal capital markets that allow them to "move" capital and liquidity across their offices, we would expect that when the default risk of a parent rises, in order to cover the losses and meet regulatory capital requirements at home, the global bank might channel funds and capital from its subsidiaries and, in the process, weaken the financial health of subsidiaries, causing their default risk to rise. Second, when the parent bank faces a shock, the perception that the subsidiaries no longer could obtain support from the parent if it were needed (i.e., the loss of the implicit guarantees) could lead to a drop in the market value of the subsidiaries and a corresponding rise in their default risk. Third, the default risk of a parent and that of its subsidiaries might be correlated, if these institutions share a common business model or focus and are exposed to similar shocks.

In this chapter, we conduct a preliminary exploration of the correlation between the default risk of global banks and their subsidiaries and offer some suggestive evidence of the factors that could amplify or dampen this correlation. We use two measures of default risk constructed on the basis of two samples of banks. First, for 93 publicly listed foreign bank subsidiaries, operating in 36 host developing countries and owned by 41% bank groups from 24 home countries, during the period from September 2008 to December 2009, we construct the distance to default measure based on Merton's (1974) structural credit risk model. This is the difference between the market asset value of the bank and the face value of its debt, scaled by the standard deviation of the bank's asset value. Hence, distance to default is inversely related to default risk. Second, following Falkenheim & Pennachi (2003), we calculate a 'synthetic' distance to default measure which can be computed for listed and non-listed foreign subsidiaries. In this case, the sample includes 175 subsidiaries in 33 host countries, owned by 94 parent banks from 44 home countries. Both measures of distance to default focus exclusively on the activities of subsidiaries in developing countries.[1] These countries were not at the core of the global financial crisis, allowing us to better identify factors that might help insulate affiliates from their parents potentially in trouble.

Our analysis shows that the correlation between the distance to default of foreign banks subsidiaries and that of their parents is significant whether we focus on publicly listed foreign banks or on both listed and non-listed foreign affiliates. Moreover, we show that this correlation is not sensitive to the sample of foreign parents considered. Also, we provide some suggestive evidence that certain bank characteristics and host regulations can affect the size of this correlation.

---

[1] Table 1 shows the number of subsidiaries and hosts countries and Table 2 reports the number of parents and home countries in our sample.

Table 1. Count of foreign bank subsidiaries across host countries in our sample.

Host Country	Number of Subsidiaries Included in the Merton Distance to Default Calculation	Number of Subsidiaries in the Synthetic Distance to Default Calculation
ARGENTINA	3	9
BARBADOS	1	3
BOTSWANA	2	3
BRAZIL	3	11
BULGARIA	1	8
CHILE	4	0
CHINA	6	6
COLOMBIA	2	2
CROATIA	2	5
CZECH REPUBLIC	1	10
EGYPT	4	7
GHANA	1	1
HONG KONG	5	11
INDIA	1	2
INDONESIA	5	9
IVORY COAST	2	3
JAMAICA	1	2
KENYA	2	2
MACEDONIA FYROM	2	3
MALAYSIA	2	0
MALTA	2	3
MOROCCO	4	1
PAKISTAN	5	5
PERU	2	5
POLAND	8	11
ROMANIA	1	9
RUSSIAN FEDERATION	1	10
SLOVAKIA	1	8

(*Continued*)

Table 1. (*Continued*)

Host Country	Number of Subsidiaries Included in the Merton Distance to Default Calculation	Number of Subsidiaries in the Synthetic Distance to Default Calculation
SOUTH AFRICA	1	3
THAILAND	1	5
TRINIDAD AND TOBAGO	1	0
TUNISIA	4	6
TURKEY	7	5
UKRAINE	3	1
VENEZUELA	1	3
ZAMBIA	1	3

The rest of the chapter is organized as follows. The next section describes the construction of the two measures of distance to default. This is followed by a section describing the data used. Subsequently, we discuss the empirical findings. The last section offers some conclusion.

2. Distance to Default Measures

Merton's distance to default is given by Equation (1)

$$dd = \frac{log\left(\frac{V_A}{X}\right) + \left(m - Div - \frac{S^2A}{2}\right)T}{S_A\sqrt{T}}, \tag{1}$$

where V_A is the market value of the bank's assets. X is the face value of debt maturing at time T. Div is the dividend rate expressed in terms of V_A. s_A is the volatility of the value of assets. Because V_A and s_A are not observed, we derive their values from simultaneously solving Equations (2) and (4) below:

$$V_E = V_A e^{-DivT} N(d_1) - Xe^{-rT} N(d_2) + \left(1 - e^{-DivT}\right) V_A, \tag{2}$$

Table 2. Count of foreign bank parents across home countries in our sample.

Parent Country	Number of Parents Included in the Merton distance to Default Calculation	Number of Parents in the Synthetic Distance to Default Calculation
Australia	1	0
Austria	1	6
Bahrain	3	3
Barbados	0	1
Belgium	2	1
Benin	0	1
Bermuda	0	2
Botswana	0	1
China	0	2
Cyprus	0	1
Czech Republic	0	2
Ecuador	0	1
Egypt	0	1
Canada	2	0
France	3	7
Germany	2	6
Greece	1	4
Hong Kong	2	2
Hungary	0	2
India	0	2
Indonesia	0	1
Ireland	1	0
Israel	0	1
Italy	2	2
Japan	2	5

(*Continued*)

Table 2. (*Continued*)

Parent Country	Number of Parents Included in the Merton distance to Default Calculation	Number of Parents in the Synthetic Distance to Default Calculation
Jordan	1	1
Kazakhstan	1	1
Lebanon	0	1
Lithuania	0	1
Luxembourg	0	2
Macedonia (Fyrom)	0	1
Malaysia	2	0
Morocco	1	0
The Netherlands	1	2
The Philippines	0	1
Portugal	1	3
Saudi Arabia	0	1
Singapore	1	3
Slovakia	0	1
South Africa	0	1
Spain	3	2
Sweden	1	1
Switzerland	0	2
Togo	0	1
Trinidad And Tobago	0	1
The United Arab Emirates	2	0
UKRAINE	0	1
The United Kingdom	3	5
The United States	2	7
Vietnam	0	1

where

$$d_1 = \frac{\log\left(\frac{V_A}{X}\right) + \left(r - Div + \frac{S_A^2}{2}\right)T}{S_{A\sqrt{T}}}; d_2 = d_1 - S_A\sqrt{T} \quad (3)$$

In Equation (1), V_E is the market value of a bank's equity, r is the risk-free rate. The volatility of the value of assets is related to the volatility of equity (S_E) through the following equation:

$$S_E = \frac{V_A e^{-DivT} N(d_1) S_A}{V_E} \quad (4)$$

We use the market value of equity for V_E and total liabilities to proxy for X, the face value of debt. Since the accounting information is on an annual basis, we linearly interpolate the values for all dates over the period, using beginning and end of year values for accounting items. The interpolation method has the advantage of producing a smooth implied asset value process and avoids jumps in the implied default probabilities at year end (Bartram, Gregory, & Hund, 2007). s_E is the standard deviation of daily equity returns over the past three months. In calculating the standard deviation, we require each bank to have at least 45 non-missing daily returns over the previous three months. T is the horizon over which default risk is computed and is set to one year. r is the one year U.S. treasury yield, which we take to be the risk free rate. We use the Newton method to simultaneously solve the two equations above. For starting values for the unknown variables, we use $V_A = V_E + X$ and $s_A = s_E V_E/(V_E + X)$. We winsorize s_E and $V_E/(V_E + X)$ at the 1st and 99th percentile levels to reduce the influence of outliers. After we determine asset values VA, we follow Campbell, Hilscher, and Szilagyi (2008) and assign asset return m to be equal to the equity premium (6%).[2]

[2] Since during recessions and market downturns the risk premium increases, as a robustness check we also computed distance to default values using a 12% equity risk premium. The correlation in levels of distance to default values using the two different equity premium values is 96%. The correlation in changes of distance to default is 99%.

The Merton distance to default measure discussed above applies to publicly listed subsidiaries for which the market value and standard deviation of equity can be inferred from their stock prices following the formulas discussed above. To compute a synthetic measure for privately held banks we follow Falkenheim & Pennachi (2003). We model market leverage (*mktlev*) and standard deviation of asset returns ($sigmaV_A$) as a linear function of accounting variables. Market leverage is measured as total liabilities divided by the market value of assets computed from the Merton model (V_A/X) described above. Similarly, the standard deviation of asset returns are computed from the Merton model (s_A), using market equity data. For each weekly observation in our sample, we run a cross-sectional regression of *mktlev* and $sigmaV_A$ on a number of accounting variables and then use the coefficients from this model to predict the value of *mktlev* and $sigmaV_A$ for the non-listed foreign banks.

The explanatory variables we use are similar to those described in Falkenheim & Pennachi (2003). We make some modifications as our sample includes international banks operating in a number of different countries. We use the book value of leverage (*Asset/Liabilities*) to proxy for market leverage. Given the significant impact earnings have on equity prices, we use three variables to capture their effects on market leverage and asset volatility. In particular, we use net income scaled by liabilities (*Net Income/Liabilities*), net income ratio squared (*Net Income/Liabilities*)^2, and the quadratic term multiplied by a dummy variable set equal to one if net income is positive and zero if it is negative (*Dummy**(*Net Income/Liabilities*)^2). The quadratic terms allow for potential non-linearities in the relationship between net income and market leverage and asset volatility. We use the standard deviation of earnings and standard deviation of liabilities growth to proxy for volatility of market value of assets.[3] Loan loss provisions (*Loan loss provisions/Liabilities*) capture differences in asset quality, net loans (*Net loans/Liabilities*) capture differences in business model, and deposits ratio (*Deposits/Liabilities*) capture differences in funding structure. We include bank size (log(*Assets*)) and a dummy variable set equal to one

[3]Liabilities growth for a given bank is measured as: log($Liabilities_t/Liabilities_{t-1}$).

(*BHC dummy*) if the institution is a bank holding company to distinguish large holding companies from smaller more independent banks. Large banks and holding companies may have more market power, greater brand recognition, and charter values. They may also be more complex, diversified and may have greater economies of scale. They are also more likely to engage in greater securitization and use of derivative products. Finally, we include eight region dummies to take into account geographical differences.[4]

We run cross-sectional regressions each week over the years 2008 and 2009 using lagged values of accounting variables and region dummies to explain market leverage and asset volatility. We then use the weekly estimated coefficients on the lagged explanatory variables for non-publicly listed banks to create 'synthetic' market leverage and asset volatility measures for these banks. These 'synthetic' measures are then used to compute weekly distance to default measures.[5] Table A.1 reports Fama–Macbeth regression results for the time period used to estimate weekly credit risk measures.[6] The results are qualitatively similar to those reported in Falkenheim & Pennachi (2003).

3. Data

Our calculations of Merton's distance to default use an extensive database of stock market prices for both publicly traded parent banks and their publicly traded subsidiaries in developing countries. In particular, we use daily stock market information from Compustat Global for international banks and firms and stock market information from CRSP for U.S. banks and firms over the period September 2008 through

[4] The region coefficients capture relative effects for each of the regions with respect to the Africa region which is not included to avoid perfect multicollinearity.

[5] We plug in the estimated values for market leverage and standard deviation of asset returns to compute weekly distance-to-default: $dd = \dfrac{log\left(m\bar{k}\bar{t}\bar{l}ev\right)+\left(m-d\,\dfrac{sig\bar{m}\bar{a}v\,A^2}{2}\right)T}{sig\bar{m}\bar{a}VA^2\sqrt{T}}$

[6] The standard errors for the coefficient estimates are based on the time series variability of the cross-sectional estimates, incorporating a Newey-West (1987) correction with three lags to account for possible autocorrelation in the estimates.

December 2009. To calculate both the Merton measure and the synthetic measure we also use bank level balance sheet data from Bankscope, a comprehensive commercial database of banks' financial statements produced by Bureau Van Dijk.

In analyzing the factors that can augment or reduce the correlation between the distance to the default of foreign subsidiaries and their parents, we examine the role of bank characteristics and host country regulations. Among the bank characteristics, using Bankscope data as of December 2006, we calculate relative bank *size* (bank assets to total system assets), *capital ratio* (regulatory capital to risk weighted assets), *equity ratio* (equity to total assets), *provisions* (loan loss provisions divided by total loans), *deposit funding* (deposits divided by total funding), *profitability* (net income divided by total assets), and *liquidity* (liquid assets divided by total assets).[7] To reduce the influence of outliers and potential data errors, we winsorize all financial variables at the 1st and 99th percentile level of their distributions

Host country-level variables come from various sources. We use data from the World Bank 2007 Bank Regulation and Supervision survey to construct different indexes of bank regulation and supervision, following the methodology proposed by Barth, Caprio and Levine (2001, 2013).[8] *Capital regulation* captures the amount of capital banks must hold and the stringency of regulations on the nature and source of capital. It is an index ranging in value from 0 to 10, with higher values indicating greater stringency. *Activity restrictions* is an index that measures the degree to which the national regulatory authorities restrict banks from engaging in securities, insurance, and real estate activities. Securities activities refers to underwriting, brokering, dealing and all aspects of the mutual fund industry. Insurance activities include underwriting and selling, and real estate activities refer to investment, development, and management. The activities restrictions index takes values from 3 (where each of the three activities is permitted) to 12 (where each activity is prohibited). *Disclosure*

[7] Note that in the ratios mentioned here assets and equity are measured as book values. We also tried running regressions using the market value of assets and equity computed from the Merton model discussed above and found similar results.

[8] The 2007 survey covers the 2005–2006 period.

requirements is an index that captures the type of information banks must disclose about their financial condition. It indicates whether the income statement includes accrued or unpaid interest or principal on non-performing loans, whether banks are required to produce consolidated financial statements, and whether bank directors are legally liable if information disclosed is erroneous or misleading. The variable ranges from 0 to 3, with higher values indicating greater bank disclosure. *Diversification requirements* is an index which measures whether regulations support geographical asset diversification. It is based on two variables: whether there are explicit, verifiable, and quantifiable guidelines for asset diversification and whether banks are prohibited from making loans abroad. The index takes values from 0 to 2 with higher values indicating more diversification. *Loan Classification Stringency* measures the actual minimum number of days beyond which a loan in arrears must be classified as sub-standard, doubtful, or loss. *Provisioning Stringency* measures the minimum provisions (as a percentage of loans) required as a loan is successively classified as sub-standard, doubtful, and lastly as loss. *Supervisory powers* is an index measuring supervisory authorities' power and authority to take specific preventive and corrective actions. The measure ranges from 0 to 14, where larger numbers indicate greater supervisory powers. *Prompt corrective powers* measures the extent to which the law establishes predetermined levels of bank solvency deterioration that force automatic enforcement actions such as intervention, and the extent to which supervisors have the requisite suitable powers to do so. The index ranges from 0 to 6 with higher values indicating more promptness in responding to problems. *Reserve Requirements* is the average level of reserves that banks are required to hold relative to their deposits and other short-term liabilities. As with the indexes discussed above, this variable also comes from the World Bank 2007 Bank Regulation and Supervision Survey. *Financial outflow restrictions* is the average of three binary variables measuring bank restrictions on lending to non-residents, maintaining accounts abroad, and on banks' investment abroad. This variable comes from the IMF Annual Report on Exchange Arrangements and Restrictions.

4. Empirical Findings

Figure 1 Panel A shows the scatter plot of the distance to default of the subsidiaries against that for the parents using Merton's distance to default calculated for 93 publicly listed subsidiaries. Panel B shows the corresponding synthetic measures following Falkenheim & Pennachi (2003) calculated for 175 foreign bank subsidiaries. It is clear from these figures that the association between the default risk of the parent and the subsidiaries in developing countries is significant. The pairwise correlation is close to 0.46,

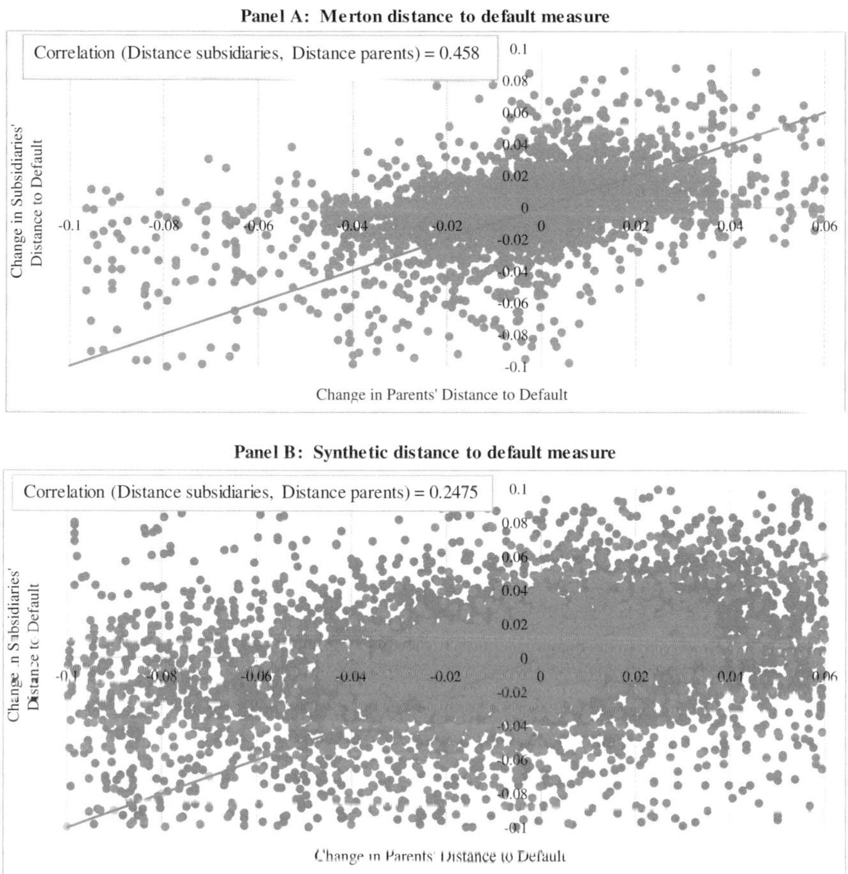

Figure 1. Plot and correlation of changes in distance to default of subsidiaries and parents.

when calculating Merton's distance to default for the publicly listed foreign bank subsidiaries and the corresponding correlation using the synthetic measure of the distance to default is 0.25. Figure 2, Panels A and B, show that the pairwise correlations remain fairly unchanged when we remove from the sample those banks with many subsidiaries, which can exert a larger influence on the calculation of the correlations, relative to banks with fewer subsidiaries.

In exploring the factors that can amplify or reduce the correlation in the distance to default between parent banks and their foreign

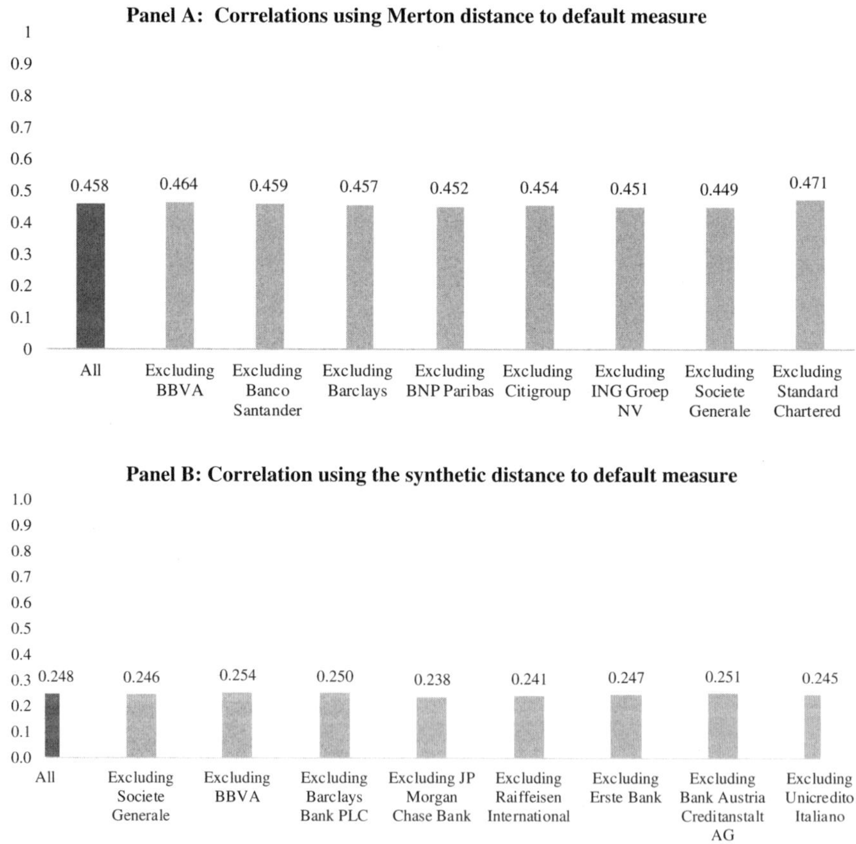

Figure 2. Correlations of changes in distance to default of subsidiaries and parents excluding parent banks with multiple affiliates.

subsidiaries, we consider two set of variables: subsidiary characteristics and host country regulations. Regarding the former, we expect "stronger" subsidiaries to be better positioned to weather an external shock and, therefore, to exhibit a lower correlation in their distance to default with that of the parent. In particular, a number of papers emphasize the role of capital, profitability, asset liquidity, and funding structure as potential buffers in absorbing liquidity and economic shocks (Allen & Gale, 2000; Repullo, 2004; von Thadden, 2004; Diamond & Rajan, 2005; Cifuentes, Ferrucci, & Shin, 2004). Similarly, we expect the correlation between the subsidiary and the parent to be lower for subsidiaries operating in countries where the regulatory authorities impose tighter regulatory regimes to help *ex ante* "ring fence" the foreign subsidiary from a parent in distress.

In Table 3 we explore the role of subsidiary characteristics in affecting the correlation in the distance to default between foreign bank subsidiaries and their parents. In particular, the table reports and compares the value of these correlations for subsidiaries which rank above and below the median in terms of size, capital, liquidity, provision, customer deposit funding, profitability, geographical distance, and cultural proximity. Across both measures of distance to default, we find consistent evidence that correlations are significantly lower for subsidiaries with higher capital (or equity) and profitability and for those that are geographical further away from the parent but that are more culturally similar. On the other hand, the evidence on the impact of customer deposit funding, liquidity, and provisions is mixed. These variables seem to influence the value of the correlation in distance to default between parents and subsidiaries, because the differences in the correlations between subsidiaries with high and low levels ratios of customer funding, liquidity, and provisions are statistically significant. However, the direction is unclear given that these differences have opposite signs across the measures of distance to default.

Regarding the role of geographical distance, one explanation for the lower correlation for those subsidiaries that are farther away might be that geographically distant subsidiaries may be less integrated into the parent group and the parent bank might find it difficult to exercise control over the local management of the subsidiary (Rajan, Servaes, & Zingales, 2000;

Table 3. Bank characteristics and differences in the correlation in the distance to default.

Bank Characteristic	Correlation for Subsidiary Characteristics Below Median (1)	Correlation for Subsidiary Characteristics Above Median (2)	Difference (2)–(1)	Z	*p*-value
Panel A: Correlations using the Merton distance to default measure					
Size	0.412	0.503	0.092	3.479	0.001
Capital ratio	0.515	0.454	–0.060	–2.112	0.035
Equity ratio	0.528	0.394	–0.134	–5.108	0.000
Customer deposits	0.512	0.401	–0.111	–4.174	0.000
Profitability	0.481	0.446	–0.035	–1.330	0.184
Liquidity	0.432	0.495	0.063	2.395	0.017
Provisions	0.525	0.408	–0.118	–4.472	0.000
Geographical distance	0.514	0.399	–0.115	–4.461	0.000
Cultural proximity (high = 1, low = 0)	0.499	0.379	–0.120	–4.410	0.000
Panel B: Correlations using the synthetic distance to default measure					
Size	0.178	0.323	0.145	7.414	0.000
Capital ratio	0.358	0.249	–0.110	4.312	0.000
Equity ratio	0.318	0.170	–0.147	–7.475	0.000
Customer deposits	0.235	0.301	0.066	3.332	0.001
Profitability	0.312	0.211	–0.101	–5.105	0.000
Liquidity	0.322	0.195	–0.126	–6.427	0.000
Provisions	0.250	0.291	0.041	2.053	0.040
Geographical distance	0.315	0.163	–0.152	–7.216	0.000
Cultural proximity (high = 1, low = 0)	0.249	0.188	–0.061	–2.470	0.014

De Haas & van Horen, 2013). At the same time, cultural proximity might reduce the correlation between subsidiaries and parents if these subsidiaries are granted more independence because the parent is more comfortable decentralizing some control when it is more familiar with the culture and business environment in the host country.

Table 4 reports the correlation between the distance to default of parent banks and their foreign subsidiaries in countries where host regulatory indexes are above and below the median. We observe that the correlation in distance to default is lower for countries with greater disclosures requirements, where supervisors have greater power, and where reserve requirements are higher. There is also some evidence that higher capital and provisioning requirements and tougher rules regarding loan classification lead to lower correlations in default risk between parents and subsidiaries. But these results are only significant when focusing on publicly listed subsidiaries for which we can calculate the Merton distance to default measure at high frequencies.

5. Conclusions

This chapter offers a preliminary non-parametric analysis of the correlation between parents' and subsidiaries' default risk. Also, we begin to explore the subsidiary characteristics and policies that can dampen or amplify this correlation. We find that there is a positive and significant correlation between parents' and subsidiaries' distance to default. This finding is robust to the measure of distance to default and to the sample of banks considered. In terms of the factors that could affect this correlation, our preliminary results indicate that higher levels of subsidiary capital and greater subsidiary management autonomy (which we proxy with greater geographical distance but closer cultural proximity) help to lower the correlation. In terms of host regulations, the most consistent findings are that higher reserve requirements, greater supervisory power and disclosure requirements lower the correlation in default risk between parents and subsidiaries. There is also some evidence — albeit less robust — that higher capital and provisioning requirements and tougher loan classification rules lead to lower correlations in default risk between parents and subsidiaries.

Table 4. Host regulations and differences in the correlation in the distance to default.

Host Regulations	Correlation for Host Regulations Characteristics Below Median (1)	Correlation for Host Regulations Characteristics Above Median (2)	Difference (2)–(1)	Z	*p*-value
Panel A: Correlations using the Merton distance to default measure					
Disclosure	0.575	0.426	–0.149	–5.265	0.000
Activity Restrictions	0.523	0.384	–0.139	–4.996	0.000
Capital Regulation	0.517	0.375	–0.142	–4.994	0.000
Loan Classification	0.510	0.374	–0.136	–4.014	0.000
Provisioning	0.466	0.261	–0.205	–3.793	0.000
Diversification	0.465	0.458	–0.007	–0.255	0.799
Supervisory Powers	0.508	0.419	–0.089	–3.372	0.001
Prompt Corrective Actions	0.454	0.463	0.008	0.317	0.752
Reserve Requirements	0.542	0.411	–0.131	–4.297	0.000
Financial Outflows	0.451	0.477	0.026	0.953	0.340
Panel B: Correlations using the synthetic distance to default measure					
Disclosure	0.271	0.228	–0.043	–2.140	0.032
Activity Restrictions	0.224	0.304	0.081	3.856	0.000
Capital Regulation	0.253	0.248	–0.004	–0.207	0.836
Loan Classification	0.256	0.249	–0.007	–0.290	0.772
Provisioning	0.253	0.210	–0.043	–1.274	0.203
Diversification	0.244	0.267	0.024	1.188	0.235
Supervisory Powers	0.292	0.200	–0.093	–4.619	0.000
Prompt Corrective Actions	0.260	0.246	–0.015	–0.701	0.483
Reserve Requirements	0.320	0.112	–0.208	–8.964	0.000
Financial Outflows	0.217	0.349	0.132	5.751	0.000

To conclude, it is important to underscore that, while interesting, the evidence we present in this chapter is only suggestive. Our analysis is non-parametric and does not control for the many variables, such as global factors and home and host developments that can also affect the correlation in default risk between global parent banks and their subsidiaries. We leave such analysis for a separate paper.

References

Allen, F. & Gale, D. (2000). Bubbles and crises. *The Economic Journal, 110*, 236–255.

Barth, J. R., Caprio, G., Levine, R. (2001). The regulation and supervision of banks around the world — a new database. *World Bank Policy Research Working Paper* No. 2588, April.

Barth, J. R., Caprio, G & Levine, R. (2013). Bank regulation and supervision in 180 countries from 1999 to 2011. *National Bureau of Economic Research Working Paper* No. 18733, January.

Bartram, S., Gregory B. & Hund, J. (2007). Estimating systemic risk in the international financial system. *Journal of Financial Economics*, 86(3), 835–869.

Campbell, J. Y., Hilscher, J. & Szilagyi, J. (2008). In search of distress risk. *Journal of Finance*, 63(6), 2899–2939.

Choi, M. J., Martinez Peria, M. S. & Gutierrez, E. (2013). Dissecting foreign bank lending behavior during the 2008–2009 Crisis. *World Bank Policy Research* Working Paper No. 6674, October.

Cifuentes, R., Ferrucci, G., Shin, H. S. (2004). Liquidity risk and contagion. *Journal of the European Economic Association, 3*(2–3), 556–566.

Claessens, S., van Horen, N. (2013). Impact of foreign banks. *Journal of Financial Perspectives*, 1(1), 29–42.

De Haas, R. & van Horen, N. (2013). Running for the exit? International bank lending during a financial crisis. *Review of Financial Studies*, 26(1), 244–285.

Diamond, D. W. & Rajan, R. G. (2005). Liquidity shortages and banking crises. *Journal of Finance*, 60(2), 615–647.

Exchange Arrangements and Exchange Restrictions (2007). IMF, *Annual Report*, September.

Falkenheim, M. & Pennacchi, G. (2003). The cost of deposit insurance for privately held banks: A market comparable approach. *Journal of Financial Services Research*, *24*(2), 121–148.

Fama, E. F. & MacBeth, J. D. (1973). Risk, return, and equilibrium: Empirical tests. *Journal of Political Economy*, *81*(3), 607–636.

Merton, R. C. (1974). On the pricing of corporate debt: The risk structure of interest rates. *Journal of Finance*, *29*, 449–470.

Newey, W. K. & West, K. D. (1987). Hypothesis testing with efficient method of moments estimation. *International Economic Review*, *28*(3), 777–787.

Peek, J. & Rosengren, E. (2000). Collateral damage: Effects of the Japanese bank crisis on real activity in the United States. *American Economic Review*, *90*(1), 30–45.

Rajan, R. G., Servaes, H. & Zingales, L. (2000). The cost of diversity: The diversification discount and inefficient investment. *The Journal of Finance*, *55*(1), 35–80.

Repullo, R. (2004). Capital requirements, market power, and risk-taking in banking. *Journal of Financial Intermediation*, *13*, 156–182.

Schnabl, P. (2012). The international transmission of bank liquidity shocks: Evidence from an emerging market. *Journal of Finance*, *67*(3), 897–932.

Von Thadden, E.-L. (2004). Bank capital adequacy regulation under the new Basel Accord. *Journal of Financial Intermediation*, *13*(2), 90–95.

Appendix A

Table A.1. Synthetic Credit Risk Scores

This table reports results from weekly Fama and MacBeth (1973) regressions of market leverage (*mktlev*) and asset return volatility ($sigmaV_A$) on lagged accounting variables. *mktlev* is total liabilities divided by the market value of assets computed from the Merton model $sigmaV_A$ is standard deviation of asset returns computed from the Merton model. The explanatory accounting variables are described in detail in the text. The time period is from September 2008 to December 2009. We report Fama and MacBeth regression coefficients as well as their corresponding Newey and West (1987) three lag corrected standard errors in parentheses. ***(**) (*) indicates significance at 1% (5%) (10%) level, respectively.

Variables	Mktlev	SigmaV$_A$
log (Assets)	−0.016***	−0.001***
	(0.001)	(0.000)
Asset/Liabilities	0.138***	0.074***
	(0.053)	(0.003)
Net loans/Liabilities	−0.084***	−0.011***
	(0.007)	(0.001)
Loan loss provisions/Liabilities	1.950***	0.074***
	(0.133)	(0.021)
Deposits/Liabilities	−0.020***	−0.002
	(0.008)	(0.001)
Net Income/Liabilities	5.584***	0.518***
	(0.189)	(0.028)
(Net Income/Liabilities)^2	0.659*	−0.405***
	(0.345)	(0.036)
Dummy × (Net Income/Liabilities)^2	25.271***	4.137***
	(1.431)	(0.238)
Std Deviation (Net Income/Liabilities)	0.437***	0.091***
	(0.127)	(0.012)
Std Deviation (Liabilities growth)	0.127***	0.020***
	(0.019)	(0.002)
BHC dummy	0.007***	−0.000
	(0.003)	(0.000)
Central Asia & Eastern Europe dummy	−0.260***	−0.028***
	(0.012)	(0.002)
East Asia and Pacific dummy	−0.189***	−0.028***
	(0.013)	(0.002)
Japan dummy	−0.252***	−0.060***
	(0.012)	(0.002)
Latin America & Caribbean dummy	−0.214***	−0.021***
	(0.013)	(0.002)

(*Continued*)

(*Continued*)

Variables	Mktlev	$SigmaV_A$
Middle East & North Africa dummy	–0.121***	–0.004**
	(0.012)	(0.002)
North America dummy	–0.255***	–0.033***
	(0.012)	(0.002)
South Asia dummy	–0.243***	-0.025***
	(0.011)	(0.002)
Western Europe dummy	–0.221***	–0.054***
	(0.013)	(0.002)
Constant	1.650***	0.022***
	(0.067)	(0.005)
Observations	95,840	95,840
R-squared	0.638	0.462

An Overview of Regulatory Stress-Testing and How to Improve It

— CHAPTER 17

▪ Matt Pritsker
Federal Reserve Bank of Boston

1. Introduction

Banks are financial intermediaries that raise funds through traditional deposits and wholesale funding sources, and other means, and then use the funds to invest in loans and other financial assets. For banks to be able to fund their activities, their funding sources must believe they will be paid back with high enough probability.

During the financial crisis of 2007–2009, the large drop in U.S. housing prices, and the accompanying losses that banks incurred on their mortgage portfolios and other assets called the financial health of many banks and their borrowers into question. As part of the response to the financial crisis, regulatory stress-tests were used to improve information on banks financial health. This paper presents an overview of why regulatory stress-testing was needed in the crisis, and how it is used today. In addition, the paper critiques current practice and suggests

---

Matt Pritsker is a Senior Financial Economist and Policy Advisor in the Division of Supervision, Regulation, and Credit at the Federal Reserve Bank of Boston. The views in this paper are those of the author and not necessarily those of the Federal Reserve Bank of Boston or of others with the Federal Reserve system.

directions for improving stress-testing. The paper concludes with a discussion of the role of regulatory stress-testing in the long-run.

2. Why was Regulatory Stress-Testing Needed?

When economic conditions are deteriorating, whether banks can access funding depends in part on how much the funding sources know about the financial strength of the banks. If indicators of banks health are reliable, then those banks that are deemed healthy enough can access funding. But, if such indicators are unreliable because they do not adjust rapidly enough to changes in economic conditions, then when conditions are deteriorating even relatively healthy banks may have difficulties funding their activities.

One lesson from the crisis is that many indicators of banks health did not accurately reflect it. As noted by Flannery (2014), measures of banks capital adequacy based on book value accounting ratios (such as book capital/book assets) moved very little during the crisis, despite the fact that the 2007–2009 crisis was the worst since the great depression, and despite the fact that other measures of banks health based on CDS spreads and the market value of banks equity as a fraction of assets moved substantially during the crisis. Other regulatory measures of banks health, such as the value at risk of their trading portfolios were also under-responsive to changes in their risk because many banks measured their risk using historical simulation, a method of risk-measurement that Pritsker (2006) shows is very slow to respond to changes in volatility.

In addition to regulatory indicators of bank health being under-responsive to changes in banks' risk, regulatory capital requirements were not stringent enough to distinguish healthy from unhealthy banks. Figures 1 and 2 present the total risk based capital ratio, and Tier 1 capital ratio for the 30 bank holding companies that participated in the most recent U.S. Comprehensive Capital Analysis and Review (CCAR) stress test.[1] The figures include data for 18 of the 19 banks, who partici-

[1] The figure shows each bank's risk-based capital ratios computed based on the capital rules that applied to the bank at each date. Because banks transitioned from the Basel I to Basel II capital rules at different dates during the period in the figures,

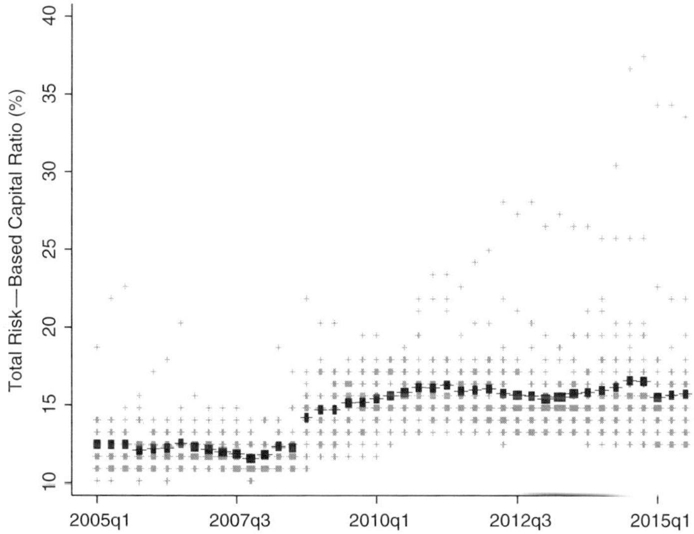

Figure 1. Total regulatory capital ratios for top 30 U.S. bank holding companies.

Notes: For the 30 banks that participated in CCAR 2015, the figure plots the time series of each banks ratio of total regulatory capital to total risk weighted assets (light plus symbols) and banks average capital ratios in each period (dark plus symbols) for a period from slightly before the 2007–2009 financial crisis until afterwards. The figures show that all of the banks that participated in CCAR 2015 satisfied Basel I and II regulatory minimums for total regulatory capital before and during the crisis.

pated in the first U.S. regulatory stress test in 2009[2] plus 12 smaller institutions that were added to the 2013 exercise. The figures shows that from 2005 through the crisis in 2009, all of the banks met regulatory minimums for their risk-based capital ratios despite many of these banks being under severe strains during the crisis period.[3,4]

---

the capital ratios are computed using rules that differ across time for a single bank and also across banks.

[2] Metropolitan Life is not in CCAR 2015.

[3] Figure 1 suffers from survivorship bias because it uses banks that survived through the crisis, not those that failed. Nevertheless, the point of the figure is that many banks that did not fail experienced significant difficulties during the crisis despite satisfying regulatory minimums.

[4] Also because of regulatory stress testing banks have been required to raise significantly more capital.

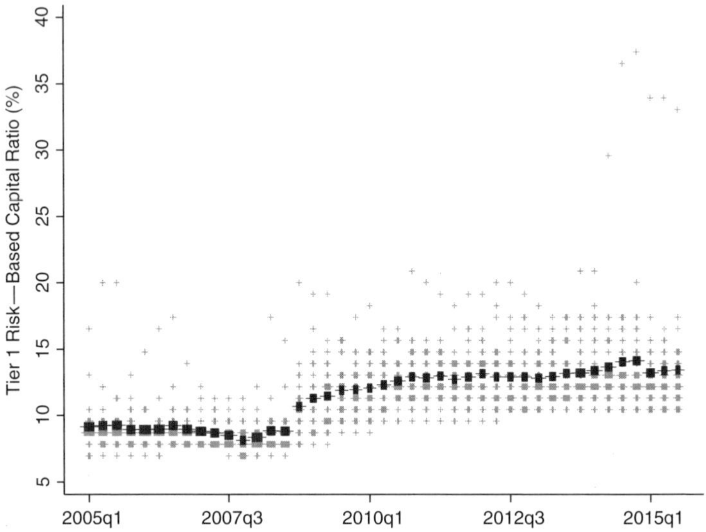

Figure 2. Tier 1 regulatory capital ratios for top 30 U.S. bank holding companies.

Notes: For the 30 banks that participated in CCAR 2015, the figure displays the time series of each banks ratio of Tier 1 regulatory capital to total risk weighted assets (light plus symbols) and banks average capital ratios in each period (dark plus symbols) for a period from slightly before the 2007–2009 financial crisis until afterwards. The figures show that all of the banks that participated in CCAR 2015 satisfied Basel I and II regulatory minimums for Tier 1 capital before and during the crisis.

During the crisis, stress-tests were used to help restore confidence in the banking system. They did so by assessing banks' ability to meet regulatory capital standards under then current conditions, as well as if conditions substantially deteriorated further with loan loss rates becoming as severe as those experienced during the great depression. By assessing banks ability to satisfy regulatory capital requirments in a severe stress-scenario, the stress-test tightened the effective capital requirement that banks needed to satisfy. Banks that could not satisfy regulatory capital requirements in the scenario were required to raise or accept additional capital. By ensuring banks would be well enough capitalized to have the strength to withstand very severe stresses, the stress-tests helped place a floor on banks net-worth and helped restore confidence in the banking system.

3. How Regulatory Stress-Testing is Currently Used

Because of regulatory stress-testings' success during the 2007–2009 crisis, since the crisis it has grown to become one of the most important parts of bank supervision activities both in the U.S. and in many other countries around the world. Because there are many similarities in how stress-tests are administered across countries, in this Chapter, I will only focus on regulatory stress-testing in the U.S. Stress-tests in the U.S. have two main parts.[5] The first part evaluates the capital adequacy of banking book positions (which are primarily loans that are valued using book-value accounting) in three regulatory macro-financial economic scenarios that are applied to all banks that are subject to stress-testing. Each banking book scenario posits the movement of approximately 30 macroeconomic and financial variables over a period of 9 quarters. The value of banks assets and cashflows are computed for each quarter in the scenario, and banks capital is deemed adequate only if it meets requirements for capital adequacy ratios in each quarter of the stress-scenearío.[6] The scenarios differ in terms of their severity: the baseline scenario represents what is expected to happen over the horizon of the stress-testing exercise; the adverse and severely adverse scenarios involve progressively worse macroeconomic outcomes than the baseline scenario. The second part of stress-testing uses three regulatory trading-book stress scenarios. The trading book scenarios are only applied to banks with very significant activity as broker–dealers in securities markets. In the most recent CCAR stress-test, the largest six U.S. Bank Holding Companies were subject to trading book stress tests, while the remaining banks were not. Each trading book regulatory stress-scenario specifies a set of instantaneous changes in 20,000 market-variables, including but not limited to changes in stock prices, interest rates, credit spreads, foreign exchange rates, and volatility and correlation surfaces,

[5] For details see Federal Reserve Board (2014), European Banking Authority (2014), and Bank of England (2014).

[6] The banking book stress-scenario results account for the scenarios' effects on the revenue component of banks' profits including also trading-book revenues.

around the world. Banks capital adequacy in the trading book is judged based on how the trading book scenarios affect the value of the banks trading book positions. The regulatory stress-testing exercise also requires each bank holding company to create a small number of its own scenarios that are tailored to its portfolio's vulnerabilities. Banks overall capital adequacy is judged on the basis of whether banks capital is adequate in the regulatory scenarios and in banks own scenarios.

In addition to assessing banks' capital adequacy, the regulatory stress-testing exercise performs other analyses including assessements of banks' methodologies for estimating losses, and banks' governance as it relates to risk measurement and management. The analysis in this article abstracts from these supplementary analyses to exclusively focus on the use of regulatory stress-testing as a tool to achieve capital adequacy objectives.

4. Critique

One of the primary objectives of regulatory stress-testing is to ensure the banking system will with high probability be able to serve the financial intermediation needs of the real sector. This in turn requires that the banking system will be well capitalized against the regulatory stress-scenarios and against the wider-set of plausible scenarios that could affect the banking system.

The extent to which current approaches to regulatory stress-testing achieve capital adequacy against a wider set of plausible scenarios is unclear. To illustrate the difficulty, suppose (for a moment) that the health of the banking sector could be represented by points on a TV-screen. Each point on the screen is one scenario the banking sector could experience. The illuminated points are those scenarios where we know the performance of the banking sector from the stress test; the sharpness of the focus at each point reflects the accuracy of the capital adequacy assessment for each scenario. Based on regulatory scenarios for the banking book, the screen would have three points that, because losses are required to be computed accurately in stress-testing, would be in nearly perfect focus. But the rest of the screen would be dark because without making additional assumptions, knowledge that the financial system is well capitalized against a few points does not ensure it is also well capitalized against other likely points. It is reasonable to assume that if the banking system is well capitalized against the regulatory scenarios, it is probably well capitalized against similar scenarios, corresponding to nearby points on the screen. But, the extent to which banks will be well capitalized against other scenarios will be unclear.

To utilize stress-testing to ensure capital adequacy against a broader set of points, at a minimum it is necessary to choose the right variables to stress, the right directions in which each of the variables need to be stressed (up or down), and the amounts by which each variable should be stressed.

Variable selection is crucial because if banks' risks are not well explained by the variables used in a stress-scenario, then ensuring banks are resilient to scenarios based on those variables does not ensure they are resilient to the risks that the banks actually face. There may be room for improvement in choosing the variables used in banking book stress scenarios since the movement of macro-variables weakly explains the profits and losses experienced by banks as noted by Guerrieri and Welch (2012).

Choosing the correct directions to stress the variables is important because if banks are exposed in different directions than those stressed, the stress-scenarios will not be stressful and may not require banks to hold the capital that they need. For example, if many banks have very significant positions that are short the stock market, then a scenario in which stock prices go down is not stressful for them. Choosing the right stress directions can be very difficult, especially in the trading book because banks can take risk in either direction: if banks are exposed to 1 variable, it can be moved up (U) or down (D), creating two possible direction choices (= 2^1). If banks are exposed to two variables, there are four possible direction choices (= 2^2): up for both (UU), down for both (DD), as well as (UD), or (DU). When there are about 20,000 variables, as there is in the 2015 CCAR trading book stress scenarios, there are $2^{20,000}$ (approximatly $10^{6,000}$) possible up-down type direction choices. Of these possible direction choices, the regulatory scenarios for the trading book choose just three of them. This raises the question of whether the chosen stress directions in the trading book are the right ones to accomplish the regulatory objective.

The above analysis of the number of possible up–down choices include among the possible choices many that are implausible. For example, moving yields up by large amounts at every even numbered annual tenor and down by large amounts at odd numbered tenors is one of the possibilites considered although it is highly implausible. Nevertheless, there are many possible plausible direction choices, and choosing correct direction choices from among the myriad possibilities is far from straightforward.

After choosing the correct variables, and stress directions, the magnitude of the resulting scenario or scenarios should be chosen so that if the banking system is well capitalized against the scenario(s) in the stress test it will also be well enough capitalized against most other plausible scenarios. This reasoning suggests that choosing a stress magnitude to achieve the objective requires the use of information on scenarios beyond those used in the stress-test.[7]

There are two relatively straightforward approaches to utilize such information in stress-testing to help stress-testing achieve its objectives. Both approaches begin from the assumption that stress tests should be based on at least the variables that banks use to model their own risks. This represents an expansion of stress-testing beyond a small number of macroeconomic and financial variables. It is useful to begin from a larger set of variables because of macro-variables weak explanatory power for explaining banks *P&L*. Based on the larger set of variables, the first approach chooses a large number of scenarios (in the thousands) and ensures the banking system is well capitalized against most of them as in Pritsker (2014), or through similar methodologies in Flood

[7] Choosing the correct scenario to achieve the objective can be complicated if banks exposures are a non-linear function of the variable movements. For example, if banks are exposed to just a single variable and earn profits from large upward or downward movements in the variable, but lose money from small moves in the variable, then the stress scenario that achieves the regulatory objective will involve small moves in the variable not large moves.

& Korenko (2015), or Breuer, Jandacka, Rheinberger, & Martin (2009). If the likely scenarios can be generated probabilistically, then ensuring the banking system is well capitalized against all but a small fraction of them ensures the banking system is well capitalized with high probability and hence satisfies the regulatory objective.[8] Because computing banks losses in a large number of scenarios is costly, it may be necessary to compute losses in scenarios less accurately. Returning to the TV picture analogy, the resulting image of knowledge of the banking system will have many more points illuminated than when using a few scenarios, but the image will be a bit blurry because of the loss of accuracy. Nevertheless, the first approach will approximately satisfy the regulators objective.

The second approach is choose a small number of stress-scenarios very well as in Pritsker II (2015). If the right scenario or scenarios is chosen, then knowledge that banks are well capitalized against them will ensure the banking system is well capitalized with high probability against other likely scenarios. To find the correct scenarios, the approach in Pritsker (2015) assumes that although banks *P&L* is driven by a large number of variables, at a portfolio level, each banks *P&L* is driven by a smaller number of economic factors. In addition, it is assumed that systemic risk is the risk that too many banks experience joint economic distress at the same time, and that this is caused by directionally similar exposures to the economic factors. This reasoning suggests that the economic factors that drive systemic risk should be identified and stress scenarios should be designed to ensure banks are sufficiently well capitalized against those factors. Pritsker (2015) describes a simulation based approach that uses information on banks exposures to the variables to identify those variables that are most important for explaining systemic risk. Given the variables that are identified as important for explaining systemic risk, the methodology further reduces the dimension of the scenario selection problem by identifying factors that explain systemic risk using the systemic-risk

[8] In the multiple scenario approach if the regulators want to increase the probability that the banking system is well capitalized, then the set of scenarios that the banking system needs to be well capitalized against needs to be increased.

variables. The identified variables and factors are used to design stress scenarios such that if banks are well capitalized against the scenarios, then systemic risk will be low. In designing such scenarios, the variables to stress, the directions in which to stress them, and the amounts they should be stressed are all solved for as part of the process.

The second approach uses one or a relatively small number of scenarios to achieve its capital adequacy objective. The reason more than one scenario may be required is that in some circumstances it may not be possible to satisfy the regulatory objective when only using one or too few regulatory stress scenarios. The second approach addresses this problem by utilizing multiple scenarios when necessary. To illustrate the conceptual difficulty with using too few scenarios in a simple setting, suppose hypothetically that regulators consider systemic risk the risk that more than 1/3 of the the banks in the banking system become significantly undercapitalized at the same time. In this setting if banks asset portfolios all have a long exposure to only one variable (such as the stock market), then ensuring that banks hold enough capital against a stock market decline of some magnitude chosen by regulators will ensure the probability that banks become undercapitalized together will be small, hence the systemic risk objective can be satisfied using one stress scenario in which the stock market declines.[9] In this example, if instead half of the banks have a long exposure to stocks while half have a short exposure, then too many banks can become undercapitalized when stocks move upward or downward enough. In this setting, a single stress scenario in which stock prices fall significantly could ensure banks hold enough capital against stocks declining, but it would not guarantee that enough banks hold capital against stocks rising in price. To ensure banks hold enough capital in this example, two stress-scenarios are required.

The multiple and few scenarios approaches outlined above have the potential to improve stress-testing practice. The advantage of these methods is they account for the distribution of the variables that affect the banks when creating stress-scenarios; and they use detailed data on

[9] In this case the stock market is both the important systemic risk variable as well as the systemic risk factor.

banks risk-exposures. It is these properties together that allows these methods to achieve capital adequacy with high probability. Realistically, however, there is uncertainty about the joint distribution of the variables that affect banks — especially in stressful times because the magnitude of the variables movements may depend on difficult to model nonlinear feed-back effects such as price declines triggering asset sales that generate further declines as in Greenwood, Landier, and David (2014) and Duarte and Eisenbach (2013). Additionally, although the data available to regulators on banks risk exposures has improved very substantially, summarizing banks exposures is very complicated, and remains a work in progress.

Given the uncertainties in distributional modeling and exposure measurement, choosing stress-scenarios will always be challenging. Going forward the multiple and few scenario approaches should be applied for a variety of plausible distributions, building on Breuer and Csiszar (2013) and Bidder and McKenna (2015), methods to choose stress scenarios should be further refined to account for uncertainties in modeling distributions and measuring exposures.

5. Summary and Conclusions

This chapter has provided an overview of the subject of regulatory stress-testing for the purpose of achieving regulatory objectives for systemic risk. The paper argued that stress-testing was needed during the 2007–2009 financial crisis to improve information about banks financial condition, and to ensure that weak banks would be recapitalized. The paper also argued that there is scope to improve the selection of regulatory scenarios to ensure that the banking system as a whole is well capitalized with high probability.

Since the 2007–2009 crisis, regulatory stress testing has been introduced, regulatory capital standards have been revised, and many new regulations have been implemented. Given the changing environment, it is important to consider what roles regulatory stress-testing should play in the long-term. In particular, given the other tools available for achieving systemic risk objectives, how can regulatory stress-testing best be applied, and to which entities and activities should it be applied?

The answer to the second question — to which entities should stress testing be applied, should depend at least in part on the ability and costs of controlling how entities contribute to systemic risks through other approaches. The answer to the first question should also depend on the costs and benefits of other approaches. In this regard, it is important to consider what role stress-testing should have in achieving capital adequacy objectives if regulatory capital standards are modified so that they become more risk-sensitive. If capital standards are sufficiently risk-sensitive, they have the important advantage that the amounts of capital that banks must hold adapts fairly rapidly to changes in the composition of banks' asset portfolios. By contrast, stress-testing has been a once a year exercise in the U.S., which means capital requirements (or other constraints on banks' capital levels) that result from stress-testing are slower to adapt to changes in portfolio composition than ideal capital standards. That said, an advantage of regulatory stress-testing is they are forward looking and can be adapted to account for changes in the economic environment and concentrations of banks risk taking. To the extent capital standards cannot be made as adaptible on their own, in the long run regulatory capital standards and stress tests both have roles to play in ensuring capital adequacy. When viewed in this light, the new approaches to regulatory stress testing that are described in this paper contribute by presenting improved ways to create forward looking stress scenarios to achieve systemic risk objectives.

References

Bank of England (2014). Stress testing the UK banking system: Guidance for participating firms, April.

Bank of England (2015). The Bank of England's approach to stress-testing the UK banking system, October.

Bidder, R. & McKenna, A. (2015). Robust stress testing. *Federal Reserve Bank of San Francisco Working Paper* No. 2015–13, September.

Breuer, T. & Csiszar, I. (2013). Sytematic stress tests with entropic plausibility constraints. *Journal of Banking and Finance*, *37*, 1552–1559.

Breuer, T., Jandacka, M., Rheinberger, K. & Martin, S. (2009). How to find plausible, severe, and useful stress scenarios. *International Journal of Central Banking*, 5(3), 205–224.

Duarte, F. & Eisenbach, T.M. (2013). Fire-sale spillovers and systemic risk. *Federal Reserve Bank of New York Staff Report* No. 645, October.

European Banking Authority (2014). Methodological note EU-wide stress test 2014. April 29, 2014, Version 2.0.

Federal Reserve Board (2014), 2015 supervisory scenarios for annual stress tests required under the Dodd–Frank act stress-testing rules and the capital plan rule, October 23, 2014.

Flannery, M. (2014). Maintaining adequate bank capital. *Journal of Money, Credit, and Banking*, 46(1), 157–180.

Flood, M. D. & Korenko, G. (2015). Systematic scenario selection: Stress testing and the nature of uncertainty. *Quantitative Finance*, 15(1), 43–59.

Greenwood, R., Landier, A. & David T. (2014). Vulnerable banks. *Journal of Financial Economics*, Forthcoming.

Guerrieri, L. & Welch, M. (2012). Can macro variables used in stress testing forecast the performance of banks. *FEDS Working Paper* No. 2012–49, July.

Pritsker, M. (2006). The hidden dangers of historical simulation. *Journal of Banking and Finance*, 30(2), 561–582.

Pritsker, M. (2014). Enhanced stress testing and financial stability. *Federal Reserve Bank of Boston Working Paper*, March.

Pritsker, M. (2015). Choosing stress scenarios for systemic risk though dimension reduction. *Federal Reserve Bank of Boston Working Paper*, June.

The supervisory capital assessment: Overview of results. Board of Governors of the Federal Reserve System, May 7, 2009.

The Role of Foreign Banks in Local Credit Booms

— CHAPTER 18

- Stijn Claessens
  Board of Governors of the Federal Reserve System, University of Amsterdam, and CEPR
- Neeltje van Horen
  De Nederlandsche Bank (DNB) and CEPR

1. Introduction

Whether foreign banks reduce or increase risks in host country banking systems has been a long-standing research and policy issue, not just since the global financial crisis.[1] On the bright side, it is evident that foreign banks can offer valuable diversification services and can absorb shocks occurring in the host market. Several empirical papers, studying crisis episodes in (mainly) emerging markets and developing countries,

We would like to thank the conference participants for their comments. Some of this paper draws on Claessens & van Horen 2015, and the database accompanying that paper is available online at http://www.dnb.nl/en/onderzoek-2/databases/bank.jsp. The views expressed in this chapter are those of the authors and do not necessarily represent those of the Federal Reserve Board, DNB or any of the institutions with which they have been affiliated.

[1]This section is partly based on Claessens & Van Horen (2013). See further papers by De Haas and Martinez Peria in this volume for reviews of the role of foreign banks in financial stability.

show that thanks to support of their parent banks, foreign affiliates do not need to rein in credit during a financial crisis in the host country, while domestic banks do have to contract their lending (see, among others, Crystal, Dages, & Goldberg, 2001; De Haas & van Lelyveld, 2006, 2010). As a result, the presence of foreign banks can act as a stabilizing force in times of crises.

On the dark side, as has been made clear again by the global financial crisis, foreign banks can be a source of instability. When faced with capital or funding shocks at home, banks might withdraw from cross-border banking activities to support lending at home. This can also translate into a reduction in the liquidity or capital that parents provide to their foreign affiliates, which in turn can have a negative impact on the supply of credit by these affiliates in the host market. There is substantial evidence of this type of shock transmission, such as Peek & Rosengren (1997, 2000) for the Japanese crisis, Schnabl (2012) for the LTCM crisis and, among others, Popov and Udell (2012) for the global financial crisis. Ongena, Peydro & Van Horen (2015) show that this shock transmission especially affects lending to and the real performance of small firms, single bank firms, and firms with less tangible assets.

It is important to realize, however, that with respect to financial stability one cannot look at foreign subsidiaries as one homogeneous group. Cull & Martinez Peria (2012) and De Haas & van Lelyveld (2014) show that foreign banks that are more funded through domestic deposits are more likely to continue lending even when their parent banks are hit by a funding shock. Claessens & van Horen (2013) show that foreign banks are also less likely to curtail lending when their market share is large, suggesting that commitments to the market matter for the degree to which foreign banks tend to withdraw. Furthermore, Cetorelli & Goldberg (2012) show that global banks actively manage their inter-office positions: when faced with a funding shock, they tend to reallocate capital within the holding towards "important" subsidiaries. While they do not study the lending behavior of subsidiaries, their results suggest that some affiliates might be forced to curb lending due to less funding from the parent, whereas other affiliates do not feel this pressure or might even be in a better position compared to domestic banks to continue to extend credit.[2]

While there is thus ample evidence that (certain types of) foreign banks can diversify host country risk, but also can contribute to importing risks when faced with a crisis at home, not much is known about the contribution of foreign banks to credit booms or the risk of a crisis occurring. In other words, while the literature has focused mainly on the ex-post manifestation and transmission of risks, the ex-ante contribution to financial vulnerabilities has hitherto not received much attention. In this paper, we therefore attempt to shed some light on how foreign banks contribute to credit booms. Specially, we focus on two related questions: (i) do foreign banks in general add to a credit boom in the country they are present in, and (ii) are there differences among foreign banks in how they relate to local credit booms?

Analyzing the pre-global financial crisis' (pre-GFC) credit booms in 93 countries, we find that foreign banks can add more than domestic banks to local booms but mainly because of their typically better financial positions. We do find, however, that it importantly matters where the parent bank is headquartered as foreign banks tend to import a credit boom from their home country to the host country, and add more to a boom in the host country if from a less well-regulated home country. Heterogeneity thus greatly matters for foreign banks' role in booms, similar to how post-crisis, foreign banks only under some conditions add to local busts. This makes assessing the risk management benefits of foreign banks more complex.

The rest of the paper is organized as follows. Section 2 describes the factors affecting credit booms and provides some reasons as to why foreign banks might play a role in credit booms. Section 3 analyses both at the country as well as at the bank level to what extent foreign banks play a role in credit booms. Section 4 summarizes the results and

---

[2] In addition, government policies can also impact the strength of the transmission. For example, De Haas, Korniyenko, Loukoianova, & Pivovarsky (2015) show that the Vienna Initiative was successful in reducing the credit contraction of a number of Eastern European subsidiaries of European banks.

provides some policy recommendations, focusing especially on the growing role of emerging market banks.

2. Factors Affecting Credit Booms

Understanding the manifestations and causes of credit booms is important as a substantial number of them either end up in subpar economic performance (63%) and/or a banking crisis (32%) (Figure 1). However, not much is known about the credit buildup phase, in large part as booms are hard to explain in general. Factors that have been mentioned as drivers of credit booms include financial liberalization and innovation, productivity gains, external shocks and monetary policy, but there remain many questions on their relative importance. And while it is evident that booms can have their own dynamics, what drives these differences is still largely unclear. Some useful new insights nevertheless come from a comprehensive study analyzing 176 credit booms in 170 countries between 1970 and 2010 (Dell'Ariccia, Igan,

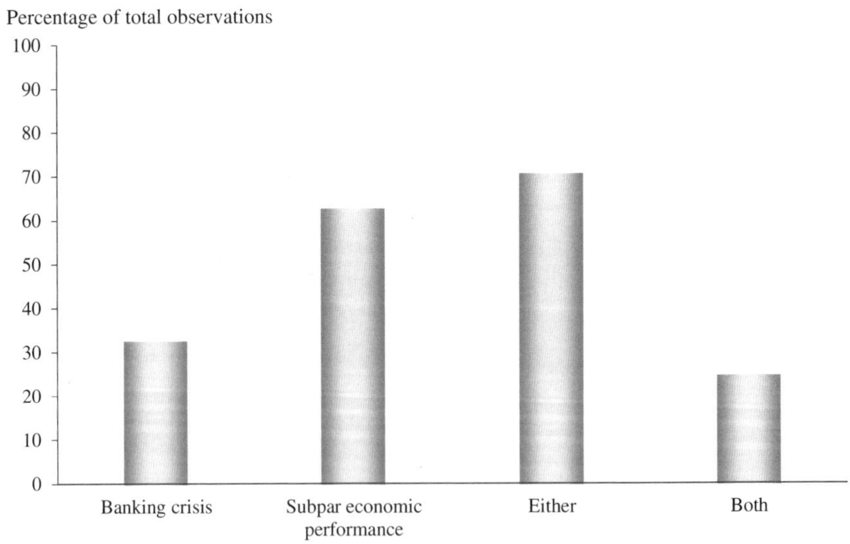

Figure 1. Credit booms followed by ...

Source: Dell'Ariccia, Igan, Laeven, & Tong (2016).

Laeven, & Tong, 2016). This study finds that credit booms are generally associated with financial reform and economic growth, with fixed exchange rate regimes, weak banking supervision and loose macroeconomic policies being more conducive to booms. It also shows that the larger and longer a boom, the more likely it ends up badly. While monetary and fiscal policies do not appear effective in limiting booms, macroprudential tools seem to be more effective in containing booms and (more importantly) limiting the impact of busts.

Even though some progress has been made to understand the drivers of credit booms, little is known about the role of foreign banks in local credit booms. Some studies, however, provide indications that foreign banks might play a role in affecting the local credit cycle. For one, global banks actively manage their liquidity across affiliates during credit cycle downturns (Cetorelli & Goldberg, 2012). This finding likely implies that they also actively manage intra-group liquidity during credit cycle upturns with direct consequences for the local credit growth of their foreign affiliates. There is also evidence for Mexico, a country where foreign banks have a large market share, that the monetary policy stances in the United States, United Kingdom and euro zone are passed on through foreign affiliates of parent banks from these countries thereby affecting local credit conditions (Morais, Peydro, & Ruiz, 2015). And Ongena, Popov, & Udell (2013) show that lower barriers to entry, tighter restrictions on bank activities and higher minimum capital requirements at home are associated with lower bank lending standards abroad, suggestive evidence that such regulations can make banks look for risks abroad and that (certain types of) foreign banks can affect credit booms. At the same time, Mehigan (2015) finds that foreign banks from home countries with higher regulatory capital requirements experienced significantly lower loan growth in the years leading up to the global financial crisis.

More generally, there is accumulating evidence that the global financial cycle is transmitted to local financial systems in large part through the activities of cross-border banks (Bruno & Shin, 2015a, 2015b; Rey, 2013). However, there exists very limited analyses on the links between foreign banks and risks to financial stability (IMF, 2015). In the next section we study more in depth if and how foreign banks are associated with credit booms in their host countries.

3. Foreign Banks and Host Country Credit Booms

To shed light on the role of foreign banks in host country credit booms we study credit growth in the three years (2005–2007) preceding the global financial crisis in 93 countries. First, we relate the size of the credit boom to overall foreign bank presence. We do this to establish whether foreign bank presence in general correlates with booms at the country level. We next explore whether certain characteristics of the individual foreign banks, including the home country in which the parent bank is headquartered, affect the contribution of a foreign bank to a local credit boom.

Our main data source is the bank ownership database of Claessens & van Horen (2015). The database contains ownership information of 5,498 banks, currently and previously active, in 138 countries.[3] For each year the bank is active it is classified as either domestic- or foreign-owned. A bank is defined as foreign owned when 50% or more of its shares are held by foreigners. In addition, for each foreign bank the home country of its largest foreign shareholder is determined. The database is very comprehensive as it covers more than 90% of bank assets in all countries. It thus provides an almost complete picture of bank ownership around the world for the period 1995–2013. The ownership data are matched to Bankscope for balance sheet information. While the database includes 138 countries, we only use a sample of countries for which all other information is available. Furthermore, we exclude countries that are offshore centers and countries where balance sheet information is available for less than 60% of the banks in 2005 and/or 2007. This leaves us with a sample of 93 countries.

[3] While coverage is comprehensive, a few limitations apply. First, as the database only include banks that report financial statements to Bankscope, it mainly covers foreign-owned subsidiaries and not foreign branches, which in general do not report separate balance sheet information. Second, the database only includes host countries with more than five active banks reporting to Bankscope in 2013. In addition, for the advanced countries in the sample, coverage is restricted to the 100 largest banks in each country in terms of 2012 assets, so smaller (typically regional) banks are not included in the database for these countries (which especially reduces the coverage of banks in the United States).

3.1. *Country Level Relationships*

We start by exploring the relationship between the (pre-GFC) credit boom and general foreign bank presence where we define foreign bank presence as the market share of foreign banks in terms of assets. Figure 2 indicates that the relationship between foreign bank presence and the pre-GFC credit boom is very weak: while positive, the correlation between the overall share of foreign banks and private credit growth between 2005 and 2007 is only 0.12. Figure 3 shows, however, that in many markets foreign banks grew faster than domestic banks did: in 63% of the host countries foreign banks increased their market share (in terms of loans) between 2005 and 2007. So, while general foreign bank presence did not appear to have added to the boom, foreign banks appear to have "replaced" domestic banks in many countries. However, Figure 4 shows that while the growth in the market share of foreign banks relates positively to private credit growth over the period 2005–2007, again the correlation is small, only 0.07 (0.13 excluding outliers).

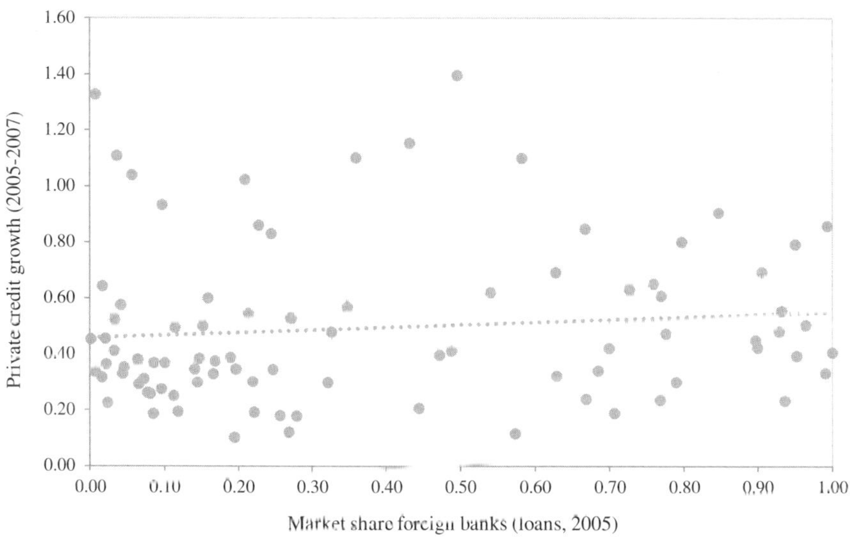

Figure 2. Foreign bank presence and pre-GFC credit boom.

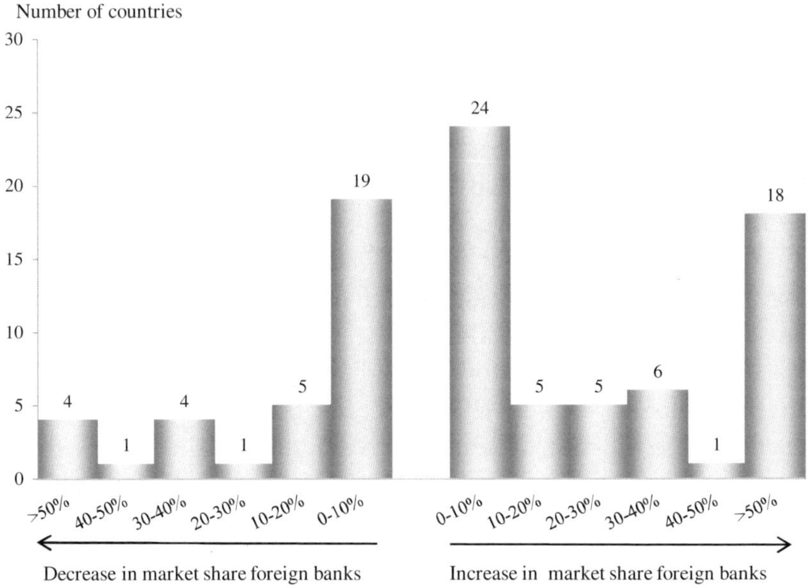

Figure 3. Growth market share foreign banks (loans, 2005–2007).

Note: Only banks are included that have loan information for both years. Banks that were only active in 2005 or 2007 are also included if the loan information is available for the year the bank is active. Countries in which less than 60% of the banks qualify are excluded from the sample altogether.

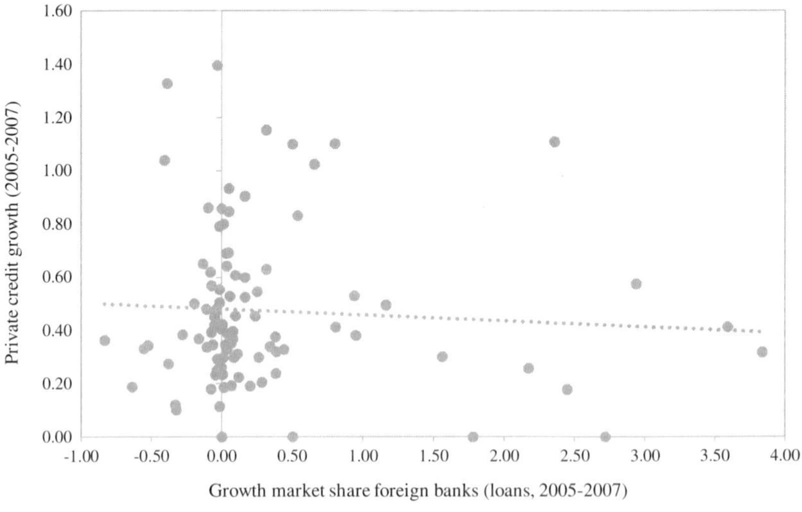

Figure 4. Growth market share foreign banks and pre-GFC credit boom.

Overall, these results suggest that the presence of foreign banks in general makes a local credit boom only slightly more likely and foreign banks' relative growth contributes little to a boom.[4] As such, it does not appear that foreign banks added greatly to domestic credit booms. But country level aggregates hide possibly important differences among foreign banks. Therefore, we next use bank-level information to explore the role of different characteristics of foreign banks.

3.2. *Bank Level Results*

To explore whether certain types of foreign banks were more likely to add to a boom than others, we next analyze the loan growth between 2005 and 2007 for 2,673 banks active in 93 countries, of which 717 are foreign owned in 2005 and 1,956 domestic owned. We examine to what extent certain bank characteristics, host country characteristics, and (in the case of foreign banks) home country characteristics affect the lending behavior of these banks in the pre-GFC period. As our database covers almost all (domestic and foreign) banks active in a country, we can, for the same country, compare the degree to which certain types of (foreign) banks contributed to a credit boom in comparison with others.

Our main variable of interest is whether the bank is foreign owned. We use ownership as of 2005, and drop banks from the regressions whose ownership changed between 2005 and 2007. As host country characteristics we consider a number of variables. Most importantly, we study the overall degree of private credit growth in the country over the period 2005–2007, since general credit growth in the host country will be strongly correlated with individual bank credit growth. In addition, we consider GDP per capita and inflation (both measured in 2005) to take into account a country's general development and macroeconomic conditions. We also include a variable called international borrowing, defined as total international borrowing by the banking sector divided by private credit (in 2005). This variable captures the extent to which the private credit boom is financed by local banks borrowing from

[4] In country level regression results controlling for some other factors (not reported), we confirm that increases in the market share of foreign banks only marginally relate to a boom.

international capital markets versus funding it domestically. Finally, we want to include a measure that captures the strength of host and home country capital regulation. For this we use the index of regulatory constraints on bank capital which comes from Barth, Caprio and Levine (2013). The index measures the regulatory approach to assessing and verifying the degree of capital at risk in a bank. Higher values indicate a more restrictive regulatory environment.

Next, we look at a number of bank characteristics that have been found in other studies to explain bank loan growth. We differentiate younger from older banks by including a dummy variable which is one if the bank has been present in the country for less than 10 years. We also include a variable that captures the market share of the bank (in terms of loans). We expect younger banks and banks with limited market share to grow faster. In addition, we include three variables that capture the health and funding structure of the bank: its solvency ratio (equity divided by total assets), its loan to deposit ratio, and its liquidity ratio (liquid assets divided by total assets).

Importantly, we consider the role of foreign banks' home country characteristics in order to analyze whether foreign banks might import a boom or other risky behavior from the home country to the host country. We include for this interaction terms of foreign bank ownership with four variables: private credit growth in the home country, the quality of capital regulation at home, a dummy whether the parent is from an OECD country and a dummy whether the foreign bank is active in the same geographical region as the parent bank.[5] All variables, their definitions and their sources can be found in Appendix Table A.1. All regressions are estimated with OLS and standard errors are clustered at the country level.

We find the following effects (Table 1). Foreign ownership by itself is not correlated with bank level loan growth. As such, being a foreign bank has by itself no differential impact on a boom. As expected, host country credit growth is strongly correlated with bank level loan

[5] The OECD group only includes the core OECD countries, and the non-OECD group includes all other countries. As such, current OECD countries like Hungary, Czech Republic, Korea, Poland, Slovakia, and Slovenia are included in the non-OECD group.

Table 1. Drivers behind loan growth.

	(1)	(2)	(3)
Foreign bank	0.036	−0.023	−0.058
	(0.027)	(0.034)	(0.164)
Host private credit growth	0.793***	0.755***	0.718***
	(0.078)	(0.067)	(0.070)
Host GDP per capita	0.004	0.009	0.007
	(0.011)	(0.012)	(0.012)
Host inflation	0.001	0.000	0.001
	(0.007)	(0.006)	(0.005)
Host international borrowing	0.089	0.109	0.089
	(0.110)	(0.107)	(0.091)
Host capital regulation	0.013	0.011	0.009
	(0.008)	(0.008)	(0.008)
Young		0.132***	0.118***
		(0.031)	(0.028)
Market share bank		−0.202**	−0.323***
		(0.084)	(0.108)
Solvency		0.748***	0.762***
		(0.259)	(0.262)
Loan to deposit		−0.016**	−0.018**
		(0.008)	(0.008)
Liquidity		0.153*	0.166*
		(0.088)	(0.090)
Home private credit growth			0.481*
			(0.248)
Home capital regulation			−0.032***
			(0.011)
Home OECD			0.043
			(0.080)
Home same region			0.109*
			(0.064)
Number of observations	1,759	1,420	1,382
R2	0.106	0.275	0.286

Note: The dependent variable Loan growth equals the log difference in loans between 2005 and 2007. All variable definitions and their sources can be found in Table A.1. The models are estimated using OLS. Regressions include a constant and the standard errors are clustered at the host country level. Robust standard errors appear in parentheses and ***, **, * correspond to the one, five and ten percent level of significance, respectively.

growth, and also makes all other host country variables (GDP per capita, inflation, international borrowing, and capital regulation) no longer significant. When we interact (in unreported regressions) the different host country variables with the foreign ownership dummy we find no significant effects. In other words, host country characteristics have no differential effect on the credit growth of foreign banks compared to domestic banks.

Importantly though bank characteristics matter for pre-GFC credit growth. Notably, young banks increase their lending more, likely as they still try to grow their market share. Market share itself is statistically significant negative, indicating that there are limits to the degree to which banks can gain further market share (since in non-OECD countries foreign banks often have large market shares, this effect plays a greater role in these countries than in OECD countries). Solvency (capital adequacy) is positive, i.e., better capitalized banks lend more, as do banks that have lower loan to deposit ratios and better liquidity positions. Again, when interacting these characteristics with the foreign ownership dummy (in unreported regressions) we find no differential effects.

Even though we do not find that foreign banks on average experience higher credit growth, or otherwise are differentially affected by host and individual bank characteristics, foreign banks tend to differ from domestic banks in many ways. And it turns out that they more likely have those ("good") characteristics associated with higher loan growth (Table 2). For example, foreign banks are especially more likely to be young and more liquid. This partly explains why foreign banks might lend more and gain market share during periods when credit is increasing in general and can partly explain why in the majority of countries foreign banks increased their market share in the years leading up to the global financial crisis.

We next study to what extent certain home country characteristics are correlated with the relative loan growth of foreign banks. We find that foreign banks more likely grow their lending faster in its host country if there is a credit boom at home, if capital regulation at home is more lax, and if they are active in the same region (which is mainly driven by banks operating within Europe). Controlling for the other home country factors, whether the parent bank is from an OECD

Table 2. Characteristics of domestic and foreign banks.

	Domestic	Foreign	*t*-test (*p*-value)
Young	0.11	0.54	0.00***
Market share bank	0.03	0.07	0.00***
Solvency	0.11	0.12	0.40
Loan to deposit	1.44	1.58	0.23
Liquidity	0.20	0.29	0.00***

Note: The tables shows the group means of selected bank characteristics for 1,956 domestic and 717 foreign banks. All variable definitions and their sources can be found in Table A.1. The last column shows the p-values from a two-sample t-test on the equality of the means and ***, **, * correspond to the 1, 5 and 10% level of significance, respectively.

country or not has no additional effect. In terms of economic impact, while bank fundamentals matter more (as reflected in how much bank variables contribute to the R-square), the overall impact of home country characteristics is not marginal. Specifically, host countries import through foreign banks about half of the credit growth at home, thus potentially introducing some significant risks to a local boom (and thereby increasing the risk of a bust). And a one standard deviation reduction in stringency of capital requirements at home is associated with a 9% points higher loan growth in the host country.

Overall, these findings suggest that it is important to not just look at foreign banks from a microprudential perspective (solvency, liquidity, etc.), but also to what happens in their home country, especially whether there is a credit boom, and how well parent banks are regulated.

4. Conclusion

Analyzing the role of foreign banks in the pre-GFC credit booms in 93 countries, we find that foreign bank presence in general played no major role. We do find, however, that better banks, often foreign, grew faster. Importantly, while foreign bank presence in general is not associated with a credit boom, we do find that foreign banks can "import" home country booms and regulatory risks. Specifically, when the parent bank experienced a credit boom at home, faced relatively lax capital regulation at home, and was headquartered in the same region (notably Europe), its foreign affiliate added more likely to a credit boom in the host country. The effects are economical meaningful, as foreign banks can, for example, import up to half a credit boom at home.

Our analysis comes with caveats. Importantly, our results are based on one, albeit very important, boom period. Whether our results generalize is thus unclear. Furthermore, there are likely other factors that might play a role in how foreign banks act abroad. For example, the structure of the banking system and the degree of competition in the home country may affect how banks operate abroad. Corporate governance has also been found to be an important factor for international active banks (see Huizinga in this volume). And there might be interactions between local lending and cross-border bank flows that we are currently unaware of. Furthermore, policy spillovers may play a role as well. For example, changes in home countries' capital adequacy requirements, macroprudential policies, or other regulatory measures are likely to affect the degree to which international active banks move some of their activities abroad or not. While, in part due to lack of data, we did not explore these factors, they are likely important. Indeed, some of these and other policies have been found to be important in the literature on liquidity shock transmission.[6]

In terms of policy, our results have a number of implications. For one, there is the need to consider foreign banks not just from a microprudential perspective (solvency, liquidity, etc.), but also keep an eye on the home country. This means supervisory agencies need to consider

[6] Buch & Goldberg (2015), summarizing a number of country-specific studies, report among the main results that the substantial heterogeneity in balance sheet characteristics affecting banks' responses to liquidity risk mainly matters for cross-border lending, and that risks of liquidity spillovers depend on whether the banks are drawing on official-sector liquidity facilities. See further www.newyorkfed.org/IBRN/index.html.

factors such as: who are the foreign banks, what is their strategy, how does their market share evolve, where do the foreign banks come from, how do they act at home, and what is the quality of the home regulation and supervision?

Second, since both the characteristics of the foreign bank and the home country matter for the degree to which there are spillovers, coordination between countries is even more important to assure that foreign banks do not unduly add to booms in the host country. This makes for (even) greater need to harmonize rules, exchange information, and cooperate among supervisory agencies, including in (weak) bank interventions and resolutions. The potential for spillovers also present an additional reason why macroprudential policies (e.g., the Counter Cyclical Buffer) are important to harmonize and reciprocate internationally.

A third set of policy implications relates to the ongoing changes in global banking which make some issues more important. One of these changes is the growing role of foreign banks from emerging markets. Since many credit booms happen in middle income countries, which are also more bank-based systems, our findings suggest that there could be an increased likelihood of importing credit booms. Furthermore, there are a need to consider the regulatory and supervisory quality in this set of countries more closely. While capital requirements in these countries is in general more stringent, supervision can be of lower quality. A relevant question thus is whether these countries can adequately perform their roles as home regulator and supervisor of foreign branches and local subsidiaries, including by making sure that their own banks are adequately capitalized and weak banks are quickly restructured and resolved. More generally, it is important that these supervisors are well equipped in terms of staff and resources to oversee their foreign affiliates.[7] These and other effects of the increased

[7] In supervision information, of course, is key. Perhaps more so than their advanced countries' supervisory counterparts, emerging market supervisors might not have access to the information necessary to properly assess risks in foreign affiliates. A related issue is that many emerging markets, as they are not members of the FSB or BCBS, are often not part of global supervisory colleges or risk management groups for international active banks, even though their banks can have substantial global activities.

importance of emerging market banks are unclear, but warrant further analysis and monitoring.

Another important change in global banking is the trend towards more regionalized banking systems. From regulatory and supervisory perspectives, increased regionalization can have some benefits. One of the principal lessons of the crisis is that banks which are "global in life are national in death," as many governments had to support their large banks (and banking systems more generally) in part due to losses on their international operations. Moreover, some national actions (or a lack thereof) have had negative effects on other countries. Therefore, international coordination in dealing with the supervision and failures of internationally active banks could provide large benefits. This is perhaps easier to achieve at the regional level, with the European Banking Union the prime example of improved coordination in several dimensions — regulation, supervision and resolution.[8] However, our findings suggest that increased regionalization can also translate into a greater likelihood of synchronized credit booms, which calls for some concern and close surveillance. More generally, changes underway in global banking make even more pressing to understand role of foreign banks not only in busts, but also in the buildup of vulnerabilities.

References

Bruno, V. & Shin, H. S. (2015a). Cross-border banking and global liquidity. Cross-border banking and global liquidity. *Review of Economic Studies, 82*, 535–564.

---

[8] Other recent, promising, policy efforts include the adoption of the so called FSB "Key Attributes of Effective Resolution Regimes for Financial Institutions" and other agreements to set out mechanisms to deal with global systemically important financial institutions that fail across some sets of specific jurisdictions. But much remains to be done here, including on modalities for burden sharing in case of actual failures where a need for government involvement in restructurings arises (see further the papers by Hüpkes and Pazarbaşıoğlu in this volume on the state of affairs on cross-border banking restructuring and resolution).

Bruno, V. & Shin H. S. (2015b). Capital flows and the risk-taking channel of monetary policy. *Journal of Monetary Economics*, *71*, 119–132.

Barth, J. R., Caprio, G., & Levine, R., (2013). Bank regulation and supervision in 180 countries from 1999 to 2011. *Journal of Financial Economic Policy*, *5*(2), 111–219.

Buch, C. & Goldberg, L. (2015). International banking and liquidity risk transmission: lessons from across countries. *IMF Economic Review*, 63, 377–410.

Cetorelli, N. & Goldberg, L. (2012). Liquidity management of U.S. global banks: internal capital markets in the great recession. *Journal of International Economics*, *88*, 299–311.

Claessens, S. & van Horen N. (2013). Impact of foreign banks. *Journal of Financial Perspectives*, *1*(1), 29–42.

Claessens, S. & van Horen, N. (2014a). Location decisions of foreign banks and competitor remoteness. *Journal of Money, Credit, and Banking*, *46*(1), 145–170.

Claessens, S. & van Horen, N. (2014b). Foreign banks: Trends and impact. *Journal of Money, Credit, and Banking*, 46, 295–326.

Claessens, S. & van Horen, N. (2015). The impact of the global financial crisis on banking globalization. *IMF Economic Review*, 63, 868–918.

Crystal, J. B., Dages, G., & Goldberg, L. (2001). Does foreign ownership contribute to sounder banks? The Latin American experience. In R. E. Litan, M. Paul, & M. Pomerleano (Eds.), *Open Doors: Foreign Participation in Emerging Financial Systems*. Washington, D.C.: Brookings Press.

Cull, R. & Martinez Peria, M. S. (2012). Bank ownership and lending patterns during the 2008–2009 financial crisis: Evidence from Latin America and Eastern Europe. *World Bank Policy Research Working Paper*, No. 6195.

De Haas, R. & van Lelyveld, I. (2006). Foreign banks and credit stability in Central and Eastern Europe: A panel data analysis. *Journal of Banking and Finance*, *30*, 1927–1952.

De Haas, R. & van Lelyveld, I. (2010). Internal capital markets and lending by multinational bank subsidiaries. *Journal of Financial Intermediation*, *19*, 689–721.

De Haas, R. & van Lelyveld, I. (2014). Multinational banks and the global financial crisis: weathering the perfect storm? *Journal of Money, Credit and Banking*, *46*, 333–364.

De Haas, R. & van Horen, N. (2013). Running for the exit? International bank lending during a financial crisis. *Review of Financial Studies*, *26*(1), 244–285.

De Haas, R., Korniyenko, Y., Pivovarsky A., & Tsankova T. (2015). Taming the herd? Foreign banks, the vienna initiative and crisis transmission. *Journal of Financial Intermediation*, 24(3), 325–355.

Dell'Ariccia, G., Igan, D., Laeven, L., & Tong, H. (2016). Credit booms and macrofinancial stability. *Economic Policy*, 31(86), 299–357.

IMF (2015). International banking after the crisis; increasingly local and safer? *Chapter 2, Global Financial Stability Report*, 55–91, Washington, D.C.

Mehigan, C. M. (2015). *Foreign bank identity: Does it Matter for credit growth*? Ireland: Mimeo, Trinity College Dublin.

Morais, B., Peydro, J. L., & Ruiz. C. (2015). The international bank lending channel of monetary policy rates and quantitative easing: Credit supply, reach-for-yield, and real effects. *International Finance Discussion Papers* No. 1137. Federal Reserve Board.

Ongena, S., Peydro J. L., & van Horen, N. (2015). Shocks abroad, pain at home? Bank-firm level evidence on the international transmission of financial shocks. *IMF Economic Review*, 63, 698–750.

Ongena, S., Popov, A. A., & Udell G. F. (2013). When the cat's away the mice will play: Does regulation at home affect bank risk-taking abroad? *Journal of Financial Economics*, *18*, 727–750.

Peek, J. & Rosengren, E. (1997). The international transmission of financial shocks: the case of Japan. *American Economic Review*, 87, 495–505.

Peek, J. & Rosengren, E. (2000). Collateral Damage: Effects of the Japanese Bank Crisis on the United States. *American Economic Review*, *90*, 30–45.

Popov, A. A. & Udell G. F. (2012). Cross-border banking, credit access and the financial crisis. *Journal of International Economics*, *87*, 147–161.

Rey, H. (2013). Dilemma not trilemma: the global financial cycle and monetary policy independence. In *Proceedings of the 2013 Federal Reserve Bank of Kansas City Economic Symposium at Jackson Hole*, pp. 285–333. Available at: http://www.kansascityfed.org/publicat/sympos/2013/2013Rey.pdf.

Schnabl, P. (2012). The international transmission of bank liquidity shocks: Evidence from an emerging market. *Journal of Finance*, *67*(3), 897–932.

Appendix A

Table A.1. Variable definitions and sources.

Variable	Definition	Source
Loan growth	Growth lending by the bank between 2005 and 2007 (log difference)	Claessens and Van Horen (2015)/ Bankscope
Host private credit growth	Private credit growth between 2005 and 2007 (log difference)	World Development Indicators (World Bank)
Foreign bank	Dummy which is one if the bank is foreign owned (2005)	Claessens and Van Horen (2015)
Host GDP per capita	GDP per capita (2005)	World Development Indicators (World Bank)
Host inflation	Inflation (2005)	World Development Indicators (World Bank)
Host international borrowing	International claims on banks divided by private credit (2005)	BIS Consolidated Banking Statistics (Immediate Borrower) and World Development Indicators (World Bank)
Host capital regulation	Composite index of regulatory oversight of bank capital, including minumum capital requirement adjusted for risk, deduction of loan losses, securities losses and foreign exchange losses not realized, fraction of revaluation gains allowed, verification of sources of funds to be used as capital, regulation of initial disbursement or subsequent injections of capital (2011)	Barth, *et al.* (2013)
Young	Dummy which is one when the bank has been present in the country for 10 years or less (measured in 2005).	Claessens and Van Horen (2015)/ Bankscope

(*Continued*)

Table A.1. *(Continued)*

Variable	Definition	Source
Market share	Loans held by the bank divided by total bank loans in the country (2005).	Claessens and Van Horen (2015)/ Bankscope
Solvency	Equity divided by total assets (2005)	Bankscope
Loan to deposit	Loans divided by deposits (2005)	Bankscope
Liquidity	Liquid assets divided by total assets (2005)	Bankscope
Home private credit growth	Private credit growth between 2005 and 2007 (log difference) in the home country of the foreign bank. For domestic banks the measure is the same as host private credit growth	World Development Indicators (World Bank)
Home capital regulation	Composite index of regulatory oversight of bank capital, including minumum capital requirement adjusted for risk, deduction of loan losses, securities losses and foreign exchange losses not realized, fraction of revaluation gains allowed, verification of sources of funds to be used as capital, regulation of initial disbursement or subsequent injections of capital (2011) in the home country of the foreign bank. For domestic banks the measure is the same has host capital regulation.	Barth, *et al.* (2013)
Home OECD	Dummy that is equal to one if the parent bank of the foreign bank is from an OECD country	Bankscope
Home same region	Dummy that is equal to one if the foreign bank is from a home country located in the same geographical region (Americas, Europe, Middle East and Africa or Asia). For domestic banks this variable takes the value one.	Bankscope

Part VI
Safety Net and Resolution Issues for Large and Cross-Border Banks

Towards a Global Solution for a Global Problem

— CHAPTER 19

▪ Eva H. G. Hüpkes
Financial Stability Board

1. Introduction

Following the financial crisis of 2007–2008 the G20 and the Financial Stability Board (FSB) undertook to put in place a global framework for regulating and resolving global banks. The FSB identified a set of global systemically important banks (G-SIBs) and set out specific policies to address the severe adverse consequences of the failure of these institutions otherwise perceived as "too big to fail". These policies include effective institutional arrangements and the preparation of concrete contingency plans that enable authorities to resolve a failing G-SIB in a manner that maintains the performance of functions that are vital for the economy and mitigates the adverse consequences of failure.

The development of common crisis management and resolution policies by authorities from the home and key host jurisdictions of global banks is a sea change from the pre-crisis world. Bilateral and multilateral policy cooperation amongst home and host authorities for G-SIBs has increased significantly. At the international level, the FSB adopted an international minimum standard for resolution (The Key Attributes of

The views expressed are those of the author and do not necessarily reflect the views of the FSB or its members.

Effective Resolution Regimes for Financial Institutions)[1] that sets out the core elements that the FSB considers necessary for effective resolution and developed guidance to assist authorities in implementing the standard. The FSB standard on Total Loss-Absorbing Capacity (TLAC) for global systemically important banks (TLAC Standard)[2] is the most recent addition to the FSB's policy framework. The effective implementation of the Key Attributes and the TLAC standard and other resolution policies is likely to lead to further changes in the ways firms operate and structure themselves. Authorities may need to adapt the ways in which they cooperate and share their supervisory and resolution responsibilities. This chapter discusses some of changes that may arise.

2. A New Paradigm — from Bankruptcy to Resolution

An important change in paradigm relates to the way failing firms are resolved. The Key Attributes set out the powers and tools that authorities should have to resolve failing financial firms in a manner that allocates the financial costs of failure not to the public, but to the firm's shareholders and creditors. Importantly they require the statutory power to restructure the liabilities of a distressed firm by writing down unsecured debt and converting it to equity.

Resolution differs fundamentally from standard bankruptcy and insolvency processes. Ordinary bankruptcy is a process that is focused on legal entities. Bankruptcy can work for individual companies, but it is messy

---

[1]The FSB adopted the *Key Attributes* at its Plenary meeting in October 2011. The G20 Heads of States and Government subsequently endorsed the *Key Attributes* (KAs) at the Cannes Summit in November 2011 as "a new international standards for resolution regimes". On October 15, 2014, the FSB adopted additional guidance that elaborates on specific KAs relating to information sharing for resolution purposes and sector-specific guidance that sets out how the *Key Attributes* should apply for insurers, financial market infrastructures (FMIs) and the protection of client assets in resolution.

[2]See TLAC Principles and Term Sheet of 9 November, http://www.fsb.org/2015/11/total-loss-absorbing-capacity-tlac principles-and-term-sheet/

and disruptive if applied to complex group structures with hundreds of financially and operationally interconnected entities located in multiple jurisdictions.[3] Resolution pays greater heed to the systemic consequences of financial failure by seeking to ensure that critical functions continue to be performed by a reconstituted institution, a newly established bridge institution, or otherwise by market participants. It relies on *ex-ante* resolution planning. Home and key host authorities should, as part of their resolution planning, identify the entity or entities within a financial group to which resolution powers would be applied. The objective is to limit resolution processes to one or a few entities, and thereby avoid the frictions that multiple legal entity-based proceedings could cause, in particular where they take place in different jurisdictions.

The legal entities to which resolution powers are applied are called 'resolutions entities' in the TLAC standard. The group consisting of the resolution entity and the subsidiaries that sit under it is referred to as 'resolution group'. A banking group can have multiple resolution entities and groups. Depending on the resolution strategy for the G-SIB in question, a resolution entity could be a parent company, an intermediate or ultimate holding company, or an operating subsidiary. Resolution strategies fall into two categories: 'single point of entry' (SPE) strategies, where resolution powers and tools are applied to one legal entity in a group structure by its home resolution authority; and 'multiple points of entry' (MPE) strategies, where resolution tools are applied to different parts of the group, by two or more resolution authorities which the FSB expects to act in a coordinated way.[4]

2.1. *SPE*

The objective of SPE strategies is to resolve the G-SIB group as a single economic entity. This strategy is appropriate where there are significant

[3] Most G-SIBs in the U.S. and Europe are legally organized in hundreds, sometimes thousands, of legally separate subsidiaries with little resemblance to the functional organization. See Caramassi & Richard (2015).

[4] See FSB Guidance on developing effective resolution strategies and plans of July 15, 2013. See http://www.fsb.org/2013/07/r_130716b/.

operational interdependencies across the subsidiaries of the G-SIB group, so that resolving them separately is not feasible.

The intent is to bail-in (write-down and/or convert) equity and other loss-absorbing instruments issued by the resolution entity. Funds will be passed down to subsidiaries within the banking group to absorb losses and recapitalize them. As long as there is sufficient TLAC at the resolution entity, material operating subsidiaries or sub-groups should, in principle, be able to continue as going concerns without themselves entering resolution.

2.2. *MPE*

Under MPE strategies, the G-SIB could be broken up into separate parts upon resolution. This strategy tends to be more appropriate where the firm's structure is more modular with fewer operational interdependencies between resolution groups. Bail-in powers would be applied to equity and unsecured debt issued by each resolution entity in the group (most likely in different jurisdictions). For example, where a resolution entity is a subsidiary, the parent's equity in the subsidiary resolution entity could be written down to zero and the holders of TLAC issued by this subsidiary who had their claims converted to equity would become the new owners of the resolution group.

3. A New Standard on Total Loss-Absorbing Capacity for G-SIBs

One of the objectives of the G20 and the FSB is to avoid the use of fiscal resources when dealing with financial crises. Apart from being deeply unpopular with the electorate, the use of taxpayers' money can create moral hazard and, in cases where the banking system is large, lead to questions about the sustainability of public debt. The Key Attributes require resolution authorities to have statutory powers to 'bail-in' shareholders as well as unsecured and uninsured creditors of a failing financial institution. This should be achieved through powers to write down the value of such claims and/or convert liabilities into equity stakes in the firm. Write-down and conversion should occur in a manner that respects the order in which creditors would normally be paid out in liquidation (the statutory hierarchy of claims). Bail-in may take the form of either a "direct" or "open bank bail-in", i.e., the write-down and/or exchange of an entity's unsecured debt for equity in the same legal entity; or "indirect bail-in" or "bridge bail-in", i.e., the exchange of the failed entity's unsecured debt for equity in a bridge institution to which all or a portion of its assets have been transferred.

To make a bail-in resolution credible, there needs to be sufficient loss-absorbing capacity in the capital and liability structure of G-SIBS. The TLAC standard seeks to operationalise bail-in by ensuring that a sufficient layer of liabilities is readily identified and available to absorb losses and recapitalise G-SIBs in resolution. It is predicated on the assumption that Key Attributes-compliant bail-in frameworks are in place in the home and key host jurisdictions where G-SIBs operate.

4. TLAC Quality, Quantity, and Location

TLAC should provide greater ex ante clarity to whom and in what order losses will be allocated. It should improve the operations of markets by reducing the distortions associated with the implicit subsidy embedded in bail-outs. To achieve those objectives TLAC must be of the right quality and quantity and in the right location.

4.1. *Quality — What Counts as TLAC, What Does Not?*

The FSB standard specifies the types of instrument that can serve as TLAC as well as those that cannot. TLAC must be available and readily bail-inable at the point of resolution. For example, short-term liabilities can be a source of vulnerability because they might not be renewed and therefore no longer available as the firm approaches the point of entry into resolution. Accordingly, they do not qualify as TLAC even though they may nevertheless be bailed in on entry into resolution.

Liabilities that are directly linked to critical functions provided by the G-SIB, such as, for example the deposit taking or payment functions, do in principle not qualify as TLAC since any write-down or conversion of such liabilities could interfere with the critical economic functions that the firm performs.

TLAC should absorb losses ahead of operational liabilities which are excluded from TLAC eligibility. This means that TLAC should in principle be subordinated to such liabilities in the creditor hierarchy. The TLAC standard provides for an exception to the subordination requirement and allows TLAC-eligible instruments to count toward the TLAC minimum requirement if they rank *pari passu* with excluded liabilities as long as they do not exceed a minimum threshold.[5] There may have to be some exceptions to this principle to accommodate resolution strategies and national laws, but the exceptions must pass the test of low risk of legal challenge based on a violation of the "no creditor worse off than in liquidation" (NCWOL) safeguard. Under the NCWOL safeguard, creditors should receive in resolution at least what they would have received if the firm were placed into liquidation. If they do not, they should be entitled to compensation.

[5] See Section 11 of the TLAC Term sheet which provides that subordination of eligible external TLAC to excluded liabilities is not required if (i) the amount of excluded liabilities (Section 10) on the balance sheet of the resolution entity that rank *pari passu* or junior to the TLAC-eligible liabilities does not exceed 5% of there solution entity's eligible external TLAC; (ii) the resolution authority of the G-SIB has the authority to differentiate among *pari passu* creditors in resolution; (iii) differentiation in resolution in favor of such excluded liabilities would not give rise to material risk of successful legal challenge or valid compensation claims; and (iv) this does not have a material adverse impacton resolvability. Also, in jurisdictions where the resolution authority may, under exceptional circumstances specified in the applicable resolution law, exclude or partially exclude from bail-in all of the liabilities excluded from TLAC specified in Section 10, the relevant authorities may permit liabilities that would otherwise be eligible to count as external TLAC but which rank alongside those excluded liabilities in the insolvency creditor hierarchy to contribute a quantum equivalent of up to 2.5% RWA of the resolution entity's Minimum TLAC requirement when the TLAC RWA Minimum is 16%, and up to 3.5% RWA when the TLAC RWA Minimum is 18%. If this option is used, authorities must ensure that the capacity to exclude or partially exclude liabilities from bail-in would not.

To ensure that TLAC is likely to be available and loss-absorbing at the point of entry into resolution, eligible instruments must be paid-in, unsecured, not be subject to set off or netting rights, and have a minimum remaining maturity of at least one year.

In addition, where the TLAC instrument is governed by a law other than the law of the jurisdiction of the resolution entity, there must be certainty that the bail-in will be legally enforceable on the basis of statutory or contractual recognition.

To enable market participants to make investment decisions based on an informed understanding of the associated risks, G-SIBs will be required to disclose the amount, maturity, and composition of their TLAC, as well as the amount, nature, and maturity of liabilities that rank equal to, or are subordinated to, TLAC instruments in the creditor hierarchy.

4.2. *Quantity — How Much TLAC is Enough?*

TLAC must be available in amounts that are sufficient to foster market confidence that vital economic functions will continue to be performed in and after resolution. For G-SIBs that are headquartered in advanced economies, the FSB's common minimum TLAC requirement has been set as follows: from January 1, 2019, resolution entities must hold TLAC instruments at least equivalent in value to 16% of the resolution group's risk weighted assets (RWAs) and 6% of unweighted exposures; from January 1, 2022, resolution entities must hold TLAC instruments of at least 18% of the resolution group's RWAs and 6.75% of unweighted exposures. G-SIBs headquartered in emerging market economies, where capital markets are less well developed, are expected to meet the lower requirement by January 1, 2025 and the higher requirement by January 1, 2028 at the latest. The FSB's minimum TLAC requirement is set with reference to both risk-weighted assets (RWAs) and unweighted balance sheet assets, as defined by the Basel III leverage ratio exposure measure.[6] The minimum TLAC requirement applies at the level of the 'resolution entity', rather than for the whole banking group.

[6] See BCBS (Basel Committee on Banking Supervision) (2014).

In addition to the common minimum, home authorities of resolution entities, in consultation with the Crisis Management Group CMG and subject to review in the Resolvability Assessment Process (RAP), should apply additional firm-specific requirements if they deem that this is necessary and appropriate to implement an orderly resolution and assure the continued performance of critical functions. In practice, the reorganisation that will be necessary following resolution may require a level of capitalisation above that required by supervisors to command market confidence.

The FSB's historical loss and recapitalization study found that the size of the minimum TLAC requirement is likely to have been sufficient to meet the loss absorption and recapitalization needs of most, though not all, systemically important global banks that failed in recent crises.[7] The minimum requirement was set taking into account post-crisis regulatory improvements and recognizing that the minimum standard will be supplemented by supervisory efforts. Overall, the economic impact analysis study concluded that the benefits from the reduced likelihood and severity of financial crises outweighed the costs that might arise from higher bank funding costs.[8]

4.3. *Location — TLAC in the Group Structure*

TLAC must be available in the right place. Location of loss-absorbing resources and their distribution in a group matters, particularly in a cross-border context. One important lesson from the global financial crisis was that cooperation easily breaks down when there is competition for resources to resolve a firm. Whereas in good times a firm can operate central control over capital and liquidity and move resources from one entity to a foreign affiliate when needed, this flexibility may disappear in a crisis.

---

[7] FSB, BCBS, and BIS (2015).

[8] Assessing the economic costs and benefits of TLAC implementation report submitted to the Financial Stability Board by an Experts Group chaired by Kostas Tsatsaronis (Bank for International Settlements) November 2015.

4.3.1. External and internal TLAC

The location of TLAC will be determined by the resolution strategy. SPE assumes that the top parent is also the single resolution entity and will act as a source of strength for its subsidiaries in times of stress. It also assumes that, in the event of failure, the parent entity will be resolved in a manner that ensures that critical operations carried out through material subsidiaries can continue. To this end, TLAC issued by the parent to third parties will be bailed in to recapitalize the parent and generate sufficient loss-absorbing and recapitalization resources that can be down-streamed to the parent's material subsidiaries or material sub-groups to maintain the continuity of their vital functions or facilitate their orderly wind-down. To provide assurances that loss-absorbing resources will be down-streamed from the parent to a material subsidiary that is located in a foreign jurisdiction, the TLAC standard requires foreign subsidiaries or groups of subsidiaries that are deemed material ("material subsidiaries" or "material sub-groups") to have on their balance sheet ("prepositioned") liabilities issued to a parent that is a resolution entity. These liabilities (referred to as "internal TLAC") should be subject to write-down and/or conversion into equity in the subsidiary prior to the bail-in of any third-party creditor claims. Such internal bail-in transactions should shift loss to the parent without necessitating the entry into resolution of the subsidiary. The new equity that is generated by way of bail-in would then be held by the recapitalized parent or, in the case of an indirect or bridge bail-in, by the newly established bridge institution.

MPE assumes that there are two or more points of entry into resolution either at holding/sub-holding or operational entity level and that sufficient TLAC is located at each of those entities. It is assumed that each of those entities will be subject to separate (albeit coordinated) resolution proceedings and that the bail-in of TLAC at those entities will generate sufficient loss-absorbing and recapitalization capacity to maintain or ensure the orderly wind-down of vital economic functions provided by those entities (or sub-groups). MPE and SPE resolution strategies can be combined. For example, an MPE resolution strategy can be the combination of two or more SPE strategies that are applied at a sub-holding level.

5. TLAC Implementation — Impact on Structure and Business

The implementation of the TLAC standard is likely to affect the ways in which firms operate and structure themselves, and lead to structural changes as in case of the reforms being undertaken on the basis of the Vickers Report and Volcker Rule.[9]

To implement the TLAC standard firms will have to review their legal and organizational structures and capital/liability structures to ensure that external and internal TLAC are issued out of the right locations and that the subordination requirement is met. They will seek to rationalize their structures to meet the various requirements in the most efficient and cost-effective way, for instance by minimizing the number of material subsidiaries or by reducing the risk-profile of their resolution entity or resolution group.

In the pre-crisis world, many global banks operated as integrated global firms managed along business lines. Some argue that in the future there will be greater functional subsidiarization with a holding structure composed of "independent" subsidiaries.[10] Whether integrated global operations can be maintained or whether structures will increasingly be compartmentalized along jurisdictional lines, with legal forms following more closely business functions, will in part depend on how resolution strategies are implemented. Structures and operations may need to change to conform with structural reform requirements, make firms more resolvable and implement the TLAC standard. A few examples of ways in which the TLAC standard may affect firm structure and operations are set out below.

5.1. *TLAC Issuance and the Subordination Requirement*

Firms will have to issue TLAC-eligible instruments out of an entity that is a resolution entity. Issuance of TLAC out of funding entities or

---

[9] Vickers Report, The Independent Commission on Banking (ICB). Final Report, Recommendations, September 2011. The "Volcker Rule," Section 619 of Title VI of the Dodd Frank Act.

[10] Global Banks: Good or Good-bye? Presentation by Huertas (2015).

subsidiaries that are not resolution entities is not permitted, subject however to certain exceptions and a phase-out provision.[11] SPE firms with a non-operating (clean) holding company as resolution entity may face restrictions on transactions that they can enter into at holding-company level. If TLAC is issued in the form of senior debt, the holding company cannot have on its balance sheet excluded liabilities that rank *pari passu* with that debt in excess of 5% of the resolution entity's eligible external TLAC. To the extent that derivatives and instruments with derivative-linked features such as structured notes are *pari passu* with senior debt, the issuance of such instruments out of the holding company (and out of any of its branches) would therefore need to be limited.

If the resolution entity were an operational entity with significant amounts of short-term deposits on its balance sheet that fall into the class of senior creditors, the parent would face limitations in regard to the amount of TLAC-eligible instruments that could rank *pari passu* and could count toward the TLAC minimum requirement. The TLAC standard provides that authorities may permit liabilities that would otherwise be eligible to count as external TLAC but which rank alongside those excluded liabilities in the insolvency creditor hierarchy to contribute a quantum equivalent of up to 2.5% RWA of the resolution entity's Minimum TLAC requirement when the TLAC RWA Minimum is 16%,

[11] Section 8 of the Term Sheet provides that External TLAC must be issued and maintained directly by resolution entities with exceptions for CET1 regulatory capital issued from subsidiaries forming part of a resolution entity's resolution group and held by third parties and regulatory capital instruments issued by cooperative banks or financial institutions affiliated to them. Regulatory capital instruments, other than CET1, issued out of subsidiaries of a resolution group and held by third parties may only be used to meet Minimum TLAC until December 31, 2021 and debt liabilities issued indirectly by a wholly and directly owned funding entity of the resolution entity prior to January 1, 2022 may be used to meet Minimum TLAC provided that the issuance is consistent with the rules set out in paragraph 65 of the Basel III framework, including that the assets of the funding entity must meet or exceed eligibility criteria (Section 9) for TLAC instruments; there is substantial legal certainty that the issued TLAC will absorb losses at the resolution entity upon its entry into resolution; and home and host authorities agree in the CMG on the issuance through the wholly owned funding entity.

and up to 3.5% RWA when the TLAC RWA Minimum is 18%, subject to certain conditions. For example, a condition is that the resolution authority has the capacity, under exceptional circumstances specified in the applicable resolution law, to depart from the pari passu treatment of creditors within the same class without such departure giving rise to a material risk of successful legal challenge or valid compensation claims.

Given this limitation, firms would have to adapt their structure and business, or issue TLAC in the form of subordinated debt. Some EU jurisdictions have adopted or are in the process of adopting legislative changes in the creditor hierarchy with the view to creating a class of bail-inable creditors that can be easily and quickly be determined.[12] Such legislative changes would enable firms with operational resolution entities to meet the subordination requirements without making changes in their liability structure and reduce the risk of violating the NCWOL safeguard.

5.2. *Recognition of the Extraterritorial Effect of Resolution Actions (Temporary Stays and Bail-in)*

The objective under any resolution strategy is that the critical economic functions can continue. Provided there is sufficient TLAC available only the capital-structure liabilities (which include TLAC) should be exposed to loss. Operational liabilities, which include derivatives and securities financing transactions, should be protected provided they rank senior to TLAC in the creditor hierarchy. However, the instinct of derivatives counterparties in times of stress may well be to seek to exercise their contractual acceleration or termination rights. The termination of large volumes of financial contracts could seriously impact the firm's ability

[12] For example, Germany adopted a law on the subordination of banks' senior unsecured debt to other senior unsecured liabilities (primarily deposits). In Italy, a government decrees was adopted that establishes depositor preference over banks' senior unsecured debt in liquidation. In France, a legislative proposal introduces the possibility for banks to issue senior non-preferred debt which, in liquidation or bail-in (in resolution), would rank below other senior liabilities (primarily deposits, but also other senior unsecured debt.

to continue to conduct its critical operations. The Key Attributes therefore provide that jurisdictions should impose a brief stay on the exercise of early termination rights that may otherwise be triggered upon entry of a firm into resolution or in connection with the use of resolution powers — subject to adequate safeguards and provided counterparties continue to fulfil all their obligations.[13] Such a stay on termination rights also needs to capture early termination rights arising in contracts of the resolution entity that are governed by foreign law or entered into with foreign counterparties as well as termination rights arising from cross-default provisions contained in contracts of the firm's foreign affiliates. In the absence of a statutory or treaty-based recognition framework that confers extraterritorial effect to the temporary stay a pragmatic approach is to rely on contractual recognition. To this end, the International Swap Dealers Association (ISDA) developed the 2014 ISDA Resolution Stay Protocol to support the cross-border enforcement of a temporary stay of early termination rights in a transaction governed by the ISDA Master Agreement for bilateral OTC derivatives have adhered to the Protocol.[14] In 2015, the Protocol was extended beyond OTC derivatives to include securities lending and repurchase (repo) agreements (collectively, 'securities financing transactions' or SFT). To ensure wide cross-border enforceability of temporary stays on close out rights in resolution all significant contracting entities within G-SIBs as well as their counter parties need to adhere to the protocol or otherwise trade on similar terms.

A similar approach will need to be adopted where a resolution entity issues TLAC under third-country law. The resolution authority must be satisfied that the TLAC instruments can be easily bailed-in. In the absence of a statutory framework that provides for quasi automatic cross-border recognition, the instruments need to include contractual recognition provisions.[15]

---

[13] See I-Annex 5 to the Key Attributes of Effective Resolution Regimes.

[14] See Geen *et al.* (2015).

[15] See Principles on cross-border effectiveness of resolution actions of November 3, 2015, available at http://www.fsb.org/2015/11/principles-for-cross-border-effectiveness-of-resolution-actions/

6. TLAC Implementation — Impact on Cross-Border Cooperation and Coordination

Implementation of the TLAC standard will also bring about changes in the manner in which home and key host authorities exercise their supervisory responsibilities with respect to global banks and how such responsibilities are shared.

6.1. *Identification of Material Subsidiaries or Subgroups*

Home authorities, together with key host authorities, need to reach a common understanding of what constitutes the preferred resolution strategy (SPE or MPE) and, on this basis, identify the resolution entity or entities that will be subject to a TLAC requirement. In addition, the host authorities should, in consultation with the home authority of the resolution entity, identify the subsidiaries or sub-groups located outside of the home jurisdiction that, based on qualitative and quantitative criteria set out in the TLAC standard and agreed by the authorities, should be deemed material. The materiality criteria set out in the TLAC standard include both qualitative as well as quantitative criteria. They can be met by one subsidiary alone or by several subsidiaries in which case they would form a material sub-group.[16] One qualitative criterion is that the subsidiary or subsidiaries have been identified by the firm's CMG as "material to the exercise of the firm's critical functions". Subsidiaries and subgroups that include banks and/or non-bank financial institutions that are deemed material will be subject to an internal TLAC requirement. Internal TLAC provides a mechanism to upstream losses from material operating subsidiaries to the parent resolution entity and thereby to stabilize the critical functions provided by those material subsidiaries or sub-groups.[17]

Under the TLAC Standard, subsidiaries that are not deemed material or part of a material sub-group are not required to hold internal

---

[16] See TLAC Term Sheet Sect. 17 a.-d.

[17] See Section 4.3

TLAC on their balance sheet. However, subsidiaries that are not economically significant for the G-SIB as a whole and as such not material for purposes of the TLAC standard may nevertheless be systemic in a host jurisdiction where they are located. Host authorities may therefore exercise their own discretion to apply TLAC or similar requirements on such subsidiaries, whether deemed material under the TLAC standard or not.[18]

The TLAC Standard stipulates that an internal TLAC requirement should be applied to material sub-groups in foreign host jurisdictions given that one of its purpose is to promote home-host cooperation in a crisis. However, the resolution entity's home authority has the discretion to apply internal TLAC requirements (or similar requirements) to domestic subsidiaries or sub-groups within its jurisdiction to facilitate the group-internal distribution of TLAC domestically.[19]

The decision on how TLAC resources should be distributed across subsidiaries, what form they should take, how much should be prepositioned, and when and by whom an internal TLAC should be bailed-in requires coordination and compromise amongst home and host authorities. The FSB's requirement to preposition a certain amount of internal TLAC at foreign subsidiaries should make host authorities confident that there are sufficient resources available in the host jurisdiction to maintain continuity of operations even in times of stress. The host authorities may not have this confidence unless adequate resources are prepositioned in the host jurisdiction and available for bail-in that can be activated by the host authority in times of stress.

However, prepositioning may drain resources from the parent that would otherwise enable the parent to allocate resources flexibly to domestic or foreign subsidiaries, or to support foreign branch

---

[18] See TLAC term-sheet Sect. 16.

[19] The proposed rule by the Federal Reserve Board released on October 30, 2015 ('proposed FRB rule'), which sets a new long-term debt requirement (LTD) and TLAC requirement for domestic firms identified by the Federal Reserve Board (FRB) as global systemic and for the U.S. operations of foreign GSIBs, requests comments on whether the material domestic operating subsidiaries of U.S. G-SIBs should be required to issue a form of internal TLAC to their parent companies.

operations which fall outside of the TLAC requirement. The TLAC standard provides for some flexibility in the determination of the internal TLAC requirement which should be within 75–90% of the external Minimum TLAC requirement that would apply to the material sub-group if it were a resolution group, as calculated by the host authority. Host authorities of material sub-groups should in consultation with the home authority of the resolution group determine the exact amount of the requirement.

6.2. *Defining the Internal TLAC Trigger*

The host authority should be able to bail-in internal TLAC and thereby recapitalize the subsidiary without having to place the subsidiary into resolution. That way, the subsidiary remains going concern. A pragmatic approach to achieve this outcome is to incorporate contractual terms in the internal TLAC instruments that set out when and how the write-down and conversion of internal TLAC will occur. The contractual internal TLAC trigger must adequately balance home and host interests. Host authorities may prefer an earlier trigger as their interest is to remove losses from the subsidiary as quickly as possible to preserve local financial stability. Home authorities may be concerned about a premature triggering of internal TLAC that drains resources from the parent and sets off a chain reaction causing other hosts to trigger internal TLAC. The FSB Standard provides that the host authority should not trigger an internal bail-in without the consent from the home authority. Only in exceptional circumstances where the consent of the home authority is not forthcoming and where the conditions for initiating domestic resolution proceedings are met should the host authority act on its own and bail-in the internal TLAC.

One of the first concrete proposals for the design of a contractual internal TLAC trigger is set out in proposed FRB rule. It provides for an internal TLAC requirement for U.S. Intermediate Holding Companies (IHCs) that are controlled by a foreign G-SIB. Under the proposed rule, the contractual trigger would enable the FRB to require the IHC to cancel internal LTD or convert or exchange it into common equity Tier 1 capital outside of resolution if the IHC is in default or in danger of default; and if any of the following circumstances apply (i) the parent or any affiliate outside the U.S. is placed into resolution; (ii) the home authority consents to the internal TLAC bail-in, or does not object following 48 h' prior notice from the FRB; or (iii) the FRB has made a written recommendation to the Secretary of the Treasury that the Orderly Liquidation Authority ("OLA") provisions of the Dodd–Frank Wall Street Reform and Consumer Protection Act of 2010 ("Dodd–Frank") are invoked. The proposed contract terms would ensure that the trigger is activated only as a last resort in times of severe stress when the foreign parent enters resolution or the home resolution authority consents or does not object or when there is a threat to domestic financial stability as evidenced by an application for resolution under OLA.

6.3. *Cross-Border Supervision*

The TLAC standard will not only give a clear focus and direction to resolution planning, it is also likely lead to a continuing strengthening of cross-border supervision. Home authorities a strong supervisory interest in the safety and soundness of foreign material subsidiaries given that the SPE parent entity will have to absorb the subsidiaries losses if internal TLAC is triggered. However, given that the parent's TLAC resources are limited and likely not sufficient to absorb losses at several subsidiaries at the same time, host authorities therefore will need to remain vigilant.

Internal TLAC balances support for a preferred group-wide coordinated resolution strategy with assurances to the host jurisdiction in the event that the group-wide strategy cannot be executed successfully. Clear and predictable requirements in the form of internal TLAC imposed by host country authorities *ex ante* appear to be far preferable to *ex post* constraints — for example, ring-fencing — that are unpredictable and imposed ad hoc when the foreign bank is under the greatest pressure.[20]

[20] Governor Tarullo (2015).

7. Conclusion

TLAC is a necessary but not a sufficient condition for successful resolution. There are number of other important resolvability conditions, including temporary stays on close-out rights, access to sufficient amounts of liquidity in resolution, arrangements that support continuity of critical services, and continuity of access in resolution to financial market infrastructure services, central counterparties in particular.[21] If implemented effectively and consistently across G-SIB home and key host jurisdictions TLAC, combined with appropriate firm structures and resolution strategies will help to provide a global solution for a global problem. If authorities and firms fail to implement these policies effectively, there is a risk that we see more local fragmentation that is detrimental to global banks and banking.

References

BCBS (2014). Basel III Leverage ratio framework and disclosure requirements. *Bank for International Settlements*, Basel, January

Caramassi, L. & Richard, J. H. (2015). Corporate structures, transparency and resolvability of global systemically important banks.

Financial Stability Board (2015). Removing remaining obstacles to resolution. *Report to the G20 on Progress in Resolution of 9 November 2015.*

FSB, BCBS & BIS (2015). 'Summary of findings from the TLAC impact assessment studies: Overview report', 9 November.

Geen, D. (2015). A step closer to ending too-big-to-fail: The ISDA 2014 resolution stay protocol and contractual Recognition of cross-border resolution, 35 Futures & Derivatives L. Rep., April. 2015, at 5, available at: http://www.cgsh.com/files/Publication/e9499fbe-a7ff-4bdd-b418-3976b6e2a00a/Presentation/PublicationAttachment/2ae1dcfc-9762-44ae-84e8-45a647bdaa47/FDLR35%233_AA_Geen.pdf

Huertas, T. F. (2015) *Federal Reserve Bank of Chicago 18th International Banking Conference* November 5, Chapter 5 in this volume.

Tarullo, D. K. (2015). Shared Responsibility for the regulation of international Banks. *Speech at the Federal Reserve Bank of Chicago*, November 5, 2015: in this volume.

[21] See Financial Stability Board (2015).

Cross-Border Bank Resolution: Recent Developments

— CHAPTER 20

- Ceyla Pazarbasioglu
  World Bank

- Ross Leckow, Barend Jansen, Marina Moretti, Wouter Bossu, Alvaro Piris, Elsie Addo Awadzi, Marc Dobler, Alessandro Gullo, Oana Nedelescu, Sven Stevenson, and Oliver Wünsch
  International Monetary Fund

1. Indroduction

Cross-border bank resolution is at the forefront of the international regulatory reform agenda. In the wake of the global crisis, a central feature of the international community's efforts to make the global financial system safer has been to end "too-big-to-fail" financial institutions. This effort has focused on identifying global systemically important financial institutions (G-SIFIs), making them more resilient through increased capital and tighter regulation and supervision, and

---

The material in this article was originally published as an *IMF Policy Paper*, June 2014, Washington D.C. It is reprinted with permission, with minor alterations to adhere to the style of World Scientific. Readers are directed to the original publication for additional information. The material in this article was the basis for the presentation by Ceyla Pazarbasioglu at the Federal Reserve Bank of Chicago's 18th annual International Banking Conference, November 5–6, 2015. At the time of the conference Ms. Pazarbasioglu was a senior advisor in the Finance and Markets Global Practice at the World Bank Group, on a secondment from the International Monetary Fund.

strengthening the resolution regime to minimize risks of financial instability and taxpayer loss should they fail. On this last dimension, the international response has centered on the work of the Financial Stability Board (FSB), in particular, the *Key Attributes of Effective Resolution Regimes for Financial Institutions* (Key Attributes) — a new international standard endorsed by the G20 leaders in 2011. The IMF has played an active role in the development of the Key Attributes, in particular through the 2010 Board paper on *Resolution of Cross-Border Banks — A Proposed Framework for Enhanced Coordination.*[1]

Consensus has been reached on a framework, but important details need to be worked out — as yet, orderly resolution of systemic cross-border banks is not a feasible option. Despite ambitious legislative reforms, more needs to be done at the country level to fully implement the Key Attributes. Moreover, international agreement and further guidance is needed in a number of areas. These include the development of mechanisms to facilitate the allocation of losses among private stakeholders, and to manage the residual risks that public funds may be needed. Greater consideration of the applicability of the Key Attributes beyond the G-SIFIs and their main countries of operation is also needed.

This chapter reviews recent progress in the development of an effective framework for cross-border bank resolution and identifies the key gaps that need to be addressed. As it has been two years since the Executive Board was last given a comprehensive briefing on cross-border resolution, an update on developments is timely.[2] The paper begins with an examination of the principal lessons learned from the recent financial crisis and the weaknesses in the international framework that the crisis exposed. It then discusses how the Key Attributes seek to address these weaknesses, and countries' progress in implementation. The paper then discusses the gaps that remain to be filled in the design of the international framework and ways to address implementation challenges.

---

[1] *Resolution of Cross-Border Banks — A Proposed Framework for Enhanced Coordination* (IMF Policy Paper, June 2010).

[2] *The Key Attributes of Effective Resolution Regimes for Financial Institutions — Progress to Date and Next Steps* (IMF Policy Paper, August 2012).

2. Cross-Border Resolution in Practice

Cross-border banks have benefits — and costs.[3] The experience of the past decade has demonstrated the benefits and potential risks presented by the rapid growth of cross-border banking. By pursuing growth opportunities beyond their borders, successful national banks export capital and banking technologies, and realize economies of scale in managing large, diversified operations. Risk is pooled across economies, and the banks' "deep pockets" often provide a credible backstop for host authorities. However, in the face of a systemic shock, these entities are also instant transmitters of financial stress. The capacity to safeguard global financial stability and minimize losses through an efficient resolution process then becomes essential.

The vast majority of cross-border finance is intermediated by a small, core set of financial institutions that are interconnected. In 2008, 145 banks globally accounted for 85% of the assets of the world's top 1,000 banks. Some of the largest cross-border groups have assets that account for several times their home country GDP. With $10 trillion of total assets, the top five largest cross-border banking groups account for about 10% of global banking industry assets. These five groups, all of which are headquartered in Europe, have over 50% of their credit risk exposures and employ roughly 60% of their staff outside their "home" country, with subsidiaries in more than 60 countries.

Resolving a cross-border bank involves enormous challenges. Financial groups develop complex international structures in order to exploit new business opportunities and maximize profits. These structures are often made up of hundreds of different entities in a web of financial and operational interdependency. When such an institution fails, authorities in different jurisdictions have to confront significant uncertainty and institutional constraints, and potentially misaligned incentives. Without an effective arsenal of resolution tools and cooperative arrangements between key

[3]The rise of cross-border banking is well documented (see e.g., *Global Financial Stability Report,* April 2014, Box 3) and the academic literature has examined its benefits and challenges. On resolution aspects, see Claessens, Herring, and Schoenmaker (2010).

jurisdictions, orderly resolution of a large cross-border financial group will prove impossible.

Incentives for cooperation in cross-border resolution are typically weak. Resolution authorities are answerable to domestic constituencies; their first responsibility is often to protect domestic financial stability and minimize any risk to public funds. Although preserving international business lines, financial links, and operational dependencies in resolution may minimize overall economic losses from a bank's failure, individual country perspectives may differ from globally efficient solutions. Unilateral "ring-fencing" operations may allow protecting systemic operations domestically at a cost or risk known with some margin of error, versus an uncertain gain from an orderly international intervention, with risk of a worse outcome. Where public funds are put at risk, bearing a share of the burden that is later perceived to be "unfair" or disproportionate could carry important political costs. "Home" — where the parent company is located — and "host" — where international affiliates are located — jurisdictions of cross-border banks can face starkly different incentives to cooperate where affiliates are either systemic for the host, but immaterial for the group; or material for the group, but not systemic for the host. In both cases, one party may have strong incentives to take unilateral action, even if this has a material impact on the group and generates spillovers for other countries.

Ex ante agreements on public sector burden sharing may not amount to credible commitments and have had little impact in practice to date. Prior to the recent crisis, even the exchange of information proved difficult, given legal constraints and sometimes conflicting national interests (Box 1). Formal agreements on sharing the public costs of resolution have been difficult to achieve in practice, as incentives to depart from their provisions in the light of actual circumstances are high. Moreover, the existence of formal burden sharing agreements that suggest that public funds will sometimes be available for resolution may increase moral hazard.

A key lesson from the 2008 crisis was that national authorities lacked both the legal tools and the cooperative arrangements needed to resolve cross-border financial groups. National authorities faced huge challenges in responding to bank failures, both of large, systemic financial

Box 1: Why did MoUs Fail to Secure Cooperation in the Global Financial Crisis?

MoUs grew in importance as supervisory cooperation intensified. Cross-border cooperation in banking supervision has existed since the 1970s, with Basel Committee work on consolidated supervision. Through the 1990s, standards focused on information flows between home and host supervisors, with cooperation in crisis times generally deemed unrealistic. Supervisory cooperation intensified in the 2000s, with work on MoUs and cooperation between banking supervisors embodied in Basel II stimulating the development of supervisory colleges. A 2006 Financial Stability Institute (FSI) survey found that 80% of bank supervisors worldwide used MoUs and informal contacts to support supervision in normal times.

Much less thought was given to cross-border arrangements on crisis management. The FSI survey found that only 19% of supervisors would make use of college arrangements to address financial stress, while 49% would resort to ad hoc meetings, and 40% had no formal arrangements at all. In 2003, EU national banking supervisors and central banks did agree on a multilateral MoU on high-level principles for cooperation in crisis management, later revised and expanded to include Ministries of Finance. The goal was to enable timely engagement and adequate information for all parties involved in a crisis, committing signatories to: (i) information exchange; (ii) joint public communication; (iii) joint contingency planning; (iv) optionally, forming cross-border stability groups; and (v) voluntary specific cooperation agreements on burden sharing. The agreement was not legally binding.

Supervisory MoUs failed to enable cooperation in the crisis. As MoUs were non binding and supervisory colleges were not empowered to make decisions, many MoU commitments — such as timely sharing of information — were quickly abandoned as domestic financial stability concerns became paramount. Supervisory colleges could not restrain unilateral action. MoUs did not provide for specific timelines or escalation procedures and had many exemptions. Differences in the

(*Continued*)

Box 1: (*Continued*)

systemic (and political) importance of banks for home and host countries resulted in misaligned incentives — which came to the fore when authorities found themselves negotiating over the distribution of significant financial commitments under intense time pressure and with no agreed process; or took unilateral action, leading in some cases to disorderly resolution and higher overall costs.

institutions, and smaller ones. Unilateral responses were the norm, leading in some cases to the breakup of groups into national components and the commitment of large amounts of public funds. In particular:

- National resolution frameworks were inadequate. Resolution authorities did not have the legal powers to restructure failing domestic or cross-border institutions or to promptly write down the claims of stakeholders. Many jurisdictions relied upon their general corporate insolvency frameworks where restructuring operations required slow, court-based proceedings and, in some cases, the consent of shareholders and creditors.
- Arrangements for cross-border cooperation were lacking. Mechanisms in national legal systems to give effect to foreign resolution measures were inadequate. The cooperative arrangements in place between the competent authorities in key jurisdictions were insufficient.
- Concerns for domestic financial stability impeded cooperative solutions. Faced with domestic financial stability concerns and significant uncertainty about risks from international operations, national authorities generally did not pursue cooperative approaches. In many cases, there was no legal authority or appetite to design group-wide resolution strategies.
- Sovereign financial strength emerged as a key factor in determining national strategies. Financially strong governments restored stability by bailing out parent banks in their jurisdictions, leaving group structures largely intact. Benefits were transmitted across borders through group access to liquidity support, in particular, jurisdictions. This minimized cross-border spillovers, but exposed authorities to high fiscal cost and political backlash — such a solution will not be feasible

in future for some countries.[4] Where credible sovereign backstops were lacking (such as in Cyprus and Iceland), authorities had to take exceptional steps to restructure banks while stemming depositor runs.

In sum, the crisis exposed three major gaps in the international framework for resolution:

- Inadequate resolution powers and tools through which to resolve a failing financial institution or group in an orderly fashion and through a least-cost approach;
- Inadequate frameworks for the enforcement of resolution measures on a cross-border basis and for coordination between authorities in different countries in the event of a cross-border failure;
- Inadequate mechanisms for loss allocation, including the ability to credibly subject bank creditors to loss in a bank failure without endangering financial stability.

3. Improving Resolution Frameworks

The Key Attributes attempt to address these gaps. They aim to enable orderly resolution while ending the distortions created by the perception that some financial institutions are "too-big-to-fail" and will be bailed out by the state. By making orderly resolution credible for large financial groups, these reforms seek to change incentives for bank creditors and contain moral hazard. Further progress is essential to maintaining the benefits from open financial markets and the efficient allocation of resources and risk-sharing globally.

A. Overview of the Key Attributes

The Key Attributes establish a new international standard for the design of resolution regimes for systemically important financial institutions

[4] For example, in the United States, the Dodd Frank Act explicitly prohibits the use of taxpayer funds to prevent liquidation of any financial institution. Taxpayers are to bear no losses from the exercise of the orderly liquidation authority (applicable to systemically important financial institutions), and all funds expended in the liquidation of a financial institution under the Act are to be recovered from the disposition of assets of such institutions or through assessments on the financial sector.

and groups.[5] They set out the powers and tools necessary to enable effective resolution and call for coordinated approaches to resolving cross-border institutions, and for allocation of losses to private creditors. They are a non-binding standard, and countries will be encouraged to implement their provisions over time.

The Key Attributes call for resolution authorities to be given a comprehensive toolkit of powers. These include the power to take control of a failing financial institution, merge ailing banks with stronger institutions, and transfer assets and liabilities to a healthy institution or a so-called "bridge bank". A key tool is the power to engage in the mandatory debt restructuring or "bail-in" of a financial institution. This is essentially a statutory power to restructure the liabilities of a distressed financial institution by writing down its unsecured debt and/or converting it to equity while the relevant institution remains open. In order to ensure the prompt and effective restructuring of the institution, all of these powers are to be exercised without the need to obtain the consent of shareholders or creditors, subject to appropriate safeguards.

The Key Attributes aim to enhance the effectiveness of cross-border resolution. They recognize that cross-border cooperation requires the ability of resolution/supervisory authorities to share information with their foreign counterparts, and mechanisms through which resolution measures taken in one jurisdiction may be enforced in another jurisdiction. To address these obstacles, the Key Attributes call for national resolution regimes to: (i) empower and strongly encourage the resolution authorities, wherever possible, to act to achieve a cooperative solution with foreign resolution authorities; (ii) empower the resolution authorities to share information with their foreign counterparts, provided that arrangements are in place for the protection of confidential information; and (iii) provide for transparent and expedited processes to give effect to foreign resolution measures.

The Key Attributes contemplate the establishment of cooperative arrangements between national resolution authorities for the resolution of

---

[5] See http://www.financialstabilityboard.org/publications/r_111104cc.pdf. *The Key Attributes of Effective Resolution Regimes for Financial Institutions — Progress to Date and Next Steps* (IMF Policy Paper, August 2012) presents staff's assessment of the Key Attributes.

SIFIs. Jurisdictions are required to put in place *Recovery and Resolution Plans* (RRPs), covering, at a minimum, domestically incorporated firms that could be systemically significant or critical if they fail. RRPs enable the preparation of concrete strategies to resolve each failing bank while safeguarding financial stability. Strategies currently under development focus on "single point of entry" (SPE) and "multiple point of entry" (MPE) approaches (Box 2). For G-SIFIs, the Key Attributes further require home and key host authorities to maintain *Crisis Management Groups* to prepare for and facilitate the management of a cross-border failure.[6] Relevant national authorities are also required to put in place for all G-SIFIs, at a minimum, institution-specific *Cooperation Agreements* that enable the execution of the agreed resolution strategy and ensure information exchange.

B. Implementation of the Key Attributes

The Key Attributes have not been fully implemented by many countries and political commitment is necessary to make meaningful progress. A 2013 peer review conducted by the FSB found that implementation within the FSB's membership was at an early stage.[7] Resolution regimes were generally more developed for banks than for other types of financial institutions, but, even for banks, lacked important powers such as bail-in or the ability to temporarily suspend early termination rights under financial contracts. The range of powers available for non-banks (e.g., insurance companies) was, in many cases, very limited. With respect to cross-border cooperation, only a few jurisdictions had established robust mechanisms to give effect to foreign resolution measures, or gave their resolution authorities clear statutory mandates to cooperate with or to share information with foreign resolution authorities. The peer review report called for more action on the part of national authorities and the FSB to promote implementation of the Key Attributes.

---

[6] CMGs should include the supervisory authorities, central banks, resolution authorities, finance ministries, and deposit insurance schemes of jurisdictions that are home or host to entities of the group that are material to its resolution, and should cooperate closely with authorities in other jurisdictions where firms have a systemic presence.

[7] FSB Thematic Review on Resolution Regimes (2013). Available at www.financialstabilityboard.org/publications/r_130411a.pdf

Box 2: Institution-Specific Resolution Strategies

Progress in developing operational strategies for the resolution of G-SIFIs has focused on two approaches: single and multiple points of entry. These strategies apply to financial groups in their entirety, which may consist of hundreds of different legal entities located in multiple jurisdictions, and give the lead in resolution to the home authority under SPE, and to individual home and host authorities under MPE. Losses of the institution in resolution will accrue and be managed at the parent level under SPE, or at the parent and subsidiary levels under MPE. Both approaches can imply the use of a range of resolution powers, including bail-in, which plays a central role, particularly in SPE approaches.

- Under SPE strategies, resolution occurs at the very top of the financial group while operating parts of the group are preserved. The home resolution authority intervenes and restructures the holding company that sits at the top of the financial group without the need for host authorities to resolve operating subsidiaries under their respective control. Shareholders and creditors of the apex institution absorb losses of the entire group through a write-down or restructuring of their equity and/or debt claims against the apex entity. Capital freed up from this exercise is "passed down" to loss-making operating subsidiaries and used to recapitalize and provide liquidity for such subsidiaries. SPE requires the ability to downstream loss-absorbing capacity to other parts of the group; and the capacity and willingness to provide liquidity support in resolution — both of which require a high level of cooperation and trust among authorities during resolution.
- Under MPE strategies, operating affiliates are resolved separately in different jurisdictions by the respective resolution authorities. Individual parts of the group are resolved in separate proceedings and losses are dealt with at the subsidiary level. Given the risks of disruption and inadequately coordinated actions, MPE requires extensive preparation and coordination to facilitate orderly resolution and preserve essential services and financial functions.

(*Continued*)

Box 2: (*Continued*)

- *Hybrid strategies are possible* — for example, core operations in key jurisdictions where the G-SIFI is active might be resolved under SPE, while stand-alone operations in other countries are resolved following an MPE approach, or closely linked regional operations might be resolved as a group in an overall MPE strategy.

The choice of resolution strategy and the structure of cross-border banks must be consistent. MPE approaches can work well where operating entities can operate on a stand-alone basis. Arrangements need to be made in order to ensure critical financial and operational services provided by other parts of the group can be reproduced, and that adequate loss-absorbing capacity exists locally. Where intra-group operations are more intensively inter-linked, or operations benefit from the size and liquidity provided by a "global" balance sheet (some capital market activity, for example), an SPE approach may be warranted. RRPs can help develop a picture of where losses might fall or liquidity needs arise in a crisis, providing input for cross-border dialogue on burden sharing and appropriate resolution strategies.

Some progress in the implementation of the Key Attributes has been made since 2013. A major step was recently taken by the European Union with the adoption in May 2014 of the Bank Recovery and Resolution Directive by the European Parliament. The Directive was explicitly intended to bring national resolution frameworks in line with the Key Attributes.

Achieving progress with recovery and resolution planning for individual cross-border groups has proven challenging. As contemplated under the Key Attributes, firm-specific Crisis Management Groups have been put in place for all global systemically important banks designated as such by the FSB, and preferred resolution strategies (SPE, MPE, or hybrid) are being discussed within those Groups and made operational. Firm-specific Cooperation Agreements are at various stages of development — their coverage remains limited to procedural aspects of cooperation, such as exchange of information, and does not include details on resolution strategies to be pursued.

Political commitment is needed to promote implementation. All FSB members have committed to fully implement the Key Attributes by the end of 2015 — yet this will require much work. The FSB will support the process through guidance, regular monitoring,[8] and peer reviews.

The Fund works with its members on strengthening resolution regimes. In the context of program support, surveillance, and technical assistance (including the Financial Sector Assessment Program, FSAP), the Fund has recommended enhancing resolution and crisis management frameworks in line with the *Key Attributes* (Box 3). Moreover, it is expected that the Fund will play an important role in assessing members' implementation of the Key Attributes: they will be presented to the Fund and Bank Executive Boards for endorsement as a standard under the Report on the Observance of Standards and Codes (ROSC) program, once the associated assessment methodology is finalized.

Box 3: Examples of Fund Advice to Member Countries on Resolution Frameworks

The Fund provides policy advice to strengthen resolution frameworks in the context of Fund-supported programs, surveillance, and technical assistance (including the FSAP). Fund advice typically addresses some of the following issues:

- *Resolution Authority*: Providing for a dedicated and autonomous resolution authority with a mandate to preserve financial stability and ensure continuity of systemically important services;
- *Early Intervention*: Strengthening powers for intervention before a firm is balance-sheet insolvent;
- *Resolution Powers and Tools*: Giving the resolution authorities a broad range of restructuring powers, including transferring a bank's assets and liabilities to another institution without shareholder or creditor approvals;

(*Continued*)

[8] See http://www.financialstabilityboard.org/implementation_monitoring/reform.htm

Box 3: (*Continued*)

- *Safeguards*: Introducing safeguards for creditors to ensure that the hierarchy of claims is respected and creditors would be no worse off under restructuring than under liquidation;
- *Legal Protection*: Providing for legal protection for officers, staff, and agents of resolution authorities for good-faith actions in resolution;
- *Resolution Funding*: Providing explicitly for emergency liquidity assistance with appropriate safeguards to protect the central bank's balance sheet, and the use of deposit insurance funds to facilitate resolution;
- *Judicial Review*: Ensuring that the legal framework does not endanger the effective implementation of resolution measures and legal certainly through appeals processes in court; and
- *Information Sharing and Cooperation*: Providing adequate legal authority for information sharing with foreign authorities and providing clear legal mandates for cross-border resolution cooperation.

4. Enhancing Mechanisms for Loss Allocation

Beyond the need for countries to implement the Key Attributes, much more work is needed to achieve a feasible framework for cross-border resolution. Remaining gaps pertain to how losses will be allocated to private sector stakeholders in a resolution, and managing residual risks that public funds will be needed in resolution. Both issues could undermine orderly cross-border resolution by leaving resolution authorities with incentives to act unilaterally in a crisis.

4.1. *Shifting the Burden to the Private Sector*

In determining how to allocate losses among private stakeholders, two particular questions require further work by the international community. These concern the development of requirements for loss-absorbing claims and the need for greater international harmonization of creditor hierarchies.

4.1.1. Making bail-in a credible option

Holders of claims targeted for bail-in must be able to absorb potential losses without generating systemic risk themselves as a consequence of their financial losses. Financial groups need to carry sufficient buffers of such claims to ensure that bail-in is not only legally feasible but also credible as a policy option. Further work at the international level is needed to ensure that this is the case and also to promote uniformity as to which claims may be "bail-inable." Doubts about whether losses can, in fact, be absorbed across a financial group, as specified in a resolution strategy, could increase incentives to ring-fence to minimize risks from the strategy failing, particularly with respect to SPE strategies, where losses are passed back to one entity.

The FSB is working on a proposal to develop "gone-concern loss-absorbing capacity" (GLAC). The purpose of GLAC is to ensure a credible buffer of liabilities beyond equity that can be subject to mandatory restructuring in a resolution and to promote a uniform international approach to this issue. A set of principles on GLAC will be presented at the G20 summit in November 2014, which is expected to cover the following issues:

- *Definition of claims that would be regarded as GLAC*: While any unsecured liability could, theoretically, be bailed in, the risks that may arise with imposing losses on uninsured deposits, interbank loans, or selected other liabilities in specific cases imply that the most likely liabilities to be eligible as GLAC are subordinated debt, senior unsecured bonds, and intra-group loans. To the extent that investors perceive the bail-in of such claims to be credible, funding costs from these sources may rise to reflect actual risks.[9] At the same time, the funding costs could fall for liabilities that are significantly less likely to suffer loss.
- *Amount of GLAC*. Enough "bail-inable" liabilities are needed to help ensure that a mandatory debt restructuring would be sufficient

[9] Recent analysis shows that the implicit funding subsidies enjoyed by G-SIFIs have declined from their crisis peaks, but remain substantial, especially in Europe. See *Global Financial Stability Report*, Chapter 3, April 2014.

to resolve distressed institutions in an orderly manner, potentially forestalling runs by short-term creditors concerned about counterparty solvency. This will depend partly on past experience with bank losses, which suggests that fiscal costs of crises averaged 13% of financial system assets[10]; as well as other considerations, such as the target capital ratio after resolution to foster market confidence, and any additional GLAC requirement (or discount) to reflect the degree of resolvability. Issuing GLAC on a significant scale may prove challenging, given the historical size of markets in unsecured debt instruments.

- *Location of GLAC*: Any difference between the place where losses are generated and the location of loss-absorbing liabilities within a group's structure can complicate the resolution of cross-border banks. This may well be the case, as financial depth and tax considerations are critical factors in deciding on where marketable bank liabilities are issued. If GLAC is not located in the jurisdictions (and within a jurisdiction, the entity) where losses are most likely to arise in distress, there must be a mechanism to move losses to where GLAC exists, or vice versa (see Box 2). The choice of jurisdictions where GLAC is located depends on the structure of the bank and the resolution strategy to be pursued.
- *Appropriate investor base*: Ensuring GLAC is held by the "right" creditors — capable of absorbing losses without socially undesirable consequences — may be critical for the credibility of bail-in. A particular example could be measures to mitigate contagion risks to other financial institutions by limiting their cross-holdings of senior unsecured debt. Additionally, as claims are traded in secondary markets, there is a risk they might quickly migrate to investors that are perceived to need protection from bail-in. Another considerations is bank governance after resolution, as conversion of GLAC into equity may create new controlling shareholders (or a more

[10] In a survey of 147 systemic crises over three decades, Laeven and Valencia (2012). Found average fiscal costs — direct fiscal outlays due to financial sector rescue packages — of close to 13% of financial system assets for all countries (2% for advanced countries and 21% for emerging market countries). This data does not fully reflect the recent crisis.

dispersed shareholding structure), that may or may not meet regulatory suitability requirements.

- *A uniform approach*: Some jurisdictions have limited the application of mandatory debt restructuring and GLAC requirements to systemic banks (e.g., the United States), while other countries plan on applying requirements more broadly (e.g., the European Union) — a common approach would better ensure a level playing field. Any GLAC framework should not discriminate on the basis of the nationality of investors when making decisions on triggering bail-in.
- *Disclosure*: Publication by banks of how much GLAC they have issued and how it would be used could help enhance fair market pricing and creditor discipline.

The amount and location of GLAC determine *ex ante* how losses accrue in resolution, aligning incentives of home and host authorities with respect to private burden sharing. This includes intra-group GLAC, such as debt of subsidiaries held by the parent. Resolution authorities must also understand how losses will be absorbed and transmitted within financial groups. In MPE approaches, each point of entry will need to issue sufficient GLAC to allow for orderly resolution. In SPE approaches, all parties must be clear on exactly how losses will be imposed on the entities within the group that issue GLAC, which will require intra-group loss-transfer agreements. These may provide for the conversion of loans from the parent company to the subsidiary into equity, or collateralized guarantees provided by the parent on borrowing by the subsidiaries. How, when, and by whom such mechanisms will be activated will need to be addressed in loss-transfer agreements.

4.1.2. Creditor hierarchy

The lack of harmonization of creditor hierarchies between jurisdictions is a key obstacle to the allocation of losses to private stakeholders. Creditor hierarchies determine the ranking/order in which losses will be allocated against the claims of various stakeholders in the liquidation of a firm. Losses are first allocated against shareholders, before subordinated debt holders and other types of creditors in ascending order.

Claims falling in the same class rank "*pari passu*" with each other and are treated in the same way in a liquidation (i.e., it is generally not possible for the liquidator to pay one but not the other).

The creditor hierarchy is an important instrument for securing the appropriate allocation of losses amongst stakeholders in both the liquidation and resolution of a bank. The creditor hierarchy for the liquidation of a bank will generally resemble that applicable in ordinary corporate insolvency proceedings, except that it will need to address creditors specific to banks, such as small depositors, the deposit insurance scheme, and the public sector providing liquidity or solvency support. In the restructuring of a bank as a going concern, the restructuring of the bank's claims will generally take into account the order of priorities applicable in liquidation, and treat all of the claims that fall into a particular class in the same manner. However, there may be instances where the resolution authority must depart from those general principles. This may be achieved by exempting certain claims *ex ante* from the imposition of losses in the going-concern resolution, even though those claims would be likely to suffer losses under the creditor hierarchy for liquidation. Another way is to empower the resolution authorities, in the resolution of a specific institution, to treat equally ranking claims in an unequal manner.[11] Unequal treatment of creditors or deviation from the established creditor hierarchy in liquidation raises the risk of litigation by affected creditors who may challenge a restructuring on the basis that their interests have been harmed. Adequate safeguards, such as a "no creditor worse off" requirement, can mitigate this risk.

Significant differences in the design of creditor hierarchies between jurisdictions can be an obstacle to cross-border resolution of branches of an international bank. If the ranking in the home country differs considerably from the ranking in the host country, the host authorities may decline to cooperate. For instance, if uninsured depositors are preferred to other senior creditors in the host country but not under home country law, the host authorities may have an incentive to ring fence instead of

[11] Key Attribute 5.1 allows flexibility to depart from *pari passu* treatment only if necessary to contain the systemic impact of a firm's failure or to maximize value for all creditors, and advocates transparency in this regard.

contributing all local assets and liabilities to a resolution per home country law.[12] Incentives for cross-border cooperation will also be undermined if the home country's creditor hierarchy discriminates against foreign or non-resident creditors or creditors of foreign branches.

Further guidance at the international level on creditor hierarchies is needed, particularly in the treatment of deposits. The Key Attributes provide some useful guidance on the hierarchy to be employed in the context of a bank resolution: Key Attribute 5.1 requires that "resolution powers should be exercised in a way that respects the hierarchy of claims", in particular, that "equity should absorb losses first, and no loss should be imposed on senior debt holders until subordinated debt has been written off entirely". The Key Attributes also permit departures from the *pari passu* treatment of claims in order to contain systemic risk or to maximize the value for creditors. With respect to cross-border cooperation, Key Attribute 7.4 provides that national resolution frameworks should not discriminate on the basis of the nationality of creditors, the location of their claim, or the jurisdiction in which it is payable. However, the Key Attributes leave important questions unanswered — in particular, on the treatment of insured and uninsured deposits in the creditor hierarchy. Greater specificity on this question would facilitate the resolution of banks, particularly on a cross-border basis.

The crisis has shown that giving preference to depositors is a useful element to mitigate the likelihood of contagion (Box 4). Depositor preference can mitigate the likelihood of contagion by providing depositors with a higher probability of recovering their claims in a bank failure. Where a deposit insurance scheme is in place, a framework that gives a preference to insured deposits mitigates the risk that the deposit insurance scheme will suffer losses; extending preference to all deposits (including uninsured) decreases the likelihood that depositors might need to be bailed in, or otherwise suffer losses. A significant number of jurisdictions already have some form of depositor preference. In providing advice on bank resolution frameworks, Fund staff typically

[12] This is not relevant for subsidiaries — due to their separate legal personality, the creditor hierarchy is that of the country of incorporation (the host country).

Box 4: The Role of Depositor Preference in Bank Resolution

Depositor preference (DP) gives depositors a preferential claim on the assets of a failed bank. It is reflected in the hierarchy of claims in the liquidation of a bank, and is also of relevance for the treatment of creditors in the resolution of banks. DP has attracted renewed interest in the context of international regulatory reform, as it affects loss allocation among various private sector stakeholders.

Existing and proposed forms of DP vary across countries, but three specific approaches are common:

- *Insured depositor preference* provides preferential treatment for insured deposits (and the deposit insurance scheme (DIS) through subrogation), and ranks uninsured deposits *pari passu* with the senior unsecured creditors.
- *General depositor preference* gives preference to all deposits, including balances above the deposit insurance limit, over senior unsecured creditors. The DIS is subrogated for insured deposits and, thus, ranks *pari passu* with uninsured deposits;
- *Tiered depositor preference* prefers insured deposits (and the DIS through subrogation) over uninsured deposits, and prefers both over senior unsecured creditors.

Different Types of Deposit Preference

Pari Passu	Insured DP	General DP	Tiered DP
All deposits (and subrogated DIS) and other senior unsecured creditors and rank *pari passu*	DIS (subrogated for insured deposits)	All deposits (with DIS subrogated for insured deposits)	DIS (subrogated for insured deposits)
	Other senior unsecured (including uninsured depositors)	Other senior unsecured	Eligible deposits over deposit insurance limit
			Other senior unsecured

Note: A higher position in the table and darker shading (within the same column) indicates a higher creditor claim.

(*Continued*)

Box 4: (*Continued*)

DP can mitigate the likelihood of contagion by providing depositors with a higher probability of recovering their claims in a bank failure. For countries with a DIS that is subrogated for insured deposits, *insured* or *tiered* DP mitigates the risk of the DIS suffering losses, thereby also contributing to shifting the burden of resolution to the private sector. By creating clear legal grounds for the preferential treatment of all deposits over other unsecured senior creditors, and signaling transparently which bank liabilities will be protected in resolution, *general* or *tiered* DP may help reduce legal challenges in case of a transfer of all deposits to another institution or the bail-in of non-deposit creditors only.

Potential benefits of changing the creditor hierarchy under all forms of DP need to be weighed against the potential impact on bank funding costs, or the availability of unsecured wholesale funding.

A significant number of jurisdictions already have some form of depositor preference. For example, Argentina, Australia, China, India, Hong Kong SAR, Indonesia, Mexico, Russia, Singapore, Switzerland, Turkey, the United States, and several European countries afford preferential treatment to at least some depositors, and similar reforms were recently introduced in the United Kingdom and the European Union.

addresses the issue of creditor hierarchy explicitly, and advocates providing depositor preference, although the exact form will depend on country circumstances, including whether or not a deposit insurance scheme is in place.

4.2. *Minimizing the Potential Burden for the Public Sector*

International regulatory reform holds out the prospect of reduced probabilities of bank failure and lower fiscal costs, should failures occur. Following the recent crisis, there is both less capacity and little appetite for any future fiscal resources to be put at risk to stem the consequences of a large financial institution's failure. Both increased capital and GLAC requirements will help impose market discipline and create better incentives for managers. Should a bank become distressed, thicker buffers of equity capital will bolster confidence and give more time for remedial action and recovery plans to work, while GLAC — should resolution ultimately be needed — can absorb losses before public funds may be needed, at least with respect to solvency support.

Nonetheless, there will always be a residual risk that public funds will be needed to preserve financial stability, at least temporarily. Emergency liquidity assistance may have to be offered on terms or against collateral that leave the central bank with some risk of loss. In some cases, state guarantees of bank liabilities (or capping losses on specific asset portfolios) may be needed to ensure continued market access. Finally, should it become apparent that GLAC cannot cover potential losses (or do so without causing fresh contagion) solvency support for systemic institutions may be needed — even if this is to be recovered later from the industry.[13] Once GLAC is exhausted, it is unlikely that private sector funding can be mobilized in the very short time periods in which a bank resolution will need to be implemented — in particular, because many legal frameworks do not enable private-sector "debtor in possession" financing for a bank resolution (whereby post-insolvency liquidity providers gain priority in the creditor hierarchy over pre-insolvency creditors).

Both liquidity and solvency support raise challenges for cross-border resolution. Liquidity support can entail significant "risk transfer" while the potential need for solvency support will create incentives to ring-fence to minimize uncertainty and fiscal risks.

- *Liquidity support*: Central banks can provide unlimited support only in their own currency — where other currencies are needed, swap arrangements have to be put in place. While the central bank that provides the other needed currency retains the risk for repayment of the swap, the counterpart central bank is exposed to foreign exchange risk.

[13] A (partially) pre-funded "orderly resolution fund" (or a deposit insurance fund) may contribute to such funding.

Additionally, central banks may need to consider accepting foreign collateral, leaving them exposed, should that jurisdiction ring-fence or take other unilateral action.

- *Solvency support*: A realistic possibility of having to put public funds at risk may create incentives to ring-fence to minimize the uncertainty arising from lower visibility on foreign operations, and the prospect that foreign creditors will be the main beneficiaries of taxpayer funds.

Ex ante agreements defining how public support would be committed to resolve a weak or failing institution are difficult to achieve in practice.[14] The *ex ante* burden sharing framework among the Nordic–Baltic countries is an important example of a non-binding agreement for public sector burden sharing in a resolution.[15] Beyond such tightly knit countries, however, the development of criteria that would guide public sector burden sharing remain elusive, and national authorities have been reluctant to make binding commitments for the use of public funds. As a consequence, the regulatory reform agenda has been directed toward the avoidance of public solvency support.

Shifting decisions and actions to the pre-crisis phase can reduce the risks that public funding for resolution may be needed. Recovery and resolution planning can help to develop a picture of structural imbalances in the distribution of assets and liabilities in a financial group from a national perspective. Information exchange alone will not change incentives for unilateral action in a crisis, and this information will be highly incomplete and risk exposures can change very quickly. Nonetheless, knowledge about where liquid and other assets are concentrated within cross-border groups, the existence of internal guarantees, and how and where losses can be absorbed with GLAC can help

[14]This issue is explored in greater detail in Schoenmaker (2010) and van Lelyvent and Spaltro (2011).

[15]It allocates public costs on the basis of the share of the bank's asset in each country and supervisory responsibility (with equal weight), and recognizes other factors — such as the share of problem assets, excessive fiscal consequences and proven early action — that may be used to alter the outcome of the model.

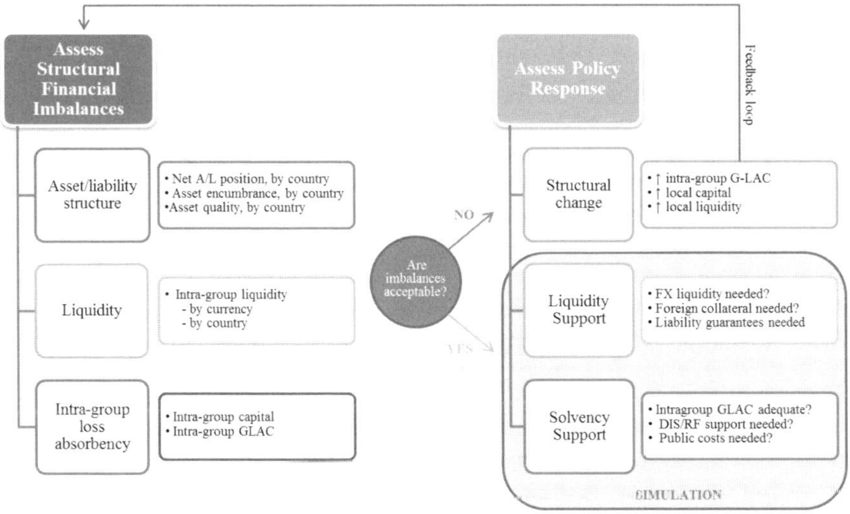

Figure 1. An effective framework.

generate a common understanding of the implications of the group's failure for each party. This knowledge can be used in an incremental process to require financial groups to adjust their structure, regulate the placement of some assets and liabilities (as with GLAC), or put in place prudential limits on specific exposures.[16] Such a procedure can also help individual hosts to manage potential risks up to acceptable levels, considering also the benefits that accrue from hosting cross-border banks. In this manner, incentives will be better aligned to ensure resolution plans will be executed in practice as agreed. An effective framework that meets these objectives would include the following elements (see Figure 1):

- Assessing structural financial imbalances between countries embedded in cross-border financial groups' balance sheets; this process can help generate a common understanding of the implications of the bank's failure for each party;

[16] The Key Attributes include scope for *firm specific* structural measures to facilitate effective resolution. These measures interact with structural *system-wide* banking reforms aimed to separate or prohibit lines of businesses deemed too risky. See Viñals, Pazarbasioglu, Surti, Narain, Erbenova, and Chow (2013).

- Determining if structural changes to cross-border financial groups are needed such that each country is satisfied with the balance between advantages of cross-border activities and the downside of potential spillover risks; and
- Assessing the potential for cross-border sovereign risk transfer or outright public costs arising from policy responses in the event of failure.

Through this process, the costs and benefits of different bank structures or resolution strategies can be assessed. The perspective of potential costs if a cross-border bank fails can help inform a "risk-based" assessment of the benefits of hosting institutions, and in what form (e.g., as a subsidiary or branch), or what risks need to be addressed by the bank, the supervisor, or in recovery and resolution planning. Three questions will help determine whether a particular configuration for a bank and resolution strategy makes sense for any one country:

- To what extent can the burden of a bank's failure be contained within the private sector?
- What burden could remain with the public sector and how can this be minimized or eliminated?
- What type of coordinated policies can be put in place to minimize *ex post* ring-fencing or unilateral decisions?

With a clearer picture of the risks, countries can assess whether the imbalances are acceptable. Key factors will be the willingness and capacity to cope with the risks of providing support in case of failure, including the fiscal and monetary capacity of each country to implement resolution strategies for failing banks. The assessment will also be guided by broader policy considerations taking into account the benefits attributed to cross-border banking, and the credibility of cooperation pledges by other countries.[17] *Ex ante* measures may be taken to ensure

[17] Local capital or liquidity requirements have a multilateral dimension, as they can impede free movement of funds, but ring-fencing in crisis is also costly, as consolidated group capital is not the relevant buffer from the national perspective. Cerutti and Schmieder (2014). Provide an argument from a stress-testing perspective, and an empirical assessment.

that imbalances are at a mutually acceptable level. Potential measures include:

- *Reducing upfront exposure by limiting cross-border risk transfer.* Measures could include requiring banks to adjust their structure, regulating placement of assets and liabilities or prudential limits on specific exposures (e.g., foreign exchange risk, liquidity) or financial flows.
- *Increasing acceptability of imbalances through agreement.* Agreement could be sought on the provision of emergency liquidity at the group level or any residual solvency support.

A system-wide perspective is important. There are gains to be derived from looking beyond individual banks where there are multiple channels of contagion between financial systems. For example, the joint support expressed by U.K. and U.S. authorities for resolution of SIFIs based in their jurisdictions using SPE-type strategies is predicated on the likely high costs across both financial systems of a failure to cooperate, as both countries are home and host of systemically relevant banks active in both jurisdictions.[18]

Cross-border simulation exercises can provide a forum for discussing alternatives to unilateral actions. Important elements include: (i) Would an ailing bank be allowed to keep up cross-border capital and funding flows? (ii) Which sources of funding could be made available in crisis? Under what conditions? (iii) Which claims would a country accept to be bailed in? (iv) What size of imbalances would a country be comfortable accepting, and under what circumstances?

Several outcomes of cooperation strategies are possible. Considering asset and liability positions in isolation, full *ex ante* ring-fencing and maximum resolvability will always be an equilibrium strategy. However, this ignores the efficiencies that may accrue from sharing critical functions. Where efficiencies appear small (for example, where locally funded operations undertake mainly basic banking functions of taking deposits

[18] *Resolving Globally Active, Systemically Important Financial Institutions,* A joint paper by the Federal Deposit Insurance Corporation and the Bank of England, December 2012.

and lending), the benefit of ease of resolution may weigh highly. Where the loss of shared platforms or a global operation has higher costs, mechanisms to offset imbalances with prior commitments to burden sharing actions could be explored (Box 5). For example, country A may be willing to accept a liability overhang in the local operations of a cross-border bank, if B is willing to provide counterbalancing resolution funding.

Box 5: Incentives to Cooperate and Subsidiarization[a]

Cross-border resolution can be helped or impeded depending on group structures — particularly banks' preference for subsidiaries versus branches. From the perspective of financial stability, a branch structure unequivocally puts responsibility for soundness on the parent institution, while a subsidiary structure can limit losses at the host level, should the parent come under stress (given local capital and liquidity requirements). The subsidiary approach may also limit the overall cost of resolution in the event of a failure, because spinning off the relatively healthy parts of the group may be easier when the group is structured as a network of independent subsidiaries rather than a fully integrated branch network.

Subsidiarization ex ante is likely to be a superior strategy to ring-fencing ex post when cross-border cooperation is unlikely to emerge. Ring fencing during a crisis has significant operational, financial, and legal risks and can of itself worsen the situation. However, if cooperative strategies are not credible and countries fear that their counterparts will act unilaterally in crisis, the host authorities may choose to protect their interests through requiring cross-border banks to hold local capital and liquidity ex ante. While subsidiarization does not preclude ring-fencing in a crisis, stand-alone-subsidiarization can reduce incentives

(*Continued*)

[a]See Fiechter *et al.* (2011). Ring-fencing cross-border banks: An effective supervisory response? *Journal of Banking Regulation*, *16*, 169–187.

Box 5: (*Continued*)

for hosts to take such action, as they have a more complete understanding and control of local assets and liabilities, and transparently requiring capital and liquidity beforehand can reduce negative effects of unilaterally impeding moving funds during a crisis.

Isolating pools of capital and liquidity could have efficiency costs and impede cross-border financial intermediation (although the extent of these costs versus the benefits of increased "resolvability" has not been established). Where operations are locally funded and assets consist of relatively straightforward loans to local counterparts, the net costs of insisting on locally resolvable structures may be low. Costs may rise if branch structures are very integrated with other parts of the group, or as the foreign banks play a more active role in intermediating international financial flows (e.g., providing significant funding to a host economy on a long-term basis). In these cases, host authorities will have to weigh the advantages of intermediation through integrated branches against a greater need for cooperation in resolution.

For heavily interconnected markets with systemic players, formal cooperation may be a better strategy.

In these cases, contagion risk and the greater reciprocal damage from severing financial flows makes it less likely that unilateral action will pay off. As an example, in December 2012 the United States and the United Kingdom stated their preference for a cooperative SPE strategy for their systemic banks. With significant interconnectedness between these financial markets, the failure of a systemic bank in either country would have a severe impact on both countries, whether the bank has a subsidiary or branch structure, so that cooperative support appears to be the least-cost solution for both.

Subsidiarization might reduce risks, but could hamper financial integration, for example, where cross-border banks provide substantial foreign funding to the economy and local sources of alternative funding are not well developed. Equally, the benefits of cross border banking in good times need to be carefully weighed against the benefits of being

(*Continued*)

Box 5: (*Continued*)

able to resolve institutions at low risk and low cost in a crisis. Increased cooperation would help countries find a better balance between constraints on cross-border capital transformation and mitigating resolution risks. Having effective dialogue, information sharing, and cooperation agreements for resolution in place would make authorities indifferent about specific bank structures. This would allow financial groups to take advantage of structures that best fit their business models without limiting their ability to manage risks during normal times and support affiliates in stressful times.

5. Cross-Border Resolution Beyond Globally Systemic Institutions

Many cross-border banks are not globally systemically important. The Key Attributes were designed primarily with G-SIFIs and advanced financial systems in mind, and set a high standard in terms of the powers and infrastructures that countries should introduce. While they, nonetheless, have broad application beyond G-SIFIs, embodying best practice and lessons from experience from a range of countries and circumstances, not all elements may be relevant to all countries. In addition, many home and host countries to cross-border banks are not FSB members or party to the fora advancing work on G-SIFI resolution. In some cases, there may be a significant asymmetry of power in interactions between G-SIFI home jurisdictions and smaller host jurisdictions where the operations are not material to the institution's overall health. This section looks at the resolution reform agenda from the perspective of small host countries and emerging and developing economies.

5.1. *The Key Attributes in Proportion*

Reforms to enhance resolution regimes should be tailored to the complexity of financial systems in different jurisdictions (Box 6). While the Key Attributes embody best practice in resolution on many core issues

Box 6: Key Attributes Beyond G-SIFIs

Many of the Key Attributes could apply to any financial institution, including those that could be systemically important in the jurisdiction concerned. However, Key Attributes 8–11, which set out best practice for resolution planning and cross-border cooperation, are only required *per se* for G-SIFIs,[a] while the majority of Fund members are neither key host nor home jurisdictions for G-SIFIs.

The impact of the failure of a bank of systemic regional importance will likely be severe for those countries directly affected, even if not felt globally. Further guidance is needed as to what best practice resolution planning and cooperation arrangements should be implemented by the resolution authorities of those countries in which such an institution is systemic. Fund and Bank staff have proposed the following approach:

- *RRPs and resolvability assessments* (Key Attributes 10 and 11) should, as a minimum, be required for all those firms designated as domestic SIFIs in the jurisdiction concerned, using relevant sector-specific methodologies. For banks, for example, this would mean domestically systemically important banks identified using the Basel Committee for Banking Supervision criteria, which include the impact that the failure of the bank will have on the domestic economy.[b] RRPs and resolvability assessments should be tailored to the complexity of the firm and its operations.
- *Crisis management groups* (Key Attribute 8) or comparable arrangements such as "resolution colleges" should be required for firms that are systemic in more than one jurisdiction and where resolution of entities in more than one jurisdiction is material for resolution of the firm. Comparable arrangements could include less formal structures

(*Continued*)

[a]While some of these Key Attributes leave open the possibility of extending to other institutions, no further guidance on which firms and what type of arrangements are specified.

[b]Comparable frameworks may be developed for other sectors in due course.

Box 6: (*Continued*)

that provide a framework for the cooperation and coordination necessary to support resolution planning and resolvability assessments for the firm in question. For example, if the firm is systemic and its resolution is material in only two jurisdictions, existing arrangements for cooperation between the resolution authorities in those jurisdictions could be sufficient without the need to formally establish a separate *crisis management group*.

- *Cooperation Agreements* (Key Attribute 9) should be required for any firm for which a *crisis management group* or comparable arrangement is required under Key Attribute 8. There would also be significant benefits in further work to define best practice *cooperation agreements* for regional SIFIs.

that are relevant for all jurisdictions, local circumstances may justify tailoring the adoption of reforms — an approach explicitly recognized in the introduction to the Key Attributes. Elements addressing some capital market functions, or the complex structures and multiple business lines of the largest institutions may not be relevant to countries with less sophisticated financial systems. In many countries insurance companies or securities firms may not present a systemic threat. In some countries it may be sufficient to replicate the economic effects of statutory bail-in powers using other resolution tools (e.g., a bridge bank). While sound resolution planning and cross-border coordination are of equal importance for regionally systemic firms (e.g., a pan-African bank), the detail required in a recovery and resolution plan would be significantly less than for a large, complex G-SIFI.

Further consideration will need to be given to loss-absorbing requirements in banking systems that are primarily deposit funded. As is the case with respect to GLAC for G-SIFIs, banks of regional or domestic systemic importance should have adequate loss-absorbing capacity (LAC) to reduce the risks to the deposit insurance scheme and/or the public sector arising from their potential failure. Further consideration will need to be given as to what form LAC requirements should take in jurisdictions with less developed capital markets, where authorities may be reluctant to allow uninsured deposits to incur losses. In such regimes, it may be appropriate to allow for the substitution of extra capital in a way that recognizes the relative cost and loss-absorbing characteristics of different liabilities. For instance, equity will absorb losses under a wider set of scenarios than bond debt, so that less may be required to substitute for GLAC, while it typically will be more expensive. While retail deposits may be more stable than wholesale deposits, they will not be suitable for absorbing losses.

5.2. *The "Small Host" Perspective*

For cooperative solutions to cross-border resolution to be credible, incentives need to be aligned between countries. When the operations of a cross-border institution are of systemic importance in a host country, but immaterial to the G-SIFI as a whole, it may not be realistic to expect an alignment of interests between jurisdictions. While legal, business, and reputational concerns can be an important factor in inducing G-SIFIs and their home authorities to assist in finding solutions to problems in host countries, this concern will be in the background if the whole institution's stability is in question. Furthermore, these small hosts often are not party to crisis management groups or core supervisory colleges where, for practical reasons, participation is limited to countries in which the G-SIFI is most exposed. Therefore, and particularly in a crisis where attention is focused on the most significant exposures and concerns, the authorities of smaller host countries may not have timely access to information that is critical for their domestic financial stability, or to a forum where their perspectives on resolution will be considered.

In these circumstances, the resolution strategies of small hosts may have to prioritize domestic financial stability. For small hosts and home jurisdictions of G-SIFIs alike, the authorities' first priority in a bank failure will be to ensure contagion is contained, critical financial services continue to function, and that economic costs are minimized. Where small hosts cannot ensure their capacity to achieve these outcomes through *ex ante* agreements on cooperative resolution strategies and burden sharing, measures ensuring local operations are resolvable through structural requirements, such as requiring local capital and liquidity via subsidiarization or asset maintenance requirements for branches, may be appropriate.[19] This approach would be consistent with MPE (or hybrid) resolution strategies, and small hosts should work with home countries to ensure this fits into the comprehensive resolution plan for the bank. While this approach may potentially have costs from a global perspective — inefficiencies from requiring local pools of capital and funding, or limitations on the scope for international bank financing of structural external deficits — these costs may be low where operations are "plain vanilla", collecting local deposits to fund lending, and also bring benefits in reducing prudential risks and increasing resolvability. Cooperation with the home jurisdiction will still have important payoffs with respect to deciding on the location and magnitude of GLAC, how critical services will be maintained, and in building trust to enable smooth resolution, should a crisis eventually occur.

6. Conclusions

Recent initiatives in international regulatory reform have made progress toward achieving an effective cross-border resolution framework. Widespread implementation of the Key Attributes will provide resolution authorities involved in cross-border bank failures with a broad set of tools for executing resolution strategies, minimizing risks to financial stability, and placing the costs of failure on shareholders and private creditors.

However, orderly cross-border resolution is still far from assured. Should a large cross-border bank fail today, it appears unlikely that the pitfalls and misaligned incentives that undermined cooperation in the global financial crisis could be avoided. Progress in the implementation of national legal and institutional reforms consistent with the Key Attributes has been mixed. More fundamentally, implementation of the Key Attributes would only partially align divergent national interests and incentives that work against cooperative cross-border resolution

[19] For a full treatment of the financial stability implications of group structures, see Fiechter *et al.* (2011).

strategies. Additional work is required at the international level on remaining gaps including:

- Defining specific proposals for GLAC (amount, eligible claims, location, and investor base; and
- Better aligning creditor hierarchies and depositor preference between countries.

Progress on minimizing residual risks that public funds will be needed to preserve financial stability is necessary to ensure that resolution strategies are credible. While a credible bail-in option would reduce the contingent need for public financial support, a residual risk remains, creating scope for misaligned incentives to undermine cooperation in resolution. Moving up decisions and actions to the pre-crisis phase could ensure incentives are aligned and authorities can credibly commit to carry through agreed resolution strategies. Such arrangements could cover (i) identifying structural imbalances on banks' balance sheets in various countries; (ii) assessing costs and benefits of different bank structures and resolution strategies, and taking action to m make these consistent with country authorities' objectives; and (iii) assessing and monitoring the potential for cross-border sovereign risk transfer or outright public costs arising from policy responses in the event of failure, and updating resolution strategies accordingly.

References

Cerutti, E. & Schmieder, C. (2014). Ring fencing and consolidated banks' stress tests. *Journal of Financial Stability, 11*, 1–12.

Claessens, S., Herring, R., & Schoenmaker, D. (2010). *A safer world financial system: Improving the resolution of systemic institutions*. London: Centre for Economic Policy Research.

Fiechter, J., Ötker-Robe, İ., Ilyina, A., Hsu, M., Santos, A., & Surti, J. Subsidiaries or Branches: Does One Size Fit All? *IMF Staff Discussion Note* 11/04. (March, 2011).

Schoenmaker, D. (2010). Burden sharing: From theory to practice, *DSF Policy Paper* No. 6; and van Leyveld & Spaltro M. (2011). Coordinating bank

failure costs and financial stability. *De Nederlandsche Bank Working Paper* No. 306.
Systemic banking crises database: An update. *IMF Working Paper* No. 12/163.
Viñals, J., Pazarbasioglu, C., Surti, J., Narain, A., Erbenova, M., & Chow, J. (2013). Creating a safer financial system: Will the Volcker, Vickers, and Liikanen structural measures help? *IMF Staff Discussion Note 13/4*.

Part VII
Corporate Governance Issues in the New Environment

Corporate Governance and Bank Risk Taking

— Chapter 21

- Deniz Anginer
  Virginia Tech and World Bank
- Asli Demirgüç-Kunt
  World Bank
- Harry Huizinga
  Tilburg University and CEPR
- Kebin Ma
  Warwick Business School

1. Introduction

Corporate managers may be more risk averse than shareholders, as corporate bankruptcy generally causes managers to lose their jobs, part of their personal wealth and their reputation. 'Good' corporate governance — promoting the interests of shareholders — may serve to counteract managers' bias against risk taking. In line with this, John, Litov, and Yeung (2008) find that 'better' corporate governance in the form of stronger investor protection brings about increased risk-taking and higher growth for an international sample of non-financial firms.

For financial institutions, the calculus regarding the optimal degree of risk taking is different compared to non-financial firms, as banks tend to be supported by the financial safety net if they become distressed. Banks, in particular, benefit from deposit insurance and may receive generous public support to prevent their failure. The financial safety net provides banks with an incentive to take on excessive risks in order to increase the value of these benefits. Hence, the association between risk taking and corporate governance may be different in the case of banks (see for example, Laeven, 2013).

Large banks may benefit relatively more from the financial safety net, as they may be deemed too big to fail by regulators (see Acharya, Anginer & Warburton, 2014; and Bertay, Demirgüç-Kunt, & Huizinga, 2013). For this reason, shareholder-friendly corporate governance may increase risk taking more in the case of large banks. Similarly, banks may gain more from increasing risk if the financial safety net is expected to be more generous. Therefore, shareholder-friendly corporate governance is likely to increase bank risk taking especially in countries with generous financial safety nets.

This chapter empirically examines the relationships between bank risk and corporate governance for an international sample of banks from 22 countries over the 2004–2008 period. We distinguish between a bank's stand-alone insolvency risk, and a bank's contribution to systemic risk to gauge the threat a bank poses to overall financial stability. Specifically, an individual bank's insolvency risk is proxied by the *Z*-score and the distance to default, while a bank's contribution to financial-sector systemic risk is represented by the marginal expected shortfall (MES) variable proposed by Acharya, Engle, & Richardson (2012), and alternatively by the CoVaR variable proposed by Adrian & Brunnermeier (2011).

Bank capitalization strategies are crucial in determining the probability of bank failure both at the individual bank level and at the systemic level. As a reflection of this, going beyond bank risk variables we in addition consider how several measures of bank capitalization are related to corporate governance.

The bank insolvency and systemic risk measures are related to an overall index of the shareholder-friendliness of corporate governance based on data from Institutional Shareholder Services (ISS) following Aggarwal, Erel, Stulz, & Williamson (2009). We in turn relate the capitalization measures to several specific characteristics of shareholder-friendly corporate governance concerning the size and composition of the bank's board, and to anti-takeover provisions as an index of the effectiveness of the market for corporate control.

We find that a bank's insolvency risk and its contribution to systemic risk are both positively associated with the overall index of the shareholder-friendliness of corporate governance. Furthermore, bank insolvency and systemic risks are positively associated with shareholder-friendly corporate governance especially for large banks and for banks located in countries with generous financial safety nets. These results are consistent with the view that shareholder-friendly corporate governance increases bank risk more if the additional bank risk significantly increases a bank's contingent claim on the financial safety net. In addition, we find that shareholder-friendly corporate governance tends to vary negatively with bank capitalization, which suggests that the positive relationship between shareholder-friendly corporate governance and bank risks in part reflects bank capitalization strategies.

In the remainder, Section 2 provides a literature review. Section 3 discusses empirical evidence on the relationship between corporate governance and bank risk. Section 4 in turn considers the empirical relationship between corporate governance and bank capitalization. Section 5 concludes.

2. Literature Review

Our analysis fits in an emerging literature that has addressed the impact of corporate governance on bank risk taking.[1] Pathan (2009) finds that small boards and boards that are not controlled by the CEO lead to additional bank risk as reflected in market measures of risk and the *Z*-score for a sample of U.S. bank holding companies over the 1997–2004 period. Chen, Steiner, & Whyte (2006), in turn, find a positive impact of option-based executive compensation and wealth on market measures of risk for a sample of U.S. commercial banks during the period 1992–2000. DeYoung, Peng, & Yan (2013) further find that CEO risk-taking incentives lead to riskier business policy decisions (regarding loans to businesses, non-interest

[1] Recent surveys are offered by Becht, Bolton, & Roell (2011) and Mehran, Morrison, & Shapiro (2012).

based banking activities, and investment in mortgage-backed securities) at U.S. commercial banks over the 1994–2006 period, especially in the second half of the sample period after deregulation and for the largest banks. Calomiris & Carlson (2014) examine bank ownership and risk-taking at U.S. banks in the 1890s, finding that higher managerial ownership is associated with lower bank default risk.

Several papers have also examined how banks with different corporate governance regimes fared during the crisis, with mixed results. Berger, Imbierowicz, & Rauch (2015) find that high shareholdings of lower-level management imply a substantially higher probability of bank failure for U.S. commercial banks over the 2007–2010 period. Fahlenbrach & Stulz (2011) find some evidence that U.S. banks with CEOs whose incentives were better aligned with the interests of shareholders in 2006 had worse share price performance during the subsequent crisis. Ellul & Yerramilli (2013) report that U.S. bank holding companies that had a strong and independent risk management function in place before the onset of the financial crisis fared better in terms of operating and stock performance during the crisis.

A higher normal, pre-crisis level of capital should increase a bank's chances of withstanding major income shocks. Confirming this, Berger & Bouwman (2013) find that higher levels of pre-crisis capital increase a bank's probability of survival during a banking crisis. Along similar lines, Beltratti & Stulz (2012) and Demirgüç-Kunt, Detragiache, & Merrouche (2013) find that banks that were better capitalized before the crisis had a better stock market performance during the crisis.

Multi-country studies of bank corporate governance and risk taking are relatively scarce. Laeven & Levine (2009) examine the relationship between bank ownership and bank risk taking for an international sample of banks. They find that greater cash flow rights of large owners are associated with greater bank risk, consistent with the hypothesis that bank shareholders favor risk-taking relative to managers and creditors. These authors also consider the interaction between bank regulation and ownership, finding that deposit insurance is associated with an increase in risk only when the bank has a large equity holder. More recently, using international data, Erkens, Hung, & Matos (2012) find that financial institutions with more independent boards and higher institutional ownership experienced worse stock returns during the global financial crisis.

Several theoretical papers consider how corporate governance affects banks. Bolton, Mehran, & Shapiro (2015) show that excess risk taking by banks can be addressed by basing executive compensation on both the stock price and the bank's CDS spread. The presence of deposit insurance and trusting debt holders, however, implies that it is not in shareholders' interests to design compensation contracts in this way. Edmans & Liu (2011) show that debt-like instruments such as pension rights are generally part of the optimal executive compensation package to reduce the agency costs of debt. John, Saunders, & Senbet (2000) demonstrate that the FDIC insurance premium can be made dependent on incentive features of top-management compensation to eliminate excess bank risk taking.

3. Bank Insolvency and Systemic Risk

In this section, we discuss empirical evidence on the relationships between bank insolvency and systemic risk measures and an index of the shareholder-friendliness of corporate governance for an international sample of banks over the 2004–2008 period summarizing some of the main findings in Anginer, Demirgüç-Kunt, Huizinga, & Ma (2015a).

3.1. *The Data*

Accounting and market data necessary to construct our bank risk measures are taken from Bankscope of Bureau Van Dijk, CRSP and Compustat Global. Data on bank corporate governance are from the Corporate Governance Quotient database assembled by ISS.

We examine two measures of individual bank insolvency risk. First, the Z-score represents the number of standard deviations that a bank's rate of return on assets has to fall for the bank to become insolvent. The Z-score is constructed as the sum of the rate of return on assets and the equity to assets ratio divided by the standard deviation of the return on assets. A higher Z score signals that a bank has lower insolvency risk. We calculate a Z-score for a bank, if at least three annual observations of its rate of return on assets are available. As a second insolvency risk variable, the distance to default measures the difference between the asset value of the bank and the face value of its debt, scaled by the standard deviation of the bank's asset value (see Campbell, Hilscher, & Szilagyi, 2008, p. 2899). The distance to default variable is computed as an annual average of weekly values.

To reflect a bank's contribution to systemic risk, we use two variables. First, following Acharya, Engle & Richardson (2012), MES is the average bank stock return when the stock market return as a whole is in the lower tail of its distribution. Specifically, MES is constructed as the average bank stock return when the market return is in its lowest 5% bracket in a given year. Second, following Adrian & Brunnermeier (2011), CoVaR is defined as the value at risk of the overall financial system conditional on a bank being in distress and the value of risk of the overall financial system conditional on a bank being in a normal state, where a bank' distress and normal states are defined as the bank's return being at the 5th and 50th percentile in a given year, respectively. Lower values for MES and CoVaR signal higher bank contributions to systemic risk.

As our corporate governance variable, we use an index of the power of minority shareholders as formulated by Aggarwal *et al.* (2009) based on individual governance attributes assembled by ISS. The individual attributes are dummy variables that take on a value of one if the characteristic is relatively shareholder-friendly and a value of zero otherwise. An overall index, called corporate governance, summarizes information on 44 attributes reflecting the board's size and composition, compensation and ownership, auditing and anti-takeover measures

Overall, corporate governance has become more shareholder-friendly over the 2003–2007 period. As seen in Figure 1, the corporate governance index increased from 0.58 in 2003 to 0.63 in 2007 for U.S. banks in part due to the passage of the Sarbanes–Oxley Act of 2002. It increased from 0.52 to 0.59 for non-U.S. banks. These differential trends in corporate governance for U.S. and non-U.S. banks (and, therefore, also for individual banks) allow us to estimate relationships between bank risk variables and corporate governance in specifications that include bank fixed effects. In the analysis, we use several bank-level control variables. The assets variable, constructed as the log of a bank's total assets, proxies for the bank's absolute size. Larger banks may

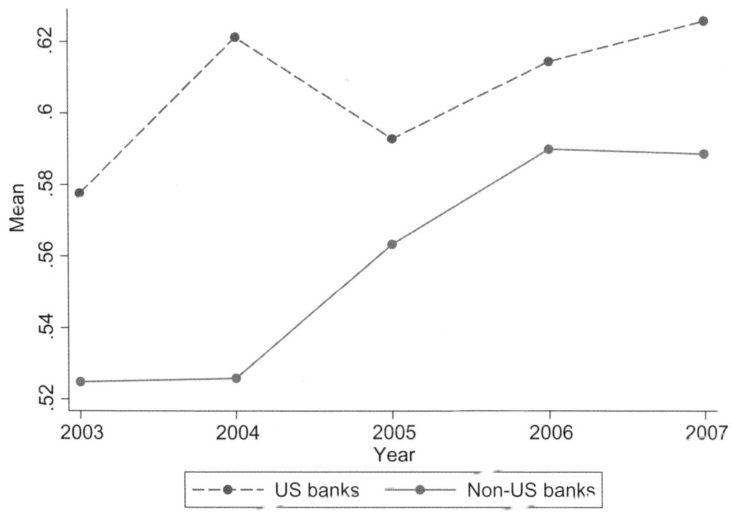

Figure 1. The evolution of corporate governance for U.S. and non-U.S. banks.

pursue riskier banking strategies, if they are considered too big to fail. In addition, the assets to GDP variable, or total bank assets divided by GDP, represents the bank's size relative to the national economy with a mean of 0.06. The overhead variable is constructed as overhead expenses divided by total assets. The average overhead variable is 0.03. Inefficient banks with large overhead expenses may choose relatively risky bank strategies to maintain a certain expected return on assets. Finally, the collateral variable is the ratio of assets that can be easily used as collateral divided by total assets. The collateral variable on average is 0.27. Banks with assets that can be used as collateral may find it easier to pursue risky banking strategies, as their financial costs may be less sensitive to overall bank risk.

We include several macroeconomic and country-level institutional control variables in the regressions. Inflation is the consumer price inflation rate. GDP growth is the rate of real GDP growth. GDP per capita is GDP per capita in thousands of constant U.S. dollars. The variable restrict is a composite index of regulatory restrictions on bank activities from Barth, Caprio, & Levine (2004). Specifically, it is an indicator of the degree to which banks face regulatory restrictions on their activities in securities markets, insurance, real estate, and owning shares in non-financial firms. Capital stringency is an index of regulatory oversight of bank capital, summarizing information about the nature and the magnitude of bank capital requirements, with higher values indicating greater stringency. Official is an index of the power of the commercial bank supervisory agency to undertake specific actions to prevent and correct problems at a bank, with higher values indicating greater power. Diversification is an index of loan diversification guidelines imposed on banks. Finally, financial freedom is an index of financial market freedoms available from the Heritage Foundation.

3.2. *Empirical Results*

We report results of estimating the following panel data model for an international sample of banks:

$$\text{Risk}_{ijt} = \alpha + \beta_0 \text{ Governance}_{ijt} + \beta_1 X_{ijt} + \beta_2 Z_{jt} + \gamma_i + \delta_t + \varepsilon_{it},$$

where Risk_{ijt} is a bank risk measure for bank i in country j at time t, Governance_{ijt} is the corporate governance variable, X_{ijt} is a set of firm-level controls, Z_{jt} is a set of country-level controls, γ_i is a set of bank fixed effects, δ_t is a set of year effects, and ε_{it} is a random error. A higher value of the Governance_{ijt} variable indicates that corporate governance better serves the interests of shareholders. Shareholders potentially stand to gain from higher bank risk to the extent that they can shift risk to debt holders and the financial safety net. Lower values of all four bank risk measures, i.e., *Z*-score, distance to default, MES, and CoVaR, point towards higher risk. Accordingly, in the estimation we expect to find that $\beta_0 < 0$. We allow for clustering of the errors at the bank level. All independent variables are lagged one year to reduce endogeneity concerns.

Table 1 provides empirical evidence on the relationships between the corporate governance variable on the one hand and proxies for bank insolvency and systemic risk on the other. In regression 1, the overall corporate governance index obtains a negative coefficient of –0.832 that is significant at the 10% level, suggesting that more shareholder-friendly corporate governance increases bank insolvency risk. Among the controls, we find that the *Z*-score is negatively and significantly related to the

Table 1. Bank insolvency and systemic risks and corporate governance.

	Z–score (1)	Distance to Default (2)	MES (3)	CoVaR (4)
Assets	–0.578***	–0.081	–0.009*	–0.014***
	(0.193)	(0.219)	(0.005)	(0.005)
Assets to GDP	–1.262*	–0.650	–0.028	0.038
	(0.647)	(0.820)	(0.020)	(0.027)
Overhead	–1.258	–3.037	–0.065	0.000
	(2.639)	(2.805)	(0.068)	(0.108)
Collateral	–0.366	–0.289	–0.003	0.018
	(0.470)	(0.581)	(0.011)	(0.014)
Inflation	–0.213	–4.588	0.386***	0.407**
	(8.318)	(12.636)	(0.132)	(0.196)
GDP growth	16.431***	25.309***	0.462***	0.431***
	(4.889)	(9.080)	(0.148)	(0.134)
GDP per capita	–0.212**	–0.181	–0.004**	0.000
	(0.093)	(0.138)	(0.002)	(0.003)
Restrict	0.048	–0.416**	–0.003	0.004
	(0.135)	(0.177)	(0.005)	(0.003)
Capital stringency	–0.047	0.130	0.001	–0.003
	(0.088)	(0.104)	(0.003)	(0.003)
Official	0.009	–0.036	–0.001	–0.000
	(0.042)	(0.052)	(0.001)	(0.002)
Diversification	0.578***	–0.693***	–0.001	0.004*
	(0.117)	(0.123)	(0.002)	(0.002)
Financial freedom	0.013**	0.019***	–0.000***	–0.000
	(0.005)	(0.007)	(0.000)	(0.000)
Corporate governance	–0.832*	–1.453**	–0.012***	–0.044***
	(0.503)	(0.595)	(0.009)	(0.014)
N	3017	2868	3069	3057
adj. R–sq	0.210	0.557	0.458	0.478

Note: The dependent variables in the four columns are *Z*-score, distance to default, MES, and CoVaR. Regressions include bank and year fixed effects. Standard errors are clustered at the bank level, and provided in parentheses. *, **, and *** denote significance at 10%, 5%, and 1%, respectively.

assets and assets to GDP variables, indicating that larger absolute and relative bank size are associated with higher bank insolvency risk. This suggests that larger banks take on more risk as they benefit from a too-big-to-fail status. The *Z*-score is positively and significantly related to the GDP growth variable, as bank insolvency risk may be reduced by economic growth. In addition, the *Z*-score is negatively and significantly related to GDP per capita. This result may reflect that banks in wealthier countries benefit from a more credible financial safety net, which induces them to take on more risk. Furthermore, the *Z*-score is positively and significantly related to the diversification variable, suggesting that guidelines promoting diversification contribute to bank safety. Similarly, the *Z*-score is positively and significantly related to the economic freedom variable, as economic freedom may enable a bank to diversify into activities that reduce overall bank insolvency risk.

In regression 2, the dependent variable is the distance to default variable. Otherwise, this regression is analogous to regression 1. In this regression, the overall corporate governance index is estimated with a negative coefficient that is significant at 5%, indicating that bank insolvency risk varies positively with shareholder-friendly corporate governance.

In regressions 3 and 4, the dependent variables are MES and CoVaR as indices of a bank's contribution to systemic risk. In both regressions, the estimated coefficients for the corporate governance variable are negative and significant at the 1% level, consistent with a positive relationship between shareholder-friendly corporate governance and a bank's contribution to systemic risk. Overall, the results of Table 1 suggest that bank insolvency and systemic risks vary positively with shareholder-friendly corporate governance.

Bigger banks may be riskier, because they expect to receive a more generous treatment by bank regulators in case of insolvency because of their too-big-to-fail status. Hence, the positive relationship between bank risk and 'good' corporate governance may be driven by the larger banks in the sample. To see whether the relationship between bank risk and corporate governance depends on bank size, we have estimated a set of regressions as in Table 1 that include an interaction term between the corporate governance variable and the assets variable. In the unreported analogous regressions 2–4, the corporate governance index obtains positive and significant coefficients in the regressions, while the interactions of this variable with assets receive negative and significant coefficients.[2] This is evidence that 'good' corporate governance increases insolvency and systemic risks of especially large banks, consistent with greater risk-shifting incentives for larger banks on account of their too-big-to-fail status.

To further investigate risk-shifting by larger banks, we have also examined how the impact of corporate governance on bank risk varies with the strength of the safety net. Countries with strong financial safety nets are more likely to bail out distressed banks that are deemed too big to fail. Thus, banks with shareholder-friendly corporate governance may be riskier if they are located in such a country. To examine this, we have estimated regressions that include a financial safety net variable that is a summary measure of the strength of the financial safety net obtained through a principal components analysis of deposit insurance design features following Demirgüç-Kunt & Detragiache (2002) interacted with the corporate governance and assets variables (the regressions also include double interactions of the financial safety net variable with corporate governance and assets). In the unreported analogous regressions 1, 3, and 4, the triple interaction term involving the financial safety net variable receives negative and significant coefficients.[3] This is evidence that 'good' corporate governance increases insolvency and systemic risks especially at banks that are large and located in countries with generous financial safety nets. Our evidence that shareholder-friendly corporate governance is related to higher bank insolvency and systemic risks especially in the case of large banks that are located in countries with generous financial safety nets indicates that banks are different from non-financial firms.

4. Bank Capitalization

Banks with more shareholder-friendly corporate governance can achieve higher insolvency and systemic risks by engaging in riskier income and

---

[2] See Anginer, Demirgüç-Kunt, Huizinga, & Ma (2015a, Table 4).
[3] See Anginer, Demirgüç-Kunt, Huizinga, & Ma (2015a, Table 5).

asset allocation strategies, or by riskier funding strategies including lower capitalization rates. In this section, we present evidence on the relationship between corporate governance and bank capitalization for an international sample of banks over the 2004–2008 period summarizing some of the main findings in Anginer, Demirgüç-Kunt, Huizinga, & Ma (2015b).

4.1. *The Data*

We consider five alternative indices of bank capitalization. First, Tier 1 capital is a regulatory capital ratio constructed as Tier 1 capital divided by risk-weighted assets, where Tier 1 capital and risk-weighted assets are calculated according to Basel rules. Tier 1 capital includes common equity and perpetual, non-cumulative preferred equity, and it can be seen as a measure of the funds cumulatively contributed by common and preferred shareholders that can be exhausted through losses while the bank remains a going concern. The mean Tier 1 capital ratio in our sample is 11.9%.

Total capital is a broader regulatory capital ratio constructed as the sum of Tier 1 capital and Tier 2 capital divided by risk-weighted assets. Tier 2 capital includes hybrid capital, subordinated debt, loan loss reserves, and valuation reserves. Subordinated debt can only be used to offset a bank's losses, after the bank has ceased to be a going concern. Thus, not all of Tier 2 capital can be considered to be a buffer to protect a bank from insolvency. The average total capital ratio is 13.7%.

Common equity is a narrower measure of bank capitalization constructed as common equity divided by total assets. This capitalization measure should be relevant to common shareholders, as it represents the capital that common shareholders have at stake. Common shareholder interests should be important to a bank's management and board, because common shareholders have voting rights. The denominator of the common equity ratio is total assets rather than risk-weighted assets, and hence insensitive to the potentially arbitrary and manipulable risk weighting of assets. The mean common equity ratio is 8.9%.

Common equity can be divided into tangible common equity and non-tangible common equity. The latter includes tax-deferred assets, mortgage servicing rights, and minority interests in financial intermediaries. The loss absorption capacity of these various items is zero (as in the case of tax-deferred assets) or limited (as in the case of mortgage servicing rights). Therefore, we also consider the Tangible equity ratio, constructed as tangible capital divided by tangible assets (i.e., total assets minus non-tangible assets). The Tangible capital ratio has a mean of 7.9%.

Banks have some discretion over the book valuation of their assets and their capital. For this reason, capitalization measures based solely on accounting data may be misguided, especially during a time of economic and financial crisis. Therefore, we consider an additional capitalization measure, denoted by Market value, that is constructed as the ratio of the market value of the bank's common equity to a proxy for the market value of a bank's total assets, computed as the sum of the book value of total assets and the market value of common equity minus the book value of common equity. This market-based measure of bank capitalization should be more accurate than corresponding accounting-based measures to the extent that bank stock investors are aware of distortions in the accounting valuation of bank assets. However, the market-based capital ratio can only be an imperfect measure of bank capitalization, as it also reflects the valuation of a bank's access to the financial safety net. Banks that are too big to fail, in particular, may have a higher market valuation than justified purely on the basis of extant bank capital, as they can count on being bailed out in case of financial distress. The average Market value ratio is 12.2%.

In the empirical work, we relate bank capitalization rates to several corporate governance features that concern the size and composition of the bank's board, and anti-takeover provisions as an index of the effectiveness of the market for corporate control. To start, Board independence is an indicator of the share of independent directors in the board; this variable ranges from 1 to 6, with a higher score indicating a higher share of independent directors. A more independent board is expected to better represent the interests of shareholders rather than of management. A more independent board, therefore, is hypothesized to favor more bank risk taking, which would serve to increase the valuation of the bank's contingent claim on the financial safety net as reflected in bank share prices. A more independent board could bring on more bank risk by condoning lower capitalization rates.

Next, Board size is an indicator of the number of board members; this variable ranges from 1 to 5, with a higher score representing a larger board. A very small board may find it difficult to stand up to management, as the burden of doing so would fall on very few board members. A very large board may similarly be unable to effectively oppose management, as it could be subject to free-rider problems among its many members. This suggests that board effectiveness — in promoting shareholder interests — may be related to board size in a nonlinear fashion, with boards of intermediate size being the most effective. Boards of intermediate size thus may favor relatively risky bank capitalization strategies. To reflect this, Board size, effective is a variable that takes a higher value if the headcount of board members is taken to imply a board that more effectively represents shareholder interests; this variable ranges from 1 to 3, with a higher score representing a more effective board. The highest score of 3 is given to a board with an intermediate number of board members between 8 and 3.

Next, the CEO chairman separation variables indicates the degree to which the roles of CEO and chairman of the board are separated; the CEO chairman separation variable ranges from 1 to 3, with a higher score indicating better separation between the two roles. Effective separation of the CEO and chairman roles should enable a board to better promote the interests of shareholders giving rise to riskier capital-related bank strategies.

As a final corporate governance feature, the anti-takeover provision variable is a dummy variable that equals one if the bank is incorporated in a country or state that allows a bank to adopt anti-takeover provisions. Such measures weaken the disciplining effect of the market for corporate control on bank management, possibly enabling managers to pursue less risky bank capitalization strategies. Consistent with this, Low (2009) founds that an increase in take-over protection in Delaware in the mid-1990s caused managers to lower firm risk.

In our capitalization regressions, we use three bank-level control variables. First, we include the Assets variable. Larger banks are expected to maintain lower capitalization rates, acting on their incentive to exploit their too-big-to-fail status. Second, Return on assets is a bank's pre-tax profits divided by total assets. More profitable banks should be able to maintain higher capital ratios, as they can more easily add to their capital buffers by retaining earnings (and not taking losses). Finally, Ownership is a dummy variable that equals one if a single owner has direct ownership of more than 10% of the bank. Concentrated ownership is expected to be associated with lower capitalization rates in line with evidence in Laeven & Levine (2009) that bank risk taking varies positively with the power of shareholders.

4.2. *Empirical Results*

Table 2 shows the results of regressions that relate bank capitalization ratios to corporate governance features for an international sample of banks over the 2004–2008 period. All explanatory variables are lagged one period to reduce the potential for reverse causation. Regressions include country-year fixed effects to control for time-varying, country-level determinants of capitalization rates such as the state of the business cycle. Standard errors are adjusted for clustering at the bank level.

Panel A shows the results of five capitalization regressions that include the board independence variable. This variable enters regressions for the four capitalization ratios based on accounting information (i.e., tier 1 capital, total capital, common equity, and tangible capital) in columns 1–4 with negative and insignificant coefficients, while it enters the market value regression in column 5 with a positive coefficient that is significant at 10%. The positive estimated coefficient in column 5 could reflect that bank capitalization varies positively with board independence, or alternatively that banks with more independent boards are higher valued, for instance because they have a more valuable contingent claim on the financial safety net achieved by riskier bank capitalization strategies.

In Panel B, the CEO chairman separation variable has a negative coefficient that is significant at the 10% level in the tangible capital regression 4, providing some evidence that a board that is not dominated by the CEO pursues a low-capitalization strategy in the interests of shareholders.

In Panel C, the board size variable enters the total capital regression in column 2 with a negative coefficient that is significant at the 10% level, suggesting that board size varies negatively with bank

Table 2. Bank capitalization ratios and corporate governance.

Panel A	Tier 1 Capital (1)	Total Capital (2)	Common Equity (3)	Tangible Capital (4)	Market Value (5)
Lagged assets	−0.008***	−0.004***	−0.005***	−0.009***	−0.002
	(0.001)	(0.001)	(0.001)	(0.001)	(0.001)
Lagged return on assets	0.736***	0.687***	1.433***	1.117**	2.701***
	(0.282)	(0.260)	(0.451)	(0.520)	(0.911)
Lagged ownership	0.002	0.004	0.006	0.007**	0.005
	(0.003)	(0.003)	(0.004)	(0.004)	(0.005)
Lagged board independence	−0.001	−0.001	−0.001	−0.001	0.002*
	(0.001)	(0.001)	(0.001)	(0.001)	(0.001)
N	2071	2149	2366	2238	2322
adj. R–sq	0.186	0.102	0.262	0.278	0.392
Panel B					
Lagged CEO chairman separation	0.000	−0.000	−0.002	−0.002*	−0.003
	(0.001)	(0.001)	(0.001)	(0.001)	(0.002)
N	1976	1984	2140	1991	2109
adj. R–sq	0.192	0.095	0.306	0.381	0.498

Panel C					
Lagged board size	–0.002	–0.002*	0.003*	–0.000	0.005**
	(0.002)	(0.001)	(0.002)	(0.002)	(0.003)
N	2110	2188	2411	2277	2367
adj. R–sq	0.207	0.120	0.287	0.284	0.405
Panel D					
Lagged board size, effective	–0.002	–0.003	–0.007***	–0.005***	–0.003
	(0.002)	(0.002)	(0.002)	(0.002)	(0.003)
N	2110	2188	2411	2277	2367
adj. R–sq	0.208	0.119	0.297	0.290	0.401
Panel E					
Lagged anti–takeover provision	0.011***	0.012***	0.007**	0.004	–0.013*
	(0.003)	(0.003)	(0.004)	(0.004)	(0.007)
N	2110	2188	2412	2278	2368
adj. R-sq	0.211	0.122	0.235	0.285	0.401

Notes: The dependent variables in the five columns are Tier 1 capital, Total capital, Common equity, Tangible capital and Market value, respectively. Regressions in Panels B-E also include the Lagged assets, Lagged return on assets, and Lagged ownership variables that are unreported. Regressions include country-year fixed effects. Standard errors are adjusted for clustering at the bank level, and provided in parentheses. *, ** and *** denote significance at 10%, 5%, and 1%, respectively.

capitalization. The board size variable, however, enters the common equity regression in column 3 and the market value regression in column 5 with positive coefficients that are significant at 10% and 5%, respectively. Hence, we cannot unambiguously establish how board size correlates with bank capitalization.

In Panel D, the board size, effective variable enters the common equity and tangible capital regressions in columns 3 and 4 with negative coefficients that are significant at the 1% level. Thus, boards of intermediate size are associated with lower capital ratios relative to un-weighted assets, while they are not materially related to regulatory capital ratios relative to weighted assets in columns 1 and 2. These results together suggest that banks with an 'effective' board size are more leveraged, and that they invest in assets with low or no risk weightings such as government bonds to keep their regulatory capital ratios at high levels.

Finally, in Panel E the anti-takeover provision variable obtains positive and significant coefficients in columns 1–3, while it has a negative and significant coefficient in the market value regression in column 5. Anti-takeover protection may enable management to pursue high-capitalization strategies as reflected in accounting-based capital ratios so as to make their jobs and wealth invested in the firm safer. The negative association between anti-takeover protection and market-based capitalization may reflect that managers create more shareholder value in the absence of anti-takeover provisions, either by influencing capitalization rates or in other ways.

Overall, the evidence of Table 2 suggests that separation of the CEO and chairman roles, boards of intermediate size, and an absence of anti-takeover provisions are associated with lower accounting-based capitalization ratios, while a more independent board, a larger board and a lack of anti-takeover provisions are associated with a higher market-based capitalization. Shareholder-friendly corporate governance may correlate positively with market-based capitalization on account of a real capitalization channel or any other channel by which shareholder-friendly corporate governance is positively related to bank valuation. The tendency of shareholder-friendly corporate governance to be negatively associated with accounting-based bank capitalization rates is consistent with the evidence presented in Section 3 that banks with shareholder-friendly corporate governance are riskier.

5. Conclusion

This chapter provides evidence that 'good' corporate governance — or corporate governance that favors the interests of bank shareholders — is associated with greater bank insolvency and systemic risks for an international sample of banks. In addition, we find that 'good' corporate governance is associated with lower levels of accounting-based bank capital.

Our finding that 'good' corporate governance is associated with increased risk taking at financial firms is consistent with earlier research showing that better investor protection reduces excessive risk-avoidance at non-financial firms explained by the fact that managers earn private benefits from reducing risk. Banks, however, are special in that they benefit from the financial safety net. The financial safety net provides banks with an incentive to take on too much risk, as banks receive financial support from the financial safety if they become distressed.

This suggests that risk taking at banks is determined by the interaction of corporate governance regimes and the financial safety net. We find empirical support for this hypothesis by showing that 'good' corporate governance increases bank risk taking especially for banks that are large and located in countries with strong financial safety nets. For these banks, more risk can be expected to increase their contingent claim on the financial safety net. 'Good' corporate governance thus reinforces the tendency for banks to exploit the financial safety net, if they are in a position to do so.

The interaction of corporate governance and the financial safety net in determining bank insolvency risk has important implications for public policy towards corporate governance at large banks. In particular, the case for more shareholder-friendly corporate governance at banks is much weaker than in the case of non-financial firms. In the case of banks, particularly large ones, 'better' corporate governance may only exacerbate the excessive risk taking resulting from the banks' incentives to exploit the financial safety net. In the second-best world where mispriced financial safety nets and too-big-to-fail policies exist, 'better' corporate governance thus may actually produce worse outcomes. To prevent this, a first priority should be regulatory and financial safety net reform to address too-big-to-fail issues and reduce moral hazard leading to excess risk taking by banks. After such reforms, the case for 'better' corporate governance at banks would become much stronger.

References

Acharya, V., Anginer, D., & Warburton, A. (2014). The end of market discipline? Investor expectations of implicit state guarantees. *New York University Working Paper*. Available at: http://ssrn.com/abstract=1961656.

Acharya, V., Engle R., & Richardson, M. (2012). Capital shortfall: A new approach to ranking and regulating systemic risks, *American Economic Review Papers and Proceedings*, 102(3), 59–64.

Adrian, T., & Brunnermeier, M. (2011). COVAR, *NBER WP* No. 17454.

Aggarwal, R., Erel, I., Stulz, R., & Williamson R. (2009). Differences in governance practices between U.S. and foreign firms: Measurement, causes, and consequences, *Review of Financial Studies*, *22*, 3131–3169.

Anginer, D., Demirgüç-Kunt, A., Huizinga, H., & Ma, K. (2015a). Bank corporate governance and financial stability: International evidence. Mimeo: World Bank.

Anginer, D., Demirgüç-Kunt, A., Huizinga, H., & Ma, K. (2015b). Corporate governance and bank capitalization strategies. Mimeo: World Bank.

Barth, J., Caprio, Jr. G., & Levine, R. (2004). Bank regulation and supervision: What works best? *Journal of Financial Intermediation*, *13*, 205–248.

Becht, M., Bolton, P., & Röell, A. (2011). Why bank governance is different, *Oxford Review of Economic Policy*, *27*, 437–463.

Beltratti, A. & Stulz, R. (2012). The credit crisis around the globe: Why did some banks perform better? *Journal of Financial Economics*, *105*, 1–17.

Berger, A. & Bouwman, C. (2013). How does capital affect bank performance during the financial crisis? *Journal of Financial Economics*, *109*, 146–176.

Berger, A., Imbierowicz, B., & Rauch, C. (2015). The roles of corporate governance in bank failures during the recent financial crisis, *Journal of Money, Credit and Banking*, forthcoming.

Bertay, A., Demirgüç-Kunt, A., & Huizinga, H. (2013). Do we need big banks? Evidence on performance, strategy, and market discipline, *Journal of Financial Intermediation*, *22*, 532–558.

Bolton, P., Mehran, H., & Shapiro, J. (2015). Executive compensation and risk taking, *Review of Finance*, *19(6), 2139–2181*.

Calomiris, C. & Carlson, M. (2014). Corporate governance and risk management at unprotected banks: National banks in the 1890s, *NBER WP* No. 19806.

Campbell, J., Hilscher, J., & Szilagyi, J. (2008). In search of distress risk. *Journal of Finance*, *63*, 2899–2939.

Chen, C., Steiner, T., & Whyte, A. (2006). Does stock option-based executive compensation induce risk-taking? An analysis of the banking industry. *Journal of Banking and Finance*, *30*, 915–945.

Demirguç-Kunt, A., & Detragiache, E. (2002). Does deposit insurance increase banking system stability? An empirical investigation. *Journal of Monetary Economics*, *49*, 1373–1406.

Demirgüç-Kunt, A., Detragiache, E., & Merrouche, O. (2013). Bank capital: Lessons from the financial crisis, *Journal of Money, Credit and Banking*, *45*, 1147–1164.

DeYoung, R., Peng, E., & Yan, M. (2013). Executive compensation and business policy choices at U.S. commercial banks. *Journal of Financial and Quantitative Analysis*, *48*, 165–196.

Edmans, A. & Liu, Q. (2011). Inside debt, *Review of Finance*, *15*, 75–102.

Ellul, A. & Yerramilli, V. (2013). Stronger risk controls, lower risk: Evidence from U.S. bank holding companies. *Journal of Finance*, *68*, 1757–1803.

Erkens, D., Hung, M., & Matos, P. (2012). Corporate governance in the 2007–2008 financial crisis: Evidence from financial institutions worldwide. *Journal of Corporate Finance*, *18*, 389–411.

Fahlenbrach, R. & Stulz, R. (2011). Bank CEO incentives and the credit crisis. *Journal of Financial Economics*, *99*, 11–26.

John, K., Litov, L., & Yeung, B. (2008). Corporate governance and risk-taking, *Journal of Finance*, *63*, 1679–1728.

John, K., Saunders, A., & Senbet, L. (2000). A theory of bank regulation and management compensation, *Review of Financial Studies*, *13*, 95–125.

Laeven, L. (2013). Corporate governance: What's special about banks? *Annual Review of Financial Economics*, *5*, 63–92.

Laeven, L. & Levine, R. (2009). Bank governance, regulation and risk taking, *Journal of Financial Economics*, *93*, 259–275.

Low, A. (2009). Managerial risk-taking behaviour and equity-based compensation, *Journal of Financial Economics*, 92, 470–490.

Mehran, H., Morrison, A., & Shapiro, J. (2012). Corporate governance of banks: What have we learned from the financial crisis? In M. Dewatripont & X. Freixas (Eds.), *The Crisis Aftermath: New Regulatory Paradigms*, CEPR report.

Pathan, S. (2009) Strong boards, CEO power and bank risk-taking. *Journal of Banking and Finance*, *33*, 1340–1350.

Vertical and Horizontal Problems in Financial Regulation and Corporate Governance

— CHAPTER 22

■ Jonathan R. Macey
Yale University

■ Maureen O'Hara
Cornell University

1. Introduction

Recent efforts to mitigate systemic risk and moral hazard in capital markets and financial institutions have run head-long into long-standing principles of corporate governance. This chapter discusses two contexts in which that is the case. The first issue relates to what we will describe as the "vertical" challenge between financial institutions and the separately incorporated holding companies that own and control them. The second issue relates to what we call the "horizontal"

The authors thank Richard Herring and participants at the International Banking Conference at the Federal Reserve Bank of Chicago for helpful discussions. They also thank Eduardo Hanmal for valuable research assistance.

challenge, or the regulatory arbitrage that occurs between the banking subsidiaries of complex holding companies and their less-regulated non-bank and shadow bank siblings. We discuss a remedy proposed in Macey & O'Hara (2015) to address problems arising from vertical challenges. We argue that problems arising from horizontal challenges are more intractable.

2. Financial Institutions and the Companies that Own Them

That corporate governance problems are particularly acute in banks is well understood (see Levine (2003); Bebchuk & Spamann (2010); de Haan & Vlahu (2013); Adams & Mehran (2012); Calomiris & Carlson (2014)). What may not be appreciated, however, is the degree to which certain unique features of banking complicate both the role of financial institutions' boards of directors and the effectiveness of their governance.

In an earlier paper (see Macey & O'Hara, 2003), we reviewed the different models of corporate governance, with a particular focus on the duties board members owe to different constituencies. We argued that these unique features of banks dictated a heightened duty of care for bank directors. We discussed the various legal cases defining the duty of care for directors, and how the courts have vacillated in their application of these duties owed by directors. In a more recent paper, Macey & O'Hara (2015), we argued that a lot has changed with respect to banking structure and practice, but little has changed with respect to the duties and obligations of bank directors. This inertia with respect to bank directors is all the more puzzling given that the Dodd–Frank Wall Street Reform and Consumer Protection Act[1] (Dodd–Frank) explicitly addressed the externalities imposed by individual banks on the financial system — yet imposed little in the way of additional corporate governance requirements on bank directors to make them responsible for limiting such risks.

[1] Pub.L. 111–203, H.R. 4173.

2.1. *An Introduction to the Corporate Governance of Banks*

Generally speaking, the problem of corporate governance stems from agency problems that emerge when the residual claims on a firm's income take the form of shares of stock that are mostly owned by people who are not involved in the management or operations of the company (see Berle & Means (1936); Jensen & Meckling (1932)). In order to ameliorate agency costs, over time corporate law has generated the general rule that fiduciary duties should be owed exclusively to shareholders (see Macey (1999)). The justifications for making shareholders the exclusive beneficiaries of the fiduciary duties owed by managers and directors are based on the fact that creditors, as fixed claimants, can safeguard their investments through a combination of pricing and the imposition of contractual protections such as conversion rights or put options (see Macey & Miller, 1993).

In our earlier paper on corporate governance problems in banks, we argued that banks are different from other firms and that the economic policies that justify making shareholders the exclusive beneficiaries of fiduciary duties do not apply with the same force to banks that they do to other types of corporations, such as manufacturing companies or technology companies. In more recent research (Macey & O'Hara, 2015), we argue that these difficulties increased in the past decade, so that banks in the post-crisis era face even greater corporate governance difficulties. Specifically, we believe there are a variety of unique features of banks relative to other firms that make them unusually risky, more fragile, and more difficult to monitor and control. We provide a short synopsis of these arguments here.[2]

First, banks' unusual capital structures give them a unique role in generating liquidity for the economy. It is well known that banks' balance sheets are highly leveraged (see Bebchuk & Spamann (2010); Flannery (1994)), with fixed claim creditors supplying 90% or more of the funding banks require to operate. Moreover, these fixed claim

[2] Our analysis of vertical problems in banking draws heavily from arguments made in our paper "Bank Corporate Governance: A Proposal for the Post-Crisis World".

liabilities generally are available to creditors/depositors on demand, while on the asset side of the balance sheet, the bank's loans and other assets have longer maturities.

The development of increasingly robust secondary markets and banks' ability to securitize assets has enabled banks to move assets off of their balance sheet. Because more transparent and liquid assets are the ones that tend to be sold either outright or as part of a pool of securitized financial assets, what is left on the bank's balance sheet tends to be the more opaque and idiosyncratic assets. Arguably these evolutionary developments in capital markets have led to a secular deterioration, rather than to an improvement in the transparency and liquidity of bank assets.

The phenomenon of holding simultaneously transparent, liquid liabilities on the one hand, and illiquid, opaque assets on the other, enables banks to serve the vital economic role of creating liquidity (see Diamond & Dybig (1986)). However, this mismatch in the liquidity characteristics and term-structure of banks' assets also leads to bank runs and other systemic problems in the financial system. With greater than a third of U.S. bank liabilities uninsured, rational uninsured depositors (and claimants) will try to be among the first to withdraw before other, more nimble creditors deplete the banks' assets. Thus, bank depositors, unlike creditors in other companies, are in a situation closely akin to the classic prisoner's dilemma. This prisoner's dilemma can lead to failures in solvent banks because the need for liquidity in the event of a run or panic can lead to fire-sale liquidations of assets, thereby spreading problems to heretofore solvent banks. For bank directors, the need to manage such liquidity risks is fundamental to a bank's survival.

Second, the existence of federally sponsored deposit insurance means that banks can continue to attract liquidity to fund their operations even after they are insolvent. Unlike other sorts of companies, it is virtually impossible for federally insured banks to become insolvent in the "equitable" sense of being unable to pay their debts as they come due in the ordinary course of business.[3] Federal insurance eliminates the

[3] In bankruptcy law and practice, there are two types of insolvency. Insolvency in the balance sheet sense means that the value of a company's liabilities is greater than the value of its assets. Insolvency in the equity sense means that the firm is unable to pay

market forces that starve non-financial firms with poor prospects of cash. The federal government has attempted to replace these market forces with regulatory requirements such as capital requirements and requirements for the "prompt resolution" of financially distressed banks. Nevertheless, it seems clear that the well-established tenet of corporate finance that there is a conflict between fixed claimants and shareholders is, as we previously observed "raised to a new dimension in the banking context."[4] In banking, neither creditors nor capital markets have incentives either to negotiate for protections against risky, "bet-the-bank" investment strategies, or to demand compensation for such risk in the form of higher interest payments.

Third, moral hazard caused by deposit insurance coupled with imperfections in the regulatory system also lead not only to sub-optimally easy access to liquidity, but also to an industry-wide reduction in levels of monitoring within the firm, resulting in a higher incidence of large losses and bank failures due to fraud.[5] The high incidence of fraud is attributable both to the lack of monitoring by creditors and to the highly liquid form of banks' assets, which makes it easy to divert bank assets to private use relative to less liquid assets such as factories and equipment.

As we discuss in Macey & O'Hara (2015), perhaps no event illustrates the endemic monitoring and other corporate governance problems in the context of the banking industry more clearly than the London whale trading loss debacle.[6] The SEC charged JPMorgan Chase

its debts as they come due in the ordinary course of business. Tabak, D. March 29, 2013, the Solvency Two Step [Web log post]. Available at: http://business-finance-restructuring.weil.com/contributors-corner/the-solvency-two-step/.

[4] Macey and O'Hara (2003) at 98.

[5] See Remarks of R. L. Clarke, The Exchequer Club, in Comptroller of the Currency News Release No. NR 1988, p. 6 noting that fraud and self-dealing were "apparent" in as many as one-third of the bank failures that occurred during the 1980s. See also Jackson and Symons (1999, p. 152), citing a study by the U.S. General Accounting Office of banks failures in 1990 and 1991 that reported that in slightly more than 60% of these failures (175 out of 286), insider lending was a "contributing factor".

[6] Kevin LaCroix, The D&O Diary, http://www.dandodiary.com/2013/09/articles/securities-litigation/a-closer-look-at-jp-morgans-920–million-london-whale-regulatory-settlements/September 20, 2013, accessed most recently on November 21, 2013.

with misstating financial results and lacking effective internal controls to detect and prevent its traders from fraudulently overvaluing investments to conceal hundreds of millions of dollars in trading losses. [7]

In JPMorgan's $200 million settlement of the SEC's enforcement action against it, the bank acknowledged significant corporate governance failures. For example, the Bank admitted that significant facts learned in the course of the various internal reviews were not shared in meetings and calls among the participants in such reviews. As a result, these facts were not escalated to JPMorgan Senior Management or communicated to the Audit or Risk Committees of the board in a timely fashion.[8]

In earlier decades, the mismatch between the maturity and liquidity characteristics of banks' assets and liabilities, their unusually high leverage, and the moral hazard caused by such institutional features as the Fed discount window, deposit insurance, and the expectation of bailouts, largely defined the unique corporate governance problems experienced by banks.[9] These characteristics remain, but the JPMorgan whale debacle underscores some important new dimensions of bank corporate governance problems: the opacity of bank activities, combined with the complexity of risk management activities involving the valuation and

---

The SEC's co-Enforcement directors Andrew Ceresney and George Canellos announced that "cases in which the defendant engaged in 'egregious intentional misconduct' may justify requiring an admission, as would the obstruction of an SEC investigation or 'misconduct that harmed large numbers of investors.'" The traditional "neither-admit-nor-deny" settlements remain a "major, major tool" used by the SEC in the majority of cases, according to the SEC. Bruce Carton, SEC to Require Admissions of Wrongdoing in Settlements of Egregious Cases, Compliance Week, June 19, 2013, http://www.complianceweek.com/pages/article.aspx?articleid=299339&pagetypeid=2&publishDate=False&timestamp=635072389785525327, accessed November 22, 2013.

[7] SEC, Order Instituting Cease-And-Desist Proceedings Pursuant to Section 21C of the Securities Exchange Act of 1934, Making Findings, and Imposing a Cease-and-Desist Order; http://www.sec.gov/litigation/admin/2013/34–70458.pdf (Order).

[8] Id Annex A at 31.

[9] See Calomiris and Carlson (2014) for a discussion of the factors leading to bank corporate governance issues in era predating deposit insurance.

control of complex asset positions, create significant monitoring difficulties for directors.[10]

2.2. *Vertical Corporate Governance: The Problem of Dual Boards*

A significant corporate governance challenge for many banks arises from their unique organizational structure: they are corporations with their own boards of director, that are entirely owned and controlled by holding companies, which are also corporations but are generally publicly held. In the case of major commercial banks such as JPMorgan Chase and Citibank, the holding companies are incorporated in Delaware, while the banks are federally chartered and under the jurisdiction of the Comptroller of the Currency. Delaware has strong, shareholder-centric corporate governance norms and rules oriented towards profit maximization. In stark contrast, the Comptroller of the Currency has only a remote interest in profit maximization. Its concern is on the safety and soundness of banks and the financial system.

Every major bank in the U.S. is now organized as some form of bank holding company ("BHC"). A BHC is defined as "[a] company that owns and/or controls one or more U.S. banks or one that owns, or has controlling interest in, one or more banks. A bank holding company may also own another bank holding company, which in turn owns or controls a bank; the company at the top of the ownership chain is called the top holder."[11]

---

[10] See also Mehran, Morrison, and Shapiro (2011) who make similar complexity and opacity arguments in their analysis of governance problems in the financial crisis.

[11] Under § 2020.1.3.1 of the Bank Holding Company Act of 1956, administered by the Federal Deposit Insurance Corporation (FDIC), a bank holding company is defined as "any company which has control over any bank or over any company that is or becomes a bank holding company by virtue of this Act.

(2) *Any company has control over a bank or over any company if*

a. *the company directly or indirectly or acting through one or more other persons owns, controls, or has power to vote 25% or more of any class of voting securities of the bank or company;*

Bank holding companies are, by definition, involved in the business of banking, and are limited by law to activities that are "so closely related to banking as to be a proper incident thereto".[12] Because the BHC controls the bank, the monitoring and control of risk must take place at multiple levels. From a regulatory perspective, the Federal Reserve "is responsible for regulating and supervising bank holding companies, even if the bank owned by the holding company is under the primary supervision of a different federal agency (OCC or FDIC)".[13] When assessing a BHC, however, the Fed will "work cooperatively" with the functional regulator of the subsidiary bank "to address information gaps or indications of weakness or risk identified in a supervised BHC subsidiary that are material to the Federal Reserve's understanding or assessment" of the BHC.[14] This structure of supervision acknowledges that Bank holding companies wield control over the banks they hold.

From a governance perspective, the holding company's board inevitably exerts control over the banks within the holding company structure, particularly where, as is often the case, the directors of the bank holding company also sit as officers and directors of the bank. As such, it is each holding company director's duty to control risk down to the level of the banks the BHC holds.[15] Consequently, directors of holding companies, like directors of the banks themselves, must be involved in the governance, risk-management, and monitoring and oversight of the

---

b. *the company controls in any manner the election of a majority of the directors or trustees of the bank or company; or*

c. *the Board determines, after notice and opportunity for hearing, that the company directly or indirectly exercises a controlling influence over the management or policies of the bank or company.*"

[12] Bank Holding Company Act, *passim.*

[13] National Information Center, *All Institution Types Defined*, http://www.ffiec.gov/nicpubweb/Content/HELP/Institution%20Type%20Description.htm (accessed January 24, 2012).

[14] The Board of Governor's Division of Banking Supervision and Regulation Bank Holding Company Supervision Manual, § 1050.1.4.1.1 (2011).

[15] For further discussion, see Gang Bai, *Asset Opacity and CEO Compensation of Bank Holding Companies*, 2011 Financial Management Association Annual Meeting, Session 099: Managerial Compensation and Financial Institutions (January 12, 2011).

banks and bank affiliates within the holding company structure. The formal corporate separateness of BHCs and the banks they control does not absolve holding company directors from involvement with the activities of their subsidiary banks even if they are directors on the board of a BHC but not on the board of the bank. It has long been observed, however, that holding companies and the banks they own and control are not truly separate as a practical matter.[16]

From both a regulatory perspective and a corporate governance perspective, bank safety and soundness is paramount. The well-known "source of strength" doctrine requires that bank holding companies provide financial assistance to support its banking subsidiaries. In particular, §225.142 of the Bank Holding Company Act provides that "[i]n supervising the activities of bank holding companies, the Board has adopted and continues to follow the principle that bank holding companies should serve as a source of strength for their subsidiary banks." This notion pervades the BHC's corporate governance and directly impacts the relationship between the BHC and its subsidiaries.

As we argued in Macey & O'Hara (2015), the Fed's BHC regulations, the principles of corporate governance developed here, as well as basic concerns about systemic risk and bank safety all indicate that bank holding company officers and directors have fiduciary obligations that guide — and when necessary, trump — corporate form. Fiduciary duties flow not only to shareholders of the holding company but also to the corporate organization itself. Thus the responsibility for bank safety and soundness must be shouldered by both holding company directors and officers and the directors and officers of their subsidiaries, particularly their bank subsidiaries.

Less clear is how the shared responsibility between the holding company board and the bank board should work in practice in the post-crisis environment. It clearly makes no sense to say that bank holding company officers and directors can ignore issues of safety and soundness that affect their subsidiary banks on the grounds that they are fiduciaries of a different corporate entity, namely the holding company. Yet, the notion that the duties and obligations of holding company

[16] Jackson (1994) and Symons & Symons (1999).

officers and directors and bank officers and directors are identical and wholly duplicative also appears problematic. To see why, consider that the OCC argues "For its part, the primary duty of the subsidiary bank's directors is to protect the bank".[17] This view is inconsistent with the duties of the directors of bank holding companies, which require directors of holding companies — like directors of other firms — to maximize value for shareholders.

The problem is simple to describe. Because they are considered to be directors of corporations, holding company directors (and bank directors, too, for that matter) ostensibly have no obligation to mitigate risk, but rather are tasked with *maximizing* the value of the company on whose board they sit. This rule makes perfect sense in the context of non-financial corporations, whose failure poses no systemic risk and whose shareholders can eliminate the firm-specific risk of the company's business antics easily and cheaply through diversification. Yet, it is the clear policy of federal banking regulators that holding companies — and particularly large holding companies whose operations pose systemic risks — should focus primarily on issues of safety and soundness. Thus, bank holding company directors are pulled in opposite directions by the legal rules that govern their behavior.

One way to reconcile the inconsistency is to recognize a basic priority: Managers and directors can only maximize profits to the extent that doing so does not conflict with relevant legal rules and regulations. In our view, this is an extremely important feature of the corporate governance landscape.

Establishing and maintaining this hierarchy, however, does not resolve entirely the tension between profit maximization and the regulatory and social goals of achieving safer and sounder financial institutions. As we have seen over the past several decades, there is plenty of room for financial institutions to engage in excessive risk-taking even after they have complied with the law. Banks, for example, can, and do invest in the riskiest assets within a particular risk-weighting class. They also look for loopholes in regulations such as the Volcker rule in order

[17] See Office of Comptroller of the Currency, The Directors Book, October 2010 (reprinted October 2013), p. 26.

to squeeze the highest returns they can for their shareholders; and, of course this quest for the highest returns involves risk, which, in turn, is not something that regulators are interested in maximizing.

The fiduciary duty to maximize profits is not the only obstacle to reaching the goal of incentivizing managers and directors of financial institutions to focus on keeping banks safe with the same intensity as directors of other companies focus on maximizing share prices. Holding company directors, like the directors of all other corporations, are elected by the shareholders. In an election between a risk-taker and a non-risk taker, the shareholders will vote for the risk-taker. Thus, among the strongest characteristics for survival in the job of bank or bank holding company directors is a strong proclivity for risk-taking.[18]

As we have discussed elsewhere, bank directors outside of the U.S. often face strictly higher burdens, with some jurisdictions viewing bank failures as a criminal offense on the part of directors. Brazil, for example, holds banks' executives and directors personally liable for the debts of failed institutions even when no fault is proven.[19] The UK government, following on the recommendation of the Parliamentary Commission on Banking Standards, recently introduced a new criminal offence for reckless misconduct in the management of a bank. This criminal liability would apply to both executive and non-executive directors of a bank.[20] The maximum sentence for the offence is seven years in prison and/or an unlimited fine.

The notion that "reckless management" is a crime is rather alien to the U.S. perspective that business failure is not a criminal offense, but rather a natural, albeit unfortunate, outcome of business judgment in an uncertain world. In our view, criminalizing bank failure is not a viable approach to resolving the difficulties of bank corporate governance. It does, however, change the calculus for bank directors with respect to the acceptable level of risk for a financial institution.

[18] This argument may explain Laeven and Levine's (2009) empirical finding that ownership by more institutional investors increases the riskiness of the bank.
[19] See Prosecuting bankers: Blind justice. *The Economist*, May 4, 2013.
[20] See Treasury (2013).

A similar change in calculus can arise from the concept found in Germany, Switzerland, and Austria called *Untreue*. This "breach of trust" is defined as "a derogation of duty that causes real harm to the institution", and it has been the basis for charges against bankers at West LB, Bayern LB, HSH Nordbank and Sal Oppenheim.[21] Indeed, the CEO of WestLB paid a fine of 150,000 euros to settle charges relating to breach of trust, and the CEO of Bayern LB is currently awaiting trial on similar charges. More intriguing are the cases involving board members of these failed financial institutions. The entire management board of the German bank HSH Nordbank is on trial for breach of trust due to risk management failures relating to a CDO and other off-balance sheet activities that resulted in the bank having to be bailed out to the tune of 30 billion Euros.[22] Similarly, seven former directors of LBBX, Germany's largest public sector lender, have been charged with breach of trust in connection with moving risky assets to special purpose vehicles allegedly to hide the riskiness of the bank.[23]

In the U.S., bank directors and managers can be criminally prosecuted for fraud and for violating the federal securities laws or provisions of the securities laws, and such was the fate that befell more than 800 bankers jailed in the aftermath of the S&L crisis. But pursuing such cases, particularly against bank directors, is notoriously difficult due to the challenge of linking wrong-doing to those actually running the bank.[24] The rarity of this outcome means that bank director behavior is unlikely to be affected.

What is clear from this review is that corporate governance problems are remarkably resilient. While some approaches have been more successful than others, in general even the most extreme outside constraints

---

[21] *Op Cit.*

[22] This duty of trust does not just attach to financial firms. Board members of the German firm Mannesmann were also charged with Untreue in connection with that firm's takeover by Vodaphone last year. See "Breach of Trust? German corporate governance is literally on trial," The Economist, February 20, 2013.

[23] See "Former board of bailed-out German bank LBBW to go on trial", Thomson Reuters, Thursday October 31, 2013 at http://uk.reuters.com/assets/print?aid=UKBREE99U0J120131031.

[24] *Op Cit*, Prosecuting bankers: Blind justice. *The Economist*, May 4, 2013.

have failed to resolve bank governance problems. In our view, this suggests using a new approach, one that explicitly recognizes the inherent difficulty of managing and controlling risk in the post-crisis era.

2.3. *Solving the Vertical Problem in Bank Governance*

Fundamental to the vertical conflict in banks is the nature of risk. Regulators of the underlying bank fear that directors will fail to control the risk of the entity, imposing costs on the entire system. Shareholders of the bank holding company worry that regulators will severely limit the bank's risk and with it any consequent return. Both concerns are valid. Yet, risk is fundamental to banking, and its banishment serves the cause of neither master.

What does serve both ends is an enhanced focus on risk management. The greater complexity of financial institutions speaks to the need to require greater expertise on the part of directors, particularly those of institutions deemed to be systemically important by regulatory authorities. The laws and regulations that govern financial institutions, particularly in the wake of Dodd–Frank, provide additional support for the argument that bank directors should be held to higher standards than the amateur standard that governs directors generally. In Macey and O'Hara (2015) we proposed new "banking expertise" requirements on bank directors, much in the spirit of the increased "financial literacy" requirements now binding on audit committees. Our proposal is particularly relevant for directors of bank holding companies, who currently face no special requirements as to qualifications.[25]

[25] Interestingly, Directors of subsidiary banks do face additional requirements. For example, the OCC notes" In addition to the citizenship and residency requirements contained in 12 USC 72, the qualifications of a candidate seeking to become a member of the Board of Directors of a national bank include (1) Basic knowledge of the banking industry, the financial regulatory system, and the laws and regulations that govern the operation of the institution: (2) Willingness to put the interests of the bank ahead of personal interests; (3) Willingness to avoid conflicts of interests; (4) Knowledge of the communities served by the bank; (5) Background, knowledge, and experience in business or another discipline to facilitate oversight of the bank;

While our proposal that bank directors have special expertise is new, the idea that corporate directors in general should have special expertise is not new, though the idea has not been well developed in the literature. Some scholars define the term "professional director" simply as directors who serve on multiple boards and adduce evidence that board membership of such professional directors correlates with improved performance for the companies on whose boards those directors serve.[26] Others use the term "professional" to refer to the particular, industry specific expertise that certain directors have.[27] We use the term in the latter sense.

Among the earliest and most persuasive appeals to require that corporate directors have substantial industry-specific expertise was made by Yale law professor, later Supreme Court Justice, William O. Douglas. Douglas argued that experts on the board "would be invaluable... in determining the course of conduct for the managers", and would be "better qualified to determine financial and commercial policy". For these reasons Douglas argued that outside experts on boards of directors "should have a position of dominance and power on the board" so that they can "make their directive influence effective" by means of their "real power over executive management".[28]

Just as the idea that some directors should be held to higher standards is not alien to the academic literature, neither is it new to policymakers. The Sarbanes–Oxley Act explicitly set higher requirements for qualified audit committees by requiring all members to be independent and at least one member to be a "financial expert" as defined by SEC rules.[29] Indeed, one motivation behind Sarbanes–Oxley was to strengthen

(6) Willingness and ability to commit the time necessary to prepare for and regularly attend board and committee meetings. See OCC, The Directors Book, 2010, p. 4.

[26] Keys & Li (2005).

[27] Pozen (2010).

[28] Douglas (1934).

[29] An "audit committee financial expert" is defined as a person who has the following attributes: (i) an understanding of generally accepted accounting principles and financial statements; (ii) the ability to assess the general application of such principles in connection with the accounting for estimates, accruals and reserves; (iii) experience preparing, auditing, analyzing or evaluating financial statements that present a breadth and level of complexity of accounting issues that are generally

audit committees to "avoid future auditing breakdowns" which were contributing to a loss of confidence in the integrity of U.S. companies and markets.[30] Our argument is that the failure of risk management at financial institutions, particularly systemically important ones, can lead to outcomes of even greater consequence. It is our belief that current steps, such as the Dodd–Frank requirement that one member of the risk committees of BHCs and SIFIs have risk management experience, are insufficient to address the magnitude of the problem of excessive risk-taking by financial institutions.

What changes are needed to address this problem? In Macey and O'Hara (2015), we suggest differential standards for both bank risk committee members and bank directors. With respect to risk committee members, we note that risk management of a complex financial institution is not something easily grasped by a typical corporate director but instead requires specialized expertise. We believe that risk management committees should be composed only of individuals who can demonstrate expertise in evaluating and monitoring the risk control systems of a bank. Allowing "amateur hour" in this oversight function at large complex financial institutions is simply irresponsible in post-crisis financial markets.

Such individuals, whom we call "banking experts", would have acquired, either through experience or education, the skills needed to monitor the risk management functions of the bank. For smaller financial institutions, this expertise may be more limited, reflecting that risk management at such institutions generally involves less complex methodologies. For large, complex financial institutions, the needed skill set will be larger, requiring familiarity with risk modeling, valuation of complex derivatives, synthetic asset replication, hedging strategies, etc.

---

comparable to the breadth and complexity of issues that can reasonably be expected to be raised by the registrant's financial statements, or experience actively supervising one or more persons engaged in such activities; (iv) an understanding of internal controls and procedures for financial reporting; and (v) an understanding of audit committee functions. See Trautman (2013).

[30] See Senate Report No.107–205 as cited in Tsacoumis, Bess, and Sappington, The Sarbanes–Oxley Act: Rewriting Audit Committee Governance, BLI Issue 3, International Bar Association.

The specific qualifications for being a banking expert could be defined in much the way that audit committee financial experts are determined.

Second, we also propose higher professional standards for bank directors. As we have argued, bank corporate governance issues pose an on-going threat to the financial system. While heightened oversight of banks is surely called for, such oversight will be successful only to the extent that the directors of financial institutions have both the incentives and the experience and skill required to be successful in carrying out their oversight responsibilities. At a minimum, we believe bank directors should be "banking literate" where such literacy is defined by an understanding of the basic functions of banking, the nature of risk in complex financial organizations, and the complex regulatory structure defining banking. Such literacy, which would a pre-requisite for becoming a director, could have been acquired through experience or through education.

There are a variety of objections to this proposal. One is that if having more qualified directors was valuable, then bank shareholders would demand this on their own. Alternatively, if higher requirements are desirable for banks, then perhaps they should be required of firms more generally. We think the response to both objections is actually the same: banks are different from other firms. As we have argued, bank shareholders do not have properly aligned incentives to limit bank risk, so externally-imposed requirements may be necessary. Other firms can adequately address corporate governance deficiencies internally, so requiring higher standards for all corporate directors is unnecessary.

Another objection to our proposal involves bank risk taking. Empirical research suggests that banks with more knowledgeable directors take on greater risk than other banks. Our proposal could thus exacerbate rather than ameliorate risk-taking at banks by placing more knowledgeable directors on boards. Our response is that relying on directors' lack of knowledge to restrain risk is surely not a formula for a safe and sound banking system. We completely agree, however, that in addition to knowledge and competence, there must also be a culture within banks that considers prudent banking to be a way of life rather than an oxymoron. Efforts by regulators to highlight the importance of cultural issues within banks should be viewed as working hand in hand with our proposals to improve corporate governance in banking.

Finally, where will all these directors come from? It will take time and effort to groom enough competent directors for all of the important financial firms in the economy. In the interim, immediately focusing on upgrading the expertise on risk committees, perhaps through focused educational programs, has to take center stage. If better directors result in creating better banks, then the returns to searching for, educating, and empowering those directors will pay off for all concerned.

3. Horizontal Governance Issues: Non-Bank Subsidiaries versus Bank Subsidiaries

Another source of conflict between financial regulation and corporate governance arises from the interactions between the bank and the non-bank subsidiaries of bank holding companies. The banks subsidiaries operate as banks, while the non-bank subsidiaries often operate as so-called "shadow banks". Shadow banking refers to traditional banking activities, particularly lending, that occurs outside of the regulated banking system and is effectuated by non-bank financial intermediaries as well. Claessens and Ratnovski define shadow banking as a non-banking institution that engages in what, from an economic and functional point of view, is the business of banking.[31] In contrast other researchers, including, Paul McCulley and Mehrling, Poszar, Sweeney, and Neilson focus on the nature of the financial assets involved in the transactions.[32]

Shadow banking includes such important financial sectors as the repo market, and the commercial paper market. Among the more important sorts of firms that operate as shadow banks are money market mutual funds, hedge funds, commercial and personal/finance companies, and broker–dealers firms. Because unregulated non-banks are active in the shadow banking system, such institutions can engage in

[31] Stijn, Claessens, & Lev Ratnovski (2014).
[32] McCulley (2007) and Mehrling, Pozsar, Sweeney, & Neilson (2013).

transactions featuring significantly higher credit risk, market risk and liquidity risk, while holding much smaller capital cushions than their regulated bank competitors.

According to the IMF, U.S. shadow banking assets exceed those of the conventional banking system and have for some time.[33] Estimates of shadow banking range from between 15 and 25 trillion dollars in the United States, between 13.5 and 22.5 trillion in the euro area, and between 2.5 and 6 trillion in Japan — depending on the measure — and around 7 trillion in emerging markets. In emerging markets, shadow banking growth is outpacing that of the traditional banking system.[34] In the U.S. the UK and the Euro area, the value of assets in the shadow banking system is greater than the GDPs of each of those countries.

Subsequent to the subprime meltdown in 2008, the activities of the shadow banking system came under increasing scrutiny and regulation in Europe, Japan, and the United States. In particular, new rules now cover money market funds (MMFs), securitization, and financial companies. Some particularly large financial companies (American International Group, General Electric Capital Corporation, MetLife, Inc., and Prudential Financial) have been designated as "systemically important financial institutions" (SIFIs) by the Financial Stability Oversight Council (FSOC).[35] A threat exists if the material financial distress of an institution or the particular characteristics of the institution could cause systemic effects throughout the U.S. economy.

---

[33] See IMF, Global Financial Stability Report, chapter Two, Shadow banking around the globe: how large, how risky? at 66, http://www.imf.org/external/pubs/ft/gfsr/2014/02/pdf/c2.pdf

[34] See IMF, Global Financial Stability Report, chapter Two, Shadow banking around the globe: How large, how risky? http://www.imf.org/external/pubs/ft/gfsr/2014/02/pdf/c2.pdf

[35] FSOC's designation authority is limited in Sections 113(a)(2) of the Dodd-Frank Act to "U.S. non-bank financial compan[ies]." See also and Section 102(a)(6). As announced in April 2015, GE Capital is being wound-down by its parent General Electric Company.

Also pursuant to Dodd–Frank, in July 2014, the U.S. Securities and Exchange Commission (SEC) issued final rules for the reform of MMFs. Certain MMFs known as "prime institutional" MMFs will be required to transact at a floating NAV and to maintain daily share prices that change according to changes in the value of the individual assets that constitute the portfolio.[36] MMFs whose customers are natural persons and government MMFs, which are MMFs that invest in government debt, may continue to use constant NAV pricing. However, in times of stress, all MMFs may impose liquidity fees and redemption gates.[37]

Another point of entry for U.S. regulators seeking to regulate the shadow banking systems is through the imposition of credit risk retention requirements in securitizations. Such requirements, known colloquially as "skin-in-the game" provisions are, strangely enough coupled with prohibitions against hedging the retained credit risk portion of the securitization. These anti-hedging provisions are strange, of course, because they increase rather than decrease the risks of the firms that are subject to the credit risk retention rules. Anti-hedging provisions are necessary, however, because their absence could exacerbate moral hazard problems that arise when the banks can effectively pass the risk off on "someone else" and so undertake unreasonably risky actions.

From a corporate governance perspective, one specific facet of the shadow banking system is of particular concern. Bank and financial holding companies can conduct banking activities not only through the downstream banks that they own and control, but also through virtually unregulated non-bank subsidiaries. Carmassi and Herring (2014) provide compelling evidence that the largest systemically important banks responded to the financial crisis by creating more complex

---

[36] Institutional prime MMFs are marketed to institutional investors, who constitute over one-half of the market for MMFs. Generally speaking, institutional prime MMFs have portfolios that are riskier than other funds' portfolios and include certificates of deposit, commercial paper, and repurchase agreements. See IMF, http://www.imf.org/external/pubs/ft/gfsr/2014/02/pdf/c2.pdf, at p. 99, footnote 60.

[37] http://www.imf.org/external/pubs/ft/gfsr/2014/02/pdf/c2.pdf, at p. 99.

corporate structures in which banking activities are now dispersed over "hundreds or even thousands" of separate legal entities.[38]

A case in point is the role played by bank mortgage company subsidiaries.

> *Mortgage companies were largely ignored (by both functional and institutional regulators), despite the fact that they had held a dominant market share (of mortgage originations) since the early 1990s. Mortgage companies were not funded by deposits, so no institutional regulator oversaw them, and their activities did not fall under the domain of any functional regulator. The Federal Trade Commission and the State Attorneys General did have the ability to bring punitive actions against mortgage companies, but only if they observed unfair and deceptive practices evidenced by a pattern of customer complaints. Before the 2007 crisis, this "repeat-complaint-oriented supervision" had little power to systematically affect mortgage company behavior, leaving them essentially free of regulatory oversight.*[39]

In a recent article, Demyank and Loutskina (2014) observe that, while defaulted mortgages originated by bank subsidiaries weakened the balance sheets and income statements of their holding company parents by increasing their reported loan losses and reducing their profits (net income), the defaults on mortgages originated by their non-bank mortgage-company subsidiaries did not.[40] Thus, rather stunningly, loan losses from mortgage defaults from subprime mortgages "have an adverse effect on a BHC's reported loan losses and net income only if they were originated by a bank subsidiary, not a mortgage-company subsidiary."[41]

Unsurprisingly, the different consequences for a bank holding company of making loans through a mortgage company subsidiary rather than through a subsidiary bank had consequences. Demyank and Loutskina document that "mortgage-company subsidiaries of BHCs originated more loans to borrowers with lower credit scores, higher

[38] See Carmassi & Herring (forthcoming).

[39] See Demyank & Loutskina (2014).

[40] Id.

[41] Id.

loan-to-income ratios, and lower relative incomes than did their bank subsidiaries. Mortgage companies were also more likely to originate loans of riskier types, such as adjustable-rate and interest-only mortgages."[42]

The incentives for holding companies to shift their riskiest sub-prime lending activities out of banks and into non-bank mortgage-companies were heightened by the Gramm–Leach–Bliley Act of 1999, which, in an effort to control risk, isolated the activities of bank and non-bank subsidiaries by erecting "formal financial barriers between the BHCs' bank and their non-depository subsidiaries."[43] In particular, BHCs were required to erect "firewalls" between their bank subsidiaries and their non-bank subsidiaries. Gramm–Leach–Bliley explicitly prohibited BHCs from bailing out troubled nonbank subsidiaries, which meant that as a practical matter "BHCs' exposure to the limited liability mortgage-company subsidiaries was indeed limited to their equity investment."[44]

Gramm–Leach–Bliley had the stated policy objective of protecting FDIC-insured banks, the federal deposit insurance fund and taxpayers from the costs associated with the failure of their non-bank/ uninsured affiliate. The so-called firewall rules of Gramm–Leach–Bliley cabin off the unregulated non-bank affiliates from their affiliate regulated banks, on paper making individual banks safer. The unintended consequence of Gramm–Leach–Bliley was that by doing so it increased systemic risk because risky activities were simply shunted from insured banks to their uninsured, unregulated non-bank affiliates within the same holding company. This shift not only led to weaker lending standards, it also led to the financial crisis.[45]

3.1. *Dodd Frank*

Several provisions in Dodd–Frank provide regulators with the tools to deal with the problem just identified. Perhaps the most keenly targeted are provisions calling for the establishment of the FSOC. The FSOC was established primarily to (a) identify risks to the financial stability of the

---

[42] Id.
[43] Id.
[44] Id.
[45] Id.

United States that could arise from the material financial distress or failure, or ongoing activities, of large, interconnected bank holding companies or non-bank financial companies, or that could arise outside the financial services marketplace; (b) promote market discipline, by eliminating expectations on the part of shareholders, creditors, and counterparties of such companies that the U.S. government will shield them from losses in the event of failure; and (3) to respond to emerging threats to the stability of the U.S. financial system.[46]

In addition, Dodd Frank requires the Federal Reserve to adopt enhanced prudential regulatory standards for the largest BHCs and designated non-bank financial companies. The stringency of these requirements increases with the size and complexity of the holding company. Further, Dodd–Frank restricts banks, bank affiliates and bank holding companies from proprietary trading or investing in a hedge fund or private equity fund, requires the Federal Reserve to impose a debt-to-equity limit on companies the Council has determined pose a grave threat to financial stability, and to establish enhanced prudential standards for large BHCs and foreign banking organizations (known as "FBOs").

These rules have the potential to mitigate problems that arise when insured and regulated depository institutions shift their riskiest activities to uninsured unregulated subsidiaries. It appears to us, however, that the rules do not go far enough. The rules are currently restricted only to SIFIs. SIFIs consist of bank holding companies with total consolidated assets of $50 billion or more as well as nonbank financial companies[47] designated as systemically important by the FSOC.

Are the issues with subsidiaries really only relevant for these mega institutions, or is it a more common phenomena across a broader spectrum of banks? To address this issue, we collected Federal Reserve/National Information Center data on subsidiaries for the U.S. financial

[46] See FSOC 2014 Annual Report, at iii, available at http://www.treasury.gov/initiatives/fsoc/Documents/FSOC%202014%20Annual%20Report.pdf.

[47] A Non-bank Financial Company is defined in Title I of Dodd–Frank as a company that is predominantly engaged in financial activities. Predominantly means that 85% of its consolidated gross revenues are derived from what are defined as financial activities by the Bank Holding Company Act of 1956.

institutions ranked 1–10, 51–60, and 76–85 based on total asset size. These data are given in Table 1.

Certainly, with respect to the subsidiary issues, the largest SIFI banks are where the bulk of the problem lies. As of year-end 2014, JPMorgan Chase, the nation's largest bank had 5,688 subsidiaries,

Table 1. Bank subsidiaries.

Rank	Name	Total Assets	Subsidiaries
1	JPMORGAN CHASE & CO. (1039502)	$2,572,773,000	5,688
2	BANK OF AMERICA CORPORATION (1073757)	$2,106,796,000	2,379
3	CITIGROUP INC. (1951350)	$1,842,181,000	1,683
4	WELLS FARGO & COMPANY (1120754)	$1,687,155,000	2,002
5	GOLDMAN SACHS GROUP, INC., THE (2380443)	$856,301,000	13,068
6	MORGAN STANLEY (2162966)	$801,510,000	9,713
7	GENERAL ELECTRIC CAPITAL CORPORATION (1631915)	$508,255,287	8,805
8	U.S. BANCORP (1119794)	$402,529,000	102
9	BANK OF NEW YORK MELLON CORPORATION, THE (3587146)	$385,303,000	1,109
10	PNC FINANCIAL SERVICES GROUP, INC., THE (1069778)	$345,243,081	895
51	CITY NATIONAL CORPORATION (1027518)	$32,610,363	74
52	FIRST CITIZENS BANCSHARES, INC. (1075612)	$30,075,113	17
53	BOK FINANCIAL CORPORATION (1883693)	$29,148,050	42
54	EAST WEST BANCORP, INC. (2734233)	$28,738,323	34
55	CULLEN/FROST BANKERS, INC. (1102367)	$28,347,544	12

(*Continued*)

Table 1. *(Continued)*

Rank	Name	Total Assets	Subsidiaries
56	SYNOVUS FINANCIAL CORP. (1078846)	$27,051,231	30
57	ASSOCIATED BANC-CORP (1199563)	$26,821,774	9
58	FIRST HORIZON NATIONAL CORPORATION (1094640)	$25,674,034	40
59	BARCLAYS DELAWARE HOLDINGS LLC (2938451)	$25,005,482	8
60	FIRSTMERIT CORPORATION (1070804)	$24,909,640	19
76	SUSQUEHANNA BANCSHARES, INC. (1117156)	$18,661,390	23
77	UMB FINANCIAL CORPORATION (1049828)	$17,500,960	68
78	FIRST NATIONAL OF NEBRASKA, INC. (1020902)	$17,465,465	20
79	FULTON FINANCIAL CORPORATION (1117129)	$17,083,180	51
80	PACWEST BANCORP (2875332)	$16,236,505	33
81	F.N.B. CORPORATION (3005332)	$16,127,090	33
82	TEXAS CAPITAL BANCSHARES, INC. (2706735)	$15,900,308	16
83	IBERIABANK CORPORATION (2291914)	$15,758,605	30
84	ASTORIA FINANCIAL CORPORATION (2504128)	$15,640,021	10
85	PRIVATEBANCORP, INC. (1839319)	$15,603,382	8

Notes: This table shows the number of bank subsidiaries for a sample of bank holding companies with $10 billion or greater of assets. A subsidiary is counted if the bank has at least a 25% or more ownership position. The data are from the National Information Center/Federal Reserve data base which can be accessed at http://www.ffiec.gov/nicpubweb/nicweb/nichome.aspx.

while Goldman Sachs had 13,068 and Morgan Stanley reported 9,713 subsidiaries. The scale of these numbers certainly suggests the potential for risk-shifting problems to arise. But even the 9th largest bank, BNY Mellon had 1,109 subsidiaries, and, in unreported results, Fifth Third, the nation's 22nd largest bank had 911 bank subsidiaries. The 50th largest bank, Popular, Inc. with an asset size of $33 billion had 74 subsidiaries, which relative to their asset size, is comparable to 10th largest bank PNC Financial's 895 subsidiaries (and $303 billion in assets). Overall, banks ranked 50–59 averaged over 40 subsidiaries, while those ranked 76–85 averaged almost 30. We believe these results suggest that vertical governance problems pose a pervasive issue in the post-crisis banking system.

4. Conclusion

There is a fundamental and perhaps irreconcilable difference between the corporate governance goals of (SIFIs) and federally insured financial institutions on the one hand, and non-federally insured, non-systemically important companies on the other hand. Because all (SIFIs) and virtually all insured banks are controlled by holding company parents, this means that different subsidiaries of the same holding companies will be subjected to different corporate governance norms. This structure creates a conflict between the goal in financial regulation of reducing the incidence of failure of (SIFIs) and the goal in corporate law of maximizing the value of the corporation for shareholders.

The conflict between bank holding companies and their underlying banks discussed in the first part of this chapter is a "vertical" corporate governance problem. The vertical conflict is exacerbated by the size and complexity of large financial institutions. It can be mitigated by impose higher professional standards on bank directors and on members of board risk committees.

The conflict between the bank and non-bank subsidiaries of bank holding companies discussed in the second part of this chapter is a "horizontal" corporate governance problem. The horizontal conflict exists among bank and non-bank subsidiaries, and is, if anything, even more difficult to resolve than the vertical governance problem.

The extent of this challenge is reflected in the immense complexity of Dodd–Frank, and particularly in the designation and regulation of entities designated as systemically important. In light of the small number of institutions designated as SIFIs, however, it appears that more work is required to mitigate the horizontal challenge, particularly as the shadow banking system remains extremely robust.

References

Adams, R. & Mehran, H. (2012). Bank board structure and performance: Evidence for large bank holding companies. *Journal of Financial Intermediation*, 21, 243–267.

Barle, A Jr. & Means, G. (1936). *The Modern Corporation and Private Property*. Brunswick (USA) and London (UK): Transaction.

Bebchuk, L. A. & Spamann, H. (2010). Regulating bankers' pay. *Georgetown Law Journal*, 98(2), 247–287.

Calomoris, C. & Carlson, M. (2014). Corporate governance and risk management at unprotected banks: National banks in the 1890s, *NBER Working Papers* No. 19806. Available at: https://www.federalreserve.gov/pubs/feds/2014/201408/201408pap.pdf.

Carnassi, J. & Herring, R. The corporate complexity of systemically important banks. *Journal of Banking and Finance*, forthcoming, 3.

De Haan, J. & Vlahu, R. (2013). Corporate Governance of Banks: A Survey. De Nederlandsche Bank Working Paper No. 386. Available at: http://ssm.com/abstract=2297770.

Demyank, Y. & Loutskina, E. (2014). A Gap in regulation and the looser lending standards that followed. *Economic Commentary of the Federal Reserve Bank of Cleveland* No. 2014–20.

Douglas, W. O. (1934). Directors who do not direct. *Harvard Law Review*, 47, 1305–1314.

Jackson, H. E. (1994). The expanding obligations of financial holding companies, 107 *Harvard Law Review 509*, 510; Symons, H. E., & Symons, E. (1999). Regulation of financial institutions, 304.

Jensen, M. C. & Meckling, W. H. (1976). Theory of the firm: Managerial behavior, agency costs, and ownership structure. *Journal of Financial Economics*, 3, 305–360.

Keys, P. Y. & Li, J. (2005). Evidence on the market for professional directors. *Journal of Financial Research*, 28(4), 575–589.

Levine, R. (2003). More on finance and growth: More finance, more growth? *The Federal Reserve Bank of St. Louis Review*, August, 31–46. Available at: https://research.stlouisfed.org/publications/review/03/07/Levine.pdf.

Macey, J., O'Hara, M. (2003). The corporate governance of banks. *Economic Policy Review Federal Reserve Bank of New York*, 9(1), 91–107, Available at: https://www.newyorkfed.oremedialibrary/media/research/epr/03v09n1/0304mace.pdf.

Macey, J., O'Hara, M. (2013). Bank corporate governance: A proposal for the post-crisis world, *Economic Policy Review Federal Reserve Bank of New York*, 22(1). Available at: https://www.newyorkfed.org/medialibrary/media/research/epr/2016/epr_2016_post-crisis-world_macey.pdf.

McCulley, P. A. (2007). Teton Reflections. Global Central Bank Focus Series, PIMCO, August/September. Available at: https://www.pimco.com/en-us/insights/economic-and-market-commentary/global-central-bank-focus/teton-reflctions.

Mehrling, P., Pozsar, Z., Sweeney, J. & and Neilson, D (2013). Bagehot was a Shadow Banker: Shadow banking, central banking, and the future of global finance. Available at: http://econ.as.nyu.edu/docs/IO/26329/Mehrling_10012012.pdf.

Pozen, R. (2010). The big idea: The case for professional boards. *Harvard Business Review*. Retrived from http://hbr.org/2010/12/the-big-idea-the-case-for-professional-boards/ar/6.

Stijn, Claessens, & Lev Ratnovski (2014). What is shadow banking? *IMF Working Paper* No. 14/25, Washington: International Monetary Fund, (2014).

Trautman, L. J. (2013). Who qualifies as an audit committee financial expert under Sec regulations and NYSE Rules?. *DePaul Business & Commercial Law Journal, 11.*

Treasury, H. M. (2013). Financial services (Banking Reform) Bill government amendments: Criminal sanctions. Retrived from https://www.gov.uk/government/uploads/system/uploads/attachment_data/file/245758/HoL_Policy_Brief_-_Criminal_Sanctions.pdf.

Tsacoumis S., Bess, S. R. & Sappington, B. A. (2003). The Sarbanes-Oxley act: Rewriting audit committee governance. *Business Law International*, 4(3), 212.

Incentive Compensation and Bank Risk: Insights from Organizational Economics

— Chapter 23

■ Edward Simpson Prescott
Federal Reserve Bank of Cleveland

1. Introduction

The main tools that bank regulators have traditionally used to limit bank risk include limits on lending concentrations, capital requirements, liquidity rules, limits on bank activities, and supervisory examination (Spong, 2000). In response to the financial crisis, not only have these tools been strengthened, but tools for regulating banks' internal governance have been developed as well. One of the more prominent tools is the regulation of the compensation practices of banks.[1]

The views expressed are those of the author and not necessarily those of the Federal Reserve Bank of Cleveland or the Federal Reserve System.

[1] Actually, there is at least one precedent for regulating compensation. The Federal Deposit Insurance Corporation Improvement Act of 1991 (FDICIA) said that "excessive compensation" was to be considered an unsafe and unsound practice as was any compensation that could lead to a material financial loss to a bank. Furthermore, the prompt corrective provisions of FDICIA restrict the bonuses paid to senior executives of banks that are significantly undercapitalized. For a discussion of these compensation regulations and their enforcement prior to the mid-1990s, see Schooner (1996).

The new focus on regulating compensation is based on the belief that compensation practices were an important factor in the run-up to the recent financial crisis. This view can be found in the Financial Crisis Inquiry Commission's report (2011, p. xix) as well as the Financial Stability Forum (2009). In the United States, the federal bank regulatory agencies issued supervisory guidance specifying that bank compensation plans should be consistent with the principle that "... a banking organization should provide employees incentives that appropriately balance risk and financial results in a manner that does not encourage employees to expose their organizations to imprudent risk;" (Federal Register, 2010). Similarly, the Dodd–Frank Act of 2010 required that federal financial regulators write rules regulating compensation at not only banks, but other financial firms too.[2] In Europe, the rules have been significantly more restrictive, even to the point of being possibly punitive. Recently, the European Banking Authority restricted bonuses to be no more than twice the level of salaries (European Banking Authority, 2015).

As for being a major cause of the crisis, compensation fails the basic timing test. Compensation practices during the boom were not that much different from before it.[3] Nevertheless, there should be some connection between compensation practices and bank risk. After all, compensation is one of the primary ways that a firm directs and motivates its employees. Under some circumstances, compensation practices could very well raise bank risk. At a minimum, it should matter for bank efficiency.

There are two classes of bankers who could conceivably have a direct impact on bank risk. The first is an individual, such as a CEO or other senior executive, who makes decisions that impact a large fraction of the firm. The second is a group of workers, such as loan officers or traders, whose actions jointly determine bank risk.

Much of the economic literature on bank risk and compensation analyzes CEOs. This focus is understandable. A CEO is the single

---

[2] For the proposed rules, see Federal Register (2011). As of December 2015, when this was written, the final rules were not yet released.

[3] A more subtle argument would be that the traditional compensation practices are fine during normal times, but during a boom they create more risk.

most influential individual in an organization and, equally important, there is data on their compensation. Nevertheless, concentrating on CEOs neglects the second group, who as a whole are paid much more. For example, JPMorgan's compensation expenses in 2012 were around $31 billion for about 250,000 employees. Of this amount, the CEO received only (in a proportional sense!) $0.0187 billion. How these employees are paid is likely to be far more important for risk than CEO compensation.[4]

This essay discusses what the economic literature has to say about the compensation of bank employees and bank risk. The empirical literature on the topic is virtually nonexistent, so the essay mainly discusses the theoretical literature on economic organization and extensions of those results to bank risk.[5] The essay will, however, discuss two case studies, including one from the mortgage industry that illustrates some important findings.

Not surprisingly, the economic literature on organizations finds that compensation matters. However, it also finds that precisely how it matters depends on the specifics of the individual job, what the job produces, how the bank is organized, and the controls and monitoring in place. These features of a bank are hard to measure and analyze for those inside an organization, let alone for an outsider like a bank

[4] While a CEO has the most power in an organization, a CEO has a limited span of control and that, along with the constraints imposed by other people in the firm, can limit what a CEO can influence. Interestingly, Fahlenbrach, Prilmeier, & Stulz (2012) find that banks have persistent risk cultures over long periods of time, which suggests that risk can be driven by a lot more than just an individual CEO.

[5] There is a small literature that studies the connection between the compensation of bank CEOs and bank risk. Its findings are mixed. Using data from the 1980s, Houston & James (1995) find little connection between the form of CEO compensation and bank risk. Using a different sample of highly leveraged banks over the 1988–1994 period, Benston & Evans (2006) find some evidence of the greater use of bonuses at banks that failed. Crawford, Ezzell, & Miles (1995) find some mixed evidence for highly levered banks using a slightly different time period. Studies of the more recent period are also mixed. Cheng, Hong, & Scheinkman (2015) do not find evidence of bank risk-taking due to managerial entrenchment. In contrast, Fahlenbrach & Stulz (2011) find that banks with CEOs whose incentives were better aligned with shareholders performed worse than other banks in the crisis.

examiner. This suggests that without detailed field work into organizations, the best one may be able to do is to restrict compensation practices that reward the most egregious risk-taking behavior.

2. Organizational Economics

The question, "What is the connection between the compensation of bankers and bank risk?" and the connected regulatory question of, "Should banker compensation be regulated and, if so, how?" are really instances of the much bigger and long-standing question, "How should a firm be organized and run?" Without an answer to the last question, there is no hope of making progress on the first two. This section describes some of the thinking and measurement that economists have done on the question of organizational structure and then ties that back to the more narrow questions about banker compensation and bank risk.

One good place to start is the classic 1972 paper by Alchian & Demsetz, which introduced the idea of agency problems and incentives into the study of the firm. Alchian & Demsetz (1972) argued that information costs were an important factor in the organization of a firm and in determining which activities were done within a firm and which were done by a market. They identified a firm as a team of workers who work together and a person who sets up the contracts that the workers operate under. They argued that measuring a team member's contribution to the team's revenue was one of the most critical problems the firm has to solve.[6]

This measurement problem is a big challenge for an organization. A firm reports its earnings at the end of a year, but figuring out a

[6] The economics literature has long used the term "team" to describe a group of people, possibly with different information sets and decisions to make, who work towards a common goal. The terminology is most associated with the work of Marschak & Radner (1972), who studied how teams coordinate decisions. Later, Holmström (1982) added private information and different goals into team-like environments. This latter development is important for our purposes because those elements are what make incentive compensation necessary.

worker's contribution to those earnings is often difficult. Firms typically use internal accounting systems that attempt to produce measures of profits at the line of business level, which will help with measurement, but these internal accounting systems are far from perfect and only push the problem down a level in the organization. Then, there is the difficult task of assessing the productivity of corporate functions, like audit, treasury, human resources, information technology, and legal, all of which are support services and do not directly produce revenue.

The importance of measurement and its importance for compensation can be seen abstractly in a simplified version of the Holmström (1982) formulation of the team problem. For a team with n workers, the production function is

$$Y = f(e_1, e_2, \ldots, e_n, \varepsilon),$$

where Y is the team's revenue, e_i is the effort of the ith worker, and ε is a random shock. The workers are risk-averse, the owner of the firm is risk neutral and, for simplicity, the owner of the firm is assumed to have enough wealth to pay the workers even if firm revenue is low.

The importance of measurement on the form of compensation can be seen in two extreme cases. For the first case, assume that there is no measurement problem. The owner of the firm knows how productive each worker is and can observe how hard he works. In this case, compensation is straightforward. Each worker supplies the level of effort specified in the contract and is paid a wage because that is the cheapest way to pay a risk-averse worker. The level of a worker's wage may depend on his productivity and the characteristics of his job, but none of his pay will vary with firm revenue.

At the other extreme, assume that each worker's effort is private information (that is, not observed by the owner of the firm), so a worker could shirk. Furthermore, assume that the uncertainty (the epsilon shock) is not observed by anyone, so the owner of the firm cannot back out the workers' effort levels from the revenue.

In this case, some sort of incentive contract will have to be used. If a wage is paid, the worker is paid the same no matter how hard he works, so he shirks. For this reason, the owner will have to tie compensation directly to the firm's revenue.[7] Just how compensation is tied to Y will depend on the production function and the utility function, but it will mean that the risk-averse worker will have to receive variable pay, be it in the form of a bonus or something else. Furthermore, it is not hard to imagine that such a contract will be limited in its effectiveness. If there are lots of workers, that is, n is large, then there can be a pretty severe free-rider problem and revenue would be very low.[8]

There are two important points to take from these extreme cases. First, the use and form of variable pay depends heavily on measurement. Second, organizations have good reasons to find ways to measure individual productivity.

Many organizational practices are designed to measure performance. One of the most common practices in banking is loan approval. In this case, a person or a group of people different from the loan officer reviews a new loan to make sure it meets the lending standards of the bank. The loan approval is important for a mundane reason, namely the loan officer may make mistakes in evaluating a loan, but it is also important for an incentive reason. A loan officer is often paid on commission, so his incentive is to generate volume, even at the expense of quality. By reviewing the loan and screening out the low-quality ones, the bank is measuring how many good loans the loan officer produces.

Approving a loan is only one example of monitoring. For example, large firms will have an audit department that makes sure other departments and workers follow the policies and procedures of the firm. Some

---

[7] Technically, what matters for compensation in incentive models is whether Y contains any statistical information about effort, which it would in this case. The precise form of optimal compensation will depend heavily on the likelihood ratio, that is, the probability of Y given that the desired effort level is taken relative to the probability if the shirking level of effort is taken. See Holmström (1979, 1982) for details or Prescott (1999) for a simple exposition in the single-agent model.

[8] It is not hard to see how there could be a free-rider problem, but some care needs to be used in setting up the model. For example, if the shock is additive and has a small impact on revenue, then the level of Y reveals a lot of information about effort levels and the free-rider problem is not that severe. Furthermore, under some conditions efficiency can be reached if the workers are risk-neutral. In these cases, group punishment, that is, penalizing all the workers if revenue is low, can be effective. See Holmström (1982).

of this auditing is done selectively. For example, each year auditors will check only a subset of policies because auditing is costly. Another example is a quality control group that checks, possibly randomly, the quality of what is produced. What an audit finds can have an effect on compensation. For example, the economic models of auditing find that compensation should be tied to whether there is an audit as well as the result of it.[9]

An important feature of monitoring and measurement is who actually carries out the monitoring. Sometimes this kind of separation is referred to as a *control* in an organization. One simple type of control is to require approval by a manager for an employee's travel expenses.[10] In this case, the control is not about risk, but instead to keep expenses down, but in other cases, ineffective controls have created a *lot* of risk. For example, Barings Bank failed in 1995 due to the actions of one of its traders, Nick Leeson. Leeson suffered losses from trading in futures in Asian markets and then used his supervision of trading and settlement operations to first hide his losses and then to take a large bet on the direction that the Tokyo stock exchange would take. His hope was that the large bet would allow him to recoup his initial losses. Unfortunately, for him and Barings, he lost so much on the bet that Barings failed.[11]

Even how the separation of duties is organized can matter. One concern is that the monitor and the person monitored might collude, that is, cooperate in a way detrimental to the organization.[12] One way to reduce collusion is to put departments like risk management and audit into a corporate function, which is under a separate budget than the lines of business that they measure.

---

[9] For early work on auditing, see Townsend (1979) and Mookherjee & Png (1989).

[10] Organizations make heavy use of controls, particularly with respect to spending money. Often, the purpose of the controls is to prevent an undesirable behavior. For example, banking has a long tradition of requiring key people in charge of financial numbers to take extended vacations away from the bank. By keeping the employee away from the bank, it is harder for that employee to perpetuate a fraud.

[11] See Kuprianov (1995).

[12] For some papers that tie collusion to organizational structure, see Holmström & Milgrom (1990), Itoh (1993), and Prescott & Townsend (2002).

Separation of duties can even involve moving responsibilities between people. Many organizations use job rotation. This is done for a variety of reasons, such as management training, but it can also be done for incentive reasons. For example, rotation is sometimes used in procurement to make sure that there is second potential producer and that the procurer is not held up in the future.[13] In all the models, these assignments of responsibilities matter for how compensation is designed.

These organizational practices affect compensation and bank risk. A very nice example of how a type of rotation interacts with compensation is contained in the Hertzberg, Liberti, & Paravisini (2010) study of loan officer rotation at a large international bank. This bank periodically moved around the lending relationships that loan officers were responsible for managing. Hertzberg, Liberti, & Paravisini (2010) report that the bank's policies effectively tied pay to loans managed by a loan officer, and they argue that the loan officer rotation, along with career concerns, mitigates the incentive that loan officers have to underreport the risk in their portfolio of loans.[14]

While measurement is critical, it can have significant costs. Not only is there the time and resources used on measurement, but tying compensation solely to measurable dimensions of output can neglect less tangible, harder-to-measure dimensions.[15] Prendergast (1999) gives the example of a baseball player who is only rewarded for hitting home runs. Late in a game with runners in scoring positions, the right strategy might be to just hit for a single, but because of his incentives he might go for the home run.[16]

---

[13] The literature has come up with a variety of reasons for job rotation including learning, reducing the ratchet effect, and information revelation. For papers along these lines, see Hirao (1993), Ickes & Samuelson (1987), Meyer (1994), and Prescott & Townsend (2006). For an example in procurement, see Demski, Sappington, & Spiller (1987).

[14] Udell (1989) looks at the related issue of loan review well after a loan has been originated. He argues that the main purpose of this review is to monitor the quality of a loan officer's loan portfolio as part of the dynamic incentive relationship with the loan officer, rather than monitoring loan quality for early-warning purposes.

[15] The economic literature refers to this problem as the multitask problem, e.g., Holmström & Milgrom (1990).

[16] An analogous example in banking is to reward an employee solely for making a loan, but not caring whether the loan goes bad in the future.

These intangibles are one good reason for subjective performance measurement. Managers can observe a lot that is not formally measured and can summarize that in a performance review. Needless to say, there are costs to subjective performance measurement. Managers, like all people, are subject to biases, such as not wanting to give negative reviews to employees. Furthermore, consistent assessment across managers is difficult to implement.[17]

The measurement problems emphasized by Alchian & Demsetz are important, but they do not capture all the factors that determine incentives. Rewards to workers come not just in the form of payments of a bonus, they also come in the future. Long-term career concerns motivate employees. The promise of a promotion and the structure of the bank's internal labor market will both have large effects on behavior.[18]

One big focus of the new compensation regulations is to require banks to use more deferred compensation along with clawbacks in the hope that this will encourage employees to act in the long-term interests of the firm. Whether this type of rule will be effective is, of course, too early to tell. As just noted, there are already long-term incentives built into many internal labor markets. Furthermore, as Jarque & Prescott (2015) point out, there are a variety of ways to implement dynamic incentives that do not rely on an explicit bonus structure or can even undo a mandated deferred compensation plan.

The list above is far from a complete list of features of organizations that affect compensation. There are also incomplete contracts, holdup problems, and the ratchet problem, to name just a few. What this short introduction to organizational economics should make clear is that the organizational structure will affect the desirability of a compensation scheme and that the multitude of organizational features at work can make it hard to identify the effectiveness of a compensation scheme even for those within an organization, let alone an outsider like a regulator.[19]

---

[17] For a discussion of subjective performance assessment, see Prendergast (1999).

[18] For discussions of internal labor markets, see Baker, Gibbs, & Holmström (1994) and Lazear & Oyer (2012).

[19] Sometimes broad patterns can be seen by supervisors. For example, in the Federal Reserve's review of compensation practices at large banks, supervisors reported that

3. A Case Study and Some Theory

There is a very nice case study of a thrift institution that illustrates how the various organizational factors discussed above can influence bank risk.[20] First Federal Savings & Loan Association of Phoenix was a fast-growing thrift that operated in Arizona in the 1970s. It used a management by objective (MBO) performance system, which tied bonuses paid to branch managers to meeting branch growth targets and to the profits of the thrift. It grew fast in 1971–1973 and management wanted it to continue to grow fast in 1974, so they set performance targets for the year to a high 15% growth rate.

First Federal's compensation system ran into a severe problem in 1974 when the economy entered a deep recession and the branches were not able to meet profit targets. Needless to say, the severe contraction forced First Federal to make the difficult choice of whether to stick with the incentive plan or to modify it to reflect the new economic conditions (this is an example of an incomplete contract). But the performance plan also seems to have neglected two interesting points about bank risk. First, by emphasizing growth at the branch level, no explicit recognition was made of the quality of a branch loans in the long run. Second, the risk to the thrift depended heavily on the correlation of the branches' performance.

The importance of the second point for compensation and bank risk can be seen in Jarque & Prescott (2014). They use a relative performance model, which is a variation of the Holmström (1982) team model, in which there is a large number of loan officers (analogous to a branch in the First Federal case), each of whom originates a pool of loans. The probability of a loan officer's pool being successful depends on his effort level, an idiosyncratic shock, both of which are private information, and a common shock to the firm.[21] The key feature of their model for bank risk is the correlation of loan officer pools. For example, if the pools are uncorrelated, then the manner in which loan officers are paid does not

they found very little explicit recognition of risk adjustment in compensation design (Board of Governors, 2011, p. 2).

[20] Harvard Business School (1975, 1980).

[21] For analyses of the relative performance model, see Holmström (1982) and Demski, Sappington, & Spiller (1987).

matter for bank risk. Loan officers' returns average out, the bank has no variation in its revenue, and there is no risk at the bank level (though there may well be a lot at the loan-officer level).[22]

More generally, the desirable mix of wage and bonuses will depend on the degree of correlation and its relation to the effects of the loan officers' efforts. Furthermore, optimal contracts make heavy use of relative performance, that is, a comparison of the loan officer's performance relative to that of the rest of the bank, which in this case would be reflected in the thrift's profits.

In Jarque & Prescott's (2014) model, one factor that determines bank risk is the degree to which the compensation scheme encourages loan officers to choose loan pools that are correlated in their success. Connecting to our earlier discussion, the role of loan review and centralized risk management here can also matter a lot. If some loans are monitored by headquarters and there is some centralized measurement of correlation, then these kinds of controls, independent of compensation to loan officers, can control correlation, thus reducing bank risk.

For First Federal, the published case study does not indicate how much discretion loan officers had and whether there was any centralized review of their loans. However, by being a thrift institution, First Federal was legally required to primarily make residential mortgage loans. Furthermore, all of its branches were in Arizona, so it was also geographically concentrated. Consequently, there should have been a substantial correlation in the returns of its branches.

Indeed, this correlation, along with management's decision to reward high growth at the expense of long-term loan quality, hurt the thrift in 1975 and 1976, when it lost money and had higher losses than its competitors. For these reasons, First Federal moved to a discretionary bonus scheme and away from its MBO system. While this move seems to have been prudent, for the reasons discussed above, a discretionary bonus system has its own set of problems, since it can reward many different types of behavior.[23]

---

[22] Compensation can still matter for efficiency. A bad compensation arrangement will lower profits.

[23] One aspect of the employment relationship that has not been discussed, but is worth noting, is that even if an employee is paid a wage, there can be a very strong

The First Federal case study illustrates that multiple organizational factors influence the connection between compensation and risk. And while a compensation scheme like the MBO system used at First Federal should raise some red flags to a bank regulator, it should also be apparent that it takes detailed examination and field work to ascertain the risk implications of the thrift's compensation system.

4. The Mortgage Line of Business

One of the lessons of the organizational economics literature is that large organizations are complicated and the connections between compensation, performance, and risk are difficult to identify precisely. In practice, analysis and investigation at the level of field work seems necessary. Some of why this is necessary can be seen by looking at compensation within the mortgage line of business.

Mortgage production is a bit like an assembly line, with different workers handling individual tasks. A loan officer needs to gather a loan application, an appraiser needs to do an appraisal, an underwriter needs to evaluate the loan application, someone needs to arrange for the loan to be funded, and often a trader needs to hedge the interest rate risk between, when the commitment is made and when the loan is made. There are also closing staffs who make sure that the paperwork and all the loan details are completed.

Even after the loan is made, there are additional steps. There are staffs who might sell the loan or securitize it, and there are servicing personnel, who keeps track of payments and handles foreclosures over the life of a loan.[24] During many of these steps there may be quality assurance staff, who check the quality of work done during the loan process. Furthermore, for all of these roles, there are managers who supervise.

For each of these roles, a bank will have a compensation plan, which can include incentives. But the compensation plans will differ because

---

incentive from the threat of firing. This can be used to encourage good or bad behavior.

[24] For a description of mortgage servicer incentives, see Cordell, Dynan, Lehnert, Liang, & Mauskopf (2008).

the roles are different. In a well-run mortgage shop, the goal for an underwriter would to be review applications at a high rate without sacrificing quality, and the incentives would reflect this. The goal for the staff who hedge interest rate risk will be to do so in the least costly way. The goal for the higher-level managers will be to make sure that the employees work efficiently, are well-coordinated, and work in a cost-effective manner, so their compensation could depend on the business line's profit and loss metrics.

These descriptions give some picture of the variation in jobs and roles possible even within just one line of business. Furthermore, there can be important variation even between similar jobs, variation that determines the incentive effects of a compensation plan. Loan origination gives one such example.

In loan origination, there are three main channels. There is a retail channel, which consists of loan officers who are the employees of the mortgage lender (often a bank, but not necessarily). There is a correspondent channel, which consists of other companies, like small banks or mortgage companies, which originate loans and underwrite them to the standards of the mortgage lender. Often, the correspondent relationship will include warehouse lending facilities to temporarily fund the mortgage. It is frequently an exclusive relationship. Finally, there is a wholesale channel, which consists of mortgage brokers who deliver completed loan applications to the lender, which then does its own underwriting. Mortgage brokers typically work with multiple lenders at once.

Retail loan officers are usually paid on commission basis. They receive a certain number of basis points on the face value of a closed loan. Prior to the Dodd–Frank Act, they also had some ability to negotiate with borrowers. Their employer would provide them with a rate sheet, which listed a schedule of interest-rate-and-discount-point combinations. If they negotiated a higher interest rate or a higher number of points, they could sometimes keep a portion of the better terms (from the lender's perspective). They could also reduce their commission if they negotiated worse terms.[25]

[25] For a given point level, a higher rate than what is on the rate sheet is called a yield spread premium, while for a given rate, a higher point level is called an overage. For

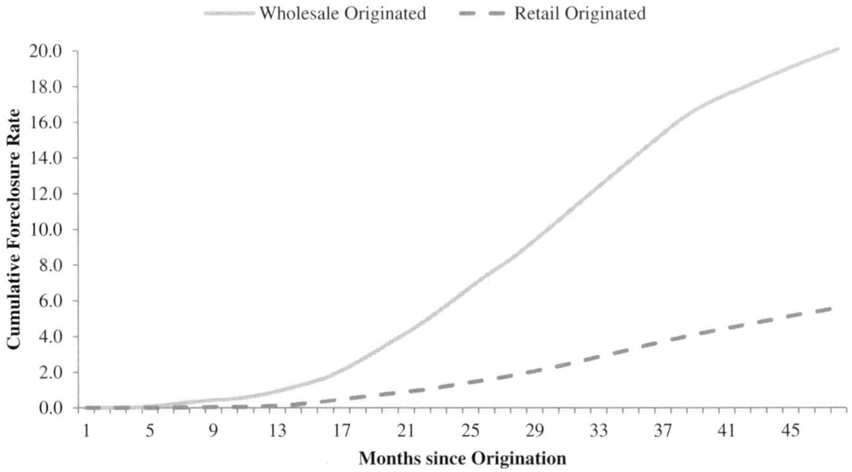

Figure 1. Cumulative foreclosure rates for adjustable-rate mortgages with a FICO score of between 600 and 650, an LTV between 85% and 95%, originated between April and July 2005 in Ohio, and classified as subprime.

Source: Author's calculations from McDash Analytics.

A mortgage broker works with a borrower and can charge the borrower fees to deliver the loan. However, like a retail loan officer, if the mortgage broker provides the borrower with a rate-point combination better (again from the lender's perspective) than that indicated on the rate sheet, the broker would receive some of that from the lender. Thus, essentially both retail loan officers and mortgage brokers were paid on a commission basis and had some ability to negotiate terms with the borrower.

Figure 1 shows the cumulative foreclosure rates for subprime mortgages that were originated in Ohio through retail and wholesale channels over the four-month period from April 2005 to July 2005. The comparison controls for several other characteristics of these loans by restricting the sample to adjustable-rate subprime mortgages with similar FICO and LTV values.

The difference in cumulative foreclosure rates is enormous. The size of both curves provides an example of the severity of the well-known

reasons unclear to me, a distinction is sometimes made between the two. Viewed from the perspective of a rate sheet, they are the same thing.

subprime problem that led up to the recent financial crisis. Less well known, however, is the differential performance by origination channel. Here are two classes of mortgages that differ not in the form of compensation paid to the originator, but only in the origination channel and the difference in their performance is dramatic.

Figure 1 is very suggestive that risk varies with origination channel, but it leaves out important borrower information that is needed for a proper comparison. In particular, mortgage brokers typically deal with borrowers who are riskier based on observable characteristics than do retail loan officers (characteristics that are in loan applications, but not in our simple comparison above). Fortunately, there is a paper by Jiang, Nelson, & Vytlacil (2014) that makes this comparison using loan-level application data obtained from an individual mortgage bank. Their study compares all of the mortgages originated by this bank from January 2004 to February 2008. They find the same result that is shown in Figure 1, namely, that the loans originated by mortgage brokers performed worse than those originated by retail loan officers (50% worse in their sample). They also find that mortgage brokers provided loans that were riskier based on the observable characteristics of the borrower. However, they find that these observable characteristics could only account for 75% of the difference in default rates between the wholesale and retail channels.[26] The rest of the difference they attribute to unobserved heterogeneity that is associated with the broker channel.

Another important feature of the bank they study was that it made a lot of loans that did not require full documentation of borrower characteristics such as income, the so-called "liar loans". They find evidence suggesting that the applicants lied about their income on low-documentation loans and that this was more of a problem on broker-originated loans than on retail-originated ones.

The evidence in Jiang Nelson, & Vytlacil (2014) implies that there are differences in risk between the retail and wholesale channels, despite

[26] They found that the correspondent channel produced lower quality loans than the retail channel as well, but that that this difference was almost completely accounted for by observables.

the very similar way that the two types of loan originators were compensated. As the earlier analysis argued, there are a variety of organizational characteristics other than compensation that influence risk. In this case, one plausible reason for the difference is that retail loan officers are employees of the firm and for the career reasons referred to earlier, may have felt that they had more to lose by bad behavior than did mortgage brokers, who deal with a wide variety of lenders.

5. Conclusion

The organizational economics perspective is quite clear about compensation: It matters for bank risk. However, it is also quite clear that precisely how compensation influences bank risk depends on the details of a job, the monitoring that is done, the assignment of responsibilities, and other organizational details. This result is a challenge for regulating compensation practices. First, compensation practices can be the wrong focus. For example, in the mortgage origination example, the origination channel was a more important source of risk than the compensation plan. Second, a simple rule may not be appropriate for all types of jobs.

Determining whether a compensation plan creates risk requires careful measurement and detailed field work within an organization. In my view, this is the most promising direction to take to determine the effect of compensation on bank risk. The two case studies described earlier give some idea of how one might go about doing that kind of assessment.

References

Alchian, A. A. & Demsetz, H. (1972). Production, information costs, and economic organization. *American Economic Review*, *62*, 777–795.

Baker, G., Gibbs, M., & Holmström, B. (1994). The internal economics of the firm: Evidence from personnel data. *The Quarterly Journal of Economics*, *109*, 881–919.

Benston, G. J. & Evans J. D. (2006). Performance compensation contracts and CEOS' incentive to shift risk to debtholders: An empirical analysis. *Journal of Economics and Finance*, *30*, 70–92.

Board of Governors of the Federal Reserve System (2011). Incentive compensation practices: A report on the horizontal review of practices at large banking organizations. Available at http://www.federalreserve.gov/publications/other-reports/files/incentive-compensation-practices-report-201110.pdf.

Cheng, I.-H., Hong H., & Scheinkman, J. A. (2015). Yesterday's heroes: Compensation and risk at financial firms. *Journal of Finance*, *70*, 839–879.

Cordell, L., Dynan, K. Lehnert, A. Liang, N., & Mauskopf, E. (2008). The incentives of mortgage servicers: Myths and realities. *Federal Reserve Board, Finance and Economic Discussion Series*, 2008–46.

Crawford, A. J., Ezzell, J. R., & Miles, J. A. (1995). Bank CEO pay-performance relations and the effects of deregulation. *Journal of Business*, *68*, 231–256.

Demski, J., Sappington, D. E. M., & Spiller P. T. (1987). Managing supplier switching. *RAND Journal of Economics*, *20*, 256–267.

European Banking Authority (2015). Guidelines on sound renumeration policies under Articles 74(3) and 75(2) of Directive 2013/36/EU and disclosures under Article 450 of regulation (EU) No 575/2013, EBA/GL/2015/22.

Fahlehnbrach, R., Prilmeier, R., & Stulz R. M. (2012). This Time is the same: Using bank performance in 1998 to explain bank performance during the recent financial crisis. *Journal of Finance*, *67*, 2139–2185.

Fahlenbrach, R. & Stulz, R. M. (2011). Bank CEO incentives and the credit crisis. *Journal of Financial Economics*, *99*, 11–26.

Federal Register (2010). Guidance on sound incentive compensation practices. 75(122).

Federal Register (2011). Incentive-based compensation arrangements, 76(72), Proposed Rules.

Financial Crisis Inquiry Commission (2011). *The financial crisis inquiry report.* New York: PublicAffairs.

Financial Stability Forum (2009). FSF Principles for sound compensation practices.

Gibbons, R. (1988). Incentives in organizations. *The Journal of Economic Perspectives*, *12*, 115–132.

Harvard Business School (1975). First federal savings (A) Case Study 9-475-072.

Harvard Business School (1980). First federal savings (B) case study 9-481-052.

Hertzberg, A. Liberti, J. M., & Paravisini, D. (2010). Information and incentives inside the firm: evidence from loan officer rotation. *Journal of Finance*, *65*, 795–828.

Hirao, Y. (1993). Task assignment and agency structures. *Journal of Economics and Management Strategy*, *2*, 299–323.

Houston, J. F. & James C. (1995). CEO Compensation and bank risk: Is compensation in banking structured to promote risk taking? *Journal of Monetary Economics*, *36*, 405–431.

Holmström, B. (1979). Moral hazard and observability. *Bell Journal of Economics*, *10*, 74–91.

Holmström, B. (1982). Moral hazard in teams. *Bell Journal of Economics*, *13*, 324–330.

Holmström, B. & Milgrom, P. (1990). Regulating trade among agents. *Journal of Institutional and Theoretical Economics*, *146*, 85–105.

Ickes, B. W. & Samuelson, L. (1987). Job transfers and incentives in complex organizations: Thwarting the ratchet effect. *RAND Journal of Economics*, *18*, 275–286.

Itoh, H. (1993). Coalitions, incentives, and risk sharing. *Journal of Economic Theory*, *60*, 410–427.

Jarque, A. & Prescott, E. S. (2014). Banker compensation and bank risk taking: The organizational economics view. Manuscript, July 30, 2014.

Jarque, A. & Prescott, E. S. (2015). Deferred pay for bank employees: Implications of hidden actions with persistent effect in time. *Federal Reserve Bank of Working Paper* No. 10–16R.

Jiang, W. Nelson, A. A., & Vytlacil E. (2014). Liar's loan? Effects of origination channel and information falsification on mortgage delinquency. *The Review of Economics and Statistics*, *96*, 1–18.

Kuprianov, A. (1995). Derivatives debacles: Case studies in large losses in derivative markets. *Federal Reserve Bank of Richmond Economic Quarterly*, *81*, 1–39.

Lazear, E. P. & Oyer, P. (2012). Personnel Economics. In Gibbons, R., & Roberts, J. (Eds), *The handbook of organizational economics*. Princeton, New Jersey: Princeton University Press.

Marshak, J. & Radner, R. (1972). *Economic theory of teams*. New Haven and London: Yale University Press.

Meyer, M. A. (1994). The dynamics of learning with team production: Implications for task assignment. *Quarterly Journal of Economics*, *109*, 1157–1184.

Mookherjee, D. & Png, I. (1989). Optimal auditing, insurance, and redistribution. *Quarterly Journal of Economics*, *104*, 399–415.

Prendergast, C. (1999). The provision of incentives in firms. *Journal of Economic Literature*, *37*, 7–63.

Prescott, E. S. (1999). A primer on moral-hazard models. *Federal Reserve Bank of Richmond Economic Quarterly*, *85*, 47–77.

Prescott, E. D. & Townsend R. M. (2002). Collective organizations vs. relative performance contracts: Inequality, risk sharing, and moral hazard. *Journal of Economic Theory*, *103*, 282–310.

Prescott, E. S. & Townsend, R. M. (2006). Private information and intertemporal job assignments. *Review of Economic Studies*, *73*, 531–548.

Schooner, H. M. (1996). Who determines when enough is enough? Refocusing regulatory limitations on banks' compensation practices. *Boston College Law Review*, *37*, 861–922.

Spong, K. (2000). *Banking Regulation: Its Purposes, Implementation, and Effects* (5th ed.). Federal Reserve Bank of Kansas City.

Townsend, R. M. (1979). Optimal contracts and competitive markets with costly state verification. *Journal of Economic Theory*, *21*, 265–293.

Udell, G. F. (1989). Loan quality, commercial loan review and loan officer contracting. *Journal of Banking and Finance*, *13*, 367–382.

Cultural Failures at Banks: A Review and Possible Solutions

— CHAPTER 24

■ Alan Morrison and Joel Shapiro
University of Oxford

1. Introduction

The years following the financial crisis were beset by an onslaught of banking scandals: LIBOR, Forex, ISDAfix, mis-selling, money laundering, tax avoidance, and others. They involved dysfunctional bank cultures that prioritized short term payoffs over long term relationships. These problems had been going on for years out of sight (or at least out of mind) of both senior managers and regulators, and came as a dramatic surprise to outside observers.

In this chapter, we will analyse the root causes of the cultural failures at these banks and possible solutions. We begin by defining culture, so as to properly understand the source of dysfunctional culture. We draw on the sociology, management, legal, and economics literatures for this task. We then ask how cultures may change, with a particular focus on how banking culture has changed in the last century. Using this

Alan Morrison is Professor of Law and Finance at Saïd Business School, University of Oxford, and a Fellow of Merton College. Joel Shapiro is Associate Professor of Finance at Saïd Business School, University of Oxford.

framework, we then explain two recent dysfunctional bank cultures: that of the derivatives and money market traders who manipulated LIBOR, and that of the foreign exchange traders who manipulated the foreign exchange fixes. Drawing upon these studies, we propose policy solutions meant to prevent and detect cultural failures.

2. What is Culture?

The way corporate culture is most commonly described is Marvin Bower's (1966) characterization as "the way we do things around here." Implicit in this statement are two key elements. First, it is difficult to describe the way things are done — including how they are done, when they are done, and what is done in response to certain events. This may arise because of a difficulty in contracting (writing the contract, enforcing it, unforeseen events) or articulating (at all or sufficiently) how to deal with contingencies. Second, it implies that things are done for a reason. Cultures can arise to solve a social (or economic) problem that cannot be handled through contracts or simple conversations. Kreps (1990) put this in economic terms; culture arises to select among multiple equilibria in a way that could not be contracted on or discussed.[1] Culture thus depends on shared values (agents evaluate outcomes in the same way) and norms (agents place the same constraints on themselves as other members of the culture).

While culture may be specific to a problem, it also depends on interactions. Therefore artifacts that spur interaction, such as the water cooler, determine the formation of a culture (Schein, 2004). Interactions also depend on language. Cultures may develop shared understandings and language to facilitate and economize on communication (Cremer, 1993; Lazear, 1999).

There are two important implications from this description of culture that have been overlooked in the debate on dysfunctional bank cultures.

The first is that cultures arise for a given network of employees, defined both by the work they do and the physical (and virtual) space

[1] Thakor (2015) discusses this and the economics literature on corporate culture in detail.

in which they interact. This means that particularly in complex organizations such as banks, there is not one specific culture, but many cultures. Moreover, cultures may extend across banks. In the LIBOR and Forex cases, which we will discuss subsequently, cultures that spanned multiple banks arose either through trading relationships between banks and/or mobility of employees across banks.

The second is that cultures are difficult for outsiders to understand. They have specific knowledge and languages that may be difficult to interpret. This will make it difficult for regulators to monitor. Moreover, it may also create a distance between senior management and rank and file employees. There are, of course, other reasons senior management may not be actively monitoring its employees. If profits are above average, the incentive to monitor is less, despite warnings of malfeasance. Also, we will see below that banks currently rely less on reputation, so again malfeasance may not be a priority of senior management.

3. Why is Bank Culture an Issue Now?

The change in investment banking culture provides important insights here. Investment banking transactions used to be completely relationship based; for example, ensuring that a long term client gets a fair price. This type of relationship involved a commitment by the investment bank to its clients that could not be codified. Therefore it was important to tie its personnel's wealth and human capital directly to the reputation and success of the investment bank, which it did through the partnership form (Morrison & Wilhelm, 2015). Over time, computerization and financial engineering codified most elements of transactions, and weakened the need to have such a culture (Morrison & Wilhelm, 2007, 2008). The partnership thus vanished and the joint stock company emerged.

In fact, almost all financial activities have become more codified and arm's length. Nevertheless, the artifacts that arose with the culture in the first place the networks, languages, knowledge, and routines remained, despite the fact that relationships, values, and norms had changed due to technology. This interaction between old artifacts and new values and norms may lead to a dysfunctional culture.

4. How do we Explain Recent Cultural Failures?

4.1. *A Brief Overview of Libor and Forex Manipulation*

LIBOR was introduced in the early 80s as a way for banks to hedge funding costs. It is now used for swaps, forward rate agreements, mortgages, and many other products (market size for products using LIBOR over $300tn, see Wheatley 2012). For a given LIBOR, a panel of multinational banks had to report their borrowing costs. There was no requirement that reports be based on transactions, and indeed sometimes there were no transactions. LIBOR manipulation generally occurred for two reasons. First, derivatives traders would ask the money market desk to manipulate the LIBOR submission to increase the payoff on their positions. These attempts were sometimes based on requests by former colleagues now at other banks. Second, management requested lower LIBOR submissions to hide credit risk from the market.

For Forex manipulation, we focus on manipulation of the WM/Reuters 4pm fix. The WM/Reuters fix was created in the early 1990s for pension valuation.[2] It began to be used for construction of indices, and many funds trade at the fix to reduce tracking error. Non-financial corporates also trade at the fix. The 4pm fix is based on actual trading using data over a one minute window. Traders had orders to buy and sell at the fix, creating a net exposure in one direction. Moving the rate increased profits (and cost clients). Traders used chatrooms to communicate with traders at other banks. They would do so to learn about orders tied to the fix from other banks, agree on the direction they wanted to move the rate, and discuss how they would move the rate.

4.2. *Analysis*

The first question we address is what was the economic problem that the cultures surrounding the LIBOR and Forex rate setting arose to

[2] "Foreign Exchange: Fix scandal might herald the end of voice broking," *Euromoney*, November 8, 2013. Available at: http://www.euromoney.com/Article/3276783/Foreign-exchange-Fix-scandal-might-herald-the-end-of-voice.html

solve? LIBOR became problematic because of the easy communication between derivatives traders and the LIBOR submitters on the money market desk. However, the co-location of the derivatives desk and the money market desk made economic sense; derivatives traders needed continual updates about interest rates in order to trade effectively and the money market desk could provide this information flow. In addition, many derivatives traders had their instruments linked to LIBOR, so an understanding of how LIBOR would be set each day was useful. This illustrates that the network that formed between the derivatives trading desk and the money market desk was based both on economic motives and locational ones. The LIBOR scandal also involved many instances of collusion; i.e., contact between banks to manipulate the rate. This appears to be a result of labor market mobility — traders contacting former colleagues who moved to other banks.

Foreign exchange traders received orders during the day to trade at the 4pm fix. As they guaranteed a trade for their clients at the fix, which was unknown at that point, the traders has substantial risk exposure to the fix. In order to mitigate that exposure, traders communicated with traders in other banks to learn about order flows. Therefore networks formed between banks based on a common goal. This, of course, subsequently facilitated collusion to manipulate the fix.

The second question we address is whether these cultures were easy for outsiders to observe. The *Financial Times* reported that[3] "Investigators are also being hampered by limited understanding of what one lawyer called the unusual 'dialect' used by forex traders. 'Most of these messages are crushingly boring and pure garbage. [But] they are difficult to decipher,' a senior banker involved in an investigation says." Forex traders used terms like "loading the ammo" and "clearing the decks". This made it difficult for regulators and management to understand what they were actually doing, both above board and below. Sir Philip Hampton, Chairman of RBS, stated that[4] "We had no controls,

[3] "Forex in the spotlight," *Financial Times*, February 16, 2014. Available at: http://www.ft.com/cms/s/0/a296da48-9579-11e3-8371-00144feab7de.html\#axzz2tfdClcDV

[4] "RBS Libor-rigging scandal: in quotes," *The Guardian*, February 6, 2013. Available at: http://www.theguardian.com/business/2013/feb/06/rbs-libor-rigging-in-quotes

absolutely. LIBOR has been going since the mid-1980s, and we had no controls in place." Therefore, whether senior management could observe the cultures or not, there was no mechanism in place to deal with them. As we pointed out above, senior management may not have had incentives to deal with manipulation as (i) it was profitable and (ii) there may have been a perceived minimal reputational damage to the firm from its discovery.

The third question we address is how these cultures became dysfunctional. As we have seen, the networks needed to manipulate were already established to solve the economic problem. Chatrooms and co-location facilitated communication. The potential for rigging was obvious. The major cost was actually detection. However, several factors decreased the likelihood of detection. First, bank holding companies have become increasingly complex in recent years (Avraham, Selvaggi, & Vickery, 2012). Second, we have already pointed out that senior managers and directors may not have understood or observed the manipulation. Even if they did, they did not have strong incentives to look into it. Third, regulators also seem to have turned a blind eye to manipulation — some regulators were informed of LIBOR manipulation[5] in 2008 and of Forex manipulation[6] in 2006.

5. Possible Solutions

In this section, we discuss ways to prevent cultures from becoming dysfunctional and what should be done if they do become dysfunctional.

Policy discussions have operated around the presumption that banks have one culture. However, we have demonstrated that there are multiple cultures at work within a given bank, and that those cultures may span banks. The most basic suggestion is to map the cultural

[5] "Barclays admitted false Libor reports to fed in '08", *CNN Money*, July 13, 2012. http://money.cnn.com/2012/07/13/investing/geithner-libor-barclays/index.htm

[6] "The lunch enquiry meetings at the heart of the Bank of England forex inquiry," *The Telegraph*, November 12, 2014. http://www.telegraph.co.uk/finance/bank-of-england/10685543/The-lunch-meetings-at-the-heart-of-the-Bank-of-England-forex-inquiry.html

networks that exist within banks, potentially with the aid of a sociologist or anthropologist, so as to be able to direct policies effectively.

One example of this is setting an appropriate "tone from the top". If such a tone was directed at the whole firm, it would have a weak effect. Tailoring it to specific networks within the firm would resonate, as it would adopt the culture and cultural understandings of the particular network. To effectively accomplish such targeting, senior management should be embedded in these networks; to listen, learn, and communicate back to the network appropriate behavior.

The president of the Federal Reserve Bank of New York, William Dudley, in 2014 suggested the use of performance bonds to correct cultural problems. Performance bonds deduct fines on the bank from the bank's deferred compensation pool. This has the effect of punishing bad behavior (rather than shareholders) and incentivizing monitoring in the firm.[7] Once again, this proposal, while very well designed, would be more effective if targeted toward networks at fault.

Just as firms use underperformance as a motivation to review employees and perhaps replace them, we suggest that outperformance should trigger formal reviews. Outperformance should be explainable, and not be a result of malfeasance. Repeated outperformance should draw management's and regulators' attention. Notice that it should not be sufficient to state that workers engaged in similar work in different firms also outperformed as a justification; collusion across banks also implies that this would be true.

Lastly, forming a professional licensing body for bankers can help in many dimensions. It can formulate and promote codes of conduct throughout the industry. It could act as a central clearinghouse for information on individual conduct. Therefore direct evidence of malfeasance could leave permanent marks. If possible, the body should be able to exclude people from the industry for misconduct. Moreover, the body might also update the records of participants (even if not directly identified in wrongdoing) in an identified cultural failure (even if not directly identified in wrongdoing). Therefore the ability to hide one's record and escape wrongdoing that may be fostered by the fluid

[7] Facilitating whistleblowing also improves monitoring at the firm.

labor market mobility of the banking sector (see a discussion in Acharya, Pagano, & Volpin, 2013) could be reduced with the presence of such a body.

6. Conclusions

The explosion of banking scandals following the financial crisis has impacted the regulatory agenda. Yet many discussions about the dysfunctional cultures that underlie these scandals do not address the fundamentals of how cultures arise and how they work. In this chapter we build on the economics, sociology, law, and management literatures to further understand culture and provide potential solutions. We note that banks have multiple cultures and cultures may span between banks. Cultures have their own languages and knowledge, and are thus difficult for outsiders to understand. Embedding management into cultural networks, increasing monitoring incentives, and promoting licensing bodies can all reduce the likelihood of cultural dysfunction.

References

Acharya, V. V., Pagano, M., & Volpin, P. (2013). Seeking alpha: Excess risk taking and competition for managerial talent. *NBER Working Paper* No. 18891, March, Cambridge, MA.

Avraham, D., Selvaggi, P., & Vickery, J. (2012). A structural view of U.S. bank holding companies. *FRBNY Economic Policy Review*, 65–81. Available at: https://www.newyorkfed.org/medialibrary/media/research/epr/12v18n2/1207avra.pdf.

Bower, M. (1966). *The will to manage*. New York: McGraw-Hill.

Cremer, J. (1993). Corporate culture and shared knowledge. *Industrial and Corporate Change*, *3*, 351–386.

Dudley, W. C. (2014). Enhancing financial stability by improving culture in the financial services industry. Speech at the workshop on "Reforming culture and behavior in the financial services industry", October 20, Federal Reserve Bank of New York, New York City.

Kreps, D. M. (1990). Corporate culture and economic theory. In James E. Alt, and Kenneth A. Shepsle (Ed.), *Perspectives on positive political economy* (pp. 90–143). Cambridge, MA: Cambridge University Press.

Lazear, E. P. (1999). Culture and language. *Journal of Political Economy*, *107*, S95–S126.

Morrison, A. D. & Wilhelm Jr., W. J. (2007). *Investment Banking: Institutions, Politics and Law*. Oxford, UK: Oxford University Press.

Morrison, A. D. & Wilhelm Jr., W. J. (2008). The demise of investment banking partnerships: Theory and evidence. *Journal of Finance*, *63*, 311–350.

Morrison, A. D. & Wilhelm Jr., W. J. (2015). Trust, reputation and law: The evolution of commitment in investment banking, *Journal of Legal Analysis*, 7(2): 363–420.

Schein, E. H. (2004). *Organizational culture and leadership*. San Francisco, CA: Jossey-Bass.

Thakor, A. V. (2015). *Corporate culture in banking, Mimeo, July*. St. Louis, MO: Washington University.

Wheatley, M. (2012). The Wheatley Review of LIBOR. Available at: https://www.gov.uk/government/publications/the-wheatley-review.

Part VIII
Policy Discussion: Where to from Here?

Understanding the Future of Banking Scale and Scope Economies, and Fintech

— CHAPTER 25

■ Arnoud W. A. Boot
University of Amsterdam and CEPR

1. Introduction

Structural changes are expected in the financial services industry. The recent focus on fintech — basically, new technology-oriented players entering the financial services industry — is one manifestation of the impact that information technology is expected to have on the industry.

This chapter will focus on the structure of the banking industry going forward. We will try to draw lessons from the (older) literature on scale and scope economies in banking, and relate these insights to the 'modern' world of information technology and fintech.

The impact of information technology on the industry is already going on for years. An important manifestation is the impact of the proliferation of information technology on financial markets. It has deepened financial markets and via changes in the business models of

Arnoud Boot is Professor of Corporate Finance and Financial Markets at the University of Amsterdam and co-director of the Amsterdam Center for Law & Economics (ACLE). He is also research fellow at the Centre of Economic Policy Research (CEPR) in London.

banks strengthened the link between markets and financial institutions. The latter runs for example via securitization and other forms of asset sales that remove assets from a bank's balance sheet allowing those assets to become tradeable. This could amplify the impact of financial market conditions on banks (Shin, 2009).

Apart from providing all kinds of benefits (e.g., diversification, liquidity), a more negative view is that the enhanced opportunities to trade assets invites 'excessive changeability' and possibly more opportunistic behavior in banks that could undermine their stability (Boot, 2014). The linkages to the financial market facilitate a proliferation of transaction-oriented banking (trading and financial market) activities possibly at the expense of more traditional relationship banking activities.

In this context also the ownership structure of banks is important. The traditional partnership model in investment banking may have contained opportunistic behavior in that partners had their personal wealth tied up in the business, and could not easily leave and liquefy their ownership claim. In a sense, the marketability of their own involvement (human capital) was severely constrained which may have countered the fluidity of banking activities itself. Also here information technology and the deepening of financial markets may have been instrumental in creating a more fluid ownership structure based on a stock market listing.

We will discuss these developments, and subsequently address — what *The Economist* has called — the fintech revolution.[1] Can we draw insights from the extensive literature on scale and scope economies in banking? We will argue that only limited insights are available. Most recent empirical work identifies some scale economies, yet faces bigger difficulties in identifying real scope advantages. And what is particularly missing in the literature, is the impact that information technology may have on the industry. 'Fintech considerations' have not been part of this literature.

The organization of the paper is as follows. In Section 2 we focus on the impact of information technology and the deepening of financial markets on the transaction- versus relationship-orientation of banks. Section 3 discusses ownership structure issues. Scale and scope

[1] 'The Fintech Revolution', *The Economist*, May 9, 2015.

economies are discussed in Section 4. Section 5 focusses on the impact of fintech on the banking industry. Concluding observations are made in Section 6.

2. Information Technology and Transaction Orientation[2]

An arguably not much contested observation is that banks have become more transaction oriented. As *The Economist* put it over 20 years ago in the context of the experience of securities firms:

"Perhaps the worst feature of the 1980s — which has subsequently returned to haunt the securities firms — was the abandonment by most of them of the old relationships with their customers. [...] "The aim was to do a deal, any deal", remembers one manager who prefers not to be named" (*The Economist*, April 15, 1995, 'Special section: A survey of Wall Street', p. 13).

While this quote was made over 20 years ago, it is interesting to note that when financial markets prosper they appear to push financial institutions away from their relationship banking franchise. As the consultancy BCG puts it (explaining the surge in transaction oriented activities in 2004–2007): "... Amid surging economies, low loan losses, and readily available cheap capital, it did not really matter whether a bank had top- or bottom-quartile capabilities [...]. All that mattered were workable sales processes" (BCG, 2010).

The modern world of information technology and deepening of financial markets has clearly induced banks to become more heavily exposed to the financial markets. Doing transactions has become easier, and hence market-linked activities like securitization and proprietary trading have become more prominent. At a more fundamental level, what this points at is the scalability of transaction-oriented activities (Boot & Ratnovski, 2016). Subject to available capital, banks can quickly increase their exposure to those activities. Relationship-based activities are more constrained as they depend on employing human

[2] This section follows in part Boot (2011) and Boot & Ratnovski (2016).

capital and engaging with potential clients. Thus transaction-oriented banking is not only more susceptible to a sudden spur in momentum, but also the feasibility of financial institutions to quickly mobilize resources and give in to such opportunities seems greater than for relationship banking activities.

The competitive dynamics plays an important role. When financial markets are exuberant, banks that abstain from, for example, trading activities — one of the financial market activities that can be expanded quickly — may look less profitable and might feel 'left behind' in the earnings game vis-à-vis other banks. This is precisely what happened with UBS, one of the bigger victims in the 2007–2009 crisis. An internal investigation in 2008 — following massive losses on subprime investments — discovered that its troublesome subprime investments were undertaken following pressure from external consultants that pointed at its fixed income activities that were lagging those of competitors. To fill this gap UBS was advised "to close key product gaps" which explicitly referred to subprime investment vehicles (UBS, 2008, p. 11).

A more subtle concern is that opportunistic trading may undermine relationship banking. Boot and Ratnovski (2016) show that banks may allocate too much capital to transaction-oriented activities and in doing so have insufficient risk-bearing capacity for relationship banking. Banks may also underestimate the risks involved, and implicitly subsidize the transaction-oriented activities at the expense of relationship-oriented activities. More specifically, proprietary trading might be granted an artificially low cost of capital. Other — mainly relationship-oriented activities — are then implicitly taxed and appear less profitable than they really are. Thus, proprietary trading could undermine a bank's competitive edge in its relationship banking business.

A related mechanism is that such transaction-oriented activities initially appear very profitable (as long as the boom lasts), and that during that time those departments — and the individuals involved in them — will gain power. What this might do is that power shifts from people engaged in more prudent relationship banking activities to those engaged in transaction activities. This may affect the overall balance of power in an institution via promotions in the corporate hierarchy, and may tilt power away from its relationship banking franchise. As a consequence relationship banking may suffer.[3]

The extensive work in the field of financial intermediation points at the distinct value of relationship banking. While we continue to believe in the importance of relationship banking, information technology, the way information can be obtained from data analysis (Big Data), and, for example, the proliferation of social media will have an impact on how relationship banking can add value. In particular, payment systems and distribution channels are changing rapidly, and this will affect the business of banking and the competitive positioning of banks as distinct financial institutions. We will come back to this when we discuss fintech, and particularly the disaggregation of the value chain that it may entail.

3. Ownership Structure: Partnerships, Stability and Institutional Franchise Value

As stated, the deepening of financial markets and information technology in general may have caused excessive 'changeability' and tradeability in the industry. We pointed at the opportunistic behavior that this may cause. An important link can be made to the ownership structure and stability of investment banks versus commercial (relationship oriented) banks.

Traditional relationship-oriented banks seem incentivized to build up *institutional* franchise value. Individuals are part of the organization as an entity, and the continuity of the organization and lasting relationships with its clientele defines its value. The value cannot be transferred and cannot readily be assigned to individual stars. In other words, the value created is an integral part of the organizational entity and not portable as part of individuals.

[3] These 'power' considerations deserve more attention in research. Much of the focus has been on remuneration contracts, while incentives running via promotion opportunities and power might arguably be as important or even more important.

Investment banks on the other hand, particularly their trading and transaction activities,[4] seem more based on the individual star concept with high marketability of individuals. As a consequence, less institutional franchise value is built up; individual franchise values dominate. If this is the only difference, then a relationship banking institution has substantial implied franchise value, while the investment bank has little implied value, and hence Keeley's (1990) analysis would suggest that an investment bank would take lots of risk, while the franchise value of a commercial bank would help curtail its risk taking.

Historically investment banks have solved the marketability problem — and the potential lack of institutional franchise value — by having partnerships. The partnership structure has two dimensions that could help jointly resolve the marketability problem, and related opportunistic, risky behavior (and star phenomenon):

- a partnership means that bankers have their personal wealth tied up in the business –they own the equity claim of the business;
- the partnership structure is such that the equity is not (optimally) marketable.

The latter implies that stars cannot take their money out, or only at a reduced value. Implicitly, this means that non-portable franchise value is created, and this value is transferred over time to future partners. Interesting examples exist where institutions have made changes that have destroyed this structure. For example, with a go-public transformation (converting a partnership in a listed shareholder owned company) the current partners effectively expropriate all franchise value that has been built up over time.[5] Even worse, once the partnership is gone,

---

[4] Activities of investment banks often are (were) relationship based, more recently trading dominates, which is not. In recent times, traders appear to have gained power within investment banks, e.g., more recent leaders of Goldman Sachs came from the trading side. In any case, we do not see the distinction between commercial banking and investment banking as an absolute dichotomy.

[5] Morrison & Wilhelm (2007, 2008) analyze the decision of major U.S. investment banks to go public. Investment banks were initially organized as partnerships. The opacity of partnerships and illiquidity of their shares allowed for successful mentoring and training in tacit non-contractible human skills, such as building

stars may no longer be 'under control.' Their financial interest is no longer tied to the firm. This may elevate risk and reduce stability.[6]

In commercial banking the enhanced marketability — and with it, transaction focus — may have opened the door for some type of star phenomenon as well. In a sense, it may have brought commercial banking closer to investment banking, and similar issues might be at play. This may have induced opportunistic behavior particularly because partnership structures in commercial banking never have been very common.

In any case, partnerships among major financial institutions are rare. The important point however is that via enhancing marketability the demise of partnerships could have undermined stability. As a caveat, all this does not mean that there might not be distinct benefits associated with these developments as well. What we have stressed is the potential downside. We are however prepared to conclude that the financial crisis has made us look more favorably at alternative ownership structures like mutuals and cooperative banks (e.g., Credit Agricole in France). It may well be that also with our thoughts about the type of ownership structure we should be more open to diversity. After all, one of the problems of the increasing intertwined nature of banks and markets is that it might make banks look more alike, and that could induce systemic risk. Diversity in ownership structures might help counter this.[7]

4. Scale and Scope Economies in Banking

What drives financial players in choosing their scale and scope of operations? This question is important because the size and particularly the complexity of financial institutions is a concern to regulators and

---

relationships, negotiating M&A deals and advising clients. They have argued that IT technology necessitated heavy investments and that that necessitated investment banks to go public. Potentially confirming this is that wholesale-oriented investment banks such as Morgan Stanley for which tacit human capital was more important than IT technology went public later than retail oriented investment banks such as Merrill Lynch.

[6] Publicly listed firms sometimes use restricted stock to create some fixity in the ownership structure, and continued loyalty of key personnel.

[7] See Berger Klapper, Martinez Peria, & Zaidi (2008).

supervisors. More recently, the question is what impact fintech and information technology will have on bank business models, and the scale and scope of banks. Research on this remains rather inconclusive, in the words of Richardson, Smith, & Walter (2010): "Indeed, the recent studies mirror the findings [...] some 15 years earlier [...] there was no predominance of evidence either for or against economies of scale in the financial sector." This precedes the fintech revolution, so it is not clear whether this remains true.

4.1. *Observations on Scale and Scope*

A first observation is that banks like to *combine* many different activities. This distinguishes banks from many of their competitors, e.g., non-banking financial institutions like mutual funds and finance companies. The latter often choose to specialize and therefore are much more transparent. Banks generally choose to diversify their activities. Although few would readily deny that some degree of diversification is necessary, banks seem to engage in a very broad variety of activities.

Particularly in Continental Europe, the size (and scope) of banks is enormous. One explanation could be that implicit or explicit government guarantees and too-big-to-fail (TBTF) concerns give artificial competitive advantages to size (Feldman, 2010). Universal banks, while not particularly efficient, might have sufficient 'protected' revenues to compete with more focused players.[8]

[8] Indeed, this is one of the complaints of more focused investment banking institutions. Universal banks can leverage their balance sheet (read: cross subsidize) to secure investment banking business (e.g., *Financial Times*, March 21, 2011, page 17: 'U.S. Banks Face Fresh Scrutiny on Lending'). Some evidence exist on TBTF benefits. Jagtiani & Brewer (2013) find that investors are willing to pay a premium when an acquisition would create a bank with assets over $100 billion. Rime (2005) finds that banks above some threshold tend to have higher credit ratings and Baker & McArthur (2009) show that banks that have more than $100 billion in assets have lower costs of capital. Beccalli, Anolli, & Borello (2015) show that scale economies are larger for banks that are designated as systemically relevant by the European Commission.

Scale and scope economies are often cited as rationale for why financial institutions tend to growth in size and complexity (scope) over time. But are scale and scope economies truly present? Sources of scale and scope economies include (see Boot, 2003; Walter, 2003): (i) information-technology related economies; (ii) reputation and marketing/brand name related benefits; (iii) (financial) innovation related economies; and (iv) diversification benefits. Information technology related economies particularly refer to back office efficiencies and distribution-network related benefits. Transaction processing offers distinct scale economies. And information technology developments facilitate an increasing array of financial products and services to be offered through the same distribution network, and thus allow for cross selling. Reputation and brand name/marketing related economies may be present in the joint marketing of products to customers. Brand image is partially marketing related, but is also related to the notions of 'trust' and 'reputation'. (Financial) innovation related economies particularly refer to large(r) institutions that might be in a better position to recoup the fixed costs of those innovations.

Diversification benefits are (at first sight) more controversial. In many cases, conglomeration may lead to a valuation discount which could point at (anticipated) inefficiencies. This is in line with corporate finance theory that tells us that investors can choose to diversify and that this does not need to be done at the firm level. However, key to the business of banking is risk processing and absorption. And confidence in a bank requires it to be safe. Diversification is then needed to be able to absorb risks and be safe. Observe also that several bank activities benefit from a better credit rating, which suggests that diversification at the level of the bank has value.[9]

---

[9] For many guarantees or contracts and activities that involve recourse, the credit standing of the guarantor is crucial for the credibility of the contract. Mester (2008) emphasizes that bank production decisions affect bank risk. Scale and scope related decisions have via diversification an effect on risk, and that in turn may affect choices about risk exposure.

4.2. Are Scale and Scope Benefits Real?

Scale and scope economies in banking have been studied extensively. In an over 15 year old survey paper Berger, Demsetz, and Strahan (1999) conclude that, in general, the empirical evidence cannot readily identify substantial economies of scale or scope. Illustrative is also Saunders (2000). He cites 27 studies, 13 of which found diseconomies of scope, 6 found economies of scope, and 8 were neutral.

An important caveat is that this research mainly involves U.S. studies using data from the 70s and 80s. Apart from potential methodological shortcomings, the results therefore do not capture the dramatic structural and technological changes in banking that have taken place since then. Furthermore, they reflect the historic fragmentation of the U.S. banking industry due to severe regulatory constraints on the type of banking (banks could engage in commercial banking or investment banking, but not both) and the geographic reach of activities (limits on interstate banking) that were present till the deregulation in the 90s (see Calomiris & Karceski, 1998).

Some more recent studies examine the existence of a diversification discount for financial institutions. Laeven & Levine (2007) confirm the existence of a diversification discount in banks that combine lending and non-lending financial services, and suggest that the potential economies of scope in financial conglomerates are not large enough to compensate for potential agency problems and inefficiencies associated with cross-subsidies.[10] Rajan, Servaes, & Zingales (2000) emphasize that, even though conglomerates trade at a discount on average, 39.3% of the conglomerates trade at a premium. They show that the interrelation between activities within the conglomerate is of crucial importance. Diversified firms can trade at a premium if the dispersion between activities low. High dispersion induces inefficiencies which point at the importance of focus within the conglomerate. In particular, one should

---

[10] Schmid & Walter (2009) confirm the Laeven & Levine (2007) results, and verify that this discount is indeed caused by diversification, and not by inefficiencies that already existed before the diversification. Chevalier (2004) shows that controlling for the pre-conglomeration performance of businesses is important: inefficiencies measured after a merger often already existed prior to the merger.

look at what type of mergers and acquisitions involve scale and scope benefits. Recent research suggests that mergers with both a geographic and activity focus are most value enhancing. Similarly, in analyzing scope and scale issues, one should focus on the type of activities. What are the scale economies in each activity? And what product-mix offers true scope economies?

DeLong (2001) looked at the shareholder gains — more specifically, the immediate announcement effect on share prices — from focused versus diversifying bank mergers in the U.S. between 1988 and 1995. She found that focused mergers, both on the level of activity and geography, have positive announcement effects. Moreover, focus in activities was shown to be more important than geographical focus, albeit the latter was important as well. Activity-diversifying mergers had no positive announcement effects. These results point at the presence of scale rather than scope economies.

The typical result in these earlier studies was, however, that even scale economies were exhausted at relatively small bank sizes. Later evidence points at more persistent scale economies. Wheelock & Wilson (2009) and Feng & Serletis (2010) find increasing returns to scale and Elsas, Hackethal, & Holzhäuser (2010) find increasing returns to scope also for larger financial institutions. Substantial scale economies are found when it comes to back-office activities and payments.[11] Apart from methodological issues (see Mester, 2010), this might be driven by information technology developments that might only have showed up in more recent data.

In this spirit, researchers have looked at whether there are scale economies in investments in IT as suggested by Boot (2003) and Walter (2003). The evidence is somewhat mixed. Erber & Madlener (2009) find no significant relationship between IT capital investments and bank productivity at the country level. Beccalli (2007) even finds a negative relationship between bank efficiency and investment in hardware and software, but a positive relationship between bank efficiency and country-level bank spending on IT consulting services. Koetter & Noth

[11] See Hughes & Mester (2015), Davies & Tracey (2012), and DeYoung (2010).

(2013) find that merely increasing IT investment does not lead to higher profitability, but that the efficiency in employing IT matters.

The impact on IT on bank business models has so far not really been empirically investigated. One could envision that on the demand side, the proliferation of savings products and their link to pensions, mutual funds and life insurance clearly pushes for joint distribution, and suggests economies of scope. IT developments might have made it possible to better exploit potential scope economies with multiple product offerings to a particular customer group, using new direct distribution channels with relatively easy access to (formerly) distant customers. But the value chain might be broken up. A question is who will have the customer interface.

5. The Impact of Fintech on the Banking Industry

A key manifestation is that fintech may lead to the disaggregation of the value chain. Interfaces (may) come about that help bundle the product offerings of specialized providers, thereby becoming a substitute for an integrated provider. The distribution related economies that we eluded to may actually lead to such disaggregation of the value chain.

5.1. *Online Platforms and Disaggregation*[12]

Online platforms will be developed that could disrupt existing financial institutions. Disaggregation of the value chain could follow from online platforms becoming the preferred customer interface. Online platforms could offer a supermarket type model facilitating access to various products and services of disparate providers along with record keeping. Technology firms such as Google, Facebook, Amazon or Apple may use a payments solution such as Apple Pay as a platform and gain direct customer interface for related products and services. Legacy financial institutions then might be relegated to serving as the back office to the platform.

The disruptive forces affecting banking — information technology and fintech in particular — may also offer new opportunities for other

[12] Our observations follow in part Greenbaum, Thakor, & Boot (2015).

businesses that have tried to enter banking. For example, Tesco, a large UK supermarket chain provides banking services to its customers under its own brand. There is also no reason why a platform should be limited to offering only financial services. A life-style oriented focus could integrate financial and non-financial offerings. The financial services platform might act as a market place where people interact directly and financial institutions serve the limited role of an advisor or broker. P2P lending has parties transacting directly without the benefit of a financial intermediary (except possibly for back office services).

New specialized lenders have arisen that seek to replace relationship lenders and traditional credit scoring with sophisticated algorithms based on Big Data mining. While still in its infancy, such analysis predicts creditworthiness by analyzing buying habits, memberships, reading proclivities, lifestyle choices and all manner of opportunistic demographic correlates. Similarly, the growing availability of inexpensive information allows for public certification of creditworthiness similar to the trustworthiness scores on eBay, or the client satisfaction scores on TripAdvisor. One could envision similar developments enabling P2P lending as well. Whether society will accept the widespread use of these data is a different matter. In any event, more and more potentially sensitive personal information can already be obtained with a few mouse clicks. Big Data may also facilitate crowdfunding, another form of direct lending involving multiple lenders and a singular borrower.

At the consumer level, we may see a (re)emergence of more community oriented arrangements. As P2P lending and crowdfunding suggest, customers may take matters in their own hands; empowerment thus. Local arrangements may emerge where communities organize their financial affairs directly.

5.2. *Payments*

An area with substantial developments is payments. This core area of banking is being coveted by technology firms and payment specialists like Google, Apple, and PayPal. Thus far, banks have maintained their central role in payments. Also, the payments innovators are not typically independent of banks, but have developed in joint ventures or other types of alliances with traditional banks. In some countries, banks themselves have managed to offer the leading online payments solution.[13]

5.3. *And Banks?*

What role will banks play in these developments? They may face challenges. As a recent report by McKinsey & Co, a consultancy, puts it: "Digitization often lowers entry barriers, causing long-established boundaries between sectors to tumble. At the same time, the "plug and play" nature of digital assets causes value chains to disaggregate, creating openings for focused, fast-moving competitors. New market entrants often scale up rapidly at lower cost than legacy players can, and returns may grow rapidly as more customers join the network" (Hirt & Millmott, 2014).

This does not mean that banks are doomed. In the past, banking institutions have shown remarkable resilience, despite questions about their viability. As far back as 1994, economists John Boyd and Mark Gertler commented on the predicted demise of banks in a well-known study titled, "Are Banks Dead? Or Are The Reports Greatly Exaggerated?"[14] At that point, the discussion was about the banks' role in lending. In particular, the question was whether securitization would undermine the banks' lending franchise. They concluded that while securitization made banks less important for the actual funding of loans, the core functions of banks in the lending process — origination (including screening), servicing and monitoring — would be preserved, as would the centrality of banks. Also, banks would typically play a role in the securitization vehicles by providing back-up lines of credit and guarantees of the commercial paper that funds many of the vehicles.

The message of that article might still have some relevance today. Banks will respond and try to be players in the fintech world. And they may have some competitive advantages.[15] Banks benefit from the anxiety of people about the safety of their liquid wealth. The financial crisis

---

[13] See Oliver Wyman (2014) and BIS (2014).

[14] Boyd & Gertler (1994) and Samolyk (2004).

[15] See also McKinsey (2010).

of 2007–2009 may have created anxiety about the stability of banks, but banks are still seen as the place where money is safe.[16] Whatever the popularity of Apple, will people trust technology companies in safeguarding their money? Being a bank with a license and an implicit guarantee from the government has value. Nevertheless, there are reasons to envision a potential decline. New competitors and the disaggregation of the value chain will put pressure on existing players.[17]

6. Conclusions

Information technology plays a leading role in the transformation of banking. Developments in information technology and the related deepening of financial markets have pushed banks to more transaction-oriented activities, including trading, at the expense of relationship banking. Banking has become more fluid, and possibly opportunistic as a result. Financial markets also facilitated investment banks in moving away from the more stable partnership model to a more fluid shareholder owned public listing.

The latest incarnation of information technology has led to a 'fintech revolution' where banks face new competitors with different — more specialized — business models forcing a disaggregation of the value chain. With technology-driven solutions they offer alternatives to key banking services including payments and lending. An important question is to what extent existing financial institutions can be leading. Can they be at the forefront of new developments? For example, by absorbing fintech players and their innovations? Or will they fade away, with new technology-linked players assuming prominence in the financial sector? Many questions, few answers.

---

[16] Vatanasombut, Igbaria, Stylianou, & Rodgers (2008) highlight that trust plays a key role in the retention of customers with online banking. They also find that perceived security reinforces trust.

[17] Much attention is devoted to the so called blockchain technology that potentially allows for a decentralized system of record keeping and transactions. A payment system based on crypto currencies (e.g., bitcoin) is the most well known application (Nakamoto, 2008; Bank of England, 2014).

Also from a financial stability point of view, the fintech revolution is challenging. We just do not know what the future structure of the industry will look like.[18] The extensive literature on scale and scope economies in banking offers little guidance on what to expect in this 'new' world.

References

Baker, D. & McArthur T. (2009). The value of the "too big to fail" big bank subsidy. *CEPR Issue Brief*, September. Available at: http://cepr.net/publications/reports/too-big-to-fail-subsidy.

Bank of England (2014). Innovations in payment technologies and the emergence of digital currencies. *Bank of England Quarterly Bulletin*, *Q3*, 1–14.

Bank of England (2015). *One Bank Research Agenda*. Discussion paper, February. Available at: http://www.bankofengland.co.uk/research/documents/onebank/discussion.pdf.

BCG (2010). *Global Corporate Banking 2010: Crisis as Opportunity*. The Boston Consulting Group. Available at: https://www.bcg.com/documents/file50789.pdf.

Beccalli, E. (2007). Does IT investment improve bank performance? Evidence from Europe. *Journal of Banking & Finance*, 31(7), 2205–2230.

Beccalli, E., Anolli, M., & Borello, G. (2015). Are European banks too big? Evidence on economies of scale. *Journal of Banking & Finance*, *58*, 232–246.

Berger, A. N., Demsetz, R. S., & Strahan, P. E. (1999). The consolidation of the financial services industry: Causes, consequences and implications for the future. *Journal of Banking and Finance*, 23(2–4), 135–194.

Berger, A. N., Klapper, L. F., Martinez Peria, M. S., & Zaidi, R. (2008). Bank ownership type and banking relationships. *Journal of Financial Intermediation*, 17(1), 37–62.

BIS (2014). Payment, settlement and clearing in various countries. Retrived from www.bis.org/cpmi/paysysinfo.htm.

[18] The Bank of England has formulated the question whether "...the distress of failure of a technology-enabled alternative finance provider have implications for financial stability" (Bank of England, 2015). The Dutch central bank has identified not just risks in the (new) fintech type operations and players, but also stability risks coming from existing institutions that could lose out in the technology race (DNB, 2016).

Boot, A. W. A. (2003). Consolidation and strategic positioning in banking with implications for Europe. *Brookings-Wharton, Papers on Financial Services*, 2003(1):37–83.

Boot, A. W. A. (2011). Banking at the crossroads. *Review of Development Finance*, 1, 167–183.

Boot, A. W. A. (2014). Financial sector in flux. *Journal of Money, Credit and Banking*, 46(1), 129–135.

Boot, A. W. A. & Ratnovski, L. (2016). Banking and trading. *Review of Finance*, 2016, 1–28.

Boyd, J. H. & Gertler, M. (1994). Are banks dead? Or are the reports greatly exaggerated? *Federal Reserve Bank of Minneapolis Quarterly Review*, 18(3), 2–23.

Calomiris, C. W. & Karceski, J. (1998). *Is the bank merger wave of the 1990's efficient?* Washington, D.C.: The AEI Press.

Chevalier, J. (2004). What do we know about cross-subsidization? Evidence from merging firms. *Advances in Economic Analysis and Policy*, 4(1), — 1218. DOI: 10.2202/1538-0637.1218.

Davies, R. & Tracey B. (2012). Too big to be efficient? The impact of implicit funding subsidies on scale economies in banking. *Journal of Money, Credit and Banking*, 46(S1), 219–253.

DeLong, G. (2001). Stockholder gains from focusing versus diversifying bank mergers. *Journal of Financial Economics*, 59(2), 221–242.

DeYoung, R. (2010), Scale economies are a distraction. *The Region*, FED Minneapolis. Available at: https://www.minneapolisfed.org/publications/the-region/scale-economies-are-a-distraction.

DNB (2016). Technological innovation and the Dutch financial sector (in Dutch). *Working Paper*, De Nederlandsche Bank (Dutch Central Bank), January.

Elsas, R., Hackethal, A., & Holzhäuser, M. (2010). The anatomy of bank diversification. *Journal of Banking & Finance*, 34(6), 1274–1287.

Erber, G. & Madlener, R. (2009). Impact of ICT and human skills on the european financial intermediation sector. In M. Balling, E. Gnan, F. Lierman, & J.-P. Schoder (Eds), *Productivity in the Financial Services Sector*, Vienna, Austria: SUERF — The European Money and Finance Forum, pp. 183–200).

Feldman, R. J. (2010). Size and regulatory reform in finance: Important but difficult questions. In *The Region*, FED Minneapolis. Available at: https://www.minneapolisfed.org/publications/the-region/size-and-regulatory-reform-in-finance-important-but-difficult-questions.

Feng, G. & Serletis, A. (2010). Efficiency, technical change, and returns to scale in large US Banks: Panel data evidence from an output distance function satisfying theoretical regularity. *Journal of Banking & Finance*, 34(1), 127–138.

Greenbaum, S. I., Thakor, A. V., & Boot, A. W. A. (2015). *Contemporary financial intermediation* (3rd ed). Cambridge, Massachusetts: Elsevier/Academic Press.

Hirt, M. & Millmott P. (2014). Strategic principles for competing in the digital age. *McKinsey Quarterly*, May 2014, 1–14. Available at: http://www.mckinsey.com/business-functions/strategy-and-corporate-finance/our-insights/strategic-principles-for-competing-in-the-digital-age.

Hughes, J. .P. & Mester, L. J. (2015). Measuring the performance of banks: Theory, practice, evidence, and some policy implications. In A. N. Berger, P. Molyneux., & J. Wilson (Eds), *The Oxford Handbook on Banking* (2nd edition), Oxford: Oxford University Press, pp. 247–281.

Jagtiani, J. & Brewer, E. (2013). How much did banks pay to become too-big-to-fail and to become systemically important? *Journal of Financial Services Research*, 43(1), 1–35.

Keeley, M. (1990). Deposit insurance, risk, and market power in banking. *American Economic Review*, 80(5), 1183–1200.

Koetter, M. & Noth, F. (2013). IT use, productivity, and market power in banking. *Journal of Financial Stability*, 9(4), 695–704.

Laeven, L. & Levine, R. (2007). Is there a diversification discount in financial conglomerates? *Journal of Financial Economics*, 85(2), 331–367.

McKinsey (2010). New but not yet Normal: Corporate and investment banking in transition. McKinsey & Company.

Mester, L. J. (2008). Optimal industrial structure in banking. In Boot, A. W. A. & Thakor, A. V. (Eds.), *Handbook of financial intermediation and banking*. Amsterdam: North Holland, pp. 133–162.

Mester, L. J. (2010). Comment on scale economies. *The Region*. FED Minneapolis.

Morrison, A. D. & Wilhelm, W. J. (2007), Investment Banking: Past, Present, and Future, *Journal of Applied Corporate Finance*, 19(1), 42–54.

Morrison, A. D. & Wilhelm, W. J. (2008). The demise of investment banking partnerships: Theory and evidence. *Journal of Finance*, 63(1), 311–350.

Nakamoto, S. (2008). Bitcoin: A peer-to-peer electronic cash system. *Working Paper*. Retrived from https://bitcoin.org/bitcoin.pdf.

Oliver Wyman (2014), Payments are Changing but how Prepared are Retail Banks?, Oliver Wyman Financial Services Point of View, 2014.

Rajan, R., Servaes, H., & Zingales, L. (2000). The cost of diversity: The diversification discount and inefficient investment. *Journal of Finance*, 55(1), 35–80.

Richardson, M., Smith, R. C., & Walter, I. (2010). Large banks and the Volcker rule, In V. V. Acharya, T. F. Cooley, M. P. Richardson, & I. Walter (Eds.), *Regulating wall street: The Dodd–Frank Act and the new architecture of global finance*. New Jersey: Wiley, pp. 181–212.

Rime, B. (2005). Do "too big to fail" expectations boost large bank issuer ratings? *Swiss National Banks, Systemic Stability Section: Working Paper*. Available at: http://www.bis.org/bcbs/events/rtf05Rime.pdf.

Samolyk, K. (2004). The future of banking in America: The evolving role of commercial banks in U.S. credit markets. *FDIC Banking Review*, 16(2), 29–65.

Saunders, A. (2000). *Financial institutions management* (3rd ed.). New York: McGraw-Hill.

Schmid, M. M. & Walter, I. (2009). Do financial conglomerates create or destroy economic value? *Journal of Financial Intermediation*, 18(2), 193–216.

Shin, H. S. (2009). Reflections on Northern Rock: The bank run that heralded the global financial crisis. *Journal of Economic Perspectives*, 23(1), 101–119.

UBS (2008), Shareholder report on UBS's write-downs, April 18 2008. Retrived from http://www.ubs.com/1/ShowMedia/investors/releases?contentId−140331&name=080418ShareholderReport.pdf.

Vatanasombut, B., Igbaria, M., Stylianou, A. C., & Rodgers, W. (2008). Information systems continuance intention of web-based applications customers: The case of online banking. *Information & Management*, 45(7), 419–428.

Walter, I. (2003). Strategies in financial services, the shareholders, and the system: Is bigger and broader better? *Brookings-Wharton, Papers on Financial Services*, 6, 1–36. Available at: http://ageconsearch.umn.edu/bitstream/26341/1/dp020205.pdf.

Four Key Factors Affecting the Future of Large, Internationally Active Banks

— CHAPTER 26

- John C. Dugan
  Covington & Burling LLP

1. Introduction

In keeping with the core theme of this conference, I will discuss four factors that I believe are critical to the future of large, internationally active banks. To do this, however, let me first set the stage with a brief discussion of the political climate affecting these firms, especially in the United States but elsewhere as well, because this climate could well have a material impact on each of these factors.

2. Political Climate

It has been eight years since the peak of the financial crisis, and during this period an enormous number of fundamental reforms have been adopted to address the problems at large internationally active banks that contributed to the crisis: Basel III capital and liquidity standards; the Dodd–Frank Act and its many implementing regulations; and

---

John C. Dugan, formerly Comptroller of the Currency from 2005–10, is a partner at Covington & Burling's Washington, DC office and chairs the firm's Financial Institutions Group.

structural reforms adopted in the U.K., Europe, and elsewhere. As a result of these reforms — along with time and changes demanded by the marketplace — large internationally active banks are by nearly any objective measure far safer than they were pre-crisis. They have much higher levels of capital and liquidity; are subject to much more intense supervision by regulators; have significantly reduced their levels of risk-taking; and, at least in the United States, have fully repaid all the government assistance they received during the crisis.

Yet despite this palpable improvement, the sharp political criticism of these banks sparked by their problems in the crisis has not seemed to decline at all; in fact, with the onset of the presidential election season in the U.S., you could make a good case that the criticism has gotten even worse. Elected officials and politicians running for political office on both the left and the right continue to call for additional sweeping changes to the structure, activities, regulation, and compensation regimes of large banks. It remains possible that, even though large banks have recently been subject to the most sweeping regulatory changes since the 1930s, the intensely populist political climate could result in even more changes in the coming years. These changes could be the result of new legislation, but they are more likely to occur, I believe, at least in the United States, through new or intensified regulatory action initiated by regulators — whether by existing regulators or new ones appointed by a newly elected Administration. While such material future changes are by no means a certainty, the potential impact of intense political criticism on regulation is real, and it certainly could shape the effect of each of the four factors that I will now discuss.

3. Proportionally Higher Capital and Liquidity Requirements

The first is the slew of requirements that require the largest banks to hold proportionally higher capital and liquidity than smaller banks. Without going into the details, the increases in the quality and quantity of capital required for these banks has been dramatic, effected through a combination of, among other requirements, the Basel III risk-based standards, the G-SIB surcharge, the Enhanced Supplemental Leverage

Ratio, and perhaps the most binding constraint of all, the requirement for higher capital to withstand stress tests established by the Federal Reserve's Comprehensive Capital Analysis and Review, or "CCAR". As a result, tangible equity capital for most large U.S. banks has at least doubled since the onset of the crisis.

A similar story applies to liquidity requirements for the largest banks. A combination of the new Liquidity Coverage Ratio, Net Stable Funding Ratio, Enhanced Prudential Standards, and intensified regulatory scrutiny has resulted in these banks also holding more than twice as much liquidity as they did pre-crisis, and in many cases significantly reducing their reliance on short-term wholesale funding.

Both types of regulatory actions have clearly made large internationally active banks safer — less likely to fail; more likely to be resolved in an orderly manner if they do fail; and less likely to cause contagious systemic damage as a result of significant financial stress.

But these enhanced requirements have also made these banks less profitable. Higher capital has translated into lower returns on equity, and higher liquidity has translated into fewer resources being "put to work" in loans and investments that produce higher returns than cash or short-term government debt. While some large banks have weathered these profitability challenges successfully, others have been struggling and have been trying to change their business models to adapt.

In this context, I think the important question affecting the future of large banks is this: will regulators keep ratcheting up capital and liquidity requirements in material ways? If they do, and if this causes a further material decline in the profitability of at least some large banks, it is obviously very likely to affect the future of their business models, creating incentives to retrench, shrink, take different risks, etc.

There are certainly levers under current consideration that regulators could pull to achieve this outcome. The Basel Committee is now discussing a whole suite of potential changes to the way that risks and exposures are calculated for purposes of risk-based capital requirements, including the measurement of trading risk, operational risk, advanced models-based credit risk, standardized credit risk, and interest rate risk; these changes — sometimes referred to by critics as "Basel IV" — could result in materially higher capital requirements. Likewise, the Basel

Committee is considering the recalibration of its leverage ratio, presumably to increase it, and the Federal Reserve is considering changes to CCAR that would have the effect of raising capital requirements for the very largest U.S. banks. In addition, the Federal Reserve has yet to propose the U.S. version of the Net Stable Funding Ratio, and when it does, this, too, could result in significantly more stringent liquidity requirements.

It is unclear whether regulators around the world want to use these tools to ratchet up requirements so significantly that they will in turn significantly affect large banks' profitability and core business models — whether as an intentional outcome or as a by-product of doing what they believe is necessary to make banks safe. Only time will tell, but this is clearly a factor that could directly affect the future of large international banks.

4. Increased Regulation of Large Bank Trading Activities

A second key factor is the intense new banking-style regulation of trading activities. This factor has not received nearly as much attention as other consequences of the financial crisis, but it is real and I believe quite important to the future business models of large international banks, especially in the United States.

There has been much discussion about the role played by "shadow banks" in causing or amplifying the financial crisis, with critics pointing to the problems of such firms as Lehman Brothers, Bear Stearns, AIG, and Merrill Lynch. All of these firms competed directly with more traditional commercial banking organizations regulated by the prudential banking regulators, but none was subject to close, prudential, bank-style regulation. At the same time, even within those organizations that operated both large traditional commercial banks and large non-bank trading operations, I believe it is fair to say that the commercial banking activities of these organizations were far more subject to extensive prudential regulation than their trading activities.

This differentiation has changed fundamentally in the wake of the financial crisis. Virtually all of the trading firms that were not subject to bank-style regulation before the crisis have either failed, been taken over by banking organizations, converted to banking organizations, or have been designated as systemically important financial institutions or "SIFIs" — and as a result, all the trading activities of the firms that have survived are now subject to bank-style regulation. In addition, the Federal Reserve has substantially increased the intensity of its bank-style regulation of the non-bank trading subsidiaries of those banking organizations that have been regulated bank holding companies since the days preceding the crisis. The net effect is that the trading activities of all large banking organizations operating in the U.S., including foreign banking organizations, are now subject to intensive bank-style regulation and supervision — and on a much more equivalent basis.

In general, I believe this significant change is a very positive development both for safety and soundness and for competitive equity purposes. Again, however, the lingering question is whether, in the current climate, this intensified regulation will be overdone and lead to further de-risking and retrenchment over time, reducing the international trading footprint of large international banks. In addition, how real is the prospect that these changes will cause existing bank trading business to move to non-banking trading firms that are not nearly as heavily regulated — which some would refer to as today's "shadow banks"? And how real is the prospect of a talent drain in the trading space from the regulated banking sector to the less regulated non-banking sector? I think these are real but perhaps less apparent challenges that large international banking organizations will face over time.

5. Resolution Planning

The third key factor is the resolution planning regime and the effect it will have on the business models of large international banks over time, especially firms that are subject to the Dodd–Frank regime in the United States. Here the single-point-of-entry concept has constituted a real conceptual breakthrough — when combined with the TLAC requirement, described below, it really is imaginable now to have a large international bank fail in a manner that causes neither seriously adverse systemic consequences nor the need for extraordinary government assistance.

Nevertheless, the resolution planning regime in the U.S. has been interpreted to require the Federal Reserve and the FDIC to jointly determine annually whether a covered firm's resolution plan is "credible". If it is not, the two agencies are empowered to jointly impose a series of escalating regulatory sanctions over time to make the plan credible, including at the end of the process by forcing divestitures and/or restructuring — or in other words, if certain conditions are satisfied, the regulators may jointly exercise an explicitly granted statutory power to "break up the bank". The first such "credibility" determinations were made in 2014, where the two agencies were generally unable to agree whether the plans were credible: the FDIC found that none of them were and sharply criticized the banks' submissions, while the Federal Reserve, after issuing some very sharp criticism as well, refused to find that the plans were "not credible" — and was sharply criticized by politicians for failing to do so. Without agency agreement, however no sanctions ensued. The process commenced all over again for the 2015 plans, with credibility determinations of 2016 released in April.

In this most recent set of releases, covering the eight largest U.S. banks, the plans of five of the institutions were deemed "not credible" by both the Federal Reserve and the FDIC, and as a result, these plans must be amended to address identified "deficiencies" and re-submitted for approval — and if the amended plans are not approved, the agencies may impose regulatory restrictions that could ultimately include forced restructuring and divestitures (if the deficiencies are not addressed within two years). The plans of two other institutions were deemed "not credible" by only one of the agencies; in these circumstances, where there is no joint determination of non- credibility, the plans do *not* need to be re-submitted for approval. Finally, the plan of one institution was essentially approved by both agencies.

This state of affairs leaves us with several important questions as the process moves forward. Will the regulators use the credibility determination as an explicit means to force large international banks to restructure and retrench? Or for those plans that that have been jointly found to be "not credible," will the banks have the means to address identified deficiencies and come back into compliance without being forced to engage in major divestitures or restructuring? And even if the banks do come back into compliance, what will be the marketplace reaction over time, especially among activist shareholders? Will these shareholders precipitate restructuring to satisfy their expectations long before regulators formally decide to go down the restructuring path? These are all important questions that could plainly affect the future business models of the largest banks — and we could observe some answers in the not-too-distant future.

6. Long-Term Debt and "TLAC": The Power of Subordination

The final factor I would like to discuss involves the recent proposals by both the Financial Stability Board and the Federal Reserve for the largest internationally active banks to hold a minimum level of Total Loss Absorbing Capacity (TLAC) in the form of equity and long-term debt, and, in the case of the Federal Reserve, the higher of a minimum TLAC requirement and a separate requirement for a minimum amount of long-term debt. While the details of the two proposals are both complex and somewhat confusing, I think the most important practical significance of each is identical and straightforward.

First, in both cases covered banking organizations will almost certainly comply through the issuance of long-term debt rather than the issuance of new equity. That is, in both cases the standard as a practical matter is really a new long-term debt requirement.

Second, both proposals effectively require the long-term debt to be ***subordinated***, either structurally, contractually, or by statute. And at least in the U.S., the long-term debt, like equity, must be subordinated to virtually ***all*** short-term liabilities of the consolidated banking organization such as deposits, commercial paper, repurchase agreements, derivatives, or any other type of short-term obligation.

Third, the new layer of subordinated long-term debt is very large. When combined with the bank's equity, it will mean that there is an enormous layer of TLAC that is subordinated to all of the company's short-term liabilities. By way of example, my back-of-the-envelope calculation shows that total TLAC for the largest G-SIBs will exceed $300 billion for each.

I believe the required subordination of this very large amount of TLAC is a true game-changer for large international banks and the financial system. It is nothing less than an audacious effort to end the fundamental problem that causes bank failures, financial panics, and the need for intense bank regulation and supervision. I am talking, of course, about ***run risk*** — the problem that modern finance has always encountered when a bank transforms its inherently short-term liabilities such as deposits into inherently longer-term illiquid assets such as loans. This maturity transformation process has long been thought to be critical to financing growth in the real economy, and has defined the core functions of banks for centuries. But it has also created the fundamental problem of run risk: short-term liability holders like depositors are incentivized to withdraw their funds at the first sign of trouble, because it is costless to do so, while the bank cannot translate its illiquid assets into cash quickly in order to meet the withdrawal demand without taking heavy losses. Indeed, the prospect of heavy withdrawals can cause banks to engage in panic "fire-sales" of assets to generate liquidity, which in turn can cause not only losses at the bank, but a severe decline in general market prices. In addition, runs caused by real problems at one bank can lead to contagious runs at healthy banks when depositors and short-term creditors decide to withdraw their funds as a precautionary measure. In short, run risk can lead, and often has lead, to financial panics and systemic damage, just as it did during the recent financial crisis.

Governments have responded to this core banking problem with many different forms of regulation intended to forestall and respond to run risk. These include, among others, safety and soundness supervision; activities regulation to constrain bank risk; liquidity requirements; capital requirements; discount window lending; and deposit insurance. Over time, this suite of regulatory tools has generally been effective at preventing runs, or at the very least, preventing runs at a single institution from mushrooming into systemwide runs and panic asset selling.

However, the regulatory response has not been foolproof, as the recent financial crisis painfully demonstrated. When traditional tools have not proved adequate to stop runs and financial panic, governments have typically taken additional extraordinary measures such as injections of government funds into financial institutions, guarantees against losses, paid assistance to healthy institutions to take over sick ones, and in some cases, full blown-nationalization — the very types of "bailouts" that occurred in 2008 and 2009. These recent bailouts, of course, led to the wave of extensive new regulation designed to prevent such "bailouts" from recurring.

The new subordinated long-term debt requirement resulting from the TLAC standards is very much a part of this new wave of post-crisis regulation. What sets it apart, however, is that it is more of a frontal assault on run risk than all of the other new regulatory requirements. Having a massive layer of equity and long term debt subordinated to all short-term claims ensures that ***all*** of an institution's "first losses" will be absorbed by stakeholders that ***cannot run***, which should provide confidence to depositors and other short-term creditors that they ***need not run***. That is, if a depositor at a bank with a trillion dollars in assets truly believes that the bank would have to sustain more than $300 billion in loss before the depositor would sustain ***any*** loss, then the depositor would have no incentive to withdraw funds in the absence of some truly cataclysmic event.

In sum, a fundamental purpose of TLAC's subordinated debt requirement is to remove the incentive to run. If successful — if a bank's short-term claimants can really be persuaded that they will suffer no losses even when a big bank fails — then it really becomes conceptually possible to imagine a large bank failing and being reorganized, downsized, or restructured in an orderly manner and without taxpayer assistance — and without runs. This would plainly be an extraordinary result. And it seems to me that, given the simplicity and audacious purpose of the new requirements, the link between subordinated TLAC and run prevention is very worthy of further study by academics, who have thus far not seemed to focus on this very important topic.

Let me make one final and related point. Academics have argued for a very long time that banks need a layer of subordinated debt that is constantly being reissued to the market in order to obtain a new and ongoing source of market discipline on bank risk-taking. Subordinated debt resulting from the TLAC requirement will make this favorite academic proposal a reality, as it is sure to result in staggered issuances by large banks of substantial amounts of subordinated long-term TLAC. Time will tell whether this continual issuance will produce a meaningful source of market discipline, but again, this an issue well worth studying.

***

As this conference has demonstrated, the future of large internationally active banks is far from clear, but I believe it is likely to be substantially affected by the four key factors discussed today.

The Last Crisis, the Next Crisis, and the Future of Large Banks

— CHAPTER 27

- Phillip Swagel

  University of Maryland

1. Introduction

The future of large banks depends on the effectiveness of the post-crisis regulatory system, which is ironic: the reaction of large banks to the 2010 Dodd–Frank law was broadly negative, even while many people working at large banks recognized that changes were needed in the wake of the financial crisis and are now striving diligently to comply with the new regime. But the success of the new regulatory regime now stands between large banks and the political forces pushing for their breakup. If the post-crisis regulatory regime does not work effectively (and is not seen as working effectively by policymakers and the broader public), then large financial institutions will be forced to make fundamental changes. The measures that large banks initially opposed may prove to be the changes that permit them to continue in their current form; their survival depends in large part on the effectiveness of the post-crisis regulatory regime.

Phillip Swagel is Professor in International Economic Policy at the Maryland School of Public Policy.

The author is grateful to Frank Medina and Bryan Sakakeeny for helpful discussions.

This chapter thus examines the future of large banks by looking at the post-crisis policy response, focusing on how the new tools and legal authorities put in place in the wake of the crisis would have been used had they been available in 2006–2008. While necessarily somewhat of an artificial exercise, such a counterfactual history is still valuable for thinking about the future of the post-crisis regulatory regime. After all, the Dodd–Frank reforms and suite of regulations from the Basel process were designed with the previous crisis — the last war, so to speak — firmly in mind.

The paper concludes by looking forward to consider how the new post-crisis legal authorities would be used in a future crisis. The exercise here is even more speculative in hazarding the nature of the next crisis — if we could know this, policymakers would work now to avoid it. Still, considering possible crisis scenarios can help policymakers assess the effectiveness of the new regulatory regime, and thus the future of large internationally active banks. The conclusion is that the most critical component of the Dodd–Frank changes for large financial institutions is the new resolution authority that is meant to make it possible for a large institution to fail while limiting the negative consequences for the broader economy. If the new resolution authority can be made to work so that large banks fail with limited broader consequences, then these institutions will no longer be "too big" in terms of systemic stability (even while arguments continue about whether their size is appropriate on other grounds, such as competition). The large banks should still expect to be treated like political punching bags, but a successful regulatory reform would allow them to continue.

Many policy steps have been taken to improve the stability of the U.S. (and global) financial systems in the wake of the financial crisis. Among other things, regulators have raised capital standards and for the first time imposed liquidity requirements on large banks; they have mandated that large banks issue long-term debt that can be converted to capital in the form of the TLAC total loss-absorbing capacity; they have required increased transparency on derivatives; they have adopted a statutory framework, regulations, and procedures to facilitate the resolution of non-banks including non-bank subsidiaries such as broker-dealers within bank holding companies; they have implemented stress tests and required large banks to develop living wills; and in the United States, the U.S. consumer financial protection bureau has been established. Some changes remain to be decided or finalized, including dozens of required Dodd–Frank rules still outstanding (21.3% of the rules had not yet been proposed as of the September 30, 2015, according to the progress report from the Davis Polk law firm).[1]

Increased capital undoubtedly contributes to improved financial sector stability, as do many of the other changes made in the wake of the crisis. The value of some changes, however, is less certain in terms of striking a balance between financial stability and economic growth. For example, while the Fed deserves credit for implementing the Volcker Rule in a way that is not as harmful to economic growth as could have been the case, the rule still fails to pass a reasonable cost-benefit test — it imposes costs in exchange for improvements in stability that could have been achieved within the pre-existing regulatory framework (since supervisors already had the authority to ensure that banks put in place appropriate risk management frameworks).[2]

Yet more worrisome are instances in which there are problems that policymakers seem to downplay or even deny. The cumulative impact of regulation on the activities of community banks is a notable example, and of both economic and social importance given the role of these institutions in providing credit to smaller local businesses that are not always well-served by larger banks. Another concern for policymakers relates to the difficulties posed by internationally active banks that "live globally but die locally." The new regulatory regime could result in bank balance sheets that are chopped up in the next crisis by the effective implementation of country-by-country ring-fencing. Because the post-crisis regulatory regime depends on cooperation between national regulators that may be difficult in the midst of a financial crisis, national regulators may adopt measures that result in the undesirable hoarding of capital and liquidity within countries rather than allowing internationally active banks to shift resources to address location-specific funding challenges. The possibility that such regulatory directives could

---

[1] http://www.davispolk.com/Dodd-Frank-Rulemaking-Progress-Report/

[2] Swagel (2013).

exacerbate a global financial crisis contrasts with the positive view of country-specific ring-fencing put forward by U.S. policymakers.[3]

It remains desirable to improve legislation and address features of financial regulation that fare poorly on the tradeoff between stability and economic costs. Senator Richard Shelby (Republican-Alabama), the chairman of the Senate Banking Committee, has put forward a bill with a number of desirable features to reduce regulatory burdens. At the same time, a case can be made as well to allow the industry to adjust to post-Dodd–Frank changes, and for policymakers to study the attendant impacts and adjust over time. To its further credit, the Fed has said that it will take this approach with the Volcker Rule.

2. The Last Crisis: 2008

If the many changes instituted after 2008 had been in place, one could imagine that the last crisis might not have taken place at all. Perhaps the advent of the Consumer Financial Protection Bureau (CFPB), for example, would have prevented the last crisis by heading off the low-quality mortgage origination at the root of the crisis. A more active regulator would have made a difference, but it is not clear that the existence of the CFPB by itself would have prevented the last crisis (and to be sure, the CFPB itself does not make this claim). The bureau is having its first experience with a crisis in the form of the difficulties experienced by users of the RushCard payments product, and the CFPB does not appear to be faring well in terms of a rapid response for people in trouble — in this case, low- and moderate-income families cut off from access to their funds by a non-bank financial institution. The RushCard situation is the sort of problem that CFPB was meant to address, but the bureau has not been adept or able. Indeed, this is an agency with a keen focus on public relations, and yet the CFPB has been relatively muted in the face of what is reported to be a crisis for those affected.[4] At the same

[3] Tarullo (2015).

[4] CFPB Director Richard Cordray put out a statement on October 23, 2015 that "The CFPB is taking direct action to get to the bottom of this situation that may have harmed thousands of innocent consumers already" and that "Further, we indicated that the CFPB is prepared to use all appropriate tools at our disposal to

time, even if the creation of the CFPB would not have prevented the last crisis, the creation of the bureau remains an important element of the crisis response — indeed, the 2008 Treasury Blueprint called for it.[5] The challenge remains for the CFPB to find the right balance between effectively protecting consumers and ensuring that its actions do not have an undesirable negative impact on innovation and growth, or needlessly cut off consumers from access to credit.

Bank funding has also changed considerably since the crisis. Large banks today are funded with much more capital than was the case going into the last crisis, both because of their own decisions and in response to regulatory changes such as those stemming from the Basel process. This is a good thing. And yet, it is again not clear that more capital alone would have prevented the last crisis (at least in the amounts commonly discussed). After all, a lesson of the collapse of Bear Stearns, Lehman Brothers, and others is that once a financial firm loses the confidence of market participants, a few percentage points of capital is not likely enough to ensure stability — once short-term creditors began to run, whether these institutions were solvent or not proved to be irrelevant because they could not meet their short-term funding needs. Even so, more capital would have helped and might have saved some firms. A similar point can be made for the post-crisis requirement of increased liquidity. Firms that arguably teetered at the brink of solvency might have made it (or survived longer) had their assets remained liquid through the crisis. AIG is often seen as the prime example of this, in that the government rescue of the firm was necessitated by a liquidity crunch. Still, AIG failed badly, not by a little — market confidence and liquidity evaporated in tandem. And as Robert McDonald and Anna Paulson

help ensure that consumers obtain the relief that they deserve." http://www.consumerfinance.gov/newsroom/statement-by-cfpb-director-richard-cordray-on-rushcard-prepaid-card-incident/ News reports into November, however, indicated that users of the RushCard continued to have difficulty accessing their funds and had suffered meaningful financial losses and personal inconveniences as a result. https://finance.yahoo.com/news/rushcard-fiasco-how-customers-aftermath-180105818.html The Bureau in early December directed the company behind the RushCard product to cooperate with an investigation, but individuals affected by the situation have obtained relief instead by having news organizations inquire on their behalf.

[5] https://www.treasury.gov/press-center/press-releases/Pages/hp896.aspx

have shown, the firm might well have been insolvent, not just illiquid as the Fed believed at the time that it extended extraordinary financing.[6]

The non-bank resolution authority created in Title II of Dodd–Frank would have been used had it existed in 2008. It is an open question whether Title II would have been used in the case of Bear Stearns, or even whether it would have been needed if the Bear situation happened in the future given the work at the New York Fed on strengthening the tri-party repo system. Still, Title II surely would have been invoked for AIG. The firm was heavily consumer facing, and its collapse would have had important implications for pensions and other forms of retirement savings. Interconnections between the constituent parts meant that there was no way to resolve part of the firm such as the financial products division without having pieces of the firm seized by individual regulators around the globe. The firm would have imploded absent the Fed's intervention, an experience that informs the FDIC's single point of entry approach to resolution — in a sense, AIG was the test case for a limited version of Title II (with the Fed rather than the FDIC providing bridge liquidity).[7] A key difference that the existence of the Title II authority will make in a future crisis is that it grants the government the authority to impose losses on counterparties in a way that was not possible in September 2008. Indeed, the Dodd–Frank Act requires those losses to be imposed on bondholders and other counterparties. Still, it is striking that there is remains a good deal of discussion in financial circles, including in the government, premised on a view that Title II is unworkable or will not be used as required in the law. An example of this can be seen in the tabulation from the Richmond Fed of the federal government safety net, which effectively disregards the new authority in assessing the size of taxpayer exposure to losses.[8] A key challenge remains for the FDIC and other regulators to address this perception that the liquidation authority cannot be used as intended.

---

[6] See McDonald and Paulson (2015).

[7] For a discussion of the FDIC approach, see Jackson, Guynn, and Bovenzi (2013).

[8] See https://www.richmondfed.org/safetynet/, and page 5 of https://www.richmondfed.org/~/media/richmondfedorg/publications/research/special_reports/safety_net/pdf/bailout_barometer_faq.pdf

The question then is whether the use of Title II for AIG would have been successful at ensuring financial market stability while avoiding costs for taxpayers. This is hard to answer — we will not know until the next financial crisis. The statute asserts that the resolution would be "orderly," presumably based on the open-ended ability to put in taxpayer money to stabilize a firm once Title II is invoked. As Morgan Ricks notes, however, bank resolution by the FDIC is "orderly" not because depositors necessarily value the FDIC's expertise at winding down institutions but rather because of the deposit insurance that shields them from losses.[9] In contrast, Title II requires losses to be imposed. The key question, then, is whether authorities will be willing to impose losses on counterparties.

In principle, market participants who purchase the securities of large banks should be aware that they are on the hook for losses in the event of a failure. This recognition should affect funding costs ahead of any crisis, so that a credible implementation of Title II would effectively contribute to market discipline on large institutions. This impact applies not just to funding explicitly designated as part of the TLAC, but to all counterparties given the wide grant of authority in Title II to impose losses. Still, it is hard to know for sure what will happen in the midst of a crisis, especially if policymakers worry that losses appropriately imposed on the funders of one firm will lead to a stampede to the exits at others. Indeed, during the crisis, the losses imposed on senior bondholders of WAMU are widely seen as having exacerbated funding pressures for Wachovia. Confidence that Title II will work as intended, including with losses imposed on counterparties, would go a long way to being able to say that the post-crisis regulatory changes have addressed Too Big To Fail by getting at "to fail" and thus making "too big" less worrisome. The key then is to have a process for failure resolution that is set down as much as possible in advance and then followed in the crisis. The FDIC especially has done a lot of good work in providing a roadmap, and must continue to flesh out the resolution process while building confidence that it will be followed.[10]

---

[9] Ricks (2011).

[10] See, for example, the May 12, 2015 speech by FDIC Chairman, Gruenberg (2015).

A challenge for the FDIC is that there are two relevant examples for how a process akin to Title II would be used, including one in an exigent circumstance, and neither instills confidence. This is not the fault of the FDIC, but illustrative of the pressures involved. The first example is the auto manufacturers' bankruptcies, a process in which political considerations appeared to have been paramount in allocating losses — the opposite of what would be desirable with non-bank resolution. And the politically-driven allocation of losses took place concurrently with discussions of the financial regulatory proposals that eventually included Title II, so it was clear that the actions taken with GM and Chrysler had implications beyond the auto sector.

The second example is the TARP bank fee included in Obama budget proposals. The law establishing the TARP required that losses be made up from assessments on the rest of the financial industry, but the TARP fee proposed by the Obama administration was problematic in two somewhat contradictory ways: first was that the fee was proposed sooner than it needed to be (at a time when it would actually have sapped financial sector stability), and second was that it then remained a proposal even when it seemed clear that the fee would not needed. That is, the administration's proposal gave the appearance, perhaps because this matched the reality, of being a revenue raiser under the guise of financial stability. Using these fees to raise revenue runs counter to the purposes vital for financial stability, which is to give confidence to market participants in the process by which Title II will be used, particularly in imposing losses.

3. The Next Crisis: 202x?

The post-crisis regulatory response can be seen as a sort of pendulum swing after the permissive environment that led into the housing bubble, which naturally raises the question whether the pendulum eventually will move back to undo some of the changes in capital and other rules. At least as of the end of 2015, it seems more likely that the pendulum will remain stuck. For the future of large banks, what matters for the foreseeable future is how the new regulatory regime works, both in normal times and in the next crisis.

One can imagine various possibilities for a future crisis. To their credit, regulators are focused on many of these. For example, federal bank supervisors have cracked down on apparently risky lending that evokes memories of the bubble, including the use of leveraged loans to fund financial engineering such as stock buybacks. Regulators have put forward analysis of potential fire sales that could result from episodes of illiquidity at mutual funds, and considered the problems that might arise from the concentration of risk at clearinghouses. (Problems at clearinghouses pose particular problems because these institutions are excluded from Title II).[11] Fed liquidity facilities seem well-targeted for other potential future financial crises such as might arise from electric grid sabotage or cyber-security problems.

On the other hand, some recent regulatory decisions seem to run counter to the idea of avoiding future crises or could make it more difficult to respond to them. The Federal Reserve is fiercely (and appropriately) independent on monetary policy, but relatively responsive to political pressures on financial regulation. The Fed's tendency to succumb to political pressure can be seen in two recent rulemakings. The first is with the Dodd–Frank requirement for risk retention on securitized lending — the so-called "skin in the game" provision — for which the Fed, under political pressure, agreed to rules that effectively eviscerated the requirement. The second example of the Fed's capitulation to political pressure is with the liquidity coverage rule, where the Fed allowed certain state and municipal bonds to count as high-quality liquid assets.[12] It is easy to foresee that the Fed would face considerable political pressure to allow similar leniency for borrowers that can mobilize significant amounts of political pressure if a future crisis involves duress among this set of borrowers. It is noteworthy that the Fed has stood up to pressure mainly from the political right on monetary policy, while demonstrating its susceptibility to pressure from the left on regulatory policy. Establishing credibility and independence on regulatory policy will be an important challenge for the Fed so that it preserves its

[11] See Steigerwald (2012).

[12] See http://www.federalreserve.gov/newsevents/press/bcreg/20150521a.htm

ability to act (or not act) even in the face of political pressure such as to assist with the financial rescue of a municipal borrower.

Other dangers in the face of the next crisis are restrictions on policy steps that might be needed. The limits in Dodd–Frank on use of the Fed's emergency powers — the so-called 13-3 authority — so far seem acceptable since broad-based lending programs can still be put in place as needed. For example, the Fed could have offered the terms of its AIG bailout to other insurers, confident that healthy firms would not have taken them (the opposite situation of the TARP capital injections, which were intentionally designed to result in broad take-up). But one could imagine more serious restrictions that tie policymakers' hands in a future crisis. Restricting intermediate steps taken by the Fed to stabilize the financial system could inadvertently allow a crisis to worsen by enough to lead policymakers to invoke Title II. The key to avoiding this discontinuity is both for the post-crisis regulatory changes to be developed, and for tools such as Title II to be available if needed.

The SEC's waiver regime also could lead to systemic problems that threaten the financial system. One can imagine a self-created issue at the SEC, as political rhetoric leads to a situation in which commissioners box themselves into a commitment not to take steps such as providing waivers to banks even when these might be necessary for financial stability. A pledge by an SEC commissioner not to vote in favor of such a waiver is akin to members of Congress who oppose increases in the debt ceiling, relying on others to take on the burden of acting in the best interest of the nation. SEC commissioners in the political majority who make a public commitment to a no-waiver regime leave themselves open to having this rhetorical bluff called by minority commissioners, with potentially fraught results for the financial system and overall economy. A broad point is that it would be useful for all participants in the regulatory system to consider issues relating to systemic risk. As Keynes pointed out, the financial system is not a morality play but a series of technical challenges to be solved.[13]

---

[13] See Krugman (2008).

4. The Future of Large Banks

The post-crisis regulatory response involves measures not only to avoid a crisis, but also to deal with them if they arise. The response to the next severe financial crisis inevitably will involve two main tools: first, the provision of liquidity from the Fed to mitigate a crisis, and then second the invocation of Title II, with its broad authority to deal with a severe crisis that threatens the stability of the financial system. Making Title II work is the key challenge of the post-regulatory response. Success would be for the FDIC both to work out implementation details with its single point of entry approach, and to convince market participants and the broader political system that the mechanism is viable.

So long as the next failure of a large bank can be addressed in a way that does not threaten the financial system and does not involve a tax payer bailout, the future of large banks is likely secure in the U.S. economy. An effective regulatory regime, with a credible Title II, will allow large banks to maintain their place in the U.S. economy.[14]

At the same time, even if everything works well, large banks will still also maintain their place in the popular and political discourse — as convenient scapegoats. But if the regulatory regime can be made to work, then large banks will be somewhat like the North America Free Trade Agreement (NAFTA), a treaty that is unpopular but continues without serious challenge because it provides economic benefits. That is, politicians might decry NAFTA, but none go so far as to suggest tearing it up. With a successful post-crisis regulatory system, large banks could have a bad reputation but remain active in the economy and provide reasonable returns for their shareholders and other stakeholders. The challenge, then, for big banks is to climb to the level at which they enjoy the same tepid support as NAFTA.

References

Gruenberg, M. (2015). A progress report on the resolution of systemically important financial institutions. *Federal Deposit Insurance Corporation*. Available at: https://www.fdic.gov/news/news/speeches/spmay1215.html.

[14] See Swagel (2012).

Jackson, T. H., Guynn, R. D., & Bovenzi, J. (2013). Too big to fail: The path to a solution. *Report from the Bipartisan Policy Center*. Available at: http://bipartisanpolicy.org/wp-content/uploads/sites/default/files/TooBigToFail.pdf

Krugman, P. (2008). Keynes' difficult idea. *New York Times: The Opinion Blog*. Available at: http://krugman.blogs.nytimes.com/2008/12/24/keyness-difficult-idea.

McDonald, R. & Paulson, A. (2015). AIG in hindsight. *Journal of Economic Perspectives*, *29*(2), 81–106.

Ricks, M. (2011). Regulating money after the crisis. *Harvard Business Law Review*. Available at: http://www.hblr.org/wp-content/uploads/2014/09/Regulating-Money-Creation.pdf

Steigerwald, R. (2012). Orderly liquidation in the shadow of the bankruptcy code presentation at the Chicago Fed. Available at: https://www.chicagofed.org/markets/orderly-liquidation-bankruptcy.

Swagel, P. (2012). Don't make banks too small to succeed. *Bloomberg*. Available at: http://www.bloombergview.com/articles/2012-09-05/don-t-make-banks-too-small-to-succeed.

Swagel, P. (2013). A modest Volcker rule. *New York Times: The Opinion Blog*. Available at: http://economix.blogs.nytimes.com/2013/12/13/a-modest-volcker-rule.

Tarullo, D. (2015). Shared responsibility for the regulation of international banks. Available at: http://www.federalreserve.gov/newsevents/speech/tarullo20151105a.htm.

The Future of Large, Internationally Active Banks

— Chapter 28

■ Mahmoud Mohieldin
World Bank Group

I am very pleased and honored to have participated in this prestigious conference on behalf of the World Bank Group (WBG). An important goal of the conference for the WBG is to help shape our upcoming Global Financial Development Report (GFDR) which will focus on the theme of Global Banking. The first of the GFDR series on the role of the state in the financial sector benefited from similar engagement with the Federal Reserve Bank of Chicago four years ago. The series successfully continued with a second report focusing on financial inclusion, and a third on long-term finance.

The decade prior to the 2008 global financial crisis was characterized by a significant increase in banking globalization, which coincided with a dramatic increase in bank size. This was manifested in

Mahmoud Mohieldin is the World Bank's Senior Vice President for the 2030 Development Agenda, United Nations Relations, and Partnerships. He is in charge of coordinating the World Bank Group's efforts to strengthen partnerships with the United Nations and multilateral development institutions. This chapter summarizes the author's comments presented at the Federal Reserve Bank of Chicago's 2015 International Banking Conference (co-sponsored by the World Bank) during the concluding session: "The Future of Large, Internationally Active Banks: Where to from Here?"

two ways: first, through a rise in cross-border lending and second, through the growing participation of banks in foreign countries, specifically in developing ones.

Benefits of globally active banks were reflected through additional capital and liquidity, financial development, and efficiency improvements through technological advancements and competition.

However, the global financial crisis led to a re-evaluation of global banking; not least because global banking was seen as partly responsible for the transmission of the financial crisis. It highlighted the importance of careful, country-level assessment of the role of international linkages in amplifying or mitigating external and internal shocks. The financial crisis also caused concern that global systemically important banks could be too big and too connected to fail.

Meanwhile, the recent IMF Global Financial Stability Report (GFSR) highlights two major developments since the global financial crisis: first, the noticeable decline of direct cross-border lending as a share of total banking assets, mainly as a result of the retrenchment of European banks; and second, the increase of intra-regional financial linkages, specifically in Asia, as a result of the share of local lending by foreign bank affiliates remaining steady, leaving market space for regional and national banks.

This conference, with high-level participation by researchers and practitioners knowledgeable on the subject, will help us think through some of these recent developments and their implications. Mainly, a rigorous examination of the potential benefits and risks is warranted. This examination would include a better understanding of how having large, internationally active banks affects economic outcomes in developed and developing markets; and, in particular, how large, internationally active banks may impact poverty, shared prosperity, and economic growth. The conference also touched upon the role of internationally active banks in ensuring a stable macroeconomic environment, which supports efforts at inclusive growth and poverty reduction, and which helps in implementing the new 2030 Agenda for Sustainable Development.

As highlighted by the 2015 GFSR, there are areas which require additional focus in order for internationally active banks to be more effective, particularly in the context of regulatory frameworks. They can better be addressed by answering the following questions: How can trust be built through cooperation, coordination, and information sharing? How can national reform efforts be synchronized with international standards and reforms? How can costly and risky divergence of accounting approaches and standards be dealt with? How can challenges associated with cross-bank disputes be tackled?

I think this conference has helped answer some of the critical questions related to the role of global banking, with an aim to inform the debate that is taking place today among policy makers, regulators, practitioners, and researchers.

From the discussions during the conference, and from my perspective at the World Bank Group, I would like to share some ideas on matters related to how best to deal with the current shortcomings in the supervision of large, internationally active financial institutions. In particular, I would like to share some reflections with you from the perspective of developing countries:

First, when considering the decline of globally-owned financial institutions and the rise of regionally-owned but internationally active banks, we must keep in mind the importance of certain political economy dynamics and the potential for geographic concentration. The extent to which these trends could be a welcome phenomenon remains to be seen, but in all cases we need to be alert to certain dynamics associated with this kind of increased regional presence in many markets.

While Asia has been mentioned a few times, we have seen similar patterns in the Middle East and Africa as well, where regional banks have gained market share after the withdrawal of many European banks. Foreign banks withdrew either because of problems in Europe or because of higher risk — actual or perceived risk — in the activities of the host countries.

The second observation is related to the challenges of cooperation and information-sharing. From a developing country's perspective you might expect that these challenges are higher and sensitivities related to sovereignty are perhaps greater.

The third observation refers to the contribution of internationally active banks to financial development. Many of the financial development indicators, particularly those on financial access and inclusion, still leave much to be desired, despite some improvements during the last decade or so. The issue of the contribution of the financial sector at large to the real economy is an area of concern for developing countries. And there are many questions that need to be answered at the country level in that regard. Some of the conference papers have tackled different aspects of this issue very well.

The fourth observation is related to assumptions developed after the Third International Conference for Financing for Development held in Addis Ababa in July 2015 about the possible contribution of the private sector and the financial sector to financing of the ambitious 2030 Agenda for Sustainable Development, which requires significant levels of funding. To what extent are we expecting contributions from the internationally active financial intermediaries in that regard?

The fifth observation, is with regard to the notion of "too big to fail," which is very relevant in developing countries. However the notion has been extended in practice to smaller banks as well. Every bank, any active bank, is there to stay. And as is being observed, even if the subsidiary is perceived as small or insignificant by the foreign bank, it might be perceived as significant by the recipient country. This may result in further complications on the rules of exit. Again, the political economy is important. While the entry of a foreign bank could be seen as a positive development for many countries in the developing world, foreign bank exits could be perceived negatively. While the foreign bank could be exiting because of problems at home or inadequate returns, the perception in the recipient country could be one of failure.

The sixth observation is related to the growing role of non-bank, non-financial institutions in providing financial services. This includes the potential for digital finance and mobile money in developing countries to enhance financial inclusion, better financial services, and better targeting of social transfers. However, they are not risk-free. For example, it may be important to consider to what extent those who are controlling mobile networks or retail business are capable of handling the financial risks associated with the management of a significant part of the payment system, social transfers, small savings, and recently, transfer of remittances across borders in many countries. The assumption is that there is collaboration and coordination between financial regulators and digital service providers, but the system has not been put to test so far. Identification of regulatory responsibility and maintaining the governance of this growing service are key.

The recent global financial crisis highlighted the role that global banks play in transmitting shocks across countries. In particular, the crisis underscored that the architecture of the global financial system is far from optimal. This is largely because international banks are operating on a global scale with global ownership, but with national authorities in charge of their supervision and resolution.

There is an absence of an international regulatory and supervisory body that can enforce common regulations. Meanwhile, we have seen good attempts at cooperation to cope with some of the challenges that the sector has been facing because of the absence of a unified system of regulation and supervision. To provide an example, there is the initiative of cooperation found in 'supervisory colleges'. These colleges are groups of national supervisors with the primary objective of exchanging information and establishing cross-border dialogue in order to ensure that supervisors are able to identify risks — and in sufficient time. And we can see the involvement of the Financial Stability Board in that regard, and their principles of good practice, being used by the supervisory colleges.

Another initiative is found in 'crisis management groups' which focus on the development of resolution strategies. Crisis management groups consist of all relevant central banks and supervisory authorities as well as authorities represented in the core supervisory college.

Though supervisory colleges and crisis management groups are certainly steps in the right direction, these bodies are self-governing and cooperation might not always happen. Hence, oversight over operations of supervisory colleges by an international body, such as the FSB, which includes a mediation and conflict resolution framework, would be useful and should be advocated. Such an oversight body should have a number of roles:

- participate in and oversee meetings of the supervisory colleges and the crisis management groups, and facilitate dialogue and collaboration;

- conduct regular surveys among home and host supervisors to assess the effectiveness of the operation of the colleges;
- review adherence to best practices.

Furthermore, despite efforts calling for better collaboration, there are many cases when information-sharing and cooperation are likely to break down. Even in advanced economies we see some examples of lack of cooperation.

For example, there are measures related to ring-fencing, which constitute implementation of preventive measures before significant problems spread, as well as accommodating measures when problems arise. There is a preference to invest more in preventive measures. In this context, I would like to refer to the FSB which has issued resolution guidelines under the Key Attributes of Effective Resolution Regimes for Financial Institutions.

The Key Attributes of Effective Resolution Regimes for Financial Institutions adopted in 2011 requires an ongoing process for recovery and resolution planning which covers, at the very least, domestically important firms that could be systemically important or critical if they fail. These attributes also introduce "bail-in" mechanisms wherein bank liabilities are written off or converted to equity, allowing the institution to continue to operate as a functioning financial entity, giving the authorities' time to reorganize or wind down parts of the bank's business in an orderly manner. These mechanisms are a way to reduce the need for taxpayer support and to limit moral hazard problems arising from institutions deemed too big to fail under the present resolution framework.

The aforementioned reforms are still a work-in-progress and will most likely be raising new implementation challenges for prudential supervisors, central banks and supervisory authorities along the way. Moreover, the proposed reforms that we discussed are for Global Systemically-Important Financial Institutions only, and it remains to be seen if they can be easily implemented for banks that are regional players or banks that are systemically important in only a number of countries. Further, the framework in place does not address the case of subsidiaries of global banks that are deemed small by the parent, but might be significant for the host.

As the abovementioned reforms are implemented and pending issues are resolved, host countries should pursue macro-prudential policies to manage global banking flows instead of relying on ring fencing measures.

Many of the issues will be addressed and discussed further in the Global Banking issue of the Global Financial Development Report.